Understanding
Religion and Science

Also available from Continuum

Christianity as a World Religion, Sebastian Kim and Kirsteen Kim

The Edge of Reason?, edited by Alex Bentley

An Introduction to Religion and Literature, Mark Knight

An Introduction to Religious and Spiritual Experience, Marianne Rankin

An Introduction to the Phenomenology of Religion, James Cox

Religious Diversity in the UK, Paul Weller

Sacred Scriptures, Joan Price

The Study of Religion, George D. Chryssides and Ron Geaves

Understanding Religion and Science

Introducing the Debate

Michael Horace Barnes

continuum

Continuum International Publishing Group

The Tower Building	80 Maiden Lane
11 York Road	Suite 704
London SE1 7NX	New York, NY 10038

www.continuumbooks.com

British Library Cataloguing-in-Publication Data
A catalogue record for this book is available from the British Library.

ISBN: HB: 978-1-4411-8200-5
       PB: 978-1-4411-1816-5

Library of Congress Cataloging-in-Publication Data
Barnes, Michael Horace.
  Understanding religion and science : introducing the debate / Michael Horace Barnes.
    p. cm.
  Includes bibliographical references and index.
  ISBN-13: 978-1-4411-1816-5 (pbk.)
  ISBN-10: 1-4411-1816-0 (pbk.)
  ISBN-13: 978-1-4411-8200-5 (HB)
  ISBN-10: 1-4411-8200-4 (HB)
  1. Religion and science. I. Title.
  BL240.3.B375 2010
  213–dc22
                        2009035039

Typeset by Newgen Imaging Systems Pvt Ltd, Chennai, India
Printed and bound in Great Britain by the MPG Books Group

Contents

Introduction

Chapter Outline

Rough relations

Relations between religion and science have often been rather rough. In the 2nd century CE the Christian philosopher-lawyer Tertullian faced criticism from more skeptical philosophers who had what we could now call a scientific attitude toward miracles. To these philosophers belief that Jesus had risen from the dead qualified easily as irrational. Tertullian invoked faith as the answer, even saying at one point "I believe [rather than know] because it is absurd." Where rational knowledge fails, faith is the answer, said Tertullian. Some of the philosophers responded disdainfully, rebuking anyone who believes things that are irrational or unsubstantiated. They called this a recipe for superstition.

In the ensuing centuries many Christians accommodated themselves, unlike Tertullian, to various schools of rationalistic philosophy. In the 2nd century CE Minucius Felix, a defender of Christianity, used the Stoic philosophers' own arguments in favor of the existence of a God who had given intelligent design to the universe. By the early 5th century Augustine, a very influential Bishop in North Africa, was careful in his explanation of the story of creation in Genesis to make that explanation conform to the best science [philosophy of nature it was called then] of his time. After the relative darkness of the early Middle Ages an intellectual renaissance occurred in Europe in the 12th and 13th centuries. Christian philosophers and theologians, eagerly drawing upon ancient philosophical sources which had been preserved and developed by Muslim thinkers, debated how Aristotle's Physics could help define the Real Presence of Jesus in the Eucharist, or how Ptolemy's astronomy might shed light on the hierarchy of angels. In the scientific revolution beginning in the late 16th century most of the scientists ("natural philosophers" they called themselves) were religious, even deeply religious in many cases.

Nonetheless, antagonism on the part of religious people toward science has been common. Augustine wanted to save Christianity from embarrassment, not to help develop science for its own sake. He believed many things which the more rationalistic philosophers of earlier times had already made fun of, as we will see. In the late Middle Ages, especially in the 13th century when the universities celebrated and adapted the science of Aristotle and other philosophers to Christian use, Church authorities twice condemned such efforts. Early in that century the authorities tried to forbid the use of Aristotle; later in the century they settled for condemning a long list of theories inspired by ancient Greek philosophy of nature. (Philosophers and theologians nonetheless used Aristotelian ideas extensively.) The later case of Galileo is well known. In 1633 the Catholic authorities in Rome compelled the somewhat overly confident Galileo to swear that the earth is stationary and does not move. In the 17th and 18th centuries people of science largely looked on in horror as courts condemned thousands of witches to death by burning or hanging. In the 19th century Darwin's theory of evolution by natural selection met at best with great caution by religious leaders, Protestant and Catholic alike. Other religious leaders flatly rejected the theory, a rejection maintained by many today. In every generation, therefore, those favoring scientific rationality have found strong reasons to be critical of religion.

Religious thinkers have their own complaints. The most common is that scientists sometimes over-reach their discipline and come to *philosophical* conclusions critical of religion. The method of science can determine much about the empirical world of nature, says this complaint, but not about things that are not natural. God is not part of nature; therefore science cannot say anything about God, argue the theologians. The sociobiologist Richard Dawkins claims nonetheless that we have enough scientific evidence about the universe to conclude that belief in God is superstition. Dawkins' conclusion goes beyond science, but seeks to give that conclusion a scientific basis.

"Scientism!" shout the theologians. Scientism is a somewhat ambiguous word. It sometimes labels the belief of many scientists that science is the only reliable method for judging truth-claims. Science may not be able to know everything, in this view, but there is no other method which provides reliable conclusions. Other times "scientism" identifies the belief that if science cannot know it, it does not exist, as though we could assume from the beginning that only the empirical world exists, the world of time and space, matter and energy. This scratches out in advance spiritual realities like God or human souls, complain the theologians. This represents a confidence the scientific method can answer even philosophical or theological issues, such as the existence of a supernatural God. Let scientists just stick to science and everything will be all right, the theologians argue.

Theologians do not mind all forms of scientism. Each year the Templeton Foundation gives an award worth more than a million dollars to a person who has contributed to a positive dialogue between religion and science. Often this award has gone to a scientist who has written on religious matters in such a way as to show compatibility between the scientist's own scientific work and religious beliefs. There has been scarcely a hint of complaint by religious believers about scientists who reach beyond science in order to speak of the spiritual or religious realm, as long as these scientists say positive things about religion or in support of certain religious ideas.

What is at stake?

Points of contention between religion and science are usually about their different fact-claims—about whether God exists or miracles happen. Relations between religions and science, however, are about much more than differences over fact-claims.

First of all, these relations also represent basic human sensibilities about *how we know* what we know. Some rely on authority; others reject authority in the end. Some seek satisfying emotional expression; others emphasize rationality.

Second, these relations include competing *value perspectives*. The excitement of new knowledge inspires many; the security of tradition restrains others. A commitment to ideals of progress dominates some; others hold a more pessimistic view about human efforts to improve life.

Third, these relations shape the *human self-image*. Religion seeks the spiritual dimension in human life and fears that science will reduce us all to organic machines. Science is fascinated by the workings of the brain as doors into better self-understanding and can find religious belief in a spiritual soul merely distracting.

Fourth, these relations touch on basic human images of *our place in the scheme of things*. Religious people often look to miracles as signs that their lives are under the care of a personal Being. Science often describes the universe as aimless, operating by only natural causes.

There are many ways to cut and sort the relations between religion and science; any single set of cuts and sorts falls short or seriously misleads. Yet too many ways of cutting and sorting leave a jumbled mess. So these chapters will employ a middling outline that tries to describe and sometimes untie a set of major knots, without addressing every intersection between religion and science. The chapters will also seek a balance between positions at odds with one another, trying to fairly represent the different positions even while offering critical analyses of them. But this book will not seek an artificial accommodation between positions. The ongoing tensions between religions and science call for a clearer exposition than that.

The emphasis in these pages will repeatedly fall on Western theisms, with particular attention to Christianity. This author knows Christianity much better than Judaism and Islam, the other two great theistic traditions. But some attempt will be made to use traditions other than Christianity occasionally to illustrate alternative religious responses to the challenges which science can make to religions.

From past to present

Over the last few centuries science has been reshaping religion in the West, even as religion has offered new ways of interpreting the findings of science. This is nothing new. As we will see, what Christians are accustomed to think of as traditional doctrines were in many cases formulated in the early centuries of Christianity to fit the best science of the times.

There are many examples of Christian belief adapting to science, which will be explored in later chapters. Belief in a spherical earth, for example, was an ancient Greek scientific idea that replaced the biblical image of a flat earth. Christians and Jews became accustomed to the Ptolemaic theory that the sun and moon and planets revolved around the spherical earth. This was unbiblical, a change in belief to conform to the science of the times. Similarly, the age of the earth as implied in the account of history in the Book of Genesis does not fit at all with the account given by modern geology. Likewise, developments in medical science have had an effect. Few today attribute illness to demonic possession or to witches, though this was once normal religious belief. Even ideas about miracles have struggled to adapt to the best science of the times as far back as the earliest days of Christianity, as has already been suggested here.

Jews, Christians, and Muslims insist that their beliefs come from God, not merely from human minds as science does. This implies that those beliefs should be independently accurate, not reliant on developments in science. In the last two centuries, however, some theologians have proposed that it is good to think of religious beliefs not as coming from God alone but as the product of an interaction between human experience, including thoughts and actions and feelings, and the presence of the divine. This could include the idea that it is natural and good that the conclusions of science should be an element in guiding religious thought, though only a minority of theologians actively suggest this.

Religious beliefs might have an impact on science also. Some have argued, for example, that the Judaeo-Christian belief in an intelligent creator helped to support the scientific quest for intelligibility in the universe. Only if a philosopher or scientist first supposes there is an intelligible order to be discovered, would the hunt to understand that order be justified.[1]

Some possible models of how science and religion may be related to each other.[2]

1. Complete separation:

    A number of theologians and philosophers of religion now insist that science and religion are so different from each other that neither should impinge on the other. Philosophers sometimes speak of science and religion as two different "language games" that are "incommensurable" with each other. Science is said to be the study of the order of nature through empirical evidence, whereas religion is an experience of that which transcends nature and is beyond empirical evidence.[3]

2. Antagonism:

    A History of the Warfare of Science with Theology in Christendom by Andrew Dickson White gives a somewhat overwrought turn-of-the-20th-century description of the relations of religion and science since the beginning of modern science in the time of Galileo as a history of head-on opposition. This book pits authoritarian and superstitious forms of religion against humanistic and enlightened science. Some books today reverse the roles, portraying science as mechanistic, arrogant, and anti-human, badly in need of religion to keep science in its place.

3. Integration:

    In late medieval times theologians presumed that traditional Christian faith would be able to integrate all the findings of science into theology. As there is one God so also there is one truth, they argued. Science and religion are one, in the end. Deists had the same assumption of unity, but they required that those parts of the religious tradition that were not scientific—miracles in particular—be rejected. Many books written in recent decades have taken either this approach or the following one.

4. Cautious Cooperation:

    Library shelves are full of books showing how religious and science are at least compatible on essential points. Many will appear in the notes and bibliography here. The extent to which this works is a question to look at again by the end of this book.

Do we have the right answers?

The fact that a great number of books propose either integration or cooperation between religion and science does not, in fact, mean that the tension between the two has been resolved. Many different ways of trying to reconcile the two differ sufficiently with each other, that we can at least say that no single answer to the problem has shown itself to be clearly superior to other answers. Many of these proposed answers will be set against one another here for comparison. The purpose, then, of this book is not to provide the right answers, but to sit in the stands of the arena and attempt to sort out the contenders, their tools, the methods of using the tools, as well as the different motivations that prod the contestants onward.

Two particular convictions will often guide observations made here about the relation between religion and science. The first is that the method of science has proven to be spectacularly successful, for the limited goal of determining which ideas about the natural world will work so well in practice that they can be treated as though they are simply the truth. Note how cautiously that claim is worded, full of qualifications. The reason for that caution will become clear in the chapters on the scientific method.

The second conviction is that religion, appearing throughout history and around the world, cannot be dismissed easily. Scientists who are also atheists think of religion as an outdated relic or as a kind of false consciousness that too many people prefer over the hard-headed ideas science provides. A few decades ago a "secularization" thesis was quite common. "Secular" here stands for whatever is non-religious. Some sociologists of religion have argued that under the impact of science society was gradually becoming more secular.

There are intelligent and well-educated people, however, whose religiousness is sufficiently important to them that they object to any science-based challenge to their beliefs. Sometimes this results in a lot of "adhockery"—ad hoc responses to this or that religious claim. A traditionalist Catholic, for example, might argue that papal infallibility makes sense, because God would have good reason to try to compensate for the human tendency to error. This argument is "ad hoc," addressed just to one particular belief. Other times the responses are more sweeping, seeking a grand synthesis about the relation between God and creation in general. This is usually the goal of those who seek to integrate their overall religious vision with science's story of the universe.

By the end of this book the reader should be in a better position to recognize the major players in the arena where religion and science meet, to describe their goals and methods, and to take at least an initial stand on the validity or value of their efforts.

Some specific points of tension

Here is a list of specific points of tension between religion and science. Not all of them have been inevitable. At times scientists or theologians have overreached their competence and made assertions that create conflict where it need not have existed. We will see this more in detail in the chapters relevant to each of the following topics.

1. Methods in Religion. "Faith and reason" are the two methods often assigned to religion and science. But the word "faith" can mean many things. Various theologies attempt to sort out and justify or critically analyze types of faith.

2. The Method of Science. The most fundamental method of science is relatively simple to describe, though difficult to justify logically. But the success of science in modern times offers a pragmatic justification—it works.
3. God. For the great Western religions, belief in God constitutes the bedrock for all other beliefs and practices. Theologians still argue about the nature, existence, and activity of God, however. Sometimes scientific theories have had an impact on theologies of God.
4. Miracles. To many science-minded people they are highly dubious. The history of belief in miracles seems to the rationalist to be a history of superstition, gullibility, and fraud. Many religious people, on the other hand, view miracles as an essential part of their tradition. Theologians disagree on how to define miracles. And everyday religious belief may not fit with what a theologian proposes.
5. Cosmic evolution. Now that the Big Bang theory of the origin of the universe holds sway, theologians ask whether the 13.7 billion-year history of the universe suggests or refutes belief in a Creator, especially one who designed or planned the course the universe would follow after the Big Bang.
6. Biological evolution. Many religious people find this theory doubly bad, because (a) it does not fit the Bible (or the Qur'an) in many ways, and (b) says that humans descended from animals which casts into doubt both the special status of humans and the basis of their morality. Biologists, however, generally find the evidence for evolution to be impressively strong.
7. Soul. Neurophysiology is making the idea of a spiritual soul increasingly an unnecessary hypothesis to account for an inner sense of self, of intellectual activity, or of inner freedom. Yet for many religious people belief in a spiritual soul is the basis of human dignity, free will, and life after death.

A fair assessment?

It is difficult to produce a fair assessment of the relations between religion and science, whether in general or on the specific points just listed. One source of difficulty is personal commitments. A great number of the books on religion and science are produced by people with already existing religious commitments. Religious people tend to hunt for the qualifications and complexities that provide at least some safeguards for religious belief.

On the other hand, many books attack religious belief and practices in the name of science. Richard Dawkins is famous for this.[4] Yet he insists that his criticisms of religious belief are fair because the preponderance of evidence is on his side. His commitment is to the scientific method as the only trustworthy means for evaluating truth-claims about how things are in the world.

Although I share Dawkins' convictions about the general efficacy of the scientific method, subject to qualification in later chapters, I have more sympathy with religion than he does. I first of all agree that it has been a source of great evils in the world. The devil's work, so to speak, has often been done in the name of God.[5] But I believe that it has also been a power for good. It has been a carrier of noble moral messages in various forms. It has brought valuable order and purpose to countless lives that would otherwise have been confused and aimless. In general, the record is ambiguous. Slave owners once justified their practice by reference to biblical ideas and practices; but religious people also led the fight against slavery in the last two centuries. Religious leaders have belonged to the aristocracy and supported its power over the weak and impoverished; but other religious leaders have defended the poor and promoted social justice.

My own training is in theology. This helps me to recognize more sophisticated forms religious thought has often taken. Religion comes in layers, just as does empirical knowledge of the world, from popular but distorted forms to highly sophisticated forms. Popular religion is often easy to criticize from a scientific perspective, as laden with superstition. But pseudo-science also abounds, a superstitious distortion of true science. A fair assessment of both religion and science can point out ways each has been distorted; it should also include an examination of what each can look like at its best.

It would seem much more like a fair exchange if religion and science could each balance the other in some way. Some theologians find science to be a positive resource for rethinking the human place and responsibility in the cosmos. Nonetheless most often modern science has put religion on the defensive, struggling to hold on to as much of its territory as possible while science nibbles at the edge of many beliefs and practices. Following chapters will illustrate this, point by point.

A long story of changes

Challenges to religion from significant changes in culture are not unusual. Some changes forced upon religion later came to be considered real advances, even by religious people. The current pressures from science should be seen in that larger historical context.

The beginnings of religion are buried in the pre-historic past. The earliest human societies were nonetheless probably much like those hunting-gathering cultures of today that until recently were relatively untouched by outsiders. These primitive tribes believe in spirits of various kinds—spirits of the dead, underground spirits who steal souls, spirits of various animals or locales. Such belief is called "animism." Hunting-gathering people do not worship these spirits. They deal with them in the same practical ways a person might deal with neighbors, some of whom are very troublesome. Hunting-gathering people also have what are called "creation" stories of primordial beings like the moon or a coyote or heron or crow who, once upon a time, did things to make the world be as it is. These beings are not worshiped either. Primitive people use a variety of objects with magic-like power or employ magical practices.

It is common to categorize primitive animism and the use of magic as either religious or at least a precursor of religion. If we decide to call these beliefs, folktales, and practices by the name religion, then one of the first great challenges to this religion appeared with the beginnings of pastoral life, based on herding cattle, sheep, or goats. When pastoral practices become central to the economic order, greater social organization becomes common, and hereditary chiefs appear as a distinct social class. The division of a group into class of rulers and the ruled intensifies with the development of agriculture, first apparently in Mesopotamia (present-day Iraq) around 10,000 years ago. The cultivation of large fields made possible large towns and even cities. These centers of population, in need of civil order, saw the strengthening of class division between the few who ruled and the many who were ruled.

This class division on earth echoed through the skies, elevating some of the spirits to rulers. The gods of polytheism were born, demanding true worship in temples and at altars dedicated to their power. These new great gods and powers overshadowed the small spirits and magic.

Literacy provided the next great challenge to religion. In the old world of Asia-Europe-North Africa literacy was invented by 5,000 years ago in the Mesopotamian Valley. The idea of using marks or symbols to represent ideas or words spread quickly to Egypt. Eventually it made its way to the Harappan culture of the Indus Valley, though this language was lost by the time of the 1700–1400 BCE migrations of Aryans into India. Around the same time writing appeared also in China.[6]

Written records of beliefs can have a disturbing effect on religion. In a large volume entitled *Ancient Near Eastern Texts Relating to the Old Testament*,[7] James B. Pritchard has assembled translations of documents or fragments going as far back as 2000 BCE. In one of these a man has a discussion with his soul about whether there really is a life after death. In print such thoughts can become wide-spread, able to raise disturbing questions for others. Another ancient Egyptian text contains a story about the Canaanite fertility goddess Astarte, who receives help from the Egyptian god Seth in defeating a sea-monster. Eventually the meeting of religions and cultures will raise questions about whether there are many fertility goddesses, or whether there is just one major one who is known by different names in different places.

Twenty-five hundred years after the first appearance of literacy, at least three different cultures were jolted by even newer modes of thought, perhaps the result of those centuries of questions about the gods. In India, China, and Greece, during something like a 200-year period, philosophy was born. India had handed down sacred texts called Vedas, collections of worship hymns and rituals (and even magical formulae) for as much as a thousand years. Sometime around 800 BCE, if the traditional dating is correct, sets of "commentaries" were added to the Vedas. These included works called the Brahmanas and the Upanishads. The focus of the latter was not worship but intellectual analysis.

In chapter 3 of the Katha Upanishad, for example, a young man named Nakiketas interrogates Death. At first Death offers explanations about various sacrificial ceremonies devoted to the gods. Nakiketas is not satisfied with these polytheistic answers, however. He wants answers to more basic questions. He asks whether the hereafter is existence or non-existence. Then he seeks to learn the ultimate purpose of human life. As Nakiketas questions, Death's discourse becomes more and more abstract, about the ultimate power or reality of the universe. Here we see the older polytheistic beliefs of India being overlaid with new philosophical reflections. Before long, at least among an intellectual elite, the gods in India were subordinate to a single Ultimate Reality called Brahman.

A similar transition took place in China. In the 5th century BCE Confucius recommended ignoring the gods and concentrating on how to organize social and civil life. A bit later Mohists offered a contrary theory of social ethics, but also ignored the traditional gods. They gave careful step-by-step abstract arguments for their positions. Taoists promoted a simpler style of life to be at peace with nature, employing both concrete examples and abstract analysis to support their position. The Taoists sought to make their lives in tune with the Tao, the underlying single source of the processes of nature.

In Greece other schools of philosophy developed. Where ancient myths of the creation and generations of the gods once explained the universe, philosophers sought more abstract answers. Thales of Miletus (a Greek city in Ionia, now the Western coast of Turkey) proposed that all things are ultimately forms that water takes. Next Anaximander, also of Miletus, thought that finite things emerged from the "unbounded," the infinite. In a few generations Plato, Aristotle, and Zeno were each tracking back the order or activities of the whole universe to single Ultimate principles. We will see later that the history of these Greek developments will turn out to be useful for understanding current issues in religion and science.

For Jews and Christians living in an ancient culture soaked with Hellenic (Greek) philosophy, this trend toward a single Ultimate as the final explanation of the universe supported monotheism. Cultural changes here also changed religious beliefs. Christians eventually learned to use many aspects of Greek philosophy to explicate their own beliefs, as we will see. Muslim philosophers did the same, although in the longer run traditional Sunni Islam became less receptive to such rational analyses.

Another great shift began in the world with the "modern" period, typically dated back to the beginnings of early modern science around 1600. For 150 years before that a spirit of rebirth—renaissance—dominated, based on ancient Greek and Roman art and literature. Leading thinkers and artists aspired to recover the achievements of the ancients. This same recovery period was also sowing the seeds of something quite new. It appeared first in a shift away from medieval Catholicism into a Reformation consciously looking backward to the era of the formation of the Christian scriptures, but in fact producing new and varied forms of religion. With older molds broken, a new form of knowledge also had room to take shape, less abstractly philosophical and more concretely empirical. Early modern science began to emerge. As science has developed, religion has been learning to dance to new tempos, even while it seeks to maintain harmony with its traditions. Change is upon us once again. The process is not often comfortable.

The process has also been complex enough that a good amount of history and philosophy can be very helpful in coming to understand the development of science and the varied relations of that science to religious perspectives. Consequently the earlier chapters here will raise a number of philosophical issues and all the chapters will include historical background. Later chapters will focus much more on specific aspects of science and their impact on religious thought. This in turn will provide a clearer sense of how religion and science might relate to each other in the future.

Part One
Methods in Religion: relations between faith and reason

Faith and Reason in Religion: Some Basics

Chapter Outline

The tension between religion and science is often described as a clash between faith and reason. The method of science pushes scientists to be as rationally objective as they can manage. Rationality and evidence, not bias or hope or a desire for esteem and wealth, is the norm that in the end gets to determine which truth-claims about the world should be accepted or rejected. Scientists often have the usual human difficulties in living up to this standard, but it remains the final standard nonetheless.

One expression of this standard is David Hume's (1711–1776) pithy saying: "A wise man proportions his beliefs to the evidence." Where evidence is weak, belief should be also; where evidence does not exist at all, there should be no belief. So at least says Hume.

A later chapter here on the limits of science makes it clear that this standard does not apply to all aspects of human life. It is true that any person starting out on a career or finding someone to marry would want to rely somewhat on evidence. A person very poor at math should not hope for a career in engineering. A person seeking a mate should note any evident boredom or animosity displayed by a potential partner. Nevertheless, at a certain point evidence is not enough. A person must make a choice, a commitment.

Neither can person's most basic values rest on evidence and reason alone. Knowing what is truly good, as well as finding within oneself the motivation to seek the good in the first place, can be difficult. Theologians and philosophers have spent many centuries disputing each others' answers about basic values; science has no way to finally resolve these disputes. (We will return to this issue later.)

A long religious tradition says that another aspect of life that lies beyond the bounds of rationality alone is precisely religious faith. The topic is clouded by the many different notions of what faith is, how it operates, how it relates to reason, and how one finds (or loses) it. To identify your assumptions about faith and how it relates to reason, you might choose among the options below. Each has been of some importance in the history of Western religious belief. This list, roughly in chronological order, provides a way to sample some of the great differences among people on this topic. Some of them will be explained more fully in the next chapter. This list is only to create a preliminary impression.

Faith and reason: nine options

1. Tertullian (2nd century CE): our human reason is weak, and the object of our faith is the God who is beyond all human understanding. We should recognize that faith therefore transcends natural reasoning, that the rational reflection of the philosophers can be the enemy of faith. "What does Athens have to do with Jerusalem?" *Faith against reason.*

2. Augustine (4–5th century CE) and Anselm (11th century): human reason is weak and, and some matters of faith are indeed beyond human reason. By the power of God we can first believe and can then reflect on our beliefs and come to a rational understanding of how they all fit together coherently and make good sense (though on some points we will have to acknowledge that the ways of God are beyond our understanding). *Faith seeking understanding.*

3. Aquinas (13th century): there are a few things that the rational mind could never grasp had they not been revealed. But our minds have sufficient clarity and power to show through reason alone the rational plausibility of many religious beliefs such as the existence of God, the immortality of the soul, and the moral law written within us. Philosophy is the handmaiden of theology (which is the "queen of the sciences"). *Faith cooperates with reason.*

4. Pascal (17th century). Reason reveals to us the inability of the human mind to find answers for the ultimate questions. The infinite lies before us, provoking us to wonder but leaving us unsure about what the ultimate truth really is. By default we have to follow our inner instinct: "The heart has its reasons which reason does not know." *Faith lies beyond reason.*

5. Schleiermacher (early 19th century). Religious faith is based on an inner experience. This is not a vague instinct. It is an experience of an ultimate unity to all things, an experience of a transcendent Wholeness, an Infinite depth upon which all finite things depend. This experience is "God-consciousness." *Faith is based on inner experience of the absolutely Independent.*

6. Kierkegaard (also early 19th century). True faith is a blind commitment. The ideal Christian is a "knight of faith" who gallops to the edge of the cliff and leaps. Abraham was correct to be prepared to sacrifice his only son Isaac at God's command. (This may be an extreme form of Tertullian's position.) *Faith is contrary to reason.*

7. New Age (a modern version of #4, but on "neo-pagan" beliefs): the most powerful way to arrive at truth is intuition. A person in tune with his or her own natural affinity with the cosmic energies will understand deeper truths from within. There is no need for outside authorities nor the rationalistic analyses of evidences. Intuitive participation in nature is the source of truth. *Intuitive knowledge replaces faith and reason.*

8. William James (early 20th century): faith can be a reasonable commitment. If we demand hard evidence for all our choices we will not choose a spouse or make friends. If a faith commitment makes us and others better off, do not wait for proof. *Faith as a reasonable free choice.*
9. Secular Humanism (19–20th century): it is irresponsible to believe anything without sufficient evidence. We should remain agnostic ("unknowing") about ideas that lack adequate evidence to support them. Anyone who knowingly clings to beliefs without adequate evidence is making superstition and prejudice legitimate. *Reason and evidence provide the only responsible basis for belief.*

Should faith be reasonable? The case of Galileo

Religious people often hesitate at this question. Some flatly say yes. Others challenge this, maintaining that faith is precisely that which operates when reason fails. A famous example from history of the tension between faith and reason may make it easier to address the question, an example which appears in a letter that Galileo wrote to the Grand Duchess Christina of Tuscany.

At a dinner with the Grand Duke of Tuscany in Florence, a philosophy professor argued that Copernicus' 1543 theory that the earth revolved around the sun was a theory in conflict with the Bible. One of Galileo's former students who was at the dinner reported that the Grand Duchess seemed to agree with the professor. Galileo quickly replied with a letter to his student in defense of Copernicus' theory, a letter Galileo revised in 1615 and sent to the Grand Duchess herself.

Galileo argued that while the Bible was God's true revelation, not everything in it should be taken too literally. God may have "condescended to popular opinion"—put things in such a way that people of earlier times might find more acceptable. Galileo's approach here has been called "accommodationism," a method in long use by Christians. It argues that scripture does indeed contain divine revelation, but there are many statements in scripture that God "accommodated" to the limits of understanding of the people of the times. If the Hebrew Scriptures had said that the world was a globe hurtling through space around the sun, people of ancient times would have laughed at such an idea and ignored the scriptures. So God accommodated the language to fit with popular belief in a flat earth under a sky-dome (a "firmament"). Later people reading the same scriptures could make their own adjustment in the light of more recent knowledge and recognize the reason God would have engaged in such accommodation.

In fact, Galileo argued, those who opposed Copernicus actually accepted an unbiblical picture of the universe. They agreed with the ancient astronomy of Ptolemy, which said the earth is a globe around which the sun and other planets circulate. The Bible instead portrayed the earth as flat with a solid dome over it. No matter, said Galileo, quoting a certain Cardinal Boronius; "the Bible is meant to tell us how to go to heaven, not how the heavens go." For things of science we must rely on <u>sense-experience</u> <u>(evidence) and rational argument</u>. God gave us powers of sensation and reasoning. We should use them. Even the great St. Augustine, Galileo noted, when pondering the 6 days of creation described in the first chapter of the book of Genesis, declared we should not make the faith look foolish to the educated by taking positions contrary to good science.[1] So do not take all of the Bible too literally, said Augustine. Galileo agreed.

Galileo's letter to the Grand Duchess Christina of Tuscany is an instance of an awkward element in the relationship between faith and reason for people of faith. On the one hand, Galileo felt bound to respect the Bible as well as his Catholic tradition. On the other hand, his physics made it reasonable to him to disagree with the common and traditional interpretation of the Bible in his day. His conclusion is that faith should indeed be reasonable, at least in the sense of not opposing scientific evidence.

In 1632, the Holy Office of the Roman Inquisition disagreed and found Galileo guilty of heresy. They said that his Copernican hypotheses "are contrary to the true sense and authority of Holy Scripture." This was not an aside. They repeated that heliocentrism ("helios" is Greek for sun) "is absurd and false philosophically, and formally heretical because it is expressly contrary to the Holy Scripture."[2] In retrospect we know that the heliocentric view Galileo supported was basically correct: the earth does go around the sun once a year. So it clearly can happen that scientific rationality produces an answer that is better than what a sacred text seems to say and than a long-standing religious tradition.

The question is how a person should proceed in attempting to figure out correct answers in such conflict. What is the *method* to be followed? Where faith and reason look like they might collide, which is to take precedence, and why? For many science-minded people, David Hume's answer is the only correct one. A person should proportion belief to the evidence; moreover, extraordinary claims require extraordinary evidence. This implies most religious truth-claims should be met with skepticism.

Defining "Faith"

The matter is complicated because the word "faith" can have many different meanings, as the earlier list indicated. Here is a simplification, reducing the notions of faith and reason to a few main points. This provides a general starting point concerning what it could mean to use faith as a method for determining what is true, such as about the orbit of the earth, about a universal flood in the days of a man named Noah, about the reality and the natural mechanism of biological evolution, or even about the existence of God. In the section entitled "Faith: Thorough Version" each of the first three simplified definitions provides examples of what might be called reasonable and non-reasonable forms, to aid in deciding whether faith should or should not have to be reasonable.

Faith: Brief Version (as a method for determining which *truth-claims* are valid)

a. The *act* of faith (the faith by which one holds something): the trust, belief, or commitment by which a person accepts certain ideas as true or accepts a certain way of life.

b. The *content* of faith (the "faith" which one holds): the particular set of ideas or pattern of life that a person accepts by an act of belief, trust, or commitment.

Faith: Thorough Version (for determining which *truth-claims* are valid)

Four major meanings of the term.

1) *Belief*: to believe that "x" is true, even though the evidence is less than compelling.

   a) Some belief is reasonable in the sense of at least being compatible with the relevant evidence, even if that evidence is not strong enough to provide "proof." (See below for meanings of "reasonable.")

   b) Some belief is non-reasonable, in the sense of being immune from standards of rationality. In this case evidence does not count, even if the evidence seems contrary to the belief ("blind faith").

2) *Trust*: to believe in someone. To trust a person's guidance.

   a) Some trust is reasonable. Long experience with a certain person could provide evidence that the person was knowledgeable, wise, morally sensitive, and caring.

   b) Some trust is non-reasonable. People trust others at times even though the evidence examined carefully would not support such trust.

3) *Choice or commitment*: to choose to accept certain ideas as true or moral standards as valid, or to make a conscious choice to trust someone or a tradition.

   a) Some choice is reasonable. E.g., #1) a. above may be a reasonable choice to make. An analogous choice could be made concerning basic values by which a person lives.

   b) Some such choice is non-reasonable. Recall Kierkegaard's "knight of faith," whose commitment to Christianity is like that of Abraham in the Hebrew Scriptures, who was willing to sacrifice his own son at God's command.

[4) *Faith as a power given by God*: an inner grace (empowerment by God from within) that enables a person to believe, trust, or make a commitment. This is the classic Christian position that only God's grace makes true faith possible, that a true and worthy act of Christian belief, trust, and commitment is not possible by human power alone. (This #4 is in brackets because it is a specific Christian belief, rather than a general definition of the word "faith," although Islam also says it is God who makes a person a believer.)]

Defining "Reason"

To repeat, the scope of science is narrower than the range of topics in religion. Science deals with questions of empirical (able to be tested against evidence) matters. Religion, unlike science, deals *also* with basic values and with questions of ultimate meaning. But religion usually makes some truth-claims about certain facts in history or in the world in general. It is about such truth-claims that religion and science may clash. So the description of "reason" given here will focus only what making judgments about factual truth (and will also eventually qualify the word "truth" itself).

Reason: Brief Version [as a means for determining what is *factually* true or not]

What does it mean to be "reasonable" rather than "non-reasonable"?

Reason consists of two major aspects:

a. *Logical* clarity and consistency: reflection clarifies ideas to make them coherent or self-consistent, and identifies how well ideas fit with other ideas.
b. Reliance on *evidence*: determining what is probably true by judging which ideas best fit with the evidence.

Reason: More Thorough Version: major elements for determining what is true

1) *Logic*: the test for consistency and clarity, as part of determining truth.
   Logic is an analysis of the interrelations and implications of ideas.
   a) "Ideas" here stands for concepts ("dog"), for propositions ("the dog is barking"), for larger descriptions ("dogs bark to communicate to other dogs"), or for theoretical explanations ("barking has evolved as a defense mechanism for dogs….")
   b) "Interrelations" stands for the possibility of comparing ideas to see whether they are compatible with each other ("That cat is barking blue?")
   c) "Implications" stands for logical relations among ideas ("If only dogs bark, and that animal is barking; then that animal is a dog.")
2) *Evidence*: the test of whether an idea is not only coherent but probably true.
   Checking all ideas (concepts, propositions, descriptions, theories) against all the available relevant evidence. This can be done directly; it can also be done indirectly by checking ideas for consistency with other ideas that are themselves based on evidence.
3) *Combination*: relying on *both* logical coherence and good evidence constitutes the full standard of reasonableness, for determining what is true. This combination can establish whether certain truth-claims are probably valid, though the chapter on the method of science will refine this claim. Judgments about the truth that conflict with logic or evidence are unreasonable judgments. Judgments that are not supported adequately by evidence but which are not refuted by it might be called non-reasonable.

Criticisms of religious faith can be vague. Sometimes critics attack only the general lack of reliance on adequate evidence. Other times they attack specific beliefs. They are not alone, however, in their vagueness. Most religious believers similarly just invoke "faith" as the justification for their adherence to a religious tradition. That "faith" might be any of the first eight on the list at the beginning of this chapter. Or it may just be an unquestioning trust in the authority of texts and leaders, fortified by a long habit of reverence toward these texts and leader. This possibility will be considered in the next chapter also.

The citizens of many countries can also pointedly note that they get to believe whatever they choose. They do not need to justify their religious choices to scientists or other skeptics, any more than they have to justify putting mustard on hamburgers. This last answer, though, will probably be frustrating to many a science-minded challenger who thinks it is irresponsible to make choices without a reasonable basis. Many attempts have been made to determine why people adopt or maintain a religious position without much concern to be very rational about it. Here is one.

Five styles of "faith" according to James Fowler

James Fowler, in *Stages of Faith* (1981) organized interviews with over 400 people and devised a complex system to categorize their responses. Fowler more or less ignored the specific beliefs, values, and practices of this religious tradition or that. His goal was to identify any psychological patterns in *how* a person appropriates the teachings and practices of the person's community or culture. He claims to have identified five stages of faith, called stages because they appear in a person's life in sequence. The following descriptions are attempts to summarize his conclusions. Not everyone, Fowler declared, goes through the entire sequence. Some seem to get comfortable at the third stage, for example, and stick to that style of faith for the rest of their lives. The stages can also be somewhat cumulative, so that a person may later draw upon elements of earlier stages in the person's life.

The first stage is characteristic of young children up to the age of 6. Fowler calls it the intuitive-projective stage. The word "intuitive" indicates that the child does not reflect upon beliefs but simply draws them in from others, especially parents and older children. The word "projective" identifies the common practice of children to invent aspects of their own world, whether it be an invisible friend or a monster under the bed. They project images out into the world from their own imagination. Ideas can take up residence in a child's head because of their emotional or imaginative appeal. We can note that adults sometimes do this also, believing in rather unlikely things like UFO visitors to Roswell, New Mexico.

The next stage in Fowler's sequence is the "mythic-literal," first appearing around the age of 7. By this age belief in Santa Claus is evaporating, and the child can recognize that the story of Little Red Riding Hood is fictional. New and longer stories take on new interest, like the life patterns of Barbie and Ken dolls or the history of the powerful dinosaurs. The new truths that children adopt now, though, are expected to be literally true. It becomes important to distinguish between fact and fiction. Authority figures, like parents, teachers, ministers or priests, deliver literal truths to live by. The various stories and information do not form a logically coherent unity. Internal contradictions are not readily noticed. (The sociologist, Robert Wuthnow identifies the same pattern in fundamentalism, though I believe that is not fair to all fundamentalists.[3] It may be as accurate just to call it a "catechism faith," which relies on memory of what authoritative sources say.)

The third stage, as Fowler describes it, is "synthetic-conventional." It is synthetic in that a young person, around the age of 11 or 12, develops an ability to entertain a more complex set of interrelated ideas, often synthesized into a coherent narrative. This style of thought has its roots in the growing ability of a child at age 9 or 10 to comprehend that the various chapters of a children's novel are logically sequential parts of a single story. The early adolescent seeks a larger life-story, of who the person is and where that person fits into her or his image of the world. This stage is called "conventional" because the child has a strong need to accept and be accepted by the others of the child's group. The understanding of life that is strongly approved by peers and community leaders, including religious leaders, seems evidently true. Fowler says he found this conformist style of faith among many adults, long after adolescence has passed.

Fowler labels the fourth stage "individuative-reflective." The second word, "reflective" is perhaps the more important. As adolescents get older, many discover in themselves a talent for rational analysis, logical argumentation, balancing the pros and cons of positions on their own. From this flows the "individuative" aspect—a person who can think out the person's own individual conclusions and values. It is only at this point of development that faith is likely to demand rational justification for a set of beliefs or practices.

This style of faith can also be called a "critical" position. The word "critical" does not necessarily mean a negative judgment. Film critics and food critics often use their knowledge and reflective abilities to end up praising a certain film or food preparation highly. What all sorts of critics do, however, is to subject whatever they are looking at or tasting to thorough analysis. Is the plot coherent? Do the photography and editing have a strong effect on the viewer? Are the sauces flavored lightly enough that the taste of the fish is not lost? Are the beans cooked to a proper firmness? Even if the answers are all a positive "yes," this is still a critical analysis. If a person supports her or his religious commitment with critical analysis, then the person is seeking a reasoned or rational faith.

The danger, here, as many a parent or teacher knows, is that the adolescent can work out a seemingly logical case for whatever that person wants to believe. Adults can do the same, for that matter. Dogmatism comes easily. There is no need to point out that this can easily be part of a religious style. On the other hand, efforts at reasoned analysis may arise precisely because a person has come to recognize problems, inconsistencies, or paradoxes in conventional accounts of life. If so, this reflective ability may lead on to another style of thought.

Fowler claims that eventually a person may develop a fifth style of faith, which he calls "conjunctive." This is partly the result of experiences of the limits of knowledge, of the ambiguities of life. For some, such experiences lead to a more flexible style of thought, perhaps still committed to a particular religious vision or tradition, but balanced by a sense that all positions are limited or imperfect. The danger Fowler describes here is cynicism, based on a sense that there are no reliable truths or values at all. The advantage can be a greater openness, including openness to religious variety and non-religion also.

As subsequent chapters here attempt to analyze various positions on the relation of science and religion, most of the writers promoting an accommodation between the two will tend to sound a lot like "conjunctive" thinkers. Scientists in general also tend to be rather conjunctive in their openness to new challenges, as a later chapter will make clear. Echoes of other styles of faith will become apparent at various points.

Some criticisms of Fowler's categorizations

Fowler's work is not very well received by many religious thinkers. First, he uses the word "faith" very broadly. It stands for just a person's basic trust whether in family, society, tradition, rationality, or a charismatic leader. Fowler ignores the doctrines and values and practices that are specific to a religious tradition.

Even more offensive to some is the implication in his findings that some forms of faith are more psychologically mature than others. That inference is almost unavoidable because Fowler claims that the stages of faith which he describes occur in chronological sequence as a person grows up. That could be taken to imply that those who do not engage at least in the critical thinking of the individuative-reflective stage or perhaps also in the conjunctive or post-critical stage have failed to develop adequately.

From the perspective of many religious people that judgment would miss what is important. Susan Kwilecki, for example, argues strongly that Fowler's categories are peripheral to the heart of religion. The standards by which religious people measure their development do not focus on the intellectual aspect as Fowler's do. They measure a person by such standards as the intensity of devotion, courage in dealing with the sorrows of life, and compassion for others.[4] The qualities of a saint do not appear in Fowler's list, nor for that matter those of a sinner. What shows up in an empirical study such as Fowler's are precisely the aspects that can be categorized by psychological surveys.

Nonetheless, the tensions between religions and science exist precisely because science promotes high standards of rationality. And, of course, the rational standards of science have often produced conclusions that seem inimical to parts or all of a given religious tradition, as we will continue to see here. Because faith has been an issue since the time of Tertullian in the 2nd century it will not be a surprise to find that theologians have been busily at work on this topic, replacing vague uses of the term with more careful analyses. That is the topic of the next chapter.

For further reading

Bishop, John, *Believing by Faith: An Essay in the Epistemology and Ethics of Religious Belief* (New York: Oxford University Press, 2007).

Collins, Francis S., *The Language of God: A Scientist Presents Evidence for Belief* (New York: Free Press, 2006). Collins, who led the successful mission to unravel the human genome, offers a somewhat conversational explication of why he can have faith.

Hancock, Curtis L. and Brendan Sweetman, eds., *Faith and the Life of the Intellect* (Washington, D.C.: Catholic University of America Press, 2003). A Collection of articles by Catholic philosophers and theologians.

Penelhum, Terence, *Reason and Religious Faith* (Boulder, CO: Westview, 1995). A Protestant Philosopher's analysis.

Modern Theologies about Faith

A "theology" is a reasoned analysis of some aspect of a religious tradition or of the overall coherence of that tradition. Theologians are generally the people in a larger religious community who apply rational or intellectual methods to the faith the community shares, including the kind of justifications for accepting or maintaining that tradition. Sometimes such analyses go by the name of "philosophy of religion." This chapter will explore more fully some of the types of religious faith discussed in the previous chapter, looking at various theologies about faith. These explorations will make it easier for the reader to evaluate the validity of any or all of these methods. Religious readers may find that they have already been implicitly relying on one or more. Science-minded skeptics about religion may find which ones they have already been rejecting, implicitly or explicitly.

Faith based on external evidence

Up until recent centuries, the use of external evidence was a predominant means for establishing the truth of the beliefs in Western religions. Jews, Christians, and Muslims alike could point to certain supernatural interventions as their starting point. For Jews it was Moses perceiving a burning bush, as well as the subsequent acts of God during the time of the Exodus. For Christians it was the miracles of Jesus, those that Jesus performed but especially the miracle of the resurrection of Jesus from the dead. Muslims marvel at the beauty and majesty of the words of the Qur'an and take this as is evidence they are from God. In the early years of Christianity many miracles were attributed to the intercession of the martyrs with God. Early Christian apologists (those who explained and defended Christianity to outside critics) relied often on the fulfillment of prophecies. The story of Jesus in the gospels includes many allusions to predictions in the Old Testament which Jesus is portrayed as fulfilling.

A major type of external evidence we will consider at greater length in later chapters, is the complex and seemingly purposeful order of the universe. Theologians and religious philosophers have claimed that only an Intelligent Designer could account for that purposeful order. Add to this the raw fact of the existence of the universe. Theologians will argue that we should ponder why there is something rather than nothing at all. Perhaps the existence of a universe can be taken as evidence of some ultimate Source of that universe. That topic will be addressed in the chapter on the existence of God.

Faith based on the internal "evidence" of personal experience

Many theologians in the last few centuries have shifted from relying on external evidence to depending more on a kind of internal evidence. The reformer Martin Luther's ideas are a major instance of this. He experienced the Holy Spirit at work in him, giving him the gift of faith through grace. That was all that he needed. Two of his standards were *sola fide* (by faith alone) and *sola gratia* (by grace alone, the power from God which enables a person to have faith).

A century later Pascal declared that "the heart has its reason which reason does not know." Pascal was convinced that at a certain point reason or rationality just ran out of steam. It could not answer some of the huge questions that the new science of astronomy posed, about the age and size and movement of the universe. It could not answer personal questions of ultimate meaning or basic morality. So trust an inner instinct or passion, Pascal urged. This happened to fit well with the earlier claim by the Reformer John Calvin, who said that God implanted in every heart a hunger to know God. The evidence Calvin used was that even the proud heathens who rejected God's authority over them, just could not help themselves and instead of turning away from divinity entirely as they wanted to, they created belief in many gods. Calvin was echoing Augustine, who said to God in Augustine's book, *The Confessions*, "You have made us for yourself, O Lord, and our hearts will not rest until they rest in you."

By the 17th and 18th centuries a more complete skepticism about religion in general began to grow among the highly educated. Augustine's and Calvin's answer no longer was very effective. In 1799 the German theologian Friedrich Schleiermacher responded to attacks on faith by the science-minded. He turned inward, as Augustine and Calvin had, but added a special claim about inner experience. We sense an ultimate Unity to things, said Schleiermacher, a Whole which is a reality on which we are absolutely dependent. This Whole embraces everything in its scope and power. This is an experience of what we also call God. Schleiermacher named this experience "God-consciousness"—awareness of the reality and presence of God.[1]

The result of this inner experience is that there is no need to rely on external evidence, said Schleiermacher. Science can neither hurt nor help true God-consciousness. In fact science is dependent, at least implicitly, on the experience of the Whole, and therefore upon religious consciousness. Science operates on the assumption that theories and evidence must all fit together into a unity. If some piece of evidence does not fit with other pieces of evidence, or with other theories based on their own evidence, then something is wrong somewhere, says the scientist. This means the scientist presupposes, at least implicitly, that there is a Whole and therefore also a wholeness to things.

Non-religious skeptics have two major complaints about Schleiermacher's notion of an experience of a Whole on which we are absolutely dependent. It is first of all too vague, the skeptics say. How does Schleiermacher get from this general inner experience of a fuzzily defined idea of the Whole, to the specific claim that this experience is a consciousness of the reality of the personal God of Western theisms? Schleiermacher's argument probably makes sense only to those who already believe in God and can easily translate this belief into Schleiermacher's more general language. Second, even if Schleiermacher insists that those who have such an experience of the Whole can call it God-consciousness, the critic can suspect that this experience is nothing more than just a glowing inner feeling, an emotional state that proves nothing about reality outside the person. Maybe it is only a consoling fiction. (We will see that fundamentalists have an entirely different reason to reject this theology.)

Faith as inner commitment

In the 19th century the Danish philosopher Soren Kierkegaard proposed the "leap of faith" described earlier here, a free inner commitment. Christianity is beyond reason, he declared. The Knight of Faith courageously leaps into the abyss, trusting that God is there. His rather dramatic example was the faith of Abraham, noted earlier here. By a special blessing from God, his son Isaac was born to him by his wife Sarah when she was past child-bearing age, according to the Hebrew Scriptures. When Isaac was older, God commanded Abraham to take Isaac to a mountain top, a sacred place, and kill

Isaac as an offering to God. As the Book of Genesis tells the story, Abraham was about to do this, until at the last minute God granted a reprieve. Kierkegaard praises Abraham's faithful willingness to obey God, even to the point of what looks absurd to the person without such faith.

By the 20th century more than one famous Christian theologian was promoting a faith similar to Kierkegaard's, now to be called "existential," implying it is rather basic and dramatic. By the early 20th century the portrait of the universe painted by science made it look even more threatening than it had to Pascal. In all its utter vastness, it gave little sign of any purpose or ultimate meaning. Science seemed to support a materialistic philosophy which declared that the universe was only dead matter drifting in accord with basic laws of nature. We humans "ex-ist"—literally stand-out—from this meaningless universe as the being that needs meaning in the form of worthwhile goals, because we are conscious beings who must make choices about what to live for. Confronted with a seemingly aimless universe that no longer gave clear external evidence of God or any other source of ultimate meaning, the German scripture scholar Rudolph Bultmann persuaded many Christians that the basis of faith lies in an inner "existential" *choice*, a fundamental act of courage, to throw oneself into faith by a free choice.

In 1896, in a lecture entitled "The Will to Believe," the philosopher William James had proposed a more modest form of commitment than either Kierkegaard or Bultmann. He compared the choice to have a general religious orientation, to the choice to accept certain people as friends or as a spouse. James argued that a religious commitment must first be at least a "live" one to the person, sufficiently interesting to make it worth considering. It must also be momentous, in the sense of having a profound effect on a person's life. It is a forced choice, in that even deciding to postpone a decision has consequences, in this case the loss of a live and momentous possibility. It is reasonable to make such a choice, James argued, just as it is reasonable to decide to marry a certain person.

Correlational theologies

In the 20th century, as an extension of "inner commitment" options, two other faith methods developed, each of them now called a "correlational theology." A German Protestant, Paul Tillich, and then later a German Catholic, Karl Rahner, are perhaps the two most famous theologians to articulate and promote versions of this approach. They both begin with a kind of deep inner awareness that we are surrounded by infinite mystery. Every answer we arrive at leads to another question. Reasoning about things never seems to finally answer the questions about life, of where it all comes from and what it all means.

Tillich said we all face an existential possibility of endless meaninglessness. He looked around for evidence that there is some ultimate meaning anyway. Like others of recent times he did not find it possible to believe in miracles as evidence of the reality of an Ultimate called God; nor could he perceive in the order of the universe a basis for an argument from design for the existence of God. Where evidence failed, he found he could still turn, in a manner similar to Bultmann's, to the inner possibility of courage in face of the threat of meaningless. He could find within himself the power to affirm Being over non-being, as he called it. Like Bultmann also, he derived his courage partly from the inspiration of traditional Christian images, especially Jesus sacrificing his life for others. Tillich "correlated" his existential need for ultimate meaning with the possibility of faith and courage he found in religious symbols. Faith in the existence of God is faith that life is ultimately meaningful. So the notion of "God" correlates positively with a person's deepest need.

Perhaps so, says the critic. But the critic then asks whether there is adequate rational evidence that there exists what Tillich calls "God" or "Being," an Ultimate Reality that provides meaning to the universe. A correlational theology might just be an inventive but inaccurate way to read the universe, in the hope of finding or asserting meaning where none really exists.

A little later in the century, the Roman Catholic theologian, Karl Rahner tried to address the critics. Like Tillich, he emphasized the issue of ultimacy. We are the being with the capacity for the infinite. By this he meant that we are able to ask endless questions and learn ever more and still be left wondering. It is like traveling toward a horizon. When we get to what we first saw as the very end of our vision, the horizon has moved; it is now further in the distance. The human capacity to question and then question again and then wonder some more keeps pushing the horizon of answers further off. There is always an endless mystery in front of us.

Rahner agreed that the infinite can threaten the meaning of our lives by presenting the possibility of endless aimlessness. All that we value and devote ourselves to may in the end be swallowed up in the utterly mindless processes of an awesomely immense universe.

This experience of infinite mystery, as Rahner puts it, is an intrinsic capacity of the human person. But Rahner notes another special aspect of most human experience: that we find ourselves able to act and choose and make lasting commitments, sometimes for the sake of others even at great personal sacrifice. All this is a stance toward life that treats it in fact as though it were ultimately worthwhile. Even many an atheist, proclaiming that the final truth about reality is that there is no ultimate value or meaning to anything, still finds the faith or hope or courage to live for certain values. Rahner calls this a kind of "anonymous" faith, an implicit affirmation that the ultimate truth about reality is better represented by the word "God," a source of ultimate value and meaning, than by the notion of endless meaninglessness.

Like Tillich, Rahner turns to his own Christian tradition. He uses the traditional Christian doctrine of grace to interpret human faith and courage in the face of infinite mystery. This doctrine proclaims that it is by the power of God acting in a person that the person is able to have such faith and courage. The fact of human courageous faith correlates here with the Christian understanding of God and grace. This courageous faith is itself evidence of a power that "always already" upholds us.

The skeptic may see two problems with this correlational theology. Like Tillich's it seeks a position that satisfies human needs. Beliefs that are satisfying, though, are not necessarily true. Further, Rahner turns to his Christian tradition, revealing that he already had faith before he tried to justify that faith. The attempt at justification might not look as strong to one who starts out a skeptic.

The analyses of the human situation offered by both Tillich and Rahner reveal more of the depth possible in religious questioning. The religious faith of many people has a focus on specific questions of whether God intervenes miraculously, or punishes the wicked and rewards the good, or will offer everlasting life after death. The correlational theologians attend to a more basic question, of whether everything in the universe is ultimately empty of meaning and purpose, or on the contrary whether it is legitimate to trust that on the deepest level human existence is part of a meaningful and purposeful unity. The chapters on the existence of God and atheism will discuss this more fully.

Radical Orthodoxy

Many theologians share a sufficiently strong conviction of the basic Christian truth and vision, so that orthodoxy—true belief—comes naturally to them. They believe they do not have to argue for the faith, whether through external evidence, internal evidence, reasoned commitments, or correlational theology. They relish the faith they have, live it, speak prophetically on behalf of it, find beauty and wonder in it. They agree with both Martin Luther and an early 20th century theologian named Karl Barth, that it is God who gives faith. If a person has it, the rule then is to live it, not waste time trying to justify it.

Radical Orthodoxy tends to reject "apologetical" theology. This form of theology does not "apologize" in the modern sense of the word. Instead it offers rational justification for belief, usually based on external evidence in some way. Apologetics, as Radical Orthodoxy interprets it, subjects Christian faith to the criterion of human rationality, a criterion that is other than faith. One already living within the faith does not need to use the rational criteria that outsiders use. Those who try to use science to support their religious faith are implying, whether they mean to or not, that faith relies on some external set of evidence and some rational analysis of that evidence, that faith must be shown to be reasonable. This then puts evidence and reason in charge of faith; it ought to be the other way around, say the Radical Orthodox.

The main issue for Radical Orthodoxy is whether to make accommodations to the larger cultural context outside of the religion. The larger culture in the West has emphasized scientific rationality. Radical Orthodoxy takes the position of an outsider to that culture, sufficiently critical of it to see little hope in it. These theologians see their faith as a call to keep a cautious distance from the culture, whether to point out its failings or try to convert it. Scientific rationality has produced a soul-less world, they complain. The culture has been guided by a false belief in progress through the use of reason instead of faith, which has led to the incredibly destructive ideologies of fascism, including Nazism, as well as the inhumane Communist states of the U.S.S.R. and China and Cambodia.

Not all theologians like this Radical Orthodoxy. Some complain it is "sectarian." Instead of engaging with the actual world of human life as it is lived and attempting to improve that world, Radical Orthodoxy rejects the world as sinful, fallen, irreligious. Radical Orthodoxy sits in judgment on the world.

Skeptics about religion reject Radical Orthodoxy on the grounds it is circular. It is faith holding itself up by its own bootstraps. It claims that a person who has Christian faith can be confident it comes from God. That presupposes first that God exists, a dubious supposition to the skeptic. Moreover there are other faith traditions in the world which have fundamental differences with Christianity. On what grounds, the skeptic may ask, can the Radical Orthodox adherents assert that their religious tradition is the one that is correct, or at least most correct. We will see more of their arguments in a later chapter on atheism.

Other theories about faith

We will eventually examine claims by evolutionary psychologists, as they call themselves, that religiousness is a result of our genes. Some claim that the social bonding and sense of dedication religion promotes provides a strong advantage to a group that shares a religion. The members of the group work together, pray together, recognize common authorities, and accept a call to be willing to sacrifice themselves for the good of the group. Religion thereby helps to preserve the group, and along with it the religion it holds.

Other evolutionary psychologists more prosaically suppose that many aspects of religion are accidental by-products of evolution. Our brains are structured in such a way, they argue, that sensory deprivation or prolonged hunger can induce a feeling of transcendence, of being in touch with a mystical or spiritual reality. We will see more of such theories later.

Each time scientists develop some new theories about religion a theologian will undoubtedly respond. In the case of evolutionary psychology, for example, the prolific religion and science writer John Haught accepts the claims of evolutionary psychology, but argues that either they do not go far enough or they go too far. They go too far when they claim that there is nothing more to know about faith than what science—a form of psychology in this case—can tell us. This is typical scientism, says Haught. It claims that the methods of science are the only valid means of discovering truth, and that what science can study is the whole truth.

More seriously, Haught argues, evolutionary psychology does not go far enough. Here are some of his words:

> Theology, unlike scientism, wagers that we can contact the deepest truths only by relaxing the will to control, and allowing ourselves to be grasped by a deeper dimension of reality than ordinary experience of science can access by itself. The state of allowing ourselves to be grasped and carried away by this dimension of depth is at least part of what theology means by "faith."[2]

Unlike Radical Orthodoxy, Haught's notion of faith is not antagonistic to scientific rationality. He praises science for its rational method. He looks for something more than this rationality, for a depth or richness of experience. These ideas are worth mentioning because they fortify the warning given at the beginning of these chapters on faith, that there are many variations of the meaning of faith. These ideas will also become relevant in the chapter on atheism. The skeptics will have a reply.

For further reading

Griffiths, Paul J. and Reinhard Hütter, eds., *Reason and the Reasons of Faith* (New York: T & T Clark International, 2005). Many chapters, all challenging secular rationality.

McCabe, Herbert, *Faith within Reason* (New York: Continuum, 2007). An articulation of how a Christian might have faith in the age of science.

Ward, Keith, *Pascal's Fire: Scientific Faith and Religious Understanding* (Oxford: Oneworld, 2006). An Anglican interpretation of the nature of faith in a time of science.

Part Two
The Method of Science: how does it arrive at its conclusions?

The Method of Science   3

By its nature science is a method. It is easy to lose sight of this because of the common practice of talking about what "science says," meaning the conclusions that have become part of accepted scientific fact-claims and theories. But the conclusions do not constitute science; the key to science is the method by which science arrives at the conclusions, and which justify holding those conclusions as the probable truth about the parts and processes of the natural universe.

People have been holding conclusions about the order of nature for countless centuries. Some of the more direct conclusions based on evidence have been correct. Somehow many groups discovered that slash and burn gardening improves the yield of crops. By paying close attention and notching sticks, perhaps, ancient groups found that the moon takes about 28 days to complete a cycle. But on the whole the range of knowledge about the natural world was hard to expand. For 2,000 years in the West, for example, no theory of what things are made of did much better than the theory that everything is made up of some combination of basic four elements, fire, air, water, earth. It was not a very effective theory.

For many of those centuries, logical reasoning tended to be a dominant method for understanding the world. On the basis of some common sense, some traditional ideas, and a bit of evidence, philosophers from before Socrates (469–399 BCE) to today have

tried to logically deduce the truth about reality. For almost 2,000 years they pitted theory against theory, philosophy against philosophy, each appealing to some evidence,
but mainly trying to show that logically speaking their theory made the most sense.
Finally in Europe between around 1200 and 1700 CE a new method emerged. We call
it modern science.

Naturalisms

This new method has a number of elements. One of them is "naturalism." Note the
plural form of the heading here; there is more than one sort of naturalism. But all of
them have in common the rule that the scientist must look for only natural causes to
explain things in the universe and not invoke supernatural causes—causes that are not
part of nature. This assumption frustrates anyone who believes that at least some
important events in history are due to supernatural intervention—intervention by God
who is "super" (above) nature. To many religious believers scientific naturalism is foolish, an unnecessary restriction on the overall search for truth.[1] No one can know in
advance, say some religious writers, that only natural causes are operating in the world.
God may be also operating, above and beyond the limits of nature and not restricted by
it. A miracle is at least partly due to more than just natural causes. No one can prove
that miracles never happen. So scientific naturalism is too narrow an approach, says
many a religious person.

Nonetheless, at a minimum a scientist, when doing science and not doing something else like philosophy or theology or writing poetry, must use what is called *methodological* naturalism. This means that whether there are miracles or not, whether there
are supernatural causes or not at work in the world, the scientist does not get to use
these sorts of causes for scientific explanations of events that occur in nature.

There are two major reasons for the rule of methodological naturalism. First, science explains how and why things happen precisely by learning what reliable and predictable activities and forces and structures exist in nature. The chemical bonding of
sodium and chlorine to form table salt is a predictable process, for example, now able
to be understood in terms of the electromagnetic interaction of the electron "shells" of
chlorine and sodium atoms. Likewise, the gravitational effect of one mass upon another
can be precisely and reliably predicted. According to most religious belief, however,
God's actions are not predictable. Human actions are not always predictable either, but
with humans there is at least the chance to investigate, to ask questions, to formulate
psychological or sociological hypotheses and then test them out. This is not the case
with the super-natural, with the divine. Theologians often speculate on apparent divine
interventions in the universe. But it can only be speculation. There is no way to inter-
rogate God. Where people say that God's supernatural power has cured someone for
God's own inscrutable reasons, the search to increase human understanding has to
end—maybe God did it for this reason or that, but we can really never know.

The second reason for methodological naturalism is the successful history of applying it. Where people have decided to look for natural causes, they have very often succeeded. We now have a polio vaccine because of the methodological naturalism that directs scientists to look for natural causes and natural cures. We no longer attribute illness to sorcery or demons.

Cosmological naturalism goes further, though few people use this name for it. This is a theological or philosophical conclusion, that even if there is a God who can do whatever God wants, God in fact has chosen not to intervene in the world. In this view God has made a world to operate entirely by its own internal order of causes. We will see this described in language which calls God the ongoing "primary" (and supernatural) cause of everything, sustaining the universe as a closed arena of events operating entirely by "secondary" natural causes.

If science could establish that God never intervenes in the world, then science could establish that cosmological naturalism is the truth. But this is difficult to do, as we will see. It is always possible, for example, that there is a God who does intervene in the world, but in ways that escape empirical observation. John Haught, classifies cosmological naturalism as one form of what he and others call "scientism." Those who claim to have valid scientific reasons for affirming cosmological naturalism, Haught says, are really stretching beyond science and arriving at a philosophical position.[2] Haught in fact does not actually attend much to cosmological naturalism, on the grounds that for him at least divine interventions are not a major aspect of religion.

There is finally what is called *metaphysical* (or sometimes "ontological") naturalism. The word metaphysical has two different meanings, unfortunately. Sometime people use it when they are talking about New Age powers and potions and realms. Theosophy, for example, a sort of New Age combination of Hindu and Platonist ideas, says there is an "astral plane" to which each human soul goes to rest between lives on earth. Some call this a metaphysical idea. But that is not the meaning of "metaphysical" when it is attached to the word "naturalism." Metaphysics in this latter case is about whatever is the ultimate truth behind everything else. In Western religions God is said to be the single Ultimate, the sole truly metaphysical reality. Metaphysical naturalism is the claim that there is no God, there is only nature. Nature itself is the sole Ultimate Reality. A scientist may believe this to be true. A scientist may think that there are no good reasons to believe in a God, or even that there are good reasons to believe no God exists. But if she or he claims that *science* can show that no God exists, this is what theologians like Haught call scientism.

The fullest form of scientism, according to its critics, is the belief that the only valid method for arriving at conclusions about reality is the method of science. Among its other faults, Haught argues, it is self-defeating. The claim that only the method of science provides reliable truth is not a scientific statement; it is a philosophical conclusion. One who supports scientism is implicitly acting as though philosophy is another legitimate way of arriving at true conclusions. On the other hand, those who apply the scientific method to any and all fact-claim issues can argue that science is the only method that has shown itself to be highly effective in actual practice, even if it will never know everything. We will see more of this issue.

Materialism and corpuscularism

Religious attacks on naturalism often associate it closely with a few other ideas: materialism, reductionism, and a mechanistic view of nature. There is some truth in this, but it is also misleading in different ways. Let's look at each of these ideas to see this.

Materialism says that only matter exists. There are no "spiritual"—non-material—realities. The traditional list of spiritual realities usually includes God, angels, demons, and human souls; sometimes it includes the popular notion of souls that got stuck somehow in the world as ghosts. In the early 17th century, many of the "natural philosophers" doing science proposed to do away with all spiritual realities except God and the human soul. Everything else was just mathematically measurable matter in motion, very regular or predictable in its motions. They called their philosophy a "corpuscularist" theory of nature. We would come close to their meaning if we called it an "atomic" theory of nature. Whatever the name, it stands for a conviction that all material reality is made up of tiny corpuscles or particles—in mathematically measurable motion.

The corpuscularists had two reasons to promote this idea. The first was to get rid of belief in "occult" forces. A long tradition based on late and rather odd versions of Platonism claimed that there were invisible (occult or hidden) magical forces which a person in tune with the harmonies of nature could control. Alchemists counted on influencing these forces to help them turn lead into gold. Physicians tried to harness these forces in order to heal. Ancient books instructing a person on how to become a magus (one who could control magical powers; plural: magi), even said that hidden (occult) magic inherent in nature would allow people to exert influence over a distance, like sending messages to another person's mind but without any normal physical means of contact. The corpuscularists complained that such invisible forces were not regular and reliable natural patterns, nor subject to mathematical analysis. The corpuscularists were put off, in fact, by Newton's description of the force we call gravity. This gravity was regular and reliable, so it was partly acceptable; but it seemed to exert its force at a distance without any physical contact, like an occult or magical force.

The second reason to promote corpuscularism was to get rid of the theory that plants and animals had souls. The ancient philosophies of Aristotle and Plato had argued that every living or animate thing must have an animating force in it. A dog gave birth to puppies because the animating force in it drove it to engage in sex; then the animating force ran the pregnant dog from within so that puppies would develop, and each puppy developed its own inner animating force to allow it to develop and grow up to be a dog. We call these animating forces "souls" ("anima" is the Latin word for a soul). The problem with souls, as far as the new science was concerned, was that they also were apparently not subject to the reliable and regular laws of nature. They had some reliability; dogs did not give birth to birds or turtles but only to more dogs. But the new scientists wanted answers that were more specific than the vague notion of souls. One or two corpuscularists went so far as to say humans had no souls either. That opinion placed a person in great danger from religious and state authorities in many places. So most declared that humans did have spiritual and free souls, as the Christian tradition had insisted from relatively early centuries.

The corpuscularist theory portrays all plants and animals as machines, complex assemblies of inert material components, whose bones and sinews operated like levers and pulleys. So this theory was also usually called a mechanistic theory. Some claimed that all material activities were running on the energy which God had imparted to the whole universe at creation; others said God continued to supply existence-power to sustain the universe. In either case, an implication of this materialist theory is that what we ordinarily call life activities in plants and animals can all be "reduced" to the level of inert or lifeless matter in mechanical motion. The human soul, most maintained, is the only thing in the world that cannot be reduced to matter in motion.

Revising materialism

Concern over "materialism" is usually based on the idea that matter is "dead" or inert. Life and mind seem to be more than what dead matter can do. By the 20th century, however, it had become clear that matter is not very inert or merely mechanical. The material universe is actually a matter-energy/space-time universe. Energy is the more basic reality; what we call matter is condensed energy. The Big Bang some 13.7 billion years ago was an enormous explosion of pure energy. Within the tiniest fraction of a second much of the raw energy began to condense, so to speak, into quarks. As things cooled down slightly more, quarks that slammed together sometimes formed stable neutrons and protons. Out of these came atoms; from atoms compounds formed; in stars heavier elements were eventually produced. All of this are forms energy takes. "Energism" in fact might be a more accurate word than "materialism" to describe the basic character of the universe as science sees it. Cosmological naturalism can be correct without implying that the universe is made of inert matter.

Another misleading bit of language is to say that this energist view of the universe is always reductionistic. The word correctly suggests an aspect of science, that the best way to understand phenomenon must include—though not restrict itself to—breaking a problem down into parts, looking for the details of the construction of a life form or a chemical interaction, and so on. Chemists, however, do not just reduce things to the physical activity of electron bonding. Chemists also note carefully which new characteristics emerge from certain complex chemical bondings. Chemists even seek to construct new chains of elements which will be able to act in ways much more complex and useful than the physics alone might suggest. Similarly, biologists do not explain life forms and activities only by looking at the chemical characteristics of things like various amino acids. They also take careful note of the genetic codes that have emerged over time. These biological codes produce chemical activities far in excess of ordinary chemical reactions.

The key word here is "emerge." Reducing things into simplicity is half of the process of science; seeing how things emerge into complexity is the other half. "Emergentism" more accurately labels much approaches to the information we have gained about how the world has come to have the forms and processes which science investigates. A person can use reductionism in science even while recognizing that from the evolution of the material universe significant properties have emerged, especially those of life and consciousness, a topic we will cover at greater length later.

The method of science

Among the dozens of different books analyzing the method of science, many have tried to pin down the "logic of discovery" and the "logic of justification" (to use the language of the chemist/philosopher Karl Popper). Philosophers of science once hoped to lay out in neat logical order the methodical steps for discovering good theories about reality, and then lay out in equally logical order the proper steps for proving that a theory is true. This is more difficult than it might seem at first.

The search for the logic of science began very long ago. The goal of ancient Greek science was formulated by Aristotle, following the lead of others before him (especially a philosopher named Parmenides). The goal was *episteme* (pronounced episTAYmay in Greek), meaning knowledge-with-certitude, as opposed to mere opinion or appearances. And the best way to achieve this seemed to be to deduce conclusions logically from reliable premises. This remained the goal for late medieval thinkers and even for many in the times of early science, but the word used was now the Latin one, *scientia*. This still meant the same as *episteme*: logically deduced knowledge, and therefore knowledge-with-certitude. Here is an example of logical deduction in the simplest form of what is called a syllogism (a structured logical argument):

1. Every A is a B
2. Every B is a C
3. Therefore every A is a C

If the premises #1 and #2 are true, then #3 *has* to be true. That is logic. But notice the "if." Establishing the truth of the premises can be difficult. From long experience people in Europe were sure that all swans are white. Then someone stumbled across the black swans of Australia. Oooops. A challenge for any logical analysis or any science, is to find a way to get highly reliable premises.

Some analyses of the method of science argue that there is no single method of science. Each of them gets its premises in different ways; each of them tests them differently. Biology does not restrict itself to the tools of physics; and physics relies on mathematics much more than biology. Astronomers use telescopes; geologists use radiometric dating. A survey of methods and tools makes it seem that there are as many methods of science as there are forms of faith. In practice, that is not true. The many sciences share an underlying single set of practices, developed over centuries of trial and error, which have turned out to be extremely effective in discriminating between theories that work as though they were true and those that do not.

The method of modern science has four main aspects. You will recognize some of them as part of what was said in Chapter 1 about what makes an idea "reasonable."

1. Identify facts and patterns.
Get the facts, the basic information about reality, as best you can. This consists of categorizing things into categories like "dog" and "tree" and "wind" and "sparks." It also consists of identifying reliable patterns such as are sometimes called "laws," like the law of gravity. Call both "facts" and "laws" by the name "fact-claims." Fact-claims are assertions about what the real world is really like (though philosophers of science remind us that these claims are, after all, still only our mental images of what the world is really like). Most of the facts and patterns we know, we were taught to recognize by others, who learned these as we do from the long history of a person's culture. So a person's culture can influence what the person sees, a point to return to.

2. Explain the facts or patterns through a hypothesis that can become a "theory."
Construct a hypothesis that could explain the facts and laws. Thus Darwin's early hypothesis of how evolution took place sought to explain why both fossils and living organisms were geographically distributed as they were, in rock layers from the past and on the surface of the earth. This, along with much other evidence, suggests that current species are descendants of earlier species. Eventually the evidence made Darwin's hypothesis into a well-functioning theory of evolution. (The line between laws and theories is somewhat arbitrary; some theories, like the theory of gravity, are only laws of a more general nature.)

3. Test both the theories and the facts-claims.
Establish how reliable and accurate the fact-claims and the theories are through two tests: First find more evidence. The facts of the fossils in the rock layers may be deceptive. Check out more rock layers, from various places in the world, but from even more depths and heights than before. Examine the layers more carefully and compare fossils more completely. Make sure the theory continues to fit with the new evidence. Second,

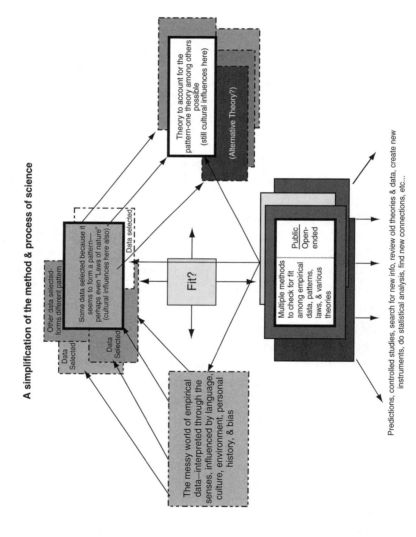

A simplification of the method & process of science

Other data selected-forms different pattern

Some data selected because it seems to form a pattern—perhaps even "Laws of nature" (cultural influences here also)

Data selected

Data Selected

Data Selected

Data selected

Theory to account for the pattern-one theory among others possible
(still cultural influences here)

(Alternative Theory?)

Fit?

The messy world of empirical data—interpreted through the senses, influenced by language, culture, environment, personal history, & bias

Multiple methods to check for fit among empirical data, patterns, laws, & various theories

Public
Open-
ended

Predictions, controlled studies, search for new info, review old theories & data, create new instruments, do statistical analysis, find new connections, etc....

Figure 3.1 A model of the method of science.

check out theories also by comparing them to all other theories that are in any way related, as are theories in evolution and geology. Comparing a theory to other theories is comparing a theory indirectly to the evidence supporting those other theories. A good theory must fit with all other relevant theories. When it does not, something is wrong somewhere.

4. The process must be a long-term public one, open to all challenges.

A crucially important aspect of science is that the method works reliably only when it is an ongoing process of investigation in which all fact-claims, theorizing, evidence and analysis must be made public. That means that in principle anyone is able to criticize the fact-claims and theories for failure to fit well with all the available relevant evidence, direct and indirect, and with the demands of logical clarity and consistency. Some critics of science, as we will see, charge that science is open to distortion and mistake because of individual interests and cultural bias. This is certainly true. It is true of any and all truth-claims that human beings make. The way in which the method of science compensates for these dangers is its practice of submitting all fact-claims and theories to public challenge by anyone, even a person with different interests and bias, over an indefinite period of time, until the use of a theory in practice over time and in many contexts has determined it to be highly reliable.

To repeat briefly: on the basis of observations of the world (the evidence) develop ideas about reality (fact-claims, laws, hypotheses, theories), then test those ideas publicly in an open-ended way to see how everything fits together. When all the ideas, categories, fact-claims, laws, theories in our minds fit very well with all other ideas, categories, etc., in particular with those that would usually be called evidence, then "so far, so good." When something does not fit, it is time to check things out again and possibly revise. As long-term wide-spread "fit" increases, the probability that the ideas are true also increases, but the public testing for fit must go on. (See Figure 3.1 for a model of the method of science.)

Networks and puzzles

Two images are especially helpful for understanding the basic method of science. The first image is that of a network of ideas. As people test one idea against other ideas they are building up an ever-larger network of ideas that support one another. As long as the varieties of ideas, fact-claims, theories, tests represented by the different boxes in Figure 3.1 all fit together coherently, each of them becomes more plausible. This can be understood as one of the strengths of science.

An earlier approach to science tried to portray it not as a network of mutually reinforcing ideas but as a set of ideas built up logically from a basic *foundational* set of truths. Descartes (1596–1650) is famous for doubting everything except the fact that he was doubting. "I think, therefore I am" are his well-known words. He wanted to use that undoubtable truth as the foundation for the whole rest of his scientific enterprise. We do not have to follow his line of thought to see how he imagined he would do this. It is enough to say that "foundationalism" has long been abandoned in scientific practice. Seeking instead to extend and strengthen and fill out the network of ideas is how science has long been functioning.

It is an amazing boot-strap operation. Identifying the "law" of gravity—the relation between mass and distance and acceleration—does not explain what gravity is, why it exists as it does, why it should or should not be that way. Nonetheless, it is a very workable law. It functions as though it is the truth. We do know more, say, about basic atomic elements and how they can bond chemically. We do not know why the quarks that make up the parts of atoms should exist as they do. But the chemistry works wonderfully well. As long as more and more things connect in a network of well-functioning ideas, they help to confirm the value of taking them as true—or at least a very good approximation of truth. The network hangs in the air, like a spider web floating in the breeze, catching more and more of the world and holding it within its patterns.

Those skeptical of Radical Orthodoxy, the position of Karl Barth and others, call it a boot-strap position too, holding itself up in the air by its own boot straps. If science also is a boot-strap affair, that would seem to undercut its validity. A major difference, though, between Barth's faith and scientific conclusions is that the latter requires extensive empirical evidence open to public challenge. The same is not true of Radical Orthodoxy.

The second image that aids in understanding the scientific method is a crossword puzzle. The clues of a puzzle (the evidence) suggest that a certain word is appropriate for a set of spaces in the puzzle. The word, however, has to fit with other words which cross it, and the other words in turn have to fit with words that cross them. So it is also with the individual conclusions even of different domain of science. Geological theories must be consonant with physics; theories in biology must not conflict with chemistry.

Science has an advantage over a crossword puzzle in that it does not have to settle for a single clue (piece of evidence) for a given set of spaces. It can and should go out and look for ever more clues that would either confirm or conflict with a given word for those spaces. Crossword puzzles also have boundaries; science does not. The goal of science is to keep finding more and more blank spaces to fill up with the relevant interconnected information. Nothing in the natural universe is intrinsically safe from scientific inquiries. On the other hand, the universe is too deeply complex for complete and final explanations of all things. Every new set of blanks filled in will reveal more that is not known.

Whether one thinks of science as network formation or crossword puzzle solving, this process is also subject to endless review by others working within the same network or puzzle or a closely connected network or puzzle. Every day people apply the network or puzzle to practical questions. These applications continue to test the network or puzzles. Although science will never know everything, there is no other method that has proven anywhere nearly as effective in providing a great deal of extremely well-functioning truth-claims about the universe.

Science as the basic human method for reliable knowledge

It is important to note this basic method is not restricted to science. It is not a unique set of rules devised for the limited activities we call science. This method is actually the everyday method we use to determine whether the oven is working or the car needs a new battery or the cat is indoors. Formulate a reasonable guess, then check it out. If the guess is right, great. If not, try another guess. When necessary get more precision in your search—checking the air pressure in your tires to explain a "hard" ride, vary the time and temperature of the chicken in the oven to determine which time and temperature will get the results you want.

Science differs from these everyday practices in two ways. The first is its extreme precision, measuring exactly, demanding very strict "fit" of (almost) all relevant evidence, controlling for variables, including potentially hidden ones.

The second is its practice of long-term public review, testing, and application by others. These repetitions by others constituted a kind of public review or testing of new truth-claims. Public reviews can take place in various ways. In the early days of the Royal Society in London, various natural philosophers would gather to watch someone exhibit a device or carry out an experiment. Leeuwenhoek, for example, in 1676 the first person to see bacteria through one of the many microscopes he constructed, met skepticism when he reported this from Holland to the Royal Society in London. He then got an English priest as well as some Dutch professional-class peers to look through his microscopes to confirm his work. He also sent microscopes to London so the Society members could take a look for themselves.

Today a major means to assure public review is publication in "refereed" journals. A person submits a description of research in the form of a scientific article. The editors of the journal send the article to experts in the field—"referees." (Sometimes the author's name is omitted. This is a "blind" review.) The experts are not told which other experts are viewing the article. These experts are individually supposed to give reasons why the article should or should not be published. The reasons have to be the kind that others knowledgeable about the field could recognize as legitimate.

In any report in physics or chemistry or geology submitted for peer review, a main thing reviewers will look for is whether the results reported could have been caused by something other than what the article claims is the cause. The reviewers will ask whether the experimental setup controlled for this or that possible variable. Geologists, for example, will ask questions about whether certain results arise under specific temperatures or pressures; whether a type of rock has the same size crystals or whether the size varies with the supposed depth of the formation of the crystals, and so on. Often such questions cannot be answered, at least not right away.

Frequently, the result of this first review process is a recommendation on how the research and/or the article could be improved. The author then has the chance to make the improvements and re-submit the article for further review. If a journal rejects an article, it is always possible to submit it to another. This process can take a long time.

Publication is not the end of the reviews. Others can use the information in the published article to test the claims further. This can be a deliberate replication of the original work in a laboratory or in the field. Someone doubtful about claims concerning superconductivity (extremely rapid conduction of electricity through some medium) at extremely cold temperatures can try to duplicate the processes the authors of the article describe. As was mentioned, published claims also get tested by anyone who tries to apply those claims to some other process. The application of published results to new contexts extends the review and testing process indefinitely.

This summary of the method of science disguises the messiness of the actual process. There are multiple possible ways to select groups of observations, multiple interpretations of what patterns prevail, multiple possible theories to make sense of it all. A critic of science can point to all this messiness and argue that there is a lot of room for error or for arbitrary judgment. The next chapter will look at this.

For further reading

Applebaum, Wilbur, *The Scientific Revolution and the Foundations of Modern Science* (Westport, CT: Greenwood Press, 2005).

Gale, George, *Theory of Science: An Introduction to the History, Logic, and Philosophy of Science* (New York: McGraw-Hill, 1976).

Silver, Brian L., *The Ascent of Science* (New York: Oxford University Press, 1998).

The Limits of Science

4

Chapter Outline

Dimensions of life beyond science

Conflicts between religion and science arise in the area of truth-claims about how things are and operate in the world. This is the realm where science is competent. It is useful to repeat, however, that there are some matters that lie beyond the reach of the scientific method.

One of those matters is the establishment of basic human values. Science can tell us much about "instrumental" values. If we want to prevent cholera, scientific investigation has taught us to secure a source of clean water. Making sure the water supply is uncontaminated is thus an important value for the sake of—an instrument for—avoiding disease. Unfortunately, this scientific knowledge could also be used to achieve a different value if we find ways to contaminate the water source of an enemy who is attacking us.

Science cannot, however, establish which basic values we *ought* to have. Should we want to be healthy? Of course, we say. But it is not the scientific method that establishes this as a value. We may want health for ourselves and others simply because we find our lives and theirs to be intrinsically valuable. Should we want to make our enemies ill? On the one hand we could thereby avoid defeat. On the other hand this particular instrument which our science provides us may be too indiscriminate, killing not just our attackers but their children also. Perhaps we judge all forms of biological warfare unacceptable. Science cannot tell us what values should take priority in such cases. Other sources of value-judgments must come into play.

Religion has usually been one of the sources of moral judgments, though religion is not the only source of morality. From before Socrates, philosophers have proposed various ethics. Secular thinkers today do the same. Significantly, one religious tradition can reject the moral standards of another religious tradition. Deciding whether to eat pork or beef, judging how many wives a man might be allowed at a maximum, taking a stand on whether war is ever legitimate, are all issues where religions have disagreed. Even within a single religious tradition there can also be differences, on sexual moralities, on the use of force or violence, on the status of women. So religion itself has problems with establishing basic moral values.

It is rather too simple, therefore, to say as some have, that science deals with truth-claims while religion deals with values, as though religion alone could do this or that religion can do this more easily. People who are science-minded and those who are not, people who are religious and those who are not, may all have value judgments and arguments to make.

Other important aspects of life are also in the end more than science can handle. In general the flow of human history is too complex for an adequate scientific analysis. Historians can engage in many generalities about how things have happened and how they have come to be as they are now. They can point to specific moments in history as especially influential. But predicting even the weather is easy compared to predicting the course of history.

Each individual life exhibits a somewhat similar complexity. The concurrence of genes and fetal development and individual nourishment and education and the countless differences in personal experiences produce unique individuals. Every individual's mental activities, from relatively simpler desire, repulsion, or excitement, to much more complex reflection and choice, are on a level of extraordinary complexity. Sociologists and psychologists and neurophysiologists try to track human patterns of causality and thereby include human life within the scope of the sciences. Functional magnetic resonance imaging (fMRI) can tell a good amount about how an individual's brain operates. But the full rich scope of individual humanness will remain beyond the reach of such studies. (A later chapter will examine this issue more thoroughly.)

The logical limits of science

Through the scientific method we have learned a great deal about the universe. But logically speaking it ought not to work very well. Here is why.

Science seems to provide a way to achieve some degree of certitude by testing fact-claims to see how reliable they are. A famous instance was the 1919 trip of the astronomer Sir Arthur Eddington to Africa to watch a total eclipse of the sun to test Einstein's theory of relativity. Einstein's theory included the claim that the gravity of a body as large as the sun would noticeably bend light rays a certain precise amount. But it is very difficult to observe anything happening near the sun because of its brightness. So Eddington waited for an eclipse. When the sun was darkened by the moon, he looked to see the position of a star whose light passed close to the sun.

The exact position of this star was already known. If Einstein were correct, as the light passed the sun, the mass of the sun would pull the light ray slightly off course. The star would appear to be in a slightly different place than it really was. Newton had predicted a small deflection would occur; Einstein's theory, however, said the deflection would be almost twice as much as Newton had indicated. Eddington looked and sure enough, the light from the star struck his telescope lens almost exactly where Einstein predicted.[1]

That sounds like good proof that Einstein was right. But consider it from a strictly logical point of view. Here is the formal logic:

> If Einstein is correct, then the light will appear off course by a certain precise amount.
> The light appeared off course by that certain precise amount.
> Therefore . . .?

Logicians would abbreviate this kind of argument as "If A, then B. But B is the case." If B is *not* the case, then A must not be correct. If Einstein were wrong, then the light would probably not appear off course to the degree it did. In that case the evidence would then have "falsified" Einstein's theory, at least on this one point. Knowing that a theory is incorrect is an important part of science. It indicates that there is a need to revise the theory or create a new one. But the light did appear as precisely off course as Einstein's theory predicted. Was his theory therefore shown to be true? To answer that consider another set of statements of the same logical form:

> If a large moose walks on this wooden bridge, it will collapse. ("If A, then B")
> The bridge has collapsed. ("B is the case")
> Therefore . . .?

Unfortunately there is no conclusion that follows from this logically. Maybe a large moose did walk on the wooden bridge. Or maybe a herd of sheep did instead. Or maybe a big wind in the night made it collapse. Or maybe termites working at it finally ate away too much of it. Or maybe a UFO landed on it. This is the problem of "alternative hypotheses." In theory, there is no end to the number of alternative hypotheses that might be formulated to explain certain events.

Similarly, perhaps also there are other causes that made the starlight fall in a certain place on Eddington's telescope that have nothing to do with Einstein's theory. No guarantees exist that a good sounding theory is the only way to account for an event. There might be some alternative theory no one has thought of yet, but which will prove to fit much better eventually with the whole range of relevant evidence and other theories. To falsify a theory is much easier than to verify it.

On the other hand, this problem is often less compelling in the concrete. In the case of Einstein's theory it is hard to figure out just what alternative causes there might be. There are no known alternatives. So Einstein's theory is more secure. Furthermore, in the case of the bridge, as with most hypotheses, a person can look for more evidence. One can look for moose droppings or sheep prints, check with the weather bureau about storms, look for signs of termite work, and even call the sheriff's office to see if UFOs have been sighted.

Thus science deals with the problem of alternative hypotheses by a refined form of what people do every day. When the evidence has been consistent as far as anyone can tell, and when there do not seem to be any alternative explanations or when all the alternatives a person can think of have been checked out, and when the theory is applied in concrete situations repeatedly and continues to work as though it is true, then a theory stands for a time as the functional equivalent of truth.

The phrase "functional equivalent of truth" is a very cautious expression. The logical limits of science make this caution necessary. The *episteme* or truth-with-certitude long sought by philosophers is a goal we will apparently always fall somewhat short of. Nonetheless, if a truth-claim about the world functions extremely well in application, allowing people to predict in fine detail certain outcomes, and to produce other outcomes that only this theory would seem to make possible, then this theory is functioning as the truth. The more evidence that builds up, the greater confidence possible in the truth of the theory. When the evidence has built up for a very long time in many different contexts, even more confidence is legitimate. When the network of ideas, with evidence connected to evidence and theory to theory, functions exactly as predicted through many tests and applications, the more probable the theory becomes. It may function so well that it would be unreasonable not to treat it as true.

Technically speaking, however—other points that philosophers make—there are two further significant qualifications. The first is that even well-evidenced scientific truth-claims are approximate. They are made in language and categories that humans can devise, based on the particular form given to experience by human senses. Facts are not mirror-images of reality; they are human interpretations that work as though they approximate reality in varying degrees. It is not possible to know exactly how well they approximate reality because to compare the truth-claims to reality exactly, it would first be necessary to know reality exactly. Even if a person happened to have what in fact is the pure and certain truth, the person could not be sure it was indeed pure and certain and not just a rough approximation or just an aspect of a larger truth.

We are aware of this partly because science itself tells us that we cannot always trust what seems to be plain evidence. Physics tells us that what our senses perceive as a solid surface is in fact a set of intersecting dynamic electromagnetic fields bound together so tightly and on so small a scale that our crude senses can only perceive solidness. Physiology tells us that the colors we see are the result of the responses of various retinal cells to different wave lengths of light. Ironically, we understand and accept these examples precisely to the degree we think science has it right on these points.

The second qualification is close to the first—that all scientific truth-claims are tentative. Because they are approximations they can be improved upon. In fact they may turn out to be rather poor approximations in comparison with a theory that arises much later. In that case what is needed is not to improve them but simply to replace them. Whether such a serious change will take place is not fully within our ability to predict. So no final verification of a theory can exist. Philosophers of science are usually careful, therefore, never to claim that science "proves" anything. Science can only provide ongoing evidence which cumulatively makes a hypothesis so well established that it can be called a scientific theory. To qualify as a theory a scientific idea must have excellent and consistent evidence in its support.

In spite of these difficulties, some ideas have meshed with so many others for so long and have been applied in so many contexts it may be reasonable not to expect any change. Our concept of "oxygen" is one such idea. In the 1770s a number of people, including famous opponents Priestly and Lavoisier, were trying to figure out what makes things burn. Long-standing tradition said combustion was a process of releasing the element "fire" (called "phlogiston" for a century or so). Lavoisier discovered that combustion was instead a rapid union of some elements with a gas he eventually called "oxygen." In less than a hundred years Dalton developed a theory of different atomic elements; Mendeleev later placed most elements in his periodic table. Further developments in atomic theory now allow us to describe in some detail just how and why oxidation takes place, thereby explaining such diverse events as combustion, corrosion, and respiration. Our knowledge of oxygen explains why acetylene torches used in China can melt iron, why the copper figures of the gods in India slowly turn green, and why an oxygen tent can help someone in New Guinea who has difficulty in breathing. The notion of diverse atomic elements, including oxygen, has fit so well and so long in so many applications it would be unreasonable not to treat "oxygen" as fact—or at least the functional equivalent of fact.

Even with the limits described here, the method of modern science has proved stunningly successful in testing ideas about reality so well and so finely as to produce an enormous body of interconnected ideas about reality that function as though they were simply the truth. In thousands of applications of these ideas in physics, chemistry, geology, biology, and astronomy, in laboratories and factories, in hospitals and military installations, the ideas prove themselves highly reliable and effective. Any that do not, cannot be treated as scientifically valid.

Whether the method of science is based on faith

Some have argued that there are various beliefs, held by a kind of secular (non-religious) faith, on which science depends. This could imply that because both science and religion are based on types of faith, they can be different but still equal in authority as sources of truth. Here is a list of some of the ways in which it has been claimed that science rests on faith of some sort.

1. Scientists have faith that previous science has been done correctly and that they can trust the claims they find in their scientific sources.
2. Scientists have faith that the universe is fully intelligible—that it runs by regular and reliable natural causes, many of which can be expressed in mathematical language.
3. Scientists have faith that human intelligence is sufficiently strong so as to be able to grasp correctly whatever intelligibility there is in the universe.
4. Scientists have faith in the criterion of "fit" with evidence and logic as the correct criterion to apply in deciding what is true or not.
5. Scientists must also, of course, have faith that the universe they think they encounter is really there and is really there in the way they experience it.

There is some truth in some of these statements, but they are misleading if they are meant to suggest that science is dependent on faith rather than evidence. Consider each of the five points:

1. It is true that few scientists would rerun any of the tests of the past to determine for themselves first-hand whether previous science has been done correctly. Sometimes scientists simply trust their peers to have done what they claim to have done. Nevertheless, unless the claims are truly useless in the sense of having no application to other scientific problems or questions, the claims will be tested by being applied. This provides evidence that the claims work—or shows that something is wrong with them. This relies on evidence, not faith.

2. The "faith" that scientists have in the intelligibility of the universe has two aspects. First, methodological naturalism is the practice of acting as though the universes were fully intelligible through knowledge of natural causes and conditions. This is the only way to get knowledge of how the natural world works. Second, the history of attempts to understand the world through naturalism shows it to be extremely effective. Revelations, inspirations, intuitions, communication from the dead, crystal balls or

magical powers have all failed to yield *reliable* results. Naturalism gives evidence of its reasonableness. Evidence is again the important word here, not faith.

3. Scientists know that their minds are limited and that some of the mysteries of the natural world may never be understood. You only succeed at what you try, however; so scientists like all of us act on the assumption that our intelligence can take us a long way if we make the effort. So far the evidence says this is a well-working assumption. It took a very long time to make the effort work. Serious attempts at it began with the ancient philosophies of the axial age, about 2,500 years ago. After a few thousand years of limited success, with no single philosophy clearly winning out, it is amazing that humans persisted in seeking intelligibility. For 2,000 years, perhaps, there was a lot of faith at work. But for the last 200 years the modern method of science, which people stumbled up in spite of reasons to doubt its efficacy, has worked exceedingly well. It is now evidence rather than faith that justifies the method of science.

4. The method of "fit," including its trust in using evidence as a major test, justifies itself both in daily life as the only effective method we have for figuring things out, as well as in the history of the success of science. We are organisms who have evolved to respond to what our senses tell us about our environment. The senses tell us when a dangerous animal is approaching or a potential mate is available for reproduction. It should be no surprise to have strong evidence that relying on evidence works. Modern science has simply learned or invented ways to discover and test evidence with enormous care and precision and subject the results of such tests to public review.

5. All of us human beings together in every culture can apply science to what seems to us to be our common world. We cannot prove the world exists, or that it exists in the way that it appears to us. But this apparent world is the only one we have to live in. And so far this universalizing science seems to work extremely well in this single apparent world. Beliefs in parallel worlds or mystical worlds or magical worlds that exist in addition to this daily world have not shown themselves to work as though they were in fact true. We avoid stepping in front of speeding buses and avoid swallowing paper clips for nourishment, because the world we live in must be treated as real if we are going to be able to continue to live at all. So, at least, says all the reliable evidence available to us.

A bit of circularity lies at the core of this set of observations. Response #4 says the evidence tells us that relying on evidence works. The challenge, however, is to justify relying on evidence as strongly as this. Is this still not an act of faith about the validity of evidence? As is so often the case with science, there is no theoretical or philosophical way to establish the validity of relying on evidence. There is only a practical or pragmatic basis for trusting evidence—what else should or could we trust, since relying on evidence is what gets us through each day alive. Has any other method shown itself in practice to be reliably effective? To repeat this one more time, relying on evidence has shown itself to work exceedingly well when done with the precision and controls used by science.

Seeking objectivity

Although science no longer expects to find absolute truth—*episteme*—it does seek to have a high degree of objectivity, to compensate adequately for the inevitable subjective bias and interests at work in whatever people do, including science.

Sometimes an investigation can be done "double blind." This is often called the gold standard of medical research. Imagine that a new drug is being tested to cure a kind of skin inflammation. To test the drug, there are some variables to take into account. It may be that this particular skin problem sometimes heals by itself. If a person is given drugs there is also often some degree of positive result even if the drug is not effective in itself. This is known as the placebo effect. "Placebo" is Latin for "I will please" (or "I will put at ease"). Being treated with an injection or capsule or pill seems to produce some positive results in a person through the psychological effect of being treated at all.[2] Natural remission ("cure") and the placebo effect can, together or separately, make it more difficult to tell whether an apparent cure is due to a specific drug or not. Ideally, then, to study whether the drug is effective, it would be necessary to "control" for the variables of natural remission and/or the placebo effect.

To test a drug thoroughly an investigator will set up four groups of people, carefully matched both for the seriousness of their skin inflammation, for comparable overall health, for habits such as exercise and diet, whether they smoke or not, and for any other factors that might influence their response to the drug. One of these groups will be monitored to see what percentage of the cases get well on their own. A second group will be given medical counseling but no treatment. A third group will be given a placebo along with their medical counseling. A fourth group will be given the drug that is being tested and medical counseling. The third and fourth groups will not be told whether they are receiving the placebo or the drug being tested. That is the first "blind" aspect of the study.

If the medical personnel administering the drug know who is getting the placebo and who is getting the actual drug, they might inadvertently indicate that in some way. Those administering the placebo, for example, might unconsciously shrug as though to say, "I do not have much confidence in this." Those who know they are administering the real drug might sound more hopeful. In the latter case the placebo effect might kick in, or do so more strongly. So the medical personnel have to be kept in ignorance also, perhaps by random assignment of supplies to them or by some other method, so they cannot know whether they are administering the placebo or the real thing. This is the second "blind." Hence the name, double blind study. The obvious intent of the method is to eliminate any subjective elements, except for the subjective intent to participate in this study, of course—and the intent to make it as objective as possible.

Not every scientific study can be done through a double blind procedure. Eddington could not do such a study with the light passing by the sun. He could nonetheless try to "control" for as many variable as possible. He did, after all, compare the track of the starlight around the sun to the track of the starlight when it does not pass the sun. More importantly in this case, the control would come through the repetition of this and other tests of Einstein's theory by other people under other conditions. Each of those other people would certainly have subjective interests, bias, and habits. Each of them, in fact, probably shares in one particular sort of interest, which is to be able to claim to have established something new or different. Some investigators, therefore, would probably be very happy to find evidence that says that Einstein was wrong or that Eddington was wrong. That would establish the abilities of these investigators in the field of physics. To do this, though, they have to produce the evidence that would convince others working in the field. The end result of all this activity by many investigators seems to be that it compensates quite adequately for subjective aspects that otherwise could produce unreliable conclusions.

The main reason to say that the compensation for any subjectivity is adequate is not that it theoretically makes sense this would happen. The four major aspects of the scientific hunt for "fit" are open to all sorts of distortions or mistakes. We human beings are notoriously guided by subjective impulses, habits, and interests. Nonetheless, the compensation for subjective elements that the method of science achieves can be called adequate because it has in fact empirically worked so well. The education of a scientist includes a lot of practice at achieving a high degree of objectivity. Those who enter the sciences may also be mostly people who are more likely to strive for a high degree of objectivity in their work. In any case, even though no person and no system is perfect, the process called "science" works terribly well. A kind of working objectivity has indeed been achieved, and achieved repeatedly.

Two case studies

A significant case of this is the story of "cold fusion." Stars produce energy by fusing elements into heavier elements. Our sun does this mainly by fusing hydrogen atoms into helium. For decades physicists have been trying to create a star-like fusion process in laboratories. The goal is to get a greater output of energy out of a lesser energy input. A successful fusion device would pay for itself in energy output. It would also be environmentally safe.

Laboratory methods have focused mainly on "hot fusion," by creating enough pressure and heat to force hydrogen to fuse into helium. So far it has always taken more energy to create fusion than the process produces. In 1989, however, the noted electrochemists Martin Fleischman and Stanley Pons announced they had produced cold fusion. They had forced heavy water—H_2O in which the hydrogen molecules have both a proton and a neutron and thus are heavier than normal hydrogen—into a lattice made of the metal palladium. They then ran an electric current through the lattice, to see if it could both break down the water into its components and then force the freed heavy hydrogen atoms to fuse into helium. Their main measurement of this was whether they got more total energy out of the compartment containing the heavy water and palladium than the amount of energy going into the compartment in the form of electricity. They claimed they accomplished this.

The news was extremely exciting; it was also met by skepticism by physicists. The only known physical pathway for this to occur ought to also release lots of spare neutrons. But Fleischman and Pons did not report significant neutron radiation. This was good in one way; the amount of neutrons freed to fly about would create radiation poisoning in anyone nearby. But it was a bad sign in another way; it cast doubt upon whether there was true fusion going on.[3]

Fleischman and Pons had good reputations as chemists. One sort of bias that was evident in the following weeks was a tendency on the part of other chemists to think that Fleischman and Pons might be on to something. The only thing that would count, however, in determining whether cold fusion worked would be the many attempts by others to duplicate the results Fleischman and Pons claimed to have produced. Professors with laboratories that could duplicate the cold fusion experiment reported that when they got to their labs the next day, their graduate students had already been at work setting things up to attempt duplication. Unfortunately, more than two decades have passed since then. Many scientists have attempted to create cold fusion. For many years *The Cold Fusion Times* has published papers of those who claim to have done it and describe in detail how they did it. But when others try to duplicate their work, the results have been disappointingly inconsistent.

Dozens, perhaps even hundreds, of scientists have had high hopes that they could create some sort of useful cold fusion. But hopes are not enough; experimenters must provide the evidence they have found a method that works. It must work reliably enough to produce confidence there are regular and reliable natural causes the scientists manipulate to produce the desired result. It may still be good that after over 20 years, many are still trying out different methods to produce cold fusion. Sometimes it can take quite a while to settle issues.

A case in point is the once-strange theory of Alfred Wegener, first published in 1915 in his book *The Origin of Continents and Oceans*, that the continents were drifting about on the planet. He provided some evidence. The geology and fossils of Brazil matched those of the indent of West Africa; the same was true of the Appalachian Mountains and the hills of Scotland. An alternative hypothesis was available, however, that there had once been land bridges connecting these regions, bridges which had subsided under the Atlantic Ocean. For most geologists it was easier to imagine land masses rising up or sinking but staying in the same place than to imagine whole continents actually drifting about. (From our current knowledge we can say that Wegener got some things wrong, in particular his notion that continents plow through the earth's crust. In fact both the continents and the crust itself are composed of "plates" which float about.) Geologists made fun of Wegener's theory, including his claim that the current numerous continents had once formed a supercontinent Wegener called pangaea ("all-earth").

Relevant evidence continued to flow in, however. Mapping the strings of volcanoes pointed to major fault lines along segments of the planet's crust. Most important was the discovery of the Atlantic Rift—a crack in the floor of the Atlantic where the crust is very thin. Magnetic measurement of parallel north-south lines of rock on both sides of this rift shows that different lines have different magnetic orientation, some to the south and others to the north. Anything that can be magnetized can do so when it is very hot; when it cools it will keep the magnetic orientation it received. The earth's magnetic field reverses itself frequently enough over hundreds of thousands of years. The north-south lines of rock along the rift contain a sequence of magnetic reversals. This makes it appear that hot rock has emerged rather continuously from the rift over the last many millions of years, became magnetized, cooled, and was then pushed to the side by newly emerging rock. Even now there is evidence that says Europe and North America are drifting apart, pushed by the active Atlantic Rift. Precise measurement from space adds to our knowledge of the pace of this separation. In all, however, it took about 50 years from Wegener's book to confirmation of his theory, in the face of long skepticism. Eventually, nonetheless, the evidence won out.

For further reading

Hackman, Sandra, ed., *The Nova Reader: Science at the Turn of the Millennium* (New York: TV Books, 1999).

Horgan, John, *The End of Science: Facing the Limits of Knowledge in the Twilight of the Scientific Age* (Reading, MA: Addison-Wesley, 1996).

Kitcher, Philip, *The Advancement of Science: Science Without Legend, Objectivity Without Illusions* (New York: Oxford University Press, 1993).

5 Criticisms of Science

Many people deeply resent the powerful presence of science in the modern world and its challenge to traditional religious perspectives. Here are the words of one critic:

> Science is not a neutral or innocent commodity which can be employed as a convenience by people wishing to partake only of the West's material power. Rather it is spiritually corrosive, burning away ancient authorities and traditions. It has shown itself unable to coexist with anything. Scientists inevitably take on the mantle of the wizards, sorcerers and witch doctors. Their miracle cures are our spells, their experiments our rituals.[1]

There is some truth in this, of course. Scientific rationality can indeed burn away the authority of tradition and replace it with the authority of logic and evidence and public review. At the same time this critic seems to be complaining that non-scientists cannot distinguish metallurgy from magic. If this is so, it reveals more of the weakness of the non-scientist than of science. In any case the quotation illustrates the strong feelings that stand behind many criticisms of science.

A source of a dislike of science may lie in its difficulty. We humans do not naturally think in the carefully rational manner science uses when doing controlled studies or fastidious testing. Over the last few million years, our brains seem to have become wired to jump to *post hoc, ergo propter hoc* (after this, therefore because of this) conclusions. Another name for this sort of thinking is "anecdotal," as in using a single event as adequate evidence. A single instance or two do not establish even a good correlation between two events, much less establish causality. Anecdotal thinking is the source of many superstitions. If you had bad luck after breaking a mirror, you might conclude that breaking mirrors *causes* bad luck. Only a large-scale controlled experiment could validly establish whether this is so.

It makes evolutionary sense we would rely on anecdotal thinking. If after walking through a desert you get sick, you may avoid deserts, regardless of whether anything in the desert caused your sickness. This mode of thought is useful because it can lead a person to avoid a locale which in fact does cause illness. If you walk through a swamp and then get sick, it may be because in the swamp a malaria-carrying mosquito bit you. Staying away from swamps is a useful lesson. So we over-generalize and become cautious about things like desert walks, which in fact do not normally make anyone sick—unless, of course a rattle snake or gila monster bites.

The same can be true in the case of so-called alternative medicine. Of all the people seeking help from alternative medicine, it should not be surprising that some of them finally do get well right after using the medicine. The hominid body has been healing itself, after all, for a few million years before there was any sort of medicine around. But *post hoc propter hoc* thinking concludes that if you first used alternative treatment and then got well, the treatment must have been the cause of the cure.

A current case of such thinking is the idea that vaccinations cause autism, or more precisely that the preservative thimerosal once used in the vaccines causes autism because the thimerosal contains mercury. Autism is an inability to be aware that other people have their own inner thoughts and feelings. Vaccinations usually occur before the age when autism can be identified. It is normal, then, that the signs of autism will appear after vaccination, if they are to appear at all. *Post hoc ergo propter hoc?* On the other hand, thimerosal is no longer used in vaccines but the rate of autism seems to be increasing, not decreasing—or at least the diagnosis has become more common. Unfortunately, many parents are skipping vaccinations. If too many do that, the diseases in question have a much better chance of re-establishing themselves in the population. Anecdotal thinking can be dangerous.

Postmodern critiques of science

In spite of its success many people are still uneasy with a science they see either as a coldly objective and deeply impersonal force, or a threat to cherished beliefs. Religious people in particular often find some conclusions of science uncomfortable. A position known as postmodernism has made available to such critics of science additional more biting critiques.[2]

The label "post-modern" may seem odd. We ordinarily think of "modern" times as the present day. In that case the postmodern would have to be the future, which is not here yet. But philosophers, historians, and others consider the whole era of the Enlightenment, along with the scientific rationality it promoted, as "modern." It was a shift from medieval and renaissance patterns to modern things like democracy and theories of human rights, the industrial revolution, capitalism—and modern (as opposed to ancient or medieval) science. Science clearly favors critical inquiry; that is part of its basic method. Science also says that any individual who can produce the relevant evidence can call in question existing beliefs. So critics of science who object to Enlightenment rationalism, modern science included, call themselves "post-modern."[3]

Postmodernism is a kind of "social constructivism," as it is called.[4] This phrase represents the claim that the various truth-claims, values, practices, social roles, and so forth of a culture are all created—"constructed"—by a given society over time.[5] This usually implies also a high degree of cultural relativism, which is the double idea (1) that every culture constructs its own social order and beliefs, and (2) that no culture should judge the beliefs and values of another culture. At best, says cultural relativism, we can only study how the various aspects of a society's culture function within that culture.

We can get a better grasp of postmodernism by dividing up its analysis of culture into four somewhat overlapping basic claims:

1) All human beliefs are part of a socio-cultural context. No one can escape this. We all have to have some culture or another to live by, a set of ideas and rules and social patterns to give form to an otherwise formless life. Without a culture we would not learn even how to talk.

2) Methods to try to transcend one's cultural context and understand other cultures are methods that have to be learned in a life lived with others, who are themselves part of a socio-cultural context. There is therefore no independent and objective standpoint from which a person can judge which socio-cultural context has the right perspective or method for evaluating other cultures.

3) The culture of scientific rationality is only one culture among many. A traditional religious community is another; a person's ethnic heritage might provide a basic cultural framework. Science happens to be a set of methods developed in Western culture, especially since the Enlightenment. People who think the culture of scientific rationality is right for determining what is true cannot show that this culture is alone valid. It might just seem so to people whose socio-cultural context has taught them to believe that.

4) Because there is no objective way to know which culture is correct, a person is fully justified in selecting or holding onto one that works effectively to give form and guidance and support and inspiration for that person, or for that person's whole community. It will usually be whatever culture a person has grown up in which can most fully fulfill this role. This can include an overall religious vision of life. If a person finds that a particular religious tradition provides a form of life that is truly vivifying and constructive for the person and the community, that is sufficient basis to devote oneself to it. (This is a kind of correlational theology.)

A 20th century Protestant theologian, George Lindbeck, has articulated an influential statement of postmodern religious thought, which he calls "postliberal" (because, among other things, it rejects the claim of Schleiermacher's liberal theology to be the basic truth about all true religions).

Lindbeck describes three major ways to understand what religion is, in order to declare the first two inadequate. The first way is cognitive or "propositional." This interpretation of religion emphasizes its function as a depository of doctrinal truths or propositions. In this interpretation, religion is analogous to philosophy or science as a source of knowledge.

The second way is the experiential-expressive. This supposes that there is some basic and universal religious experience which major religions of the world share, such as an experience of the "sacred" or the divine or the Whole. Each of the religions expresses a different response to this basic experience. The expressions constitute different religious traditions. Each religion is a path up a different side of the same mountain, toward the One Ultimate Reality which everyone can experience. Schleiermacher's notion of religious experience is an instance of this sort of definition of religion.

The third way to understand a religion, Lindbeck's own postliberal position, is as a "cultural-linguistic" product of a culture's history. Religions are each a "comprehensive interpretive scheme" (CIS) of life, produced in the history of a culture and encoded in that culture's language. Some today like to refer to a CIS as a "master narrative" or even a "meta-narrative," the story behind all other more limited stories. In any case, a CIS is the web of truth-claims, values, and practices which tell people what is most worth living for, tells them how to live in a way that reinforces that basic worth, and helps to make it part of the person's life.

In a CIS the doctrines and stories and ethical standards are intimately tied to a set of rituals and sentiments and institutional forms. Lindbeck insists that although a religion's truth-claims may have great importance, they are subordinate to the larger pattern of the overall interpretative scheme. "The cognitive aspect, while often important, is not primary."[6]

Can we test a comprehensive interpretive scheme to see whether it is true or valid? Lindbeck declares that religious statements must meet an "intra-systematic" criterion of truth. This means that doctrines must be coherent with (fit with) the overall scheme of the religious tradition, with its stories and values and practices and symbols. Lindbeck struggles, however, with the question of whether religious doctrines are also "ontologically" true, as he calls it, that is whether they are valid truth-claims about how the world really is—"objectively" true, as we might say. Certain doctrinal statements such as "God is the Creator," for example, or "the soul is immortal" sound like ordinary truth-claims. From within a tradition, Christianity in this case, these doctrines may be intended as universal truths about how reality really, objectively is. But from the postliberal perspective of Lindbeck, different religions may each legitimately make quite different universalist-style truth-claims. Each set of truth-claims is legitimate if it functions as a coherent part of its own comprehensive interpretative scheme to guide a person in how to live. Ultimately there is no objective way to determine which CIS is truly objectively correct, or even whether any of them are.

Many religious thinkers today who criticize science favor a position like Lindbeck's postliberal version of postmodernism in religion. We can see this by running through the four-step description of the method of science as described in the chapter on the method of science (and illustrated by Figure 3.1). That description will be referred to as the "model" of the method of science.

Postmodernism and the model of the scientific method

The first aspect of the model of the scientific method in Chapter 3 is to pay attention to the facts, to basic evidence. The second aspect is to try to identify patterns among the facts. Unfortunately, the postmodernists argue, even basic evidence is clouded and colored by various factors, and the process of identifying facts and finding patterns is not purely objective. Clearly, every person who starts looking at reality to get the direct evidence is actually bringing some degree of past conditioning, preferences, images, or bias to bear. Most ideas about reality work well enough that they seem trustworthy. That the ground is solid, air is breathable, apples can be eaten, all seem to be simple facts. But at least on some occasions the ground could turn out to be quicksand, the air poisonous, and the apple made of wax.

The phrase most often used to indicate the difficulty of seeing the facts and patterns free from prior prejudice and training is to say that our ideas (facts, patterns) are all "theory-laden." The phrase is a bit too serious. The distinction between a dog and a horse is partly learned but is not usually what we call "theory." The phrase does remind us, nonetheless, that it would be difficult ever to see things exactly as they are in themselves, that there is always some conditioning of our perceptions in one way or another. It is also a reminder that we are usually not aware how much our perceptions are thus conditioned. Instead we tend to think we are objectively seeing the facts just as they are.

A good example of the variable interpretation of supposedly plain facts is what is meant today by "moon." We see this now as a large rock in the sky, orbiting the earth the way the earth orbits the sun. Eight hundred years ago in Europe the moon was not seen as ordinary rock. As part of the perfect heavens it had to be made of a special heavenly kind of element. Because the heavens were a realm of perfection, the moon's orbit had to be a perfect circle. Because continuous motion was known to be unnatural (by nature all things eventually slow down and stop, said medieval Europeans, echoing Aristotle), there had to be some force or being constantly at work that propelled the moon through the sky. Christian theologians speculated whether each such heavenly body had an angel pushing it. Moreover, the moon could exert a spiritual power over people, sometimes causing lunacy (in Latin moon = *luna*), just as Mars provoked a martial spirit in people and Mercury caused a mercurial one. This influence was perhaps an overflow of the power from the being or force that kept the moon in motion.

Notice for now, the postmodernist might say, how various parts of this all "fit" together. "Moon" takes on its meaning to people from the network of ideas about heavenly bodies, the size and age of the universe, the position of the earth in the universe, the nature of orbits, and so on. Ideas about the heavens, the universe, orbits, etc., take their meaning in turn from religious beliefs, or from a toy that whirls rocks on a string, or from prior scientific theories learned in school. Every basic "fact" is actually an interpretation of how the world is. Each such interpretation is based on other "facts" which are also interpretations of reality. The facts people learn are influenced by parents, by the language of the culture, by religious traditions, by the science of their society, by their peculiar individual experiences growing up, and so forth. The criterion of "fit" can evidently support a wide variety of ideas, some of which we do not think of as valid at all now. As the culture changes, so does the outcome of applying the rule of "fit."

The third part of the model of science is to devise a hypothesis to account for the particular patterns among the facts. Here too social influences may dictate which hypotheses are devised and selected. Many a historian of science, for example, has noted that Darwin's theory of natural selection echoes the capitalist economic theories of his time. First came Adam Smith and followers, proclaiming that free competition among entrepreneurs will eliminate those who do not produce good quality products at acceptable cost. Then came Darwin, saying that competition among organisms will eliminate those who are inferior in survival talents. Had Darwin lived in a different social context, might he not have come up with a significantly different hypothesis to explain the existence of a variety of species, now and in the past?

It is such analyses as these that allow critics of science to argue that the method of science itself is a peculiar network of rules and restrictions produced in the cultural context known as the "modern" European Enlightenment.[7] This implies that those who do not accept the norms of this modernity should feel free to use other methods to determine what is true. Religious people today do not have to accept scientific rationality as valid always and everywhere. They are free to reject any encroachment science might be making on religious belief by relying on some form of faith rather than rationality.

Further support for the postmodernist interpretation of science

Thomas Kuhn, a famous historian of science, describes scientific theories somewhat as Lindbeck treated any CIS (comprehensive interpretive scheme), as though there were only social agreements and not an objective set of standards for determining which physics theories are correct. He calls major new developments in science "paradigm shifts."[8] A paradigm in grammar is a model. (A model of how to add "ing" to a word, for example, by first dropping an "e" at the end of a word.) Kuhn claimed that such shifts in science are not entirely logical. Instead he portrayed them as a series of social shifts, wherein various scientists talking to each other slowly get accustomed to new paradigms, a new way of seeing things, a new "interpretation." Here again is a "social construction" process at work. Kuhn speaks as though atomic theory, for example, maintains its hold in physics because it is part of the social milieu of physicists.

Physicists like to think they are relying on objective evidence. Kuhn responds by claiming that the method of science is really based on certain values. Values are not like objective truth- claims. Values are much more likely to represent social traditions. If science is based on values, that might make it even more socially dependent. Here is an often-cited passage in which Kuhn describes the values he has in mind:

> First, a theory should be accurate: within its domain, that is, consequences deducible from a theory should be in demonstrated agreement with the results of existing experiments and observations. Second, a theory should be consistent, not only internally or with itself, but also with other currently accepted theories applicable to related aspects of nature. Third, it should have broad scope: in particular, a theory's consequences should extend far beyond the particular observations, laws, or sub-theories it was initially designed to explain. Fourth, and closely related, it should be simple, bringing order to phenomena that in its absence would be individually isolated and, as a set, confused. Fifth—a somewhat less standard item, but one of special importance to actual scientific decisions—a theory should be fruitful of new research findings: it should, that is, disclose new phenomena or previously unnoted relationships among those already known.[9]

A postmodernist concludes that values clearly vary from culture to culture. It is difficult to get people to agree on values. The values used by the method of science are values promoted in the time of the European Enlightenment. Science is thus guided by culturally constructed values. Science cannot therefore be truly objective.

To such analyses of the method of science, postmodernists add a historical claim, by pointing to theories which scientists in general once considered to be the simple truth but sometimes turned out to be quite wrong. Newton thought space was like an immense unchanging empty box in which events took place. Einstein described space instead as a characteristic of matter-energy itself, so that the expansion of matter-energy creates and carries its own space with it. Once phlogiston explained combustion; later oxygen did.

A massive example of a paradigm shift that might seem to support Kuhn's analysis, is the case of the theory of the four basic elements. In one form or another this theory dominated Western ideas for over 2,000 years. We can trace it back to at least the 5th century BCE, when the Greek Alcmaeon of Crotone in Sicily, a Pythagorean, argued for a connection between basic elements and bodily humours. The theory was extended to explain major differences in the four ages of a person's life, childhood, youth, maturity, and old age, each dominated by a humour. Democritus and Aristotle supported a similar theory. For about two thousand years Western "science," based on these theories, held that everything material on earth was composed of these four basic physical elements.

Classical Greek Philosophy of Nature: the 4 Elements

FIRE	Hot	Dry	Very light
AIR	Hot	Moist	Medium light
WATER	Cold	Moist	Medium heavy
EARTH	Cold	Dry	Very heavy

Relations of the 4 elements to (1) the seasons, and (2) human biology and (3) human personalities

1. The Seasons
   Summer: Hot and Dry, dominated by the element Fire
   Autumn: Cold and Dry, dominated by the element Earth
   Winter: Cold and Moist, dominated by the element Water
   Spring: Hot and Moist, dominated by the element Air.

2. The four "humours" of human biology and typical diseases
   Yellow bile = hot and dry—liver disorders
   Black bile = cold and dry—constipation
   Phlegm = cold and moist—catarrh and chest problems
   Blood = hot and moist—over-indulgence; gout, diarrhea.

3. Human temperament
   Choleric—an excess of fire/yellow bile; a tendency to anger and aggressiveness
   Melancholic—an excess of black bile; a tendency to sadness and pessimism
   Phlegmatic—an excess of water; a tendency to calmness and patience
   Sanguine—an excess of blood; a tendency to happiness and optimism.

Clearly the theory of the four basic elements all "fits" rather well together. On the basis of knowledge of the four elements and their major characteristics and effects, physicians could explain and treat both human biological and psychological characteristics. (In fact we still call medical people "physicians" because the profession was once grounded in physics—the four elements and their interaction.) Yet we now think this physics, along with its related explanations of the seasons as well as of human biology and psychology, to be simply incorrect. Does this imply that applying the method of "fit" is always done in a way that is relative to what that particular culture has "constructed" as its basic view of how things work? If so, then science is culturally relative. Postmodernism rests its case.

In defense of the method of science

The four-element theory did indeed provide a base for a complex of other theories which all fit together nicely. But coherence among theories is only part of the test for "fit." The other major test is that each theory fit with the relevant evidence.

The theory of the relation between the seasons and various elements sometimes fits with the evidence, depending on where one lives. Summers are certainly warmer than winters, but whether they are drier than winters is only an approximation. Autumn can be cooler and drier, but also cooler and wetter, again depending on where one lives. The hurricane season in the Southern U.S. extends well into Autumn, bringing with it lots of rain. The Mediterranean seasons were sorted to fit with the four elements in accord with normal Mediterranean weather.

Evidence also counted a bit in establishing the relation between the four humours and certain health conditions. (For some reason the word "humours" retains its British spelling even in the U.S.) An excess of phlegm often accompanies chest problems. A cold or pneumonia produces phlegm in the throat. On the other hand, when either is accompanied by a fever, the condition is not cold and moist but warm and moist. The evidence here goes contrary to the theory.

Numerous lovers of theory in general accepted the Four-humour theory of illness nonetheless, perhaps just because it "made sense." Not just the facts of sickness and stages of life, but also an explanation of those facts now seemed available. This theory also had the advantage in the minds of many that it was fully naturalistic. It abandoned belief that gods or spirits were the causes of disease, in favor of the supposition that natural elements explained disease.

None of this was subjected to careful comparative ("controlled") testing, however. The ancients did know a lot about the use of various healing herbs, about diet and exercise and fresh air. Ancient medicine was usually empirical, attending to evidence, not trusting to four-humour theories alone. The Babylonians and Egyptians kept catalogues of specific conditions and various potions or procedures for each. So they had some successes in healing. But given what we know now empirically about microbes, both bacterial and viral, about the actual functioning of the lungs and heart and circulatory system, as well as the nervous system and the lymphatic system, much of the four-humour theory is not much more than a bit humorous, in our modern meaning.

Today in India, China, Africa, and other places, "traditional" medicine, as it is often called, is still practiced. A traditional Indian healer will consider which "chakra" might be involved in a diseased condition.[10] A traditional Chinese healer will address imbalances of "chi." While some traditional medical practices may have some empirically valid effect, much of the theory behind them shares one important similarity to the theory of the four humours—few of them are really very effective, and at times may distract from an approach that is more effective. The evidence now indicates rather clearly that "modern" medicine, when long and carefully tested, provides a much greater and more reliable cure rate.

The critics of modern science sometimes argue it is presumptuous and arrogant to claim that ancient traditions are not valid; they argue it is foolish to overlook the wisdom of the ages when that might contribute to health today. A special charge is that it is Western pride, including prejudice against foreign traditions, that induces people to reject those traditions.

In fact, the 2,000+ years history of theories of four elements, seasons, physical health, and human psychology shows that ancient and long-accepted traditions of the West can also be rather ineffective and useless. Respect for tradition is often unwise. The elimination of smallpox and near-elimination of polio from the world shows that modern sciences and their methods of controlled testing are effective as no other methods have proved to be.[11]

The single biggest problem with the postmodern attacks on the efficacy of science is that they fail to account for the incredible success of the method of modern science. Recall that for a great many centuries an intellectual elite in various territories—ancient Greece, Persia, India, China, early Islam, medieval Europe—tried to figure out the world. Greater health, wealth, and power would go to those who did. All these many early attempts at science accomplished relatively little. Some like Aristotle and Archimedes did fairly well. It is impressive, for example, to read Aristotle's reasoning, based on the evidence he had, about the cycle of water evaporating from oceans, condensing in the sky, and then falling as rain to nourish land crops, strengthening his analysis by entertaining all the alternative interpretation and determining which theory fit (yes, there is that word again) best logically and with the evidence. Around the world and over centuries, however, no method produced the sort of extensive and reliable results that the modern method has.

What of those culturally constructed values that guide science, according to Kuhn? In fact these are not "values" in the sense of moral or aesthetic values; they are instead criteria of "fit"in disguise. Read the lines by Kuhn cited above again, and he turns out to be saying this: predicted consequences should fit with the theory; ideas must be consistent—fit with—each other; additional data and theories should fit with the one a person is working with; the theory works well when it can show how many ideas fit together; the theory should fit with new phenomena. These are all aspects of the universal method of science of testing for "fit." Yes, this is a "value" in science. But it is not a value in which scientists have blind faith, or which they accept because it is part of their social context. Instead it is the only basic method we have in life in general for testing out ideas regardless of culture. It has also proven itself to be very effective when applied carefully.

Consider also the claim made earlier that Darwin's theory is a product of his culture and time, that it is just an application of the basic theory of capitalism to biology.

Perhaps so. But the origin of the theory is not nearly so important as the process of testing for "fit" with the available relevant evidence, and with other theories which have also been tested against the evidence. Even if Darwin's theory fit with his social context, that "fit" is not the one that counts. Darwin amassed and described a wide range of evidence to support his theory in 1859. A hundred and fifty years later the relevant evidence has expanded enormously. So far, so good.

A universally valid method

Science seeks knowledge that is universally true. One of Newton's great achievements, for example, was to work out the math which could show that gravity applies to the heavenly bodies the same as it does on earth. Science today proposes that everywhere in the universe every mass "attracts" every other mass in direct proportion to their masses and inversely proportional to the square of the distance between them. Science proposes that all the planets and stars of the universe are composed of atoms. Scientists also think of the basic method of science as a universally valid means to determine empirical truth, truths which can be tested by natural means such as the human senses or instrumentation. Common in postmodern critiques of science are attempts to deny that science is universally valid.

In spite of postmodern claims to the contrary, both the results and the basic method of modern science are successfully in use around the world. It does not matter whether a person has been raised on Confucian or Marxist values in China, the method of science and its results are the same there as in Buddhist-secular Japan, Hindu India, and Muslim Cairo. Postmodern relativism and social constructivism do not adequately attend to science's success, especially to its universal applicability. We have sound reasons therefore to suppose that the method of science will work everywhere for everyone who learns how to apply it. Its efficacy has been demonstrated in practice over the last 200 years in a great variety of ways.

This universal effectiveness of science poses a special challenge to religion. The great variety of religions, some of which differ from each other on very fundamental claims about the universe and how it works, have not yet found some reliable way to figure out which of them is more probably correct. Each religious group appeals to its own tradition or sacred sources, albeit sometimes insisting that these too constitute a universally valid set of truth-claims or practices.

Once again, a reason we should not be surprised that the method of science works everywhere is that our sensory apparatus is not hopelessly out of touch with the real world. Philosophers sometimes follow the odd path of Descartes, mentioned in Chapter 3, who doubted everything he possibly could, in search of something that cannot be doubted. This extreme degree of skepticism does not fit well, however, with either everyday common practices nor with our evolutionary history. As suggested earlier in the section about why science is not based on faith, in everyday life our senses need to be pretty good at experiencing the world as it is, at least on the gross level of ordinary sight and sound and feeling. Without good sensory reception we would be constantly falling off curbs, bumping into trees, driving our cars into each other, failing to find food or putting harmful things in our mouths. We do not ordinarily attend to the thousands of specific sensory experiences we have to get right every day in order to stay alive and generally unharmed and healthy. This is true of people everywhere and throughout history.

Our evolutionary history makes sense of this. Whichever organisms have sharper awareness of potential enemies, odd sounds in the bushes, signs that the fruit of a tree is ripe, or that the quarry hunted is close by, are the organisms who will more likely survive to pass on those abilities to the next generation. Organisms which have poorer sensory powers will be more likely to die off. This is true also of our hominid ancestors through countless centuries.

There is even some evidence that the categories we form on the basis of our experience are not entirely arbitrary, not entirely dependent on a particular culture's history. When it comes to classifying various plants and animals, for example, people in a wide variety of cultures seem to have a somewhat common "folk biology." Scott Atran, an expert in this, offers numerous examples. People in any culture tend to classify organisms that interbreed as the equivalent of what we call a species. They all distinguish between grasses and grains and bushes and trees.[12] After a few million years of primate evolution our human senses and minds are fairly good at forming highly workable impressions of visible reality. So all in all it should not be a surprise that science works as well as it does, once we stumbled across the full method.

Science can still be used for great harm, of course. It often does not "work" for the good of everyone when it is applied. China's Three Gorges Dam is an awesomely large work of engineering and science. It will end up pushing 1.5 million people out of their homes. It will provide badly needed electricity, but will flood an enormous amount of farmland. Not surprisingly there have been protests, from both within and from without China about the social cost as well as the cost in food-production.

The method of science cannot make people who use science all wise, peaceful, compassionate, generous, and honest. The public nature of science does enforce a certain honesty. Do not bother to try to lie because when you are caught—and you will be as people try to duplicate or apply the results you claim you got—you will not just be socially disgraced, you will have been caught being unscientific. A scientist can still cheat and lie, of course, when she or he decides to sell or share or use the results of good science. But all these problems are not the result of the method of science itself; they exist because people who create, understand, and use science are human beings.

Why did modern science appear when and where it did?

Postmodernists treat modern science as a set of socially constructed values and methods, peculiar to the culture of the European Enlightenment. If indeed the method of science is universally effective, then a fascinating historical question is why the scientific method developed fully first in Europe rather than springing up in cultures around the world. There could be a variety of reasons for this, too many to describe in detail here. Here are a few common speculations.

The sociologist Rodney Stark, among others (see those mentioned in the Introduction) proposes that monotheism helped. The God of Western religions has long been described as the one who planned or designed the universe with perfect intelligence. Belief in this, Stark argues, led people to expect the universe to be rationally comprehensible and therefore able to be studied rationally.

Belief in the intelligibility of nature would indeed seem to be a pre-requisite for science. But it is not enough. The ancient Stoics had this belief also; they did not produce modern science, even though they lived in the rationalistic atmosphere of Hellenic philosophy.

A significant contributing factor in European history was the rise and development of somewhat independent universities at places like Bologna, Salamanca, Paris, and Oxford in the 12th and 13th centuries. Neither fully under control of the Church nor of the local civil ruler, the faculty of these places allowed themselves a lot of room to speculate and argue. Additionally, the European university faculty were learning a lot about ancient Greek science as well as Muslim work building on that science. Europeans especially learned from the Muslims of Spain, often with the help of Jewish translators. European faculty delighted in all this new knowledge, and as they argued with each other they developed highly rationalized methods of disputation, including extensive development of the rules of logic. (Perhaps it also helped that the faculty of the universities were all celibate—or supposed to be. With no families to care for, they had to do something with their time.)

An interest in empirical research developed from at least the 13th century. Aristotle did some good empirical analyses, but left a heritage of preferring abstract philosophical analysis to getting one's hands dirty in the lab or field. Roger Bacon at Oxford and Albert the Great at the University of Paris nonetheless told people to get more empirical. A 14th century movement known as "nominalism" agreed (Chapter 9 will say more on this). The "humanists," 15th century scholars of ancient arts and rhetoric, were often also devoted to alchemy, which required a great deal of trial and error (mostly error) laboratory work, as they sought ways to turn base metals into silver or gold.[13]

Europeans also turned out to be fascinated by mechanical gadgets. By the 13th century bell-tower clocks had become somewhat common in Europe, perhaps powered by weights slowly dropping. China had mechanical clocks by the 11th century; Islam by a couple centuries later. For reasons unknown, however, it was the Europeans of the 15th and 16th centuries who invented microscopes and telescopes, thermometers and barometers, and many other mechanical devices for measuring or inspecting or testing aspects of the physical world.

The development of the method of modern science in Europe may also have been an unforeseen consequence of Gutenberg's movable type in the 15th century. Philosophical ideas, including what we call early attempts at science, were then no longer the possession of the few who could afford to have texts hand-copied or had the time to attend a university. In the early 17th century, much of the communication of new scientific ideas among people was still by way of handwritten letters and reports. But printed sources began to count more and more. People all over Europe were now able to read each others' ideas and to try them out themselves. Without realizing what a powerful effect this would eventually have, Europeans were engaged in public and long-term testing of ideas. China invented and used movable type, however, long before Europe, and did not develop modern science.

The science which has been developing for these past centuries turned out to have serious impact on religious beliefs. The next section begins to address this impact, in two chapters, one on God and the other on atheism. These chapters will be somewhat philosophical, but they will prepare the way for the more concrete topics which follow them.

For further reading

Ben-Ari, Moti, *Just a Theory: Exploring the Nature of Science* (Amherst, NY: Prometheus Books, 2005).

Downing, Crystal, *How Postmodernism Serves (My) Faith: Questioning Truth in Language, Philosophy and Art* (Downers Grove, IL: IVP Academic, 2006). A bit too postmodern to be easily readable, but the introduction can be helpful on this topic.

Haack, Susan, *Defending Science—within Reason: Between Scientism and Cynicism* (Amherst, New York: Prometheus Books, 2003).

Part Three
God and Atheism

The Reality and Nature of God in Western Religion

6

The two chapters of Part Three will take up the question of whether there is a God. Not all questions about God's existence will appear in these chapters. Later chapters will examine some arguments about whether there has to be a Designer or Planner of the universe. This chapter will address more basic questions about belief in God. Whether God should be thought of as intervening in the world will be briefly touched on in this section, but Part Four, on miracles, will cover that issue more thoroughly.

As promised in the Introduction, this chapter will be both historical and philosophical, not directly focused on science. It provides material that will become important in evaluating the arguments of atheists as well as interpretations different theists give to the idea of God. Relations between religion and science obviously depend on the nature of the religion and its beliefs. If there is no God at all, metaphysical naturalism rules. Scientists can use naturalism as their method without concerns about overstepping its limits. If a tradition says instead that there is indeed a God, but not one who gets involved in any way in the universe, then cosmological naturalism is fully justified. If a given religious tradition insists that God intervenes in special ways in history and the universe, followers of that tradition might complain that even methodological naturalism is inadequate for discovering all that is going on in the world.

Prior to God, the gods

The last part of the Introduction noted that polytheism preceded monotheism. In the 10th century BCE there was no belief in a single supreme Creator God. There were a few quite powerful "high gods," as anthropologists have sometimes named them. In Egypt around 1350 BCE for a brief 20 years the pharaoh Akhenaton had tried to eliminate the worship of all gods except his special sun god, Aton. This may be an unusual premature moment of monotheism. It is hard to be sure. It might also have just been a political move to restrict the power of the many priests in charge of the worship of other gods. But until the first millennium BCE, in all the great cultures of the world, there were many gods, not just one. They demanded sacrifices and praise; they wanted humans to feed and glorify them. These gods were normally of ambiguous moral character, at best. Even those which were not vain, petty, and greedy, were often quite cruel.

This is true even of the original religion of those who one day would become the Jews, who in their turn would pass on their monotheism to Christianity and Islam. Yahweh, the god who appeared to Moses, is described in the earliest texts as a mountain-top god like many other mountain-top gods in that era. In the territory of Palestine some of those who were the ancestors of the people of the later Judaic kingdom centered on Jerusalem worshiped a mountain god under the name El Shaddai. Others referred to their god with the general name of elohim (a plural form of el, meaning a god). According to archeological evidence, a god named Yahweh was sometimes associated with Astarte, a goddess of fertility more often linked to Baal, god of fertility and rain. All of these gods, including even Yahweh at first, could be cruel, angry, jealous. He demanded the slaughter of those who stood in the way of his people. Or so those people believed.[1]

By the time of the Babylonian Exile, however, in the 6th century BCE (to be explained further in Chapter 11 here), the Jewish exiles had begun to think of their Yahweh in a new light. Mercy and loving-kindness were much more often attributed to this God. The Jews gave to the world a God of justice and compassion. God also became much more awesome, becoming God with a capital "G." Before long it was no longer permitted to use God's sacred name, YHWH. (In English today many Jews will spell the name G*d.) Circumlocutions such as "the Lord" became common, and the kingdom of God was often referred to more cautiously as the kingdom of heaven.

As the Introduction noted, this shift in ideas about God was parallel to similar shifts in India and China and Greece around the same era. In all these places an intellectual elite began to ruminate on what is Ultimate, on the origin of everything, on the nature of everything, on the meaning and purpose of everything, if any. They found their answers in belief in an Ultimate Reality. In India it was Brahman, in China the Tao, in Greece various philosophers each proposed an answer.

Because many major cultures around the world began to speculate about the Ultimate Reality during, this era, around the 7th or 6th century B.C.E., the philosopher Karl Jaspers called it the "axial" age, as though human history turned on its axis in a new direction. The metaphor can mislead, because belief in a single Ultimate was sometimes just an overlay upon an ongoing polytheism, or it was a philosophical idea which had to compete with ongoing polytheism. The search for a single Ultimate was a significant development in human thinking nonetheless.

Belief in many gods implies that there is no ultimate coherence to what happens in the universe. What one god does another can undo. As one god acts, another can be acting contrary, limiting the power of the first god. The gods were also quite human-like, changing their minds at times, moved by various emotions, choosing to do this or that. So there was no way to predict what would happen tomorrow. The world was a place of fundamental uncertainty. But when Taoist and Hindu thought, when Jewish monotheism and Greek philosophy developed, they all believed that there was a single Ultimate Power behind things. Therefore, they concluded, all things ultimately have a single coherent order to them.

Belief in a Single Ultimate and the origins of science

The various practices that led to modern science go back all the way to the axial age. Those practices include as a special element the attempt to discover an overall rational order to things. We have seen the significance of this in considering the method of science: everything has to fit together; therefore everything can be tested against everything else. In the web or crossword puzzle of ideas in science any lack of fit says that there is some error somewhere in the puzzle. It is not a coincidence that this axial age was also the time when formal logic was developed, particularly in Greece but also in other places. Logic seeks a coherent fit among ideas. This is the time period when philosophy, science, and theology started shining, all of them forms of systematically logical reflections on how things all fit together intelligibly.

As was mentioned, this might have been at first just an act of faith in the intelligibility of reality. Or it may have been a normal extension of what people everywhere need to do, which is to expect that their ideas about reality do not contradict one another, and that yesterday's experiences provide some basis for predicting tomorrow's. It was not until the modern forms of science appeared that the assumption there is an overall rational order to things began to pay off and thereby give evidence it is true.

Explicit naturalism appeared in these early times. Philosophers in the various cultures attributed less and less to the gods and more and more to the regular order of nature. A major effect of this new rational approach was often the death or subordination of the old gods. In Greece philosophers were accused of being atheists, because some of them thought it was irrational to believe in the gods. In Babylon, the prophet Isaiah spoke for the newly developed monotheism of Judeans in exile. He declared that the other gods were only sticks and stones in the temples, not real gods at all. In India, the gods were subordinated to the incomprehensible Ultimate Reality called Brahman. In all these places most people in fact tended to retain belief in the old gods. That was their family tradition; that was how they knew how to live. The familiar faces of the gods were more welcome in the home than ideas about some impossible-to-understand Ultimate Reality. But where there was an intellectual elite, people trained in the methods of rational analysis that their culture had recently developed, there also was a tendency to see the old stories as false stories.

In Greek a word for a story is "mythos." As old myths began to appear to the educated as false, explanations of how the universe works were "demythologized." Sometimes this just meant treating the myth as symbolic of deeper and more abstract truth. But inasmuch as the gods were often pictured doing cruel, immoral, and childish things, many of the philosophers wanted people to give up all belief in these gods and seek a single changeless Ultimate. Philosophy contended against philosophy, each claiming to have the correct unifying basic understanding of nature, but with none of them having sufficient and clear evidence they were correct. In the midst of such disagreements, there was ample room for Judaic, and then Christian, notions about a single Ultimate God.

The existence, nature, and activity of God

There are three major aspects to belief in God. The first is the belief that God exists; the second is the set of beliefs about the nature of God; the third is the set of beliefs about how God acts in creation or history.

Belief in the reality or existence of God, of course, anchors the other beliefs in Western theism, whether Judaic, Christian, or Muslim. If God did not exist, then beliefs about God's revelation in Torah or New Testament or Koran would be at best a vague symbol; the Christian belief in Jesus as the incarnation of God would be at best a pious poetic expression. If it can first be shown that God exists, then much else about these religions can be more plausible.

Beliefs about the nature of God are as important as belief in God's existence. Before a person can claim that God exists it is necessary to define "God." Otherwise it is like a claim that "gawmp" exists. A person cannot decide whether any "gawmp" exists without first knowing what it is. People who grow up in a culture in which the name of God is used often have a feeling that they know what it means. But they may be only just slightly clearer than they are about "gawmp." A person may think of God as kind and loving, and yet as dooming millions to hell. A person may think of God as the Infinite and Eternal Cause of all existence, yet speak of this God as though God were a finite being alongside of, albeit superior to, all other beings. Religions have found it difficult to be both clear and consistent about what God is like.

A list: three notions of god

1. **The Everyday God**, powerful, loving, miracle-working, anthropomorphically described as though finite in some sense. This is the God of the everyday imagination of Christians and Jews, and perhaps also Muslims. This God is the most powerful Being in the universe, but also person-like, with human-like qualities, albeit fully perfect in these qualities. This God may be thought to change His (almost never Her) mind in response to prayer, acting in history by working miracles. Miracles can count as empirical evidence of the existence and activity of God. This notion conflicts even with the methodological naturalism of science, which must act as though all events in the universe are due entirely to natural causes.

2. **The Cosmic God**, God of many religious scientists and science-minded philosophers. This God is evident to the rational mind through the evidence of the extraordinarily complex order of the cosmos. In past centuries the complex construction of the eye or hand was sufficient evidence to show that there had to be a God to have designed and created the universe, like a master clockmaker might design and create a clock. This God need not do any miracles at all. The main work of this God is planning, creating, setting in motion, and now sustaining the entire universe in operation in accordance with the eternal plan and purpose. This notion of God can fit with both methodological and cosmological naturalism.

3. **The Metaphysical God**, God of philosophers and mystics. This defines God as the Infinite beyond (and within) all finite realities. It is the Uncaused Cause, Absolute (totally independent) Beingness, eternal Mystery. It is a God about whom little can be said and then only in a carefully qualified way: This God is outside of time and unchanging, for time is change; beyond all dependency on any other power and therefore unaffected by anything that a creature does—although this God may have somehow taken into account from all eternity the acts of all creatures already. This God is perfect personness, goodness, truth, beauty, and unity, though in a way beyond conception. This God is actively sustaining the universe in existence for some ultimate divine purpose; but it is hard to say such a God could intervene to do miracles, and it would be incorrect to say that this God can have changes of mind. It is *experienced* by the mystics, they say, and described metaphorically as a light so pure it blinds human consciousness. It cannot be grasped by

mind, imagination, words, or images. This is incompatible only with metaphysical naturalism, which denies any reality to God at all.

In general the Jewish and Christian scriptures have countless passages that imply an imaginable God as a free and active agent, planning and guiding events in the universe. This is a somewhat anthropomorphic image of God. (See notion #1 on the list.) The Qur'an has passages which also seem to imply a person-like God, though Muslim scholars emphasize verses which stress the total transcendence of God, beyond all human imagination. There are other ways of speaking of God, however, especially through the interaction of early Western theistic religions with Hellenistic philosophy. Of the three religions Christianity engaged most fully and at greatest length eventually with the philosophical traditions.

In the early days of Christianity the best theoretical scientists, according to the opinions of the day, were the philosophers who argued about the order and basic composition of the universe. The Introduction notes that Stoic philosophers argued there was a divine pattern inherent in the order of the universe. The order of the cosmos was evidence of a rational principle called the Logos which lay at the heart of the universe. The Epicureans, on the other hand, opted for an atomist philosophy which portrayed the gods and humans alike as subject to an all-encompassing unplanned flow of natural forces. The basic "stuff" of the universe was atoms— minute uncuttable particles. All things were composed of these atoms. Two basic forces acted on the atoms. One was "chance," the unpredictable or random flow of atoms through space, bumping into each other and holding together in larger and larger conglomerates. The second force was the sum of the laws of nature that operated ineluctably, imposing some degree of "necessity" upon the course of events. So all history was just chance and necessity operating on atoms in space, without divine guidance or plan. It was in this context that Christians had to explain to Stoics, Epicureans, and to each other for that matter, just how their God related to the overall course of nature.

From the earliest days of Christianity theologians also found attractive a set of ideas about God inspired by Plato's thought, ideas that made it difficult to portray God in one's imagination at all. Platonists in general came to argue that there was a fully Perfect, Eternal, and Changeless One, the Ultimate Reality, from which the rest of the universe emanated, like light and heat from the sun. The universe was thus composed of the "overflow," as it were, of the Ultimate One. For most Platonists, this process of overflow had always been going on. The One and the universe were both everlasting. Because the One was infinite it was beyond all categories; therefore it was beyond what the human mind can grasp. It is legitimate to assert that the One exists, said the Platonists; it is not legitimate to claim to understand it.

Aristotelians shared the belief of the Platonists that the universe had always existed. Aristotle argued that the motions of the universe—change of qualities, movement from place to place, increases or decreases in size or power—had been going on forever. Therefore, he argued, there had to be an everlasting Unmoved Mover to account for this endlessly ongoing motion. Otherwise everything would have run down, so to speak, and have ground to a halt. The Unmoved Mover could not itself be moving; if it were then a person would have to look for some other Mover to account for that motion. The only type of reality that can cause motion without moving is something highly attractive. Other things will move toward it, even while it remains motionless. Whatever is attractive is in some sense "good." So Aristotle's Unmoved Mover is the supreme Good.

Defining God

Philo of Alexandria

The ancient philosophers—Stoic, Epicurean, Aristotelian, and Platonist—thought the God in whom the earliest Christians believed was an "everyday god," who actively intervened in historical events. This seemed to the philosophers to be too undignified for the highest divinity. This Christian God appeared to the Stoic and Platonic philosophers to be rather like a super-Zeus, an exaggerated version of the old Greek belief in a high and powerful but imperfect and limited god.

In the Judaic and Christian tradition, the earliest theological thinker who insisted that God is truly Ultimate was Philo of Alexandria in Egypt. Alexandria was an intellectual center in the ancient world, the home of a very famous library. "Philosophers"—i.e., the learned and the scholarly—gathered in Alexandria to have access to the resources of this wonderful library. They wrote in Greek, the intellectual language of the time.

Philo was one of these scholars. There were many Jews living in Alexandria, whose families had been in Egypt for generations, some of them since the 6th century B.C.E., when Babylon had conquered Jerusalem and many Jews had fled. Philo of Alexandria adapted his Jewish faith to what he thought was the best philosophy and science of the times. He insisted that God is the changeless Ultimate One, as Platonists said. But the God of Judaism is also an active Creator. The world is not God's overflow. It is created by God out of nothing. God is not the supreme reality at the top of the universe, so to speak. Nor, for that matter, is God a rational force inherent in nature, like the Stoic Logos. Instead the entire universe is radically other than God, as God's creation. God is independent of the world; it is God who made the world to exist. This is Philo's form of a "metaphysical" God.

After Philo, Christians in Alexandria and elsewhere reflected on their own belief in God. They agreed with Philo that God must be superior even to the One of Platonism. So Christians also would end up sometimes emphasizing God's utter transcendence of all categories of the universe, and therefore also the categories of human thought.

Philo influenced many thinkers, Christian and Muslim and Jews. Whenever people began to think about what they meant by the word "God," they ran up against two basic alternatives: either God is a finite being or God is truly infinite. If God is finite, then no matter how powerful, intelligent, enduring, and loving this God might be, He [they did not think it might be a She] would be a limited being. Limit implied the possibility of being surpassed. What could be surpassed was potentially second or inferior. The word "God" did not seem to be the right word for something that could be inferior to anything.

Anselm of Canterbury

Anselm (1033–1109), Archbishop of Canterbury, addressed this in a famous work called the *Proslogion*, written around 1078 CE. Anselm asked whether the definition of the word "God" allows God to be second to anything else, inferior to anything else, more limited than anything else, in any way whatsoever. Anselm made people explicitly aware that they define the word "God" as standing for whatever Reality it is that cannot even possibly be second to, inferior to, or more limited than anything else. That implies that if a person has an image of God as limited in any way, or even having some potential to be inferior to something else, then God would be reduced to the status of a god, perhaps possessing enormous power, but no longer the absolutely Ultimate Reality behind everything else.

Anselm therefore ended up defining God in a manner which Philo would have approved, as "that than which nothing greater can be conceived." This concept of "God" has been a Western way to answer the human question about what is the absolutely Ultimate. Here are a few of the lines of the famous analysis by Anselm in his *Proslogion*. He is attempting to show that a reasonable person must define God as necessarily existing.

> CHAPTER II. That God Truly Exists[2]
> [I]t is one thing for an object to exist in the mind, and another thing to understand that an object actually exists. Thus, when a painter plans beforehand what he is going to execute, he has [the picture] in his mind . . . However, when he has actually painted it, then he both has it in his mind and understands that it exists because he has now made it. Even the fool, then, is forced to agree that something-than-which-nothing-greater-can-be-thought exists in the mind, since he understands this when he hears it, and whatever is understood is in the mind. And surely that-than-which-a-greater-cannot-be-thought cannot exist in the mind alone. For if it exists solely in the mind even, it can be thought to exist in reality also, which is greater.
>
> * * * *
>
> You exist so truly, Lord my God, that You cannot even be thought not to exist. And this is as it should be, for if some intelligence could think of something better than You, the creature would be above its creator and would judge its creator—and that is completely absurd. In fact, everything else there is, except You alone, can be thought of as not existing. You alone, then, of all things most truly exist and therefore of all things possess existence to the highest degree.

Thomas Aquinas (1225–1274)

Over 200 years later Aquinas provided a now classical instance of a metaphysical approach to God. Because it is very abstract, it illustrates that not all concepts of God need be anthropomorphic. (That will be significant when reflecting on the objections to belief in God in the next chapter.) His theology has been dominant in Catholic, Anglican, and some Protestant thought up to recent years. He offered five arguments in favor of the existence of God. The last two of these will appear in later chapters. The first three are actually summed up in the 3rd argument. It is rather dense, difficult to wade through, so here is a summary before looking at Aquinas' words.

→There are two key elements. The first is Aquinas' claim that if you look at the things and events in the universe, you realize that these things and events are "contingent," meaning "dependent." They are as they are, or happen as they happen, because of what causes them to be or act that way. Everything is caused by something else.

Sometimes a cause is prior in time to the effect, as in the case of one billiard ball first rolling toward then hitting the other ball, and making it move. Some causes are simultaneous with their effect, like the pool table holding the billiard balls on its surface up off the floor, and the floor holding up the pool table at the same time. In either case what is going on is contingent, dependent, caused. Aquinas' wording will look odd. He says it is possible for things in the world to be and not to be. By this he means that whatever does exist could cease to exist. Its existence is contingent.

Aquinas extends this claim of contingency to the question of why anything exists at all. A physicist today still does not really have an answer to that. Physics says that the sum of all matter and energy remains the same. We can move things around and exchange energy, but we can neither increase nor decrease the sum total of the stuff of matter-energy in the universe. That is a working law, very dependable so far, but there is no way to show that this has to be the case. If Aquinas knew of this rule of modern science, he could say that it does not answer the question of why the matter-energy exists at all, nor where it gets its power of never diminishing (or growing).

There are only two basic options, Aquinas thought. The universe is either "necessary"—it cannot not-exist; it is non-contingent as a whole. Or it is contingent—it does not exist necessarily; it could have not existed. If the universe could not-exist, at some point it would have ceased to exist. But it was odd that a universe full of things that are contingent could itself be ultimately non-contingent. So we can ask both why the universe exists at all and why it continues to exist; and we can least speculate on what it would take to make a universe exist. Here are Aquinas' words:

> The third way [to show God exists] is taken from possibility and necessity, and runs thus. We find in nature things that are possible to be and not to be, since they are found to be generated, and to be corrupted, and consequently, it is possible for them to be and not to be. But it is impossible for these always to exist, for that which can not-be, at some time is not. Therefore, if everything can not-be, then at one time there was nothing in existence. Now if

this were true, even now there would be nothing in existence, because that which does not exist begins to exist only through something already existing. Therefore, if at one time nothing was in existence, it would have been impossible for anything to have begun to exist; and thus even now nothing would be in existence—which is absurd. Therefore, not all beings are merely possible, but there must exist something the existence of which is necessary. . . . Therefore we cannot but admit the existence of some being having of itself its own necessity, and not receiving it from another. . . . This all men speak of as God.

A skeptical scientist today could challenge this argument as too speculative. We can assert that Big Bangs can happen because apparently at least one did, and maybe those strange phenomena we call "black holes" are involved in something like Big Bangs a lot. But it would seem impossible to answer the more basic question of why there is energy-stuff in existence to go bang in the first place. The scientist would want to see mathematical analyses or be able to analyze the types of forces involved. Without such specifics, any speculation seems too vague or general, to be a real answer. (We will eventually see, though, that some cosmologists also speculate about how a universe might arise out of a fluctuation in a quantum vacuum.)

Add to this complaint Aquinas' mind-stretching question about series of causes. If everything exists or acts according to how it is caused, how deep down does the string of causes go? The famous physicists Stephen Hawking tells of a woman who came up to him after a talk about the universe. She disagreed with his description of the universe. She said the world rests on a giant elephant, which in turn rests on the back of a giant turtle. When asked what the turtle rests on, she said after that it is "turtles all the way down." This raises Aquinas' sort of question (which he actually borrowed from Aristotle) about whether there is an absolutely infinite set of layers of causes, or whether there is a "first cause" that underlies the whole stack of other "secondary" causes that constitute the universe. The same question pops up if a person thinks of a temporal series of causes, stretching back in time forever. Is there instead a first cause which at some finite time ago brought universe into being?

The notion of a "first cause" is strange. It cannot be truly first if it is caused—contingent or dependent on—anything else whatsoever in any way whatsoever. To say it the other way around, if there is a first cause that means it is uncaused. If it exists, it does not owe that existence to any other cause. Therefore it has its own power of existence. If it exists at all, it exists "necessarily," not able to not-exist. So Aquinas concludes that it is reasonable to say there must be a necessarily-existing Uncaused Cause, adding that everyone calls this God. Because this is the cause of the whole of the universe, it is legitimate to think of it as Creator.

Aquinas also concludes that this first cause of everything would have to be infinite. If it were finite, we could ask why it has the particular limits it has. But that would be to look for some explanation—actually some cause—so that the first cause would turn out not to be first after all; something else explains some aspect of it. Anselm would agree for his own reason: if God were less than infinite, then we could think of something greater than the less-than-infinite God. If it is infinite, however, it is beyond all categories, and just like the One of the Platonists and Philo, it is beyond human comprehension.

Aquinas also argues that this Uncaused Cause must be completely simple, in the sense of having no parts, no internal differentiations. If it did, one aspect would not be the same as another aspect. Each of the two aspects would therefore be limited. Limitations are finite characteristics. The Infinite Cause cannot have such limitations.

Talking about the Uncaused Cause

Aquinas concludes that addressing the question of how there can exist anything at all produces an extremely bare-bones general answer: a necessarily existing infinite and incomprehensible Uncaused Cause. The skeptical scientist would again say this tells him or her nothing to lay hands on, nothing that can be empirically tested, nothing that explains other specifics about events in the world. The scientist would be correct in this. But Aquinas also thinks the word "incomprehensible" can be modified a bit.

Aquinas insists that we can legitimately apply concepts to God. We can do this by way of what is often called "analogical predication." He argues we can assert *that* God is truly good, perfect, infinite, and so forth, but must immediately qualify this assertion by adding that we cannot really comprehend what this is like in the Infinite which is God. Predicating (applying) ideas to God is only analogous (partly alike, partly different) to regular speech.

The theological argument goes something like this. Every effect is first somehow in the cause of that effect. The motion of a billiard ball hit by the cue ball is receiving that motion from the cue ball. Or to borrow a standard example from Aquinas' time, the rock in the field gets warm in the sun because the sun first has the warmth which it is imparting to the rock. In this second case, notice that "first" does not have to be restricted to "prior in time"—the sun keeps on imparting warmth to the rock. The rock stays warm as long as the sun keeps shining. Similarly, the universe keeps existing as long as God continues to maintain its existence.

Whatever is real in the universe, if it comes from the Uncaused Cause, is somehow first "in" the Cause. In fact, Aquinas argues, it is first in the Cause in an absolutely unlimited way—identical with the simple power of existence of that Cause. The various things in the universe are limited forms of existence, each having its own characteristics and activities. Some real aspects of the universe are power or energy, goodness, life, consciousness. Somehow all these things must be in the Infinite Cause or they would not be part of this universe. Because they exist in the Cause in a way we cannot really understand, we are not applying these ideas to God in the same way we apply them to things we can understand. We can grasp what life and consciousness are in human form, for example. We can say *that* the Cause must possess the fullness of these, but we cannot say or imagine or grasp how they exist "in" the Cause.

Thus, for Aquinas human language is correct, but inadequate. It is literally true that God is perfect goodness, but not in a way that the human mind can grasp. God does have infinite power—omnipotence. God does have unrestricted knowledge—omniscience. But God possesses these attributes in a manner no human mind or imagination can grasp. Thus a finite mind can apply words to what is beyond all words; it is how to think of what is beyond all thought—God.

This argument for the reasonableness of belief in God produces an extremely metaphysical notion of God. Anthropomorphic language about God gets swallowed up in the philosophical qualifications which say that words which describe God as loving or merciful, or even stern and just, are true, but not in the way any human can grasp. It would lead a person to think that this sort of philosophizing about the Ultimate is a strange Western aberration. That is not so.

For comparison: Taoism and the Hindu tradition

As noted earlier, talk about an Ultimate is not restricted to Western religions. The human mind everywhere seems capable of raising questions bigger than it can answer. In the philosophical Taoism of China, the Tao is said to be the formless which gives rise to forms. The person who claims to understand the Tao does not understand it. The person who knows the Tao acknowledges that it cannot be understood.

The earliest collection of Taoist sayings is the little book entitled *Tao Te Ching* [Pronounced Dow Duh Jing] The title is literally "Way-Power-Book," which is rendered better in English as "The Book of the Power of the Way." Its origins seem to be in the 5th century BCE. Of its 81 brief statements here are #1 and #56:

> The Tao that can be told of is not the eternal Tao;
> The name that can be named is not the eternal name.
> The Nameless is the origin of Heaven and Earth (1)
>
> He who knows [the Tao] does not speak.
> He who speaks does not know. (56)

The eternal Tao cannot be "told" or "named." The person who speaks—who tells about the Tao—obviously does not understand that the Tao is beyond what speech can express.

Similarly, ancient Hindu reflections on the Ultimate Reality came face to face with the incomprehensible. Hymn 129 of Book X of the *Rig Veda*, a major sacred text of Hindu tradition, wrestles with the question of the origin of all things. (If the traditional date assigned to this hymn of ca. 800 BCE is correct, this may be the very first known instance of reflection in writing on the nature of the Ultimate Reality.) The passage is very puzzling. With little or no previous philosophy as a guide, it has many more questions than answers, and not all the attempts at answers fit with each other.

> Then was not non-existent nor existent:
>> there was no realm of air, no sky beyond it.
> What covered it, and where? and what gave shelter?
> Was water there, unfathomed depth of water?
> Death was not then, nor was there aught immortal:
>> no sign was there, the day's and night's divider.
> The one thing, breathless, breathed by its own nature:
>> apart from it was nothing whatsoever.
> Darkness there was:
>> at first concealed in darkness this All was indiscriminate Chaos.
> All that existed then was void and formless.
> By the great power of Warmth was born that Unit.
> Thereafter rose Desire in the beginning,
> Desire, the primal seed and germ of Spirit.
> Sages who searched with their heart's thought
>> discovered the existent's kinship in the non-existent.
> Transversely was the severing line extended:
>> what was above it then, and what below it?
> There were the begetters, there were mighty forces,
>> free action here and energy up yonder.
> Who verily knows and who can here declare it,
>> whence it was born and whence comes this creation?
> The gods are later than this world's production.
> Who knows then whence it first came into being?
> He, the first origin of this creation,
>> whether he formed it all or did not form it.
> Whose eye controls this world in highest heaven,
>> he verily knows it—or perhaps he knows not.

Aspects of this fascinate historians of religion and philosophy. The mention of some watery primordial chaos echoes ideas from ancient Mesopotamian texts, some of which have echoes in the first chapter of Genesis also. Perhaps the person who wrote this "hymn" had heard the Mesopotamian myths about the original waters of chaos. The notion of a transverse line that divides that which is above from that which is below appears also in Plato's writings. If this text is indeed from the 7th century BCE Plato may have borrowed from it. But the dating is uncertain, so the borrowing might have gone the other way. These may be signs of the flow of ideas and speculations across the ancient world of Eurasia.[3] In any case, the Hindu tradition, developing from two major cultural traditions which happened to intersect in India, ended up eventually with two concepts of the Ultimate.

One tradition identified a cosmic Self (note the capital letter) named the Atman (which means something like "Breath" or "Spirit"). The individual soul or self within each person is actually just a drop of the ocean that is the cosmic Self. The major goal of life should be to finally and completely escape from the constant pattern of reincarnation all are caught up in, and never have to be born again. If a person achieves this, then the soul or self that resides within each individual is dissolved back into the cosmic Self. The individual self ceases to exist as individual.

A different Hindu tradition settled upon an all-embracing cosmic Power called Brahman—not to be confused with Brahmin, the name for the priestly caste of India. It alone is truly real; it is Reality. Whether the universe and all the living beings within it are themselves real therefore became a question for the philosophers of India to address over the centuries. Those who say that Brahman is the Ultimate also say that the Atman is just a different way of approaching Brahman. In fact Brahman-without-attributes, similar to Aquinas' incomprehensible God, is the most accurate way to speak of the Ultimate.

Additional notions of the Ultimate

The three major options in Western thought listed earlier—the everyday God, the cosmological God, and the metaphysical God—do not begin to exhaust the possibilities of notions of the Ultimate. Add some ancient Greek notions, whether the Stoic Logos or the Platonic One or Aristotle's Unmoved Mover. Do not forget the Tao, the Atman, and Brahman. Here are two more possibilities just to stand as extra reminders of the difficulty of establishing both the nature and existence of a God.

First is "God" as defined by Benedict Spinoza (1632–1677), whose position is pantheism. "Pan" is Greek for "all." Pantheism says all that exists is divine. Nature is God and God is nature. Modern science, says Spinoza shows us that God/nature operates in accord with the patterns we call the laws of nature. God/nature, therefore, makes modern science possible in the first place. This fits well with a Cosmic God, one who does not interrupt the patterns of natural law. To do so would be to act contrary to the divine nature. (Einstein sometimes used Spinoza'a language about "God," though Einstein declared he was not really a believer.)

The God of process theology, based on the philosophy of Alfred North Whitehead, is quite a different Cosmic God. Whitehead postulated the existence and activity of an all-encompassing divine Being with two major aspects or "poles." The eternally changeless aspect is the divine nature, a repository of unqualified values. The changeable aspect is the divine "Person" who perceives every event in the universe, evaluates the possibilities for greater value in each subsequent event, and lures each event toward that next best possibility. The ongoing all-pervasive lure of God accounts for the billions of years of cosmic evolution toward greater complexities and richness and consciousness. No single activity of God looks particularly divine or miraculous. It is the cumulative effect of God's "luring" that is evidence of the all-inclusive divine activity in the world.[4] Because all of the universe operates within this divine influence, process theology promotes what it calls "panentheism," "all-within-God-ism."

Wrestling with ideas about the Ultimate

The religious ideas most people are used to are the ordinary everyday ideas learned by teenage years, usually focused on the everyday anthropomorphic God. Thoughts about the Ultimate are the product of sophisticated philosophizing or theologizing. Science is also quite sophisticated. It goes beyond everyday methods of seeing which ideas fit with each other and with the evidence. Science instead applies carefully complex means of getting precise data and highly developed rational techniques of analysis. It may well be legitimate to compare everyday religion to everyday beliefs about the world. But, as the Introduction noted, many a religious thinker insists that if religious thought is to be compared to science, it should be the sophisticated forms of religion that are set in relation to the sophistication of science.

The religious case would be stronger, nonetheless, if there were only a single notion of the Ultimate. With so many alternatives, it is more difficult to say that one of them is the correct one to balance against metaphysical naturalism's claim that the Ultimate Reality is the natural universe itself, nothing more. Religion might settle for a claim that we should have reverence for the universe which gives us life and sustains us, echoing the attitudes of Spinoza. But the traditional theisms would not settle for this.

What this entails in the face of skepticism about religion will become clearer after a look at forms of atheism in the next chapter, along with some initial religious responses to atheism.

For further reading

Armstrong, Karen, *A History of God* (New York: A. A. Knopf, 1993). An ambitious and thorough description of 4,000 years of religious belief, from the time of the gods onward. It includes a description of the God of Islam also.

Cobb, John B. and David Ray Griffin, *Process Theology: An Introductory Exposition* (Philadelphia: Westminster Press, 1976). Two leading U.S. process theologians have produced this fairly readable summary. Ch. 3 is on God.

Haught, John F., *What is God? How to Think about the Divine* (Mahwah, NJ: Paulist Press, 1986). Five ways to think about God, each based on aspects of life with profound depth or endless openness. God gets forgotten, Haught insists, when people restrict themselves to science, because science is concerned with the knowable. God is precisely the unknowable Mystery.

Morris, Thomas V., *Our Idea of God: An Introduction to Philosophical Theology* (Downers Grove, IL: InterVarsity Press, 1991). This is as clear as a book can get about ideas this abstractly philosophical. Every chapter is dry but excellent.

7 Science-Based Atheism and Some Religious Responses

The National Academy of Science (NAS) is the most prestigious scientific group in the U.S. A person can be nominated only by other members and must be elected by the members. Up to 72 can be elected each year (as well as 18 foreign associates), but there are, of course, many thousands of scientists and engineers in the U.S. In a recent survey about two thirds of the NAS members said they did not believe in God. Usually the annual Gallup Poll on belief in "God or some higher power" finds that over 90% of Americans say yes to this, making the U.S. one of the most religious of the North Atlantic nations. The NAS has only about 33% saying yes. Thus science and either atheism or agnosticism go together in the minds of the majority of leading U.S. scientists.[1]

In the interaction between science and religion, belief in God has been challenged by the bare fact that science does not use the concept of God. That is the point of "naturalism" as a method. The growth of science has also made miracles less plausible. Many think too that the theory of evolution undercuts belief in a Designer and Providential Orderer for the universe. None of this disproves God's existence. But over the last few centuries God has increasingly become a "God of the gaps," as one person put it.[2] As science described more and more aspects of the universe, God's activity could be found only in smaller and fewer gaps in the natural order, where science had not yet explained how certain things could happen naturally, without God's intervention.

A famous example begins with Newton's speculation that God might have to intervene in the universe to keep the whole thing from starting to wobble and fly apart. The particular problem Newton had in mind was that Jupiter might be slowing down and Saturn speeding up, because of their gravitational pull on each other. Newton's fear was that if God did not intervene eventually Jupiter would spiral down into the sun and Saturn would fly out into space. God probably had to step in regularly and adjust the mechanism of the universe, Newton proposed. By the early 19th century, however, the astronomer Laplace had solved the problem with some excellent math work. He showed that Jupiter and Saturn had a regular 900-year pattern of oscillation because of their influence on each other. In the long run the slowing and speeding up reversed and then reversed again, creating an extremely long-term stability.

Another famous astronomer of the time, Frederick William Herschel, reported on a meeting between Laplace and Napoleon, who was Laplace's former student, at a country villa for some vigorous discussion. Laplace explained his theory of planetary oscillations. He went further and presented his theory of how the entire universe could have evolved from primordial matter in motion. Napoleon is supposed to have remarked: "But what about God?" Napoleon's question was based on an assumption that the universe needed the idea of God to explain it. In a somewhat legendary version of this meeting, Laplace is said to have responded: "Sire, I have no need of that hypothesis." Laplace thought he had closed the gaps. There was no left-over unexplained evidence that required the God-hypothesis to explain it.

Laplace did not say he had disproved God's existence. Perhaps a concept of God is needed to account for the existence of any universe at all, as Aquinas had argued. Moreover the relatively few disbelievers in those days stood in opposition to generations of intelligent and informed people, to whom the existence of God was highly plausible. Surely, the argument went, the few agnostics and atheists were not probably more correct than the thousands of philosophers and theologians whose belief in God was firm and part of a highly rational analysis of the world. It would turn out, though, that the existence of God would remain under attack.

The problem of evil and skepticism

From ancient times Christianity and Judaism alike faced a severe theological challenge. It is not directly involved in the encounter of religion with science; it is a moral issue, not a scientific one. But atheists often add this problem to their quiver of objections. The problem is a simple one: God is said to be perfectly good, omnipotent, and omniscient. Yet there are many great evils in the world. Why?

The word "evil" can be misleading; it would be better to speak simply of great suffering. When someone says "evil" in English the person usually means to label a particular person who acts with bad motives. We do not call tornadoes evil, destructive as they may be; we do not call malaria evil either. The traditional phrase "the problem of evil," however, uses the single word "evil" to name anything that constitutes human suffering, whether from disease, debility, disaster, or death.

There is little doubt that the world is full of suffering, both from the actions of other people and also from natural causes. Once smallpox killed millions; so also have influenza, bubonic plague, malaria, and cholera. Droughts, floods, earthquakes, tsunamis, and hurricanes add to human misery. In 1755 a great earthquake off the coast of Morocco shook the city of Lisbon with such great force that thousands died under the walls of collapsing buildings; others died from the many fires caused by the fallen candles and lamps. Many jumped on ships in the harbor, seeking safety. But twice the water in the harbor retreated out to sea, leaving the ships stranded on the river bottom. Both times the water returned as enormous tsunamis. The refugees on the ships died also. European theologians and philosopher found themselves addressing an old question: If God has all power, all knowledge, and is all good, why does God allow such evils to take place?

The book of Job, an ancient tale rewritten often, had already put thought to the suffering of those who seemed to be good people. Today the book *When Bad Things Happen to Good People* by Rabbi Harold Kushner, has been selling well for over 20 years. Why would God allow good people to seriously suffer, Kushner asks, as they often seem to? A famous ancient version is attributed to the pagan philosopher Epicurus in the 4th century BCE:

Is God willing to prevent evil, but not able?	Then he is not omnipotent.
Is he able, but not willing?	Then he is malevolent.
Is he both able and willing?	Then whence cometh evil?
Is he neither able nor willing?	Then why call him God?

In the 4th century A.D a Christian apologist named Lactantius repeated these questions, as did Augustine a century later, both struggling with possible answers. In the 11th century Otloh of Emmerah confessed he had lost his faith for a while, partly because the scriptures sometimes seemed to contradict each other, but also because of how much suffering existed. A good God, Otloh concluded, should not allow such suffering. Skeptics agree. Victor J. Stenger, in his *God, the Failed Hypothesis*, devotes a chapter to the problem of evil as part of his overall, mainly scientific, argument against belief in God. He pointedly attacks the notion of God he says most religious people hold, the everyday God who supposedly possesses the means and the power to control everything, but fails to prevent natural disasters and diseases.[3]

Masters of suspicion

In the 19th and early 20th centuries, influential atheists offered explanations as to why most people in history believed in God in spite of the fact, in the opinion of these atheists, such belief was incorrect. Many of the atheists had a common theme: they cast suspicion on belief in God by portraying it as a fiction that people construct or accept in order to alleviate certain anxieties of life. A 20th century philosopher named Paul Ricoeur identified Nietzsche, Marx, and Freud as "masters of suspicion." For Nietzsche we can substitute the name Feuerbach, whose ideas were then used by both Marx and Freud. All three of these are full "reductionists," reducing religious beliefs and practices to underlying human psychological processes. Religions usually claim they come from God, from "above," so to speak. These masters of suspicion say that religions come from below, from our own human needs and imagination.

Ludwig Feuerbach (1804–1872)

In a work entitled, *The Essence of Christianity*, Feuerbach said that we humans tended to "project" into the sky above us some of our own ideas about ourselves. We create God in the human image and likeness, he claimed.

Feuerbach began with the observation that the human mind is open to the infinite. He did not mean we really can grasp the infinite; he meant only that human knowing is open-ended. We can ask questions, come up with an answer or a variety of answers, but realize that there are endlessly more questions and possible answers. We can even ask endless questions about the methods we use to produce and evaluate answers, as Chapter 2 indicated.

Feuerbach forcefully raised the terrifying questions which Tillich and Rahner later addressed. These are the questions which came to be called "existential." These are questions about whether there is any ultimate purpose or value to human life. Perhaps everything is a random and ultimately useless process, coming from no place in particular with no particular ultimate meaning or goal. That is what a universe would be like without something like a God who provides an ultimate purpose or fulfillment. The thought of such a universe frighten us, Feuerbach claimed. We grow uneasy about the ultimate value of our lives.

Thoughts such as this also reveal to us our own finite and fallible nature. We are able to conceive of ultimate perfection, but this only makes us all the more aware of our limits and imperfections, Feuerbach argues. We become anxious about ourselves, fearful of our potential for mistakes, convinced we are weak beings caught in immense forces of nature. So we seek some Perfect source of help and guidance and purpose. Our sense of the infinite allows us to dream up the possibility of a Supreme Reality that is infinitely Perfect. We call it "God." In order to imagine the perfection of this Infinite God we look to the best aspects of our own human nature, exaggerate those aspects into perfection, and then attribute those aspects to God. We make this God distinct from us by contrasting our imperfections and finiteness with the unlimited perfections of this God. But it is really our own idealized selves we are worshiping when we worship God, said Feuerbach.

To Feuerbach this "projection" of a grand human image into the sky is not just a pleasant fantasy. It is a way we rob ourselves of self-confidence. It is we humans who have the power of goodness and creativity and freedom. If we did not have these powers in ourselves we would not be able to use these images to create a model of God. But conscious of our limitedness, afraid to take on too heavy a responsibility, we tell ourselves that we are not really very good or creative at all, that our freedom is rarely used for anything but doing harm. This is especially evident in the Christian doctrine of original sin, which declares that every person is born sinful and corrupt. So we conclude that we should leave things in God's hands. By this we sacrifice our autonomy and make ourselves dependent on an imaginary God. Feuerbach called this a kind of self-alienation, whereby we come to treat our own abilities and strengths as alien to us. Here are a few words from Feuerbach, who writes rather obscurely. It summarizes his claim that religion is self-alienating, though he calls it a "differencing" in this translation.

> Religion is the disuniting of man from himself; he sets God before him as the antithesis of himself. God is not what man is—man is not what God is. God is the infinite, man the finite being; God is perfect, man imperfect; God eternal, man temporal; God almighty, man weak; God holy, man sinful. God and man are extremes: God is the absolutely positive, the sum of all realities; man the absolutely negative, comprehending all negations. But in religion man contemplates his own latent nature. Hence it must be shown that this antithesis, this differencing of God and man, with which religion begins, is a differencing of man with his own nature.[4]

What humans need to do, said Feuerbach, was to recapture a sense of their own value by recognizing that there is no God, that there is only the human inner potential for "divine" goodness and creativity and freedom, potential which we must develop in order to improve life. The impulse at work here is humanism—an affirmation of the worth and potential of the human person—in a purely worldly ("secular") form. "Humanism" is a word to remember; it will appear again later here.

Theologians responded to Feuerbach by saying that he was only attacking the everyday, somewhat anthropomorphic God of popular religion. A sophisticated theology of God such as that of Aquinas recognizes that God is not merely human nature made perfect. God is the Infinite, the Absolute, Ultimate Mystery. Feuerbach's rejoinder is that the Infinite is not the God of religious people; it is just a bunch of philosophical abstractions which theologians play with to keep belief in God safe from the critical skepticism of people like Feuerbach. He insists that the actual religious belief of most people pictures God as an anthropomorphic everyday god, the first of the three images of God described in the previous chapter.

The response by believers to Feuerbach's challenge will probably depend on what type of faith they have and what sort of God they can accept. In any case, the idea that God is beyond all human categories goes back at least to Philo and extends through Anselm and Aquinas and later theology, as we have seen. It was not dreamed up, as Feuerbach suggests, to meet the challenge of 18ᵗʰ and 19ᵗʰ century skepticism about anthropomorphic images of God.

Karl Marx (1818–1883)

Where Feuerbach had spoken generally of religion as a human creation based on a sense of human finiteness, Karl Marx focused on the specific problems of the oppressed. Marx said relatively little about religion. His most famous statements appear in an 1844 article on Hegel's *Philosophy of Right*. Religion is an illusion, Marx said (i.e., God and other supernatural beings are illusory), used by people to express their misery caused by the conditions of life in this world. They do this by contrasting this life with an idealized world to come, and by contrasting the callous rulers of this world with an idealized otherworldly leader who is God. Religion is therefore the cry of the oppressed, an expression and sign of their distress. Religious otherworldliness promises pie in the sky in the great by and by; it thus becomes the opium by which people dull their awareness of their current pains in this world.

Critical analysis of religion is the "prerequisite of all criticism" because all critical analysis of human social and political and economic life has to start with the recognition that all these forms of life are products of human history just as religion is. (Marx here foreshadows the arguments adopted by postmodernists.) If we can become aware that even the religions are just the product of human thought in history, then we can recognize that so are all social, political, and economic forms. In that case, for the first time in history we will be able to deliberately choose to accept, reject, or change these forms. We can thus take power over the conditions of our own lives. We can overcome the self-alienation of which Feuerbach accused religion. Though Marx's statements are brief, they are rather strong; here are his own famous words from the article just mentioned:

> The foundation of irreligious criticism is this: Man makes religion, religion does not make man. Religion is indeed man's self-consciousness and self-awareness so long as he has not found himself or has already lost himself again.
>
> Religious suffering is, at one and the same time, the expression of real suffering and a protest against real suffering. Religion is the sigh of the oppressed creature, the heart of a heartless world, and the soul of soulless conditions. It is the opium of the people.
>
> The abolition of religion as the *illusory* happiness of the people is the demand for their *real* happiness.

Marx claimed that the theories he and Friedrich Engels worked out constituted the first truly "scientific" theory of socialism. Attempts in the former U.S.S.R., in China, and in other places to follow Marx's program for society turned out rather disastrous. But Marx was inspired by a compassion for the oppressed, a compassion that has its roots, many have claimed, in the Judaic-Christian ethic of love of neighbor. If this is so, then, ironically, Marx's criticism of religion as he saw it operating in Europe, was a criticism inspired by that same religion. He offered a vision of justice, freedom, and equality for all human beings. It is also all the more ironic, therefore, that the regimes which have operated in his name have destroyed so much freedom, justice, and equality. On the other hand, liberation theology movements of Latin America have sometimes found inspiration in his ideas because of their concern for liberation from oppression.

Sigmund Freud (1856–1939)

Freud invented psychoanalysis and called it a science. It supposes that there are non-conscious memories, feelings, anxieties, and compulsions present and working in people in ways that people are unable to recognize because they repress them, keeping them out of conscious awareness to avoid the discomfort or threat they carry with them. So Freud "reduced" a lot of human ideas and behavior to non-conscious psychological structures of the mind. He did this to religion also.

Freud proposed a number of rather odd theories about the origin of religion. His most aggressive criticism of religion appears in a small work entitled *The Future of an Illusion.* He began with the assumption that religious beliefs are unfounded. Historically they originated with belief in spirits and in gods, which Freud considered superstition. The idea of a single supreme God came later. Freud thought that people tended to anthropomorphize the forces of nature, by a process he called the "humanization" of nature, in order to deal with the threat of death and suffering to which nature (or "fate") subjects us. Though he does not say so, he is repeating ideas from Feuerbach. Here is an excerpt from *The Future of an Illusion* summarizing his thought.

> With the first step, which is the humanization of [the forces of] nature, much is already won. Nothing can be made of impersonal forces and fates; they remain eternally remote. But if the elements have passions that rage like those in our own souls, if death itself is not something spontaneous, but the violent act of an evil Will, if everywhere in nature we have about us beings who resemble those of our own environment, then indeed we can breathe freely, we can feel at home in the face of the supernatural, and we can deal psychically with our frantic anxiety. We are perhaps still defenseless, but no longer helplessly paralyzed; we can at least react; perhaps indeed we are not even defenseless; we can have recourse to the same methods against the violent supermen of the beyond that we make use of in our community; we can try to exorcise them, to appease, them to bribe them, and so rob them of part of their power by thus influencing them.

> ★ ★ ★ ★

> For there is nothing new in this situation. It has an infantile prototype, and is really only the continuation of this. For once before one has been in such a state of helplessness: as a little child in one's relationship to one's parents. For one had reason to fear them, especially the father, though at the same time one was sure of his protection against the dangers then known to one.[5]

Freud mentions the response of a religious person who says that Freud fails to acknowledge the more sophisticated notion of God as the Infinite. There is a kind of "oceanic feeling" a person experiences that is an experience of the Infinite. This is a truer sense of God, says the respondent, probably echoing Schleiermacher, than Freud's anthropomorphic father-figure. Like Feuerbach, however, Freud responds in turn by saying that the Infinite is not the real God of religion. The God to whom people pray, from whom they ask for help, upon whom their hopes for eternal happiness rests, is a human-like God, Freud insists.

Jean Paul Sartre (1905–1980)

Sartre was one of the most famous atheists of the 20th century. He refined the concept of "existentialism," already in use by a religious thinker, Gabriel Marcel. Sartre was anything but religious, though. He was convinced that the findings of modern science had banished God completely from the universe. Early 20th century astronomers found evidence that the universe was almost immeasurably large, by finding that some apparent stars were themselves entire galaxies of stars, and that there were endless numbers of these galaxies. The human race is lost and insignificant. As far as Sartre was concerned, the theory of evolution also indicated that the rise and development of life on the planet was unplanned, aimless, and brutal. We will examine these topics, of astrophysics and of evolution later. For now it is enough to indicate that Sartre used these ideas to explain and justify his own existential anxiety.

He insisted that because there is no God, we humans are utterly on our own. We are free; that is our nature as conscious beings. So we have full responsibility for our own lives. Echoing Feuerbach, Sartre insists we should not hand that responsibility over to a non-existent God. Sartre declared that even if God did exist, that would not absolve us of the responsibility to make our own choices. To maintain our humanness we would have to keep in our own hands the right to create our own values, to write up our own commandments. The notion of "God" is, as Feuerbach said, an act of self-alienation, whereby we give up the core of our humanness which is our inner freedom, and hand over authority to this Being in the sky. The idea of God is actually a threat, therefore, to our humanness. It is therefore good that there is no God, says Sartre, even though awareness of this exposes us to the absurdity of our situation, as the beings who need values and purpose, in a universe where everything is ultimately meaningless.

Richard Dawkins (1941–)

Feuerbach and Sartre were both philosophers, not scientists. In spite of the claim by Marx and Engels that they had discovered the laws of "scientific socialism," there is little that is really science in it. Freud said his psychoanalytic theories were scientific, but his analysis of religion is highly speculative. Nonetheless, these masters of suspicion offered answers to an important question: if there is no God, as these skeptics thought, why do so many intelligent people believe there is. Those who now use science as a springboard to atheism can thus presuppose the arguments of the masters of suspicion, as well as of atheistic existentialism. All this contributes to the position of the sociobiologist, Richard Dawkins, probably the most famous atheist in the English-speaking world today. It would be more accurate, in fact, to call him a public anti-theist.[6]

Sometimes Dawkins speaks in a mild voice. He most frequently argues that there is no rational basis for belief in God in the apparently aimless universe which science describes. He and Sartre are alike in this. He also complains about belief in God based on inner experience:

> Some people believe in God because of what appears to them to be an inner revelation. Such revelations are not always edifying but they undoubtedly feel real to the individual concerned. Many inhabitants of lunatic asylums have an unshakable inner faith that they are Napoleon or, indeed, God himself. There is no doubting the power of such convictions for those that have them, but this is no reason for the rest of us to believe them.

At other times, however, Dawkins complains in unsparing terms about what he sees as the irrationality inherent in religion:

> Much of what people do is done in the name of God. Irishmen blow each other up in his name. Arabs blow themselves up in his name. Imams and ayatollahs oppress women in his name. Celibate popes and priests mess up people"s sex lives in his name. Jewish *shohets* cut live animals' throats in his name. The achievements of religion in past history—bloody crusades, torturing inquisitions, mass-murdering conquistadors, culture-destroying missionaries, legally enforced resistance to each new piece of scientific truth until the last possible moment—are even more impressive. And what has it all been in aid of? I believe it is becoming increasingly clear that the answer is absolutely nothing at all. There is no reason for believing that any sort of gods exist and quite good reason for believing that they do not exist and never have. It has all been a gigantic waste of time and a waste of life. It would be a joke of cosmic proportions if it weren't so tragic.[7]

Dawkins even has a specific argument against belief in the existence of God, an argument based on his understanding of evolutionary theory. It is, more precisely, an argument directed against those who claim that the universe is so complexly ordered (a topic of a later chapter) there must be a divine Designer of the world. We humans can design things because of the complexity of our central nervous system. Whoever designed us would have to be orders of magnitude more complex. If God designed the universe, says Dawkins, God would have to be enormously more complex than human beings. But if this kind of complexity is a sign of design, then God would also have to have been designed by another designer—and so on endlessly. So the whole idea of a Designer God is self-contradictory, concludes Dawkins.

Religious responses to atheism

McGrath against Dawkins

We can begin a review of a few religious responses to atheism by considering the ideas of the philosopher Alistair McGrath. He has written a book entitled *Dawkins' God* (Blackwell, 2005) in which McGrath argues that it is rational to believe in God, and that it is Dawkins who is being irrational in his attacks on religion. McGrath begins by addressing Dawkins' complaint that religion leads people to do bad things. That is true, McGrath acknowledges, but not most religious people. Moreover religion does good things for people—McGrath claims there is an empirical positive correlation between religiousness and a sense of well being.

McGrath's key response, however, addresses a charge made by Dawkins that some religious thinkers try to preserve belief in God by the invocation of "mystery." It is the goal of science to dissolve mystery, Dawkins says. Religion which promotes belief in and even submission to "mystery" is irrational. You may hear echoes of Feuerbach once again in this.

McGrath's response is that a sense of mystery is not irrational; it is an acknowledgment of the inevitable limits of human consciousness, open to the infinite but never able to have infinite understanding or knowledge. McGrath is here doing what many a theologian has done, to point out that Dawkins does not show much knowledge of sophisticated theology, including theology about the limits of human knowledge of God. Dawkins, like Feuerbach and Freud, rails against belief in an anthropomorphic God. When he faces the theologians' God, the Infinite Mystery, his response is similar to that of Feuerbach and Freud. They all insist that the God of theologians is not the God of most religious people. Religious people, they complain, do not address their prayers to Infinite Mystery; they do not hope that Infinite Mystery will intervene in their lives; they do not make acts of personal dedication to something as impersonal as Mystery. So say these skeptics.

The choice here remains awkward for religious people. As was noted, most religious believers probably do not treat God as the Infinite Mystery, not even with the help of Aquinas' "analogical predication," which asserts that God is perfect Personness, Goodness, Love, and so forth, but in an infinite and changeless manner beyond all human comprehension. Most religious people probably do want to have an image of God that is closer to that of a Supreme Father-figure, who listens and responds with comfort and help. On the other hand, when Feuerbach and Freud claim that religious people want this sort of God, Feuerbach and Freud do so to support their own atheism. They prefer an image of God upon which it is easier to throw suspicion. The God who is Infinite Mystery is safer from their attacks.

Karl Rahner and Infinite Mystery

The most influential Catholic theologian of the 20th century, some of whose ideas we saw in Chapter 2, shares McGrath's Anglican understanding of God. McGrath does not fully spell out his theology of God. Here is a more thorough exposition of what McGrath probably has in mind, as expressed in the thought of Rahner. Here is a two-step version of Rahner's basic theology. He focuses on the "existential" questions, ideas about life's ultimate possible meaning.

1. We humans are peculiar beings with a capacity for the infinite.
As Feuerbach said, each thought we think and each choice we make is one of an endless possible range of thoughts and choices. Each time we formulate a thought out of our experiences, says Rahner, we are rising above ("transcending") those experiences, as it were, sitting up higher than them and looking down on them in order to ask what it was we experienced: was it a dog? a marshmallow? a hot-air balloon on a warm summer day? We do a similar thing when we make a choice. We rise above (transcend) options and look down upon them in order to ask ourselves whether we want door #1 or door #2.

Our human lives are also made up of many things that are not thoughts and choices. Like rocks we are material; like trees we are alive; like snails we move about; like chimpanzees we use tools. But the particularly human thing about us is to be able to think consciously about such things and make conscious choices about them in a way that keeps rising above (transcending) any one occasion or option. We can reflect on how good or bad a certain course of action might be. We can thereby evaluate the possible courses of action. But it is not easy to say what is good or bad, so before we evaluate the course of action we might first have to evaluate what we mean by "good" or "bad," and even reflect on how we make such evaluations.

All of this illustrates what is meant by saying that we have a capacity for the infinite. It is a way to label the fact that except for eventual death, there is no prior limit to the various ideas and reformulation of ideas and evaluation of ideas and reformulation and reevaluation. Human life is lived in the presence of endless openness to the always more.

If God were less than the absolutely Infinite, God would then be smaller than the reach of the human mind. God would not fit the definition even of that-than-which-nothing-greater-can-be-conceived. Moreover, contrary to those like Dawkins (not famous for atheism until after Rahner's death) who think of God as just more supremely complex than humans, Rahner could appeal to Aquinas' reminder that the Cause of everything else must not be like anything else. It is infinite simplicity, not supreme complexity. To the human mind it is therefore endless mystery.

2. There are four possible basic styles of response to the endless mystery.

The first is to ignore it. Because the capacity for thought and choice are endless, a person could argue, it will only drive a person crazy to worry about such things. Would it not be more reasonable just to settle for the practical issues of life, about how to develop a work skill, raise a family, be a decent neighbor and friend, contribute to the lives of others until death arrives? Rahner calls this "unconcern." It is actually a way of covering up concern, he claims—a move to replace potential anxiety or despair with more comforting thoughts.

The second style of response is a thorough atheism which affirms that all things are part of an ultimate meaninglessness. A fully consistent atheism might imply that one should simply drift through life aimlessly or live with a fundamental cynicism about all goals and values. Sartre's view leaves a person open to this response.

The third is a nominal atheism. This is the situation of a person who says that all things are part of an ultimate meaninglessness, but who makes this an atheism in name only, Rahner claims, by living deliberately and uncynically, as though life were actually meaningful after all, showing this by dedication to values of friendship and family, by courage in the face of bigotry, by endurance in the face of the burden of caring for someone who is alone. If all things are really part of ultimate meaninglessness, such heroic acts of love and courage are at least logically foolish. They will mean nothing in the end, will be swallowed up in the aimless dark eventually. But such atheists live as though they have an implicit faith that being a person in this universe is ultimately meaningful. They act like anonymous theists.

The fourth style of response to the fact of mystery is to treat that endless mystery, which we all face just because we are human, as Mystery (with a capital "M"). That is a symbolic way of representing an option open to any person, which is to trust that the ultimate truth about reality is best represented by acts of personal qualities such as courage and love and humaneness. This is a trust that the personness that is our identity is a better symbol of the ultimate than words like "cold" and "dark" and "aimless" and "meaningless." Whoever does this, says Rahner, has just done the equivalent of affirming the reality of God, and of God as somehow the perfection of Personness.

Rahner's analysis provides an example of what a more sophisticated theological approach can look like. It especially makes clear again that the attacks of the masters of suspicion on belief in God tends to work best against a more anthropomorphic interpretation, against aspects of the "everyday God." A fundamental religious trust that there is an ultimate value and purpose in being human is less susceptible to the kind of specific attacks made by Feuerbach, Marx, Freud, and Dawkins. This trust stands in opposition also to Sartre's belief in the ultimate meaninglessness of reality.

John Haught makes this point by dividing atheisms into two types, soft-core and hard-core.[8] Soft-core atheism attacks an anthropomorphic God who supposedly runs the universe. Feuerbach, Freud, and Dawkins fall into this category. When this God is eliminated, according to these skeptics, we can then just calmly get on with life, without all the evils and oppressions they believe religion produces or supports. Hard-core atheism, on the other hand, looks into the depths. It moves on past belief in an anthropomorphic God, to face the possibility of ultimate meaninglessness. When God is entirely removed, says Sartre, we must acknowledge that there is no ultimate foundation for our values; we must make them up. There is no ultimate ground for the trust that life has some ultimate purpose. It will be difficult to then calmly get on with life. Somehow we must find the courage to face the absurdity of our situation.

Hard-core atheism makes it clear that the deepest questions within religion are not the daily practical ones, of whether God will help a person in a particular situation, or whether certain rules have been ordained and will be enforced by God. The most profound "God-question" is whether all existence lacks any ultimate meaning. For this no super-Zeus will do; only a metaphysical Ultimate suffices. So argue the theologians.

Belief in God and the structures of the mind

Between the skeptic and the believer stands a group of people who use scientific understanding of the operations of the human mind to explain why people believe in God or other invisible agents. These theories could be used to imply that the mind tricks us into believing things that are not true. On the other hand, at least one person argues that these theories imply that atheism is unnatural. This is Justin Barrett, who provides one of the more succinct analyses.[9]

Barrett builds upon the work of Stewart Guthrie, whose 1993 book, *Faces in the Clouds*, provides an extensive argument that we humans are hard-wired to anthropomorphize, thereby partly bolstering Freud's claim on this. Guthrie argues that Freud got it partly wrong, though, when Freud said it is more comforting to deal with a "humanized" nature. Guthrie argues that a divine being who can punish severely and even send a person to eternal punishment is hardly comforting. Guthrie argues that, comforting or not, we cannot help ourselves; we are hard-wired by our genes to anthropomorphize. The bulk of his book consists of countless examples of anthropomorphizing, making a convincing case that we do a great deal of it. The further question for both Guthrie and Barrett is why we do it so extensively.

Barrett coins a phrase to sum up his and Guthrie's answer: a mental "hypersensitive agency detection device" (HADD). Barrett begins with the neurophysiology which has investigated the structures of the mind. By the early 20th century it was already clear that certain parts of the brain carried out rather specific tasks. Broca's area, near the left ear, is important for speech. A line of grey matter running down the middle of the crown controls various muscle groups. Functional magnetic resonance imaging (fMRI) of blood flow in the brain can now provide much more detailed information about brain structures and their functions. MRI results, for example, can tell whether a person likes or dislikes goose liver paté by differences in blood flow in emotion centers in the mid-brain. Barrett calls some of the structures of the brain "devices."

One of those brain devices is attuned to the activity of other conscious beings. It is very important for survival and success for humans to be able to detect when other conscious agents are around and active. This includes possible enemies, hiding in the bushes, ready to attack. It includes dangerous animals, intent on finding a meal. Guthrie notes that a rustling in the bushes may be no more than the wind. Jumping to the conclusion the rustling is caused by a potentially dangerous conscious being, on the other hand, will save the person on those occasions when it is indeed a dangerous animal or person. Thus a tendency to anthropomorphize can be an excellent survival device. Survival includes the chance of having descendants to whom one may pass on the tendency to anthropomorphize.

The human environment also includes friendly humans, whose intentions are important, whether as a possible mate or ally. Barrett points to several studies which indicate that some structures of the brain are especially attuned to recognizing both friend and foe, perhaps reading their emotions through their facial expression or body language. It is these structures, as well as the general tendency to anthropomorphize, which Barrett labels HADD.

It is natural for us humans to assume that where no visible cause of an event is apparent, that there must be a cause nonetheless—an invisible one. It is extremely natural, Barrett argues, that we human beings think of these causes as "agents." Even the wind and the weather, the mountains and rivers, are readily interpreted as signs of an agent or agents. They might be spirits, gods, or God.

Barrett adds several psychological studies about the tendencies of children to equate the status of such invisible beings with the status children attribute to their parents and most adults in general. These studies tend to confirm some of Freud's claims about how children view their parents. To young children, adults have immense knowledge and power. They are the repository of the rules of life. They are the guardians and guides and protectors. Barrett argues that this early inclination is a strong base on which elevated notions of God are built. Eventually a child learns at first hand the fallibility and limitations of adults. There is no equally obvious evidence of divine fallibility or limit.

Unlike Freud, Barrett does not use these observations to conclude that theism is incorrect. As a psychologist he does not grant himself the right to judge philosophical or theological matters. He concludes, in fact, that atheism is unnatural. It has been rare in history. Now, Barrett thinks, we know why. Only a culture which teaches people to go against their natural inclinations to anthropomorphize, could produce and sustain atheism, he says. Nonetheless, it is easy to see that a skeptic could use Barrett's analysis to claim that belief in God or other spirit beings is not based on good evidence or reasoning, but on innate tendencies which are not necessarily religious at all.

(A small side observation flows from Barrett's work. Surveys of religiousness almost always indicate that more women are religious than men, or that they take their religion more seriously. It is also the case that on average women are better than men at interpreting the emotions and thoughts of others, at being sensitive to others' feelings, at maintaining social connections. Autism is the extreme case of an inability to be aware of others as having inner thoughts and intentions. Something like nine out of ten autistic people are men. Women's greater social sensitivity may explain their tendency to have a greater sense of relation to even invisible personal beings.)

A theologian might respond to a skeptic by arguing that having a special sensitivity to the presence and activity of something like a divine Being might in fact provide the starting point for a valid path of religious discovery. Andrew Newberg and others propose something like this, by starting with brain states that seem quite comparable to mystical experience. These experiences diminish a sense of time and spatial location; they create a sense of being in the presence of an Infinite Mystery such as Rahner describes. Newberg does not quite say that religious experience is valid or correct. His language borders on this sort of judgment, nonetheless.

> Our minds are drawn by the intuition of this deeper reality, this utter sense of oneness, where suffering vanishes and all desires are at peace. As long as our brains are arranged the way they are, as long as our minds are capable of sensing this deeper reality, spirituality will continue to shape the human experience, and God, however we define that majestic, mysterious concept, will not go away.[10]

Most religious people nonetheless favor a somewhat more anthropomorphic God, one who loves, is personally involved in people's lives, often through divine interventions. The next few chapters on miracles will make this point clearer.

For further reading

For atheism or skepticism

Dennett, Daniel, *Breaking the Spell: Religion as a Natural Phenomenon* (New York: Penguin, 2007). An appeal to religious people not to believe in the supernatural.

Shermer, Michael, *How We Believe: Science, Skepticism, and the Search for God* (New York: Holt, 2003). Shermer provides social science explanations for religious belief.

Steele, David Ramsay, *Atheism Explained: From Folly to Philosophy* (Chicago: Open Court, 2008). A clear recent review of relevant evidence and arguments.

In defense of belief in God

Haught, John, *Deeper Than Darwin: The Prospect for Religion in an Age of Evolution* (Boulder, CO: Westview Press, 2003). This argues for a position similar to Rahner's.

Lennox, John C., *God's Undertaker: Has Science Buried God?* (Oxford: LionHutton, 2007). Lennox answers in the negative, surveying most of the topics in religion and science.

Ward, Keith, *Pascal's Fire: Scientific Faith and Religious Understanding* (Oxford: Oneworld, 2006).

Part Four
Miracles: does God intervene in natural processes?

Belief in Miracles Today

8

The Hebrew Scriptures have specific stories of divine intervention. The story of the Exodus from Egypt, placed around 1200 BCE, portrays God as quite active, sending various plagues, parting the Red Sea, providing manna in the desert for the Hebrew wanderers to eat. In Christian tradition, belief that Jesus was born of a virgin and was resurrected from the dead imply special acts by God in history. Islam is based on the special revelations God gave to Muhammad through the agency of Jibril (Gabriel) over a twenty-two-year period (from 610 to 632, the year of Muhammad's death). There are more notions of "miracle," however, than these examples suggest.

Defining "Miracle"

In search of clarity about the word "miracles," consider these six possibilities:

1. Miracles in an analogous or poetic sense.
People often toss the word "miracle" around as a synonym for being lucky or as a name for anything deeply moving. "It is a miracle she escaped that accident alive" may mean only "She was lucky to get out." We also speak of the miracle of birth even when we think it is an entirely natural event, because the birth of a child is wondrous. Even an atheist may call some events miracles, in this loose sense of the word.

2. Preternatural "miracles" (a medieval category).[1]
Those who believe in spirits and gods and souls may think of them as not part of nature. Nature is defined as material reality, different from the spiritual. Spiritual beings are then said to be "preter" [alongside of] nature. With superior knowledge and long experience demons, for example, can affect material things in ways that are so startling that people call them miracles. In the end, though, they are thought to be doing nothing more basically unusual than what any person does by choosing to manipulate nature in some way. Their acts are like stage magic which consists mainly of tricks and slight of hand, to cause wonderment and awe.

3. Supernatural miracles: "miracle" in the strict sense of the word.
This definition of miracle begins with the belief that the material universe operates by built-in and reliable laws of nature. The whole universe follows such laws. But God who created all the laws of nature is not bound by them. God can speed them up or slow them down (make a lily bloom suddenly). God can make them do what they otherwise could never do (raise a person from the dead). These are the only true miracles, as interventions by a power that is fully superior to nature (super-natural) and outside of nature's limitations.

4. The universe as the one single (ongoing) miracle of creation.
Traditional theists believe the universe was created by God out of nothing. The universe is therefore not "natural" in its origin but was caused by the Supernatural Being called God. The fact that the universe exists at all is therefore a miracle, a supernatural act. Every part or aspect of the universe is part of that single enormous miracle. The universe can operate entirely by natural causes, as cosmological naturalism says, and still be this one miracle. It is a single *ongoing* miracle if Aquinas was correct, that God must continuously sustain the existence of this contingent universe.

5. Pre-planted wonders.
Wondrous events may happen as they do because God, from the beginning foresaw all possible events and arranged things so the flow of *natural* causes would intersect at many points in the future to produce effects that are unpredictable to human minds. Thus the cure of a certain disease happens without divine intervention, by causes that intersect at a certain point in history to bring about the cure in a way that is utterly surprising and therefore looks like a special "intervention" by God, though it was actually pre-planted as part of the single miracle of creation and was then carried out by entirely natural causes. This also fits with cosmological naturalism.

6. Special wonders in a universe without any laws of nature.
Imagine a universe in which God does everything that happens. The regularity of most events is not due to the operations of reliable natural forces, but because God customarily acts in a reliable way. God normally makes the earth continue to rotate, so the sun rises every day. But God could make the earth stop rotating for a few hours, and for those hours the sun would appear to stand still in the sky. Because this event would be

surprising it would be called a "wonder." In Latin the word for that is *miraculum*. This view of God's activity is called "occasionalism"—every occasion that occurs is done directly by God; only some of them are surprising.

For most Jews and Christians, definition #3 is the important one in the meeting between religion and science. To whatever extent some aspect of some event has occurred only because God has intervened, to that extent that event is no longer explicable through natural causes alone. Even methodological naturalism falls short in such cases. A claim that a divine intervention occurred is simultaneously a claim that science is inadequate to explain the event.

The traditional Islamic belief is closer to #6. God is the primary cause of every event, and not just in the sense that God sustains everything in existence. Rather God is the true cause of every specific event. It is good that science studies the patterns of natural events. It is a mistake, however, to think that those patterns operate as independent "secondary" causes. No cause and no effect is independent of the will of God for each of those occasions. All forms of naturalism, which treat events in the world as though they are due only to natural causes, misses the reality of the divine will as the cause of each and every event, says traditional Islam.

Support for belief in miraculous interventions (definition #3) is easier if this belief is left as just a general assertion, without adding any claims that this or that specific historical event is due to divine intervention. Sorting through some specific or concrete claims about miraculous intervention can give a better indication of what might be plausible or not. Here are some specific beliefs from history against which a person can test her or his ideas about supernatural and preternatural interventions.

1. Trial by ordeal: an early medieval method for determining guilt or innocence. It included holding a hot poker in the palm until it burned the skin. If the skin healed without serious infection, that was a sign from God of the person's innocence.
2. Relics to repel invaders: from the 6th to the 15th centuries the dead body of an important saint, or some part like a skull or a hand, would draw the power of the saint to the area to give protection against invaders. (Relics were used for many purposes.)
3. Blessed church bell power over storms: large church bells, because they had been blessed by a priest with holy water, could drive away thunder and lightning. Popular during the 12th to 16th centuries.
4. Succubi and Incubi: a demon would take on form as a human woman, seduce a man to get his semen (demons did not have their own), then change into male form and materialize in a woman's bed at night to make her pregnant. Numerous such pregnancies were claimed up to the 16th–17th centuries.
5. Comets and lightning as signs sent by God: up to the 17th century such heavenly events were considered divine messages.
6. Disease, insanity, and afflictions of livestock caused by demons or witches. A frequent belief up to the 18th century in Europe, when witches were last burned or hanged.
7. King's touch: the kings of France and England could cure certain diseases by the touch of their hands. God gave such power to those God appointed to rule over others.

8. Earthquakes, volcanoes, flood, disease, as punishments from God: the story of Sodom and Gomorrah is a classic biblical instance, in which God rained down sulphur and fire.
9. The appearance of the Blessed Virgin Mary to children at Lourdes, Fatima, and Medjugorje (in a Croatian section of southwest Bosnia beginning in 1981).
10. The power of prayer to overcome disease.

The first seven items on this list are no longer part of ordinary belief. Most people think of these ideas as superstitions. The last three on the list, however, are part of some contemporary religious belief. There has been a gradual shift since ancient times away from many forms of belief in supernatural or preternatural interventions, but not a total abandonment of such beliefs by everyone. The shift has largely come about because of the acceptance of certain standards of rationality or of naturalism, especially through the development of science. It is an interesting question, of course, as to why so many beliefs have been abandoned while others are still in force.

At least five types of challenges exist to belief in miracles in the strict sense (and to preternatural miracles also). The first is still the challenge which scientific naturalism presents. Methodological naturalism, technically speaking, does not eliminate the possibility of miracles. They would just lie outside the range of explanations science allows itself to use. In practice, however, science intends to explain everything it can (without supposing it will eventually explain everything) through natural causes. It seems to be succeeding rather well at this. So the person who looks for miracles now also appears unscientific, at a time when science is eliminating or reducing disease and other afflictions far better than centuries of prayers for miracles.

The second problem is to *identify*, among all the events of life, those events which are due to more than solely natural causes. One who believes firmly in miracles could say that some divine activities go completely undetected. Miracles would thereby occur without anyone knowing it. On the other hand, no matter how wondrous a given event may seem, in the end there is no surefire way of determining it was not due to natural causes alone. Awed observers of the event may just be ignorant of the natural causes at work.

The third problem with miracles, as we have already seen, is that this belief is closely linked to anthropomorphic ideas about God, ideas which are more easily challenged by the masters of suspicion and other atheists. The God who does miracles may seem to be a powerful Agent or Doer who changes his mind, selects certain occasions to act and not others, just as a human person might.

A fourth and related problem is, again, how to explain evil. If God is pictured anthropomorphically like a powerful Being with the ability to intervene and help people in times of need, why have so many great disasters occurred. Could God not warn people of a coming earthquake or tsunami? Could God not intervene to wipe out a contagious disease? Even if the Holocaust is due to evil human free choices, does God have to let those free choices work out their full course of suffering, fear, and death?

Finally, by contrast with an anthropomorphic view, the traditional philosophical notion of God as the Infinite and Incomprehensible Ultimate portrays that Ultimate as necessarily changeless. Whatever this Ultimate does or has done would then logically have to be part of a single creative act—the one miracle of creation in which all else that will ever happen is already included. This is a religiously odd position, because it is a *theological* argument against the reasonableness of belief in miracles. The deists, believers in the regularities of the laws of nature, will make this point rather strongly, as we will see. Schleiermacher had his own theological reasons for supporting this conclusion also. It will turn out that other 20th century theologians will agree.

(The theological puzzles continue. If God is absolutely changeless, how is it possible for God to begin to create a universe? Would not God have to have been always, changelessly, producing whatever exists? That might even explain the law of the conservation of matter and energy. A typical theological answer is that God eternally, changelessly, decreed that the universe would come into being when it did, and then time began. Before that, time did not exist. God has been and remains utterly outside of time. Interestingly, modern physics says time is an attribute of matter-energy, so if physicists could agree that once there was no universe whatsoever, then they might agree that once there was no time—though the word "once" then becomes rather peculiar. Fortunately, such puzzles are more philosophical than scientific, so we can pass over them here.)

Types of religion according to how God acts in time and space

Categories concerning miracles have now become as complex here as some of the categories about the meaning of the word "faith." One way to simplify is to draw together what we have seen so far and offer just four choices of world-views in relation to the topic of miracles.

1. Strong supernaturalism.
This includes belief in a God who intervenes frequently in history and nature—i.e., performs many miracles, gives many signs, delivers messages through prophets. Pentecostals and other fundamentalists usually take this view. It can also includes belief in constant activity by spirit-beings such as angels, saints, and demons, as causes of disease, insanity, strange weather, victory in war.

2. Occasional supernaturalism.
Supernatural interventions do occur but only occasionally. Perhaps most of the work of God appears in inner guidance and comfort. The exceptions are regular miracles like the transubstantiation of the bread and wine in the Catholic mass, or irregular miracles like the sudden healing of a sick person.

3. Naturalistic religion.

Religious cosmological naturalism (as in the Deism of the 17th and later centuries in Europe) says that there are no miracles but that there is a God, Designer and Creator of the world. In this perspective God has made the world and given it over to human minds and hands to care for. This can be expressed as belief that God performs one single miracle of creating-sustaining the universe. (There will be more on Deism in a later chapter.)

4. Naturalistic un-religion.

This is metaphysical naturalism, which says that the natural universe is all that there is, as far as we can tell. There is therefore no good reason to believe in any supernatural or "spiritual" realities, neither God nor the soul, and certainly no miracles. Our powers of thought and choice are natural (not acts of a spiritual, non-material soul). This may be agnosticism, which is a claim that there is inadequate evidence to know whether there is a God. Or it may be atheism, which is a claim that there is no supernatural reality of any kind, including God.

Item #3 on this list was a crucial turning point in Europe in modern centuries. It broke with centuries of belief in the intervention in this natural world order by supernatural beings outside of the laws of nature. Where previous generations had seen many signs of God and preternatural beings interrupting the regular order of the world, deists saw only the regular order. This was the effect of—or the companion of—early modern science. This four-part distinction among types of universes will be useful to keep in mind.

Religious believers are usually happy to say that *in addition* to the forces of nature the hand of God is also at work. As was mentioned earlier, it is often hard for religious people to understand why anyone should object to this belief. Many things, after all, are beyond human understanding. It should be counted a blessing, perhaps, that some events are the special work of a loving and attentive God, giving a sign of encouragement, healing the sick, saving lives, watching over people. If people cannot understand fully or predict what miracles God will perform, perhaps the best thing to do is to accept that fact rather than obstinately or arrogantly demand that all events become intelligible to limited human minds, as some scientists seem to do. Naturalism is a fine working assumption for scientists, but is it not at least possible that some specific events have causes from beyond nature? Once again, it may help to look at some specifics before trying to answer this religious response.

Miracles in medicine

As far back as ancient Greek times there were medical and philosophical opinions that disease is a result of natural causes, not supernatural ones. Today we tend to agree. To probe current ideas we can address the particular case of cystic fibrosis (CF).

The symptoms of cystic fibrosis have been quite clear for a long time. Various body tissues cannot get water in and out of the cells properly. The lungs clog up with phlegm, making it difficult to breathe. A child with CF requires daily thumpings to loosen up the phlegm. These are half-hour sessions of light pounding on the back and chest (now there is a machine to do this). Another symptom is poor digestion. It is difficult for the child to be well-nourished.

The references here are to children because until recently a child with CF did not live beyond the teenage years. Now with careful attention to lungs and nourishment, many have lived even very much longer. But the children and their parents must still acknowledge the possibility of a relatively early death, and with the reality of many difficulties on a daily basis.

In past centuries a disease of this sort, with no evident physical cause, might have been attributed to the work of demons or perhaps even to God who has been thought to afflict people for some good divine reason. A first step in looking for a specific natural cause instead, was to recognize that CF is due to a recessive gene. A child suffers from CF only if both parents have this gene and the child inherits two copies, one from each parent. A long search finally identified the particular gene segment of the human genome that was different in those suffering from CF from that of people not afflicted by it. By a happy coincidence this particular gene segment had already been identified as the segment which had the code for producing a particular protein, which in turn was essential as a gate-keeper for chloride ions, allowing them passage into epithelial cells. Epithelial cells are a component of the lining of the lungs, the intestines, and the reproductive organs. Anything which disturbs their proper functioning will also disturb breathing, digestion, and fertility.

A few decades ago, however, none of this was known. Would it have been legitimate in the year 1950, for example, for a person to claim that the cause of CF was supernatural? No one could prove that CF was due to natural causes alone. As long as there was no specific, accurate, and clearly defensible scientific explanation of this disease, would not a person be justified in keeping open the possibility of supernatural (or preternatural) intervention? Is it legitimate, in fact, to continue to believe today that it is not truly genetic inheritance but divine intervention that causes CF? We do know that CF exists where a child inherits the same certain gene from both parents. But maybe that just disguises the intervention of God.

The idea that CF is due to some non-natural cause probably strikes most people as unreasonable. Naturalism of some sort or another tends to prevail in the case of diseases which have been identified as part of a pattern, even when the cause is not known. Enough natural causes for various diseases are now known that the working assumption is that natural causes account for all diseases. But what about cures of incurable medical conditions? Practices at the shrine at Lourdes provide a test for ideas about this.

Miraculous cures?

In 1858 a teenager named Bernadette Soubirous claimed to have seen an apparition in the hills near her town in southwestern France. Eventually, she said that the apparition declared "I am the Immaculate Conception." This in fact is not a name, but was a newly approved doctrine of the Catholic Church, declaring that when Mary was conceived in her mother's womb she did not inherit the taint of original sin, thereby helping to make her worthy to be the mother of God, as Christian doctrine has it. Eventually the woman appearing to Bernadette told her to rinse herself in a stream, which in fact did not exist. But, as the story goes, Bernadette dug in the place where the stream was supposed to be and uncovered a spring. The water of that spring at Lourdes is still associated with miraculous cures.

There is a quasi-official medical board at Lourdes, set up with the approval of the local bishop in the late 19th century and then re-established in the 20th century. This board evaluates significant claims of cures of severe medical conditions. Medical expertise is put to use to evaluate whether something beyond a natural cause might have been at work. Interestingly, the medical board is not allowed to say explicitly that any cure is miraculous, on the grounds that the supernatural is outside of the realm of their competence. They must restrict themselves to declaring that some cure is beyond what can be explained medically. At that point, however, the judgment and relevant documentation is passed on to the bishop of Lourdes. He appoints a commission to examine the cases. So far, of the thousands of claims made, relatively few have been classified as beyond medical explanation. Though some say there have been a few thousand cures, only 67 (as of 2009) have been accepted by the bishop's commissions. In each case, the bishop of Lourdes can then inform the bishop of the dioceses from which the cured person has come. That local bishop can do as he thinks best in response.[2] Evidently, the Catholic Church is very cautious about claiming that any of the cures are truly miracles. The medical board imposes stiff requirements.

1. The diagnosis of the illness must be examined and determined to be correct.
2. The prognosis must be very clear, classifying the illness as permanent or soon terminal.
3. The cure is rather quick, complete, and lasting.
4. No known medical treatment could have produced the results of #3.

In the 60 or so years since the medical board was first set up, there have been a few million sick visitors. God seems to be a bit sparing with miracles if less than one in 50,000 supplicants have been cured. Or it may not be surprising that once in 50,000 times nature itself does something extremely unusual, without any supernatural intervention. The fact that there is no medical explanation available might mean only that there are many things we do not know about natural processes.

This is an instance, then, when naturalism and supernaturalism contend to interpret certain events in the world. It is an instance where religion and science meet directly. This confrontation can be avoided by the use of cosmological naturalism. Or it can be avoided just by eliminating a medical panel to identify potentially miraculous cures, so that methodological naturalism can apply undisturbed. But belief in cures by God as well as other miracles is extremely important to the religious faith of many people.

Putting prayer to the test

Religious people who pray for the health of loved ones and neighbors might rely happily on modern medicine also. Taking a belt-and-suspenders approach by using every source of possible health could sound wise. This method has been put to an odd sort of test, however, using scientific method to try to determine the efficacy of prayer, through a study funded by the Templeton Foundation in 2005.[3]

The Foundation provided $2.4 million to see how large-scale praying might affect patients recovering from heart surgery. About 1,800 patients at six different hospitals were divided into three groups at each hospital. Two of these groups did not know whether they were going to be prayed for or not. One of these two in fact did not receive prayers; the other did. A third group was told they were indeed going to be prayed for, as they were. Three large religious groups, two of them Catholic and one Protestant, were enlisted to pray for 14 days for two of the three groups, totaling 1,200 patients, 600 of whom knew the prayers were being offered for them. At the end of two weeks, the relative health of the members of each group was evaluated by teams that did not know who was to have received prayers and who not.

When the numbers were all properly crunched, the outcome was rather unimpressive. Those who were prayed for fared no better than those who were not. One odd result: those who had been told explicitly that they were going to be the object of prayers did slightly *worse* than the others. Perhaps hearing that a massive number of prayers were to be made on their behalf, some have speculated, made these patients more fearful that they were in the direst need of prayer, which in turn made them more pessimistic about their health.

Theologically speaking, this study is at least very odd. It treats prayer as though it were a certain kind of power of persuasion or even an energy of sorts, to get God to do good things, and implies that sheer quantity of prayer counts. One person compared these prayers to form letters sent to Congress, which usually ignores them, but in this case sent to God. The outcome of this study is consistent with both metaphysical naturalism (there is no God to respond to prayer) and cosmological naturalism (God exists but does not intervene). Nonetheless, a religious believer could argue that perhaps God does intervene, but not for a test such as this study, or not to group prayers for strangers, or not in ways that fit the "outcomes" measures of the study, and so on.

The Templeton Foundation has a lot of money and probably does not miss a few million dollars; and no one was hurt by this experiment. That is not always the case where a religious belief tells people, especially parents, to avoid medical doctors. The practice of some Christian Science adherents is one such case.

The Church of Christ Scientist ("Christian Science") was founded by Mary Baker Eddy (1821–1910). Christian Science inhabits a universe described by a mixture of ideas from India and from Platonism in the West. "Prayer" is really getting in touch with the power of spirit over matter. God is infinite Spirit; material existence is a kind of error, a falling away from true existence as spirit. Thorough understanding of this puts one in touch with spiritual power, which can overcome limitations of matter, including disease. Jesus healed the sick and insane in the New Testament using this power. His disciples also could heal, so the power can be used by anyone with the right knowledge and purity of intention.

Speaking very precisely, Christian Science healing should not be classified as dependence on miracles, in the sense of special divine interventions. Christian Science followers say that these healings instead can be done by being in touch with a spiritual power that is in fact that which is most real in the universe. Nonetheless, Christian Science recommends relying on the power of this sort of prayer rather than using modern medicine. (Eddy made an exception for having broken bones set by a physician.) The result has sometimes been death, even of children whose parents refuse to consult a physician or do so too late.

On this last point several small Christian fundamentalist groups are similar to Christian Science, except that they do expect divine intervention, and insist that prayers to God, not medicine, should be the source of cures. This belief also has led to the death of a number of children, according to a study by Seth Asser and Rita Swan. They searched through years of newspaper reports about faith healings to find instances of children who died. They classified several hundred of these deaths according to cause of death. This included a variety of conditions, such as bowel obstruction, appendicitis, bacterial diseases, and diabetes. A group of pediatricians, who did not know the actual specific cases of death, evaluated how successful modern medicine usually is in dealing with each type of condition. Of 172 dead children, 140 suffered from the categories of illness judged by the pediatricians to be diseases or conditions that can be cured or corrected 90% of the time by modern medical methods. In those cases, relying on faith healing instead of medical aid was apparently fatal to the children, Asser and Swan concluded.[4]

Conclusion

Many ordinary religious people seem to restrict their expectation of miracle to aspects of life that are not subject to tests or medical evaluation. They hope God may work in hidden ways, to provide strength or a sense of consolation. This relative modesty in making claims about miracles may be the result of the history of modern science, using naturalism in some form, and closing gaps where once only a supernatural explanation seemed to work. The theologians have taken up this issue frequently, ever since the beginning of modern science. But to understand modern theological positions, as described in Chapter 10 here, some earlier history will help first. Chapter 9 will provide that.

For further reading

Geivett, Douglas R., and Gary R. Habermas, eds., *In Defense of Miracles: A Comprehensive Case for God's Action in History* (Downers Grove, IL: InterVarsity Press, 1997).

Hume, David, *Writings on Religion* (La Salle, IL: Open Court, 1992) Introduction, notes, and editorial arrangement by Antony Flew, including Flew's analysis of "On Miracles."

Nickell, Joe, *Looking for a Miracle: Weeping Icons, Relics, Stigmata, Visions & Healing Cures* (Buffalo, New York: Prometheus Books, 1993). A leading investigator for the journal *Skeptical Inquirer*, Nickell has been uncovering mistaken or fraudulent miracles for many years.

Williams, Terence C., *The Idea of the Miraculous: The Challenge to Science and Religion* (New York: St. Martin's Press, 1991). A philosophical defense of belief in miracles.

9 A Brief History of Christian Thought on Miracles

Early Christian beliefs

The attitude of educated Romans and Greeks to early Christian beliefs was made worse by the fact that Christianity at first appeared to be what today we would call a cult. It was not a legitimate traditional religion like Judaism, it seemed, but rather a recently invented variation of Judaism. People then looked at new variations of old religions with the same suspicion that people now look at current revisions of Christianity like the Unification Church ("Moonies"). A similar problem for the credibility of Christianity was that the people who wrote the Christian scriptures were apparently not very well educated because they wrote in simple, even crude, Greek. Then as now, the beliefs of uneducated people are not always very informed or critical.

The philosophers themselves could not agree, however, on what the universe was really like. As we have seen, Epicureans thought the universe was unguided and unplanned, that things just happened according to the random working of the regular forces of nature. The Stoics rejected chance; they claimed that the *Logos*, the divine principle of rational order, ruled everything. The old gods had to follow the rational order of nature just as people did. No one could escape the laws of nature. This philosophy was science as they knew it: the attempt to rationally understand nature.

The Stoics' complaint was not that Christians believed in an invisible and powerful God. It was the interruption of the rational order (logos) of things by God that was objectionable. The same God who the Christians claimed created the order of nature, then turned around and violated the laws of that same nature. This God was apparently inconsistent, operating against his own original intention in setting up reliable laws. This charge was taken seriously by some Jews and Christians. They had to face repeatedly the question of whether their beliefs stood in the way of a rational understanding of nature because of belief in a God who interrupted the order of nature, who might do what nature would never do on its own.

As the Introduction mentioned, one of the first attempts to respond to the philosophers' complaints was by a 2nd century Christian named Minucius Felix, who wrote a dialogue called the *Octavius*. To set the stage for his Christian ideas, he gave the first words in this heated exchange to an imaginary Stoic philosopher who mocked Christian beliefs:

> What monstrous absurdities these Christians invent about this God of theirs . . . that he searches diligently into the ways and deeds of all men, yea even their words and hidden thoughts, hurrying to and fro, ubiquitously; they make him out a troublesome, restless, shameless and interfering being, who has a hand in everything that is done, interlopes at every turn . . . .

In response to his own imaginary attack by a Stoic, Minucius Felix promoted belief in God precisely on the basis of the order of nature. He borrowed an early version of the "argument from design" from the Stoics themselves (we will see more about this in the chapter on the cosmos).

Not all Christians thought they had to try to live up to the rational standards of the philosophers. Recall Tertullian's question, in the list of types of faith at the beginning of Chapter 1, implying that Athens (philosophy) and Jerusalem (religion) have nothing in common. Irenaeus, 2nd century bishop of Lyons and an influential theologian, used arguments borrowed from the Skeptics, another philosophical school of the times. He cited the inability of "physicists" to know things like where migrating birds spent the winter, or of the storehouse in the sky of hail and snow, or of the source of the Nile, or what the precise differences were among various fluids, metals, and rocks. "On all these points we may indeed say a great deal while we search into their causes, but God alone who made them can declare the truth regarding them."[1] Scripture teaches us what we need to know here in this world; in the new world to come God will teach us the rest. Irenaeus thereby devalues the role of the scientific inquirer.

Augustine on miracles

The influential theologian Augustine (364–430 CE) had a variety of ideas about miracles. He was sure God had worked miracles because the Bible was full of miracle stories, though he speculated that maybe God had worked miracles only in biblical times, but not later. But then Augustine came to accept the common Christian belief that God worked miracles in association with the shrines of Christian martyrs, who had given their lives rather than give up their faith. Augustine nonetheless remained unsure how to explain miracles or even how to define them consistently. He ended up with perhaps four different theories.

Augustine sometimes speaks as though nature does not have its own reliable order of causality. Every event is due to God's action, as in the last of the six definitions of "miracle" given in the previous chapter. The sun rises each day because before dawn each day God turns to the sun and says "All right, get up and do it again."[2] Every plant that flowers is being told to flower by God. Here all things are miracles in the sense of resulting from specific divine interventions. But only some of them evoke wonder; so only some are named "miracula" (wonders). Here is an often quoted passage from Augustine's to this effect:

> While man plants and waters, who draws up the moisture through the roots of the vine except God who gives the growth? But when water was changed into wine with unaccustomed swiftness at the Lord's command the divine power was revealed, as even fools acknowledge.[3]

In these words Augustine blurs the distinction between the regular and the extraordinary events in nature. All of them are God's direct work. This is the dominant view of God's activities in Muslim tradition also, mentioned in the previous chapter as "occasionalism."

In other places Augustine speaks of miracles in a way that even the Stoics could find sufficiently rational, by treating all of the order of the universe as though it were a single grand miracle, with some special events pre-planted in it. Wondrous events result from sequences of natural causes, which God planted as "seeds" from the beginning of creation, to sprout and grow at the proper time in God's plan. God set up events like a set of dominoes carefully arranged to produce a particular sequence when set in motion. These seeds are called either "causal reasons" or "seminal reasons." Though such wondrous events startle people, they nonetheless flow from the intersection of natural causes that God lined up at the beginning of creation as part of nature's own "secondary" causality, with God as the "primary" cause.[4]

These first two notions of miracles do not fit comfortably with each other. One says that every event was an individual act by God; the other that there was only one general act of God which is the planning-creating-sustaining of the universe with seeds of all future events planted from the beginning. It is not surprising that Augustine tended more strongly to favor a third notion, which mixed the first two. God did indeed plan and create an orderly universe, says Augustine, which normally operates by natural causality. God created the universe, however, with loose joints in its sequence of natural causes, some slack spaces where God could intervene as needed.

> God, however, did not place all causes in the original creation but kept some in his own will . . . . Nevertheless those which he kept in his own will cannot be contrary to those which he predetermined by His own will; for God's will cannot contradict itself. He established them, therefore, in such a way that they would contain the possibility, not the necessity, of causing the effect which would proceed from them.[5]

The order of nature, therefore, did not produce events by the steady flow of natural causes alone, as the Stoics said, nor by natural causes which the Epicureans called "necessity" at work (laws of nature), mingling with chance. The sequence of cause and effect was left deliberately loose by God so it would be possible for God to intervene in it rather easily without overthrowing it. Natural laws, chance, and God all had room to operate.

Augustine also has a fourth category of wondrous events, those caused by preternatural beings rather than God. Augustine accounted for belief in the gods of polytheism by supposing that they were actually demons, servants of Satan or Satan himself, who used their superior knowledge to perform wonders, such as a stage magician does. The sciencefiction writer Arthur C. Clarke is supposed to have said that if a sufficiently advanced race of beings should arrive from another planet, we would not be able to distinguish their technology from magic. Augustine thought this of demons.

Of these four interpretations of wondrous events in the world, only the second fits fully with both methodological and cosmological naturalism. The idea that all wondrous occasions are produced by only natural causes, albeit according as God arranged all things from the very beginning, would allow a scientist to trust that natural events, no matter how wondrous, are the product of regular and reliable and therefore intelligible natural causes. The other three notions are either fully or partly in conflict with even methodological naturalism, because they suppose that some events are not due entirely to natural causes. The search to explain things comes to an end where such non-natural causes are at work.

Augustine is sure in the end that some divine intervention does occur. He notes that skeptics challenge Christian miracles saying, "If you wish us to believe these things, satisfy our reason about each one of them . . . ." Augustine responds, "We should confess we could not, because the final comprehension of man cannot master these and such-like wonders of God's workings . . . ."[6]

Augustine was not unreasonable to think this. His mental model of the universe was as compatible as he could make it with the science of the times, even while retaining the belief that God intervened on many occasions. If the philosophers thought to the contrary that the world was fully intelligible, they could not prove it. The world in fact seemed to be full of wonders that challenged belief in its regularity and reliability. If a person was a rationalist like the Stoics, all that their reasoning had to go on was a certain degree of regular order in the universe, capped by philosophical speculation that maybe the rational order, like turtles, went all the way down. Speculation is not evidence, however. It will not be until the success of modern science that this rationalist approach toward nature becomes more firmly grounded in evidence. Meanwhile Augustine could hold a different view of the work of those he called the "physicists," the philosophers of nature.

> For even these men, gifted with such superior insight, with their ardor in study and their abundant leisure, exploring some of these matters by human conjecture and others through historical inquiry, have not yet learned everything there is to know. For that matter, many of the things they are so proud to have discovered are more often matters of opinion than of verified knowledge.[7]

Augustine was correct, of course, that a lot of science in his day was speculation rather than well-tested conclusions. It is also true still today that science does not know everything. Augustine's basic, attitude, however, is one that fit with his era, the early 5th century CE. This is the beginning of the early Middle Ages, the period that later could rightly be called the dark ages (or at least rather dim ages).

The early medieval universe, from around 500 to 1000 CE, filled up with miraculous interventions. The search for an understanding of the overall unity of things was almost forgotten. The spirit of rationality did not die out entirely. A manuscript probably from 7th century Ireland testifies to this. Attributed to an otherwise unknown "Augustulus," the title is *On the Miracles of Sacred Scripture*.[8] The author attempts to show that each of the biblical miracles could have had a fully natural cause. His view was rather unusual, however.

Wealth began to return to Western Europe again in the 10th century and later, partly because of better weather and partly because of technological advances in farming. With wealth came leisure for learning. The late Middle Ages (ca. 1000–1450) became a time of explosive renewal of rational thought, though with severe disruptions in the calamitous 14th century. (The same was true in China in roughly these centuries.)

The absolute and ordained powers of God

The 11th century marks the beginning of late medieval times, the "high" Middle Ages. By the 12th century major universities were founded in various cities. By the 13th century scholars were working furiously to revive the ancient sciences. The degree of nature's reliability continued to be a significant issue. In fact, the main contention concerning God's power was not just whether God performed miracles but whether God could do absolutely anything God chose.

The problem was partly theoretical. Because medieval theology said God is perfect goodness and perfect power it would seem logical for God to make as perfect a universe as possible. Given God's choice to make any universe at all (a puzzle in itself), then logically speaking God would seem to have to make this single universe that exists "the best of all possible worlds," to use Leibniz's later phrase.[9] But God is supposedly also perfectly free. Cannot God make any kind of universe God wants? Theorizing minds sought a fully rational explanation of creation. The more tradition-oriented believers, however, did not want God's power subjected to the demands of logical rationality.

The conflict took an interesting form, in the argument over whether God can restore a fallen virgin.[10] In the 4th century, Jerome had declared that not even God can restore a virgin to her (or his) original virginity. His point was to urge people never to lose that virginity. A famous theologian of the 11th century, Peter Damien, strongly disagreed. He insisted God can do whatever God wants. In this case God could wipe out the whole universe and then create it all over again, but this time with a person's virginity preserved.

This could be a striking way to resolve the question of naturalism. God could even make the universe over and over again millions of times, each time to work by natural causes alone. If there is some aspect of events in some entirely naturalistic universe which God does not want, then God can create a new universe with that aspect changed. So an entirely naturalistic universe would not be a restriction on the divine power.

In fact, however, such thorough-going naturalism was avoided. By the 13th century at least two noted theologians, Albertus Magnus and Thomas Aquinas, accepted an approach that preserved room for divine interventions, by accepting a distinction between God's absolute power and God's "ordained" power. The word "absolute" here means completely unlimited. God can indeed do whatever God wants, whenever and however God wants. The ordained power, on the other hand, is the way in which God "ordained" from all eternity to limit the application of the absolute divine power. God apparently chose to create a universe that operates mainly, but not entirely, by regular and reliable natural causes. Albert and Thomas agreed that God freely chose to apply God's own absolute power within these limitations.

The 14th century philosophical movement known as nominalism was part of the continuing dispute over God's power.[11] Nominalism stressed the distinction between God's absolute power and God's ordained power in order to stress the former and thereby emphasize the freedom God had in making this world. (By "world" they meant the universe, as they knew it, tiny in comparison with ours.) They even argued that the order of this world (universe) might be only one of a potentially infinite number of different worlds that God might have made out of God's infinite power. Every world might have different patterns of causality. Perhaps the regular patterns of *this* world were rather arbitrary, or at least certainly not logically necessary. The nominalists argued, moreover, that God has the freedom to change even the rules of this world or to suspend them at any time.

The order of this universe was therefore so dependent on God's utter freedom, that no amount of deduction or logical analysis could determine what it was like. The only way to determine what God had chosen to do was to go look. The intelligibility in things can be discovered only empirically rather than being deducible logically from first principles.[12] This left open the possibility that God might have made this (or some) universe so tightly run by reliably regular secondary causes that there was no room for miracles. Nominalism nonetheless argued that only an empirical investigation could discover just what sort of order this universe does have.

It has turned out that the degree of orderliness in the universe discovered by modern empirical science is so great that miracles have become less plausible. The irony, therefore, is that the notion of God's sovereign freedom that first preserved space for God to work any miracles that God chose, ended up promoting the empirical method which has cast doubt upon miracles. This also may be a reason that modern science developed in Europe in following centuries—a lot more people decided to go out and look instead of just theorizing.

For further reading

Fridrichsen, Anton Johnson, *The Problem of Miracle in Primitive Christianity* (Minneapolis: Augsburg Publishing House, 1972).

Kee, Howard Clark, *Medicine, Miracle, and Magic in New Testament Times* (Cambridge: Cambridge University Press, 1986).

Ward, Benedicta, *Miracles and the Medieval Mind: Theory, Record, and Event* (Philadelphia: University of Pennsylvania Press, 1982).

Skepticism and Modern Theologies about Miracles

10

Chapter Outline

The modern world began in the Enlightenment, the time when the new science was developing, when economies began to operate less by royal decree and increasingly by capitalist or laissez-faire rules, when political order shifted increasingly toward some degree of democracy, when individualism came to be praised over allegiance to authority and custom—and when traditional Christianity began to develop in new ways, sometimes very reluctantly.

As natural philosophers (scientists) pursued explanations through reliably regular patterns of nature, they were successful enough to encourage an expansion of their basic hope, that the events of nature would indeed prove to be intelligible in this way. William Gilbert (1544–1603) thought that the movement of a compass was part of the *natural* power of magnetism. The activity of the heart and blood to William Harvey (1578–1657) was not something done by a supernatural force but by a natural "spirit." To Edmund Halley (1656–1742) the appearance of a comet was not a special sign sent by God but part of an orbit that could be explained by natural causes. To Benjamin Franklin (1706–1790) a lightning bolt was a manifestation of a natural fluid to be called electricity, not a warning from God. The irregularities in the speeds of Saturn and

Jupiter to the Marquis de Laplace (1749–1827), was a natural oscillation, not a sign that the universe needed divine tending to keep it running smoothly as Newton had once supposed.

Perhaps it was in a negative reaction to all this intellectual skepticism about miracles that there was a resurgence of popular belief in the miraculous. The historian Keith Thomas claims that in the 16th and 17th centuries in Europe belief in miraculous healing and in divinely inspired prophecies increased enormously.[1] Witch hunts especially represented a widespread belief in active preternatural beings and in the reality of pacts with real demons.[2] Nonetheless, the supernatural was being squeezed out of many things. God was becoming "the God of the gaps," as noted earlier.

Deism and miracles

This long history of ideas about miracles in the West culminated in a rather striking movement in the 17th and 18th centuries known as "deism." This was a name given to those 17th and 18th century thinkers who said true religion was rational religion. They proposed that the basic religious truths were knowable to all rational people everywhere. Tired of vicious wars of religion (1618–1648 saw the devastating Thirty Years' War, rooted in Catholic-Protestant differences in Europe; England had civil wars in the 1640s over religious differences), many sought to avoid bloody fights over religious doctrines. The power of reason, they believed, was a common human heritage. Its use in science showed its power. Surely God wanted people to follow their God-given reason as the single and unifying guide, rather than follow any of the conflicting religious traditions, over which people were enthusiastically killing each other.

The major beliefs which deists claimed could be known by all reasonable people were articulated by Lord Herbert of Cherbury as early as 1645:

1. There is a God, whose supreme intelligence planned and created the marvelous order of nature which science was uncovering.
2. This God ought to be worshiped.
3. True worship of this God is awe and admiration of the divine handiwork and a dedication to live virtuously in accord with the rational order which God had made.
4. A person should repent of all failures to worship and live virtuously.
5. God will reward and punish people in accord with how they live, in this life or the next.

Some deists allowed a few miracles. In 1696, for example, John Toland's "Christianity not Mysterious" only partially rejected miracles. Toland said God did supernaturally reveal some things, such as His own existence, but such things are also knowable by reason.[3] Toland rejected as absurdities such beliefs as "transubstantiation and other ridiculous fables." Toland claimed he was defending Christianity, but the Anglican parliament in Ireland banned Toland's book because it revised Christian doctrines which did not fit his test of reasonableness. Later, Samuel Clarke in his 1742 Boyle lectures allowed room for God's special revelatory activity, as well as for miracles in biblical times done by God or Jesus to confirm the validity of revelation.[4] But traditionalists were not entirely placated by this.

Other deists went further and sought a way around all miracle stories. Descartes responded to those who saw God's hand moving the clouds by saying that he would explain the nature of clouds through natural causes and remove any reason to marvel at them.[5] Thomas Woolston, in his *Discourse on Miracles* (1728–1729) proclaimed the miracles of Jesus to be allegories. He argued that to accept them as literally true, would be to accept absurdities, improbabilities, and incredibilities.[6] Matthew Tindall in his *Christianity as Old as the Creation* (1730) argued that in any case revelation could not really be helpful, because only rational analysis could determine whether any supposed revelations were true.[7] Thomas Jefferson eliminated all miracles from his truncated version of the gospels.

The method of the arguments used by Deists varied, at first resting on rather abstract rational argumentation. Descartes argued mostly on the basis of logical analysis. Even if our sense experience (evidence) did not show that God made the world to operate with complete regularity, we would still know from reason that as God is immutable God would not act differently at some times and places, but rather would continue to sustain the same laws of nature always and everywhere.[8] Boyle similarly offered the argument that God was powerful and intelligent enough to get things right the first time around, without a need for miraculous tinkering. Deists' method eventually shifted from abstract rational argument to more empirical study. In 1872 Francis Galton, for example, used statistical analyses of empirical patterns to refute the belief that prayers evoked miracles. His studies showed that in spite of their prayers, the clergy lived no longer than physicians or lawyers; that ships with missionaries sank as often as others; and that religious lands had their full share of evil.[9]

David Hume "On Miracles"

The single most famous English-language analysis of the credibility of miracles was put forth by the Scottish philosopher David Hume (1711–1776), as the tenth chapter of his *An Enquiry Concerning Human Understanding* (a book that appears in many different editions). Early in the chapter he sets down his famous basic rule: "A wise man proportions his belief to the evidence." In the case of miracles, the main evidence is testimony, particularly of those miracles which occurred in the beginning of a religious tradition like Christianity.

Hume first defines miracle as that which goes against constant experience. Even if an event were rare but still within the range of what people experience sometimes as part of natural occurrences, they would not call it a miracle. Only if the event is clearly contrary to constant experience of what natural causes produce, would anyone call the event a miracle. Constant experience is evidence; it ought to lead a person to be dubious about any exceptions to it.

Then Hume returns to the point about testimonies of miraculous events and proposes a general rule. Set the probability of the truth of the miracle against the probability that the testimony is incorrect. Might there be a case when it would be a greater miracle that the testimony is mistaken? In that case one could accept belief in the lesser miracle, the miraculous event which the testimony claims happened. Hume then proceeds to give several reasons why it is quite normal and not at all miraculous for testimony to be mistaken.

First, people are not always sufficiently knowledgeable or critical. An example today would be the many people persuaded by demonstrations of ESP (extra-sensory perception—and other psychic powers) such as mind-reading or moving objects with mental power alone. Today the stage magician James Randi ("The Amazing Randi") has demonstrated time after time, using his knowledge of the stage magician's craft, how these ESP feats are actually accomplished, using only normal natural means rather than ESP powers.

Second, Hume argues, we all take pleasure in feelings of surprise and wonder, so much that we give credence to claims that are extremely improbable. The other side of that coin is that a person is always tempted to tell a good story and perhaps make it even better in order to evoke a little awe in others. When travelers tell of their adventures, the stranger the story the more interesting it is, both to tell and to listen to. The traveler—or the one testifying to a miracle—ends up working harder on the rhetoric than on the evidence. The extreme case is fraud, where in support of religious belief or to make money or to get attention, a person invents a story and even fakes the evidence for it.

Third, Hume insists, miraculous events seem to happen much more often, according to the reports we hear, among what Hume calls "ignorant and barbarous nations." The tone of that phrase expresses an 18th century sense of British superiority over other cultures. Many people in Great Britain, of course, believed strongly in miracles. Many of the educated looked down upon those beliefs also, but consoled themselves with the thought that they, the educated, at least knew better.

Fourth, Hume continues, many of the religions of various cultures in the world are supported by miracle stories. The Buddha's mother was made pregnant by a god and delivered the baby Siddhartha through her side without discomfort. Yet the Buddha's eventual proclamation of how to achieve salvation conflicts with the Judaic account. Jesus' miraculous resurrection is the basis for Christian belief. Muslims deny it happened and appeal to the miraculous revelations to Muhammad as the basis for their way of life. In such cases, Hume argues, the miracles of one religion repudiate the miracles of another.

Hume concludes from all this that even if a miracle or a set of miracles had great and strong testimony on their side, it would still be more probable that someone was in error than that an actual miracle occurred. Be rational, Hume insists; do not let down the standards of evidence.

Among the many critics of Hume's position two present-day Evangelical Christians can serve as examples. C. John Collins argues against Hume's starting point.[10] Events in the universe do give consistent and strong evidence that events happen in accord with the laws of nature—except when people intervene. Pick up a rock from the ground; that moves the rock contrary to the law of gravity. If there is another intelligent and free Being called God, says Collins, that Being may also do what humans do. This is not a violation of the laws of nature, any more than picking up rocks violates nature, though it does make nature do what it would not do entirely on its own. (He may be borrowing this argument from C. S. Lewis' book, *Miracles*. We will see this analogy challenged in Chapter 19.)

This argument assumes that human actions are in some sense not fully natural. Collins thinks of the human person as a combination of natural body, perhaps, and spiritual soul. We will look at this notion of the person in some final chapters here. But in any case, when a bird picks up straws to build a nest in a tree, it also is going contrary to what gravity alone would do but without thereby violating the laws of nature. Neither Collins nor Hume would think of the bird's action as miraculous.

Norman Geisler, a prolific writer in defense of a traditionalist view of Christianity, charts what he sees as several flaws in Hume's account.[11] The first of these is what Geisler sees as Hume's prejudice in favor of naturalism. To say that miracles are highly improbable ignores the belief that (1) God has the power to do whatever God wants, that (2) God has good reason to create miracles as signs to guide people, and that (3) we have adequate evidence that God has in fact acted in history in miraculous ways. Hume is correct that testimony can be in error. But the testimonies in the New Testament, for example, are multiple. In Paul's first letter to the Corinthians, he says that over 500 people saw the risen Jesus. (Oddly none of the rest of the New Testament, all written later than Paul's time, repeats this striking claim.) These testimonies, says Geisler, are fairly consistent though not perfectly so, and thus are not the same single testimony repeated many times. These witnesses were even willing to die for that to which they testified, which is good evidence they were not just entertaining the crowd with enjoyable stories. This satisfies Geisler that the Christian miracle stories, unlike those of other religious traditions, are to be trusted.

Schleiermacher and liberal theology

We have seen in Chapter 2 that near the end of the Enlightenment, Friedrich Schleiermacher (1768–1834) addressed what he called the cultured despisers of religion, in his great work of 1799, *On Religion*, only decades after Hume had his say. Recall that Schleiermacher defined religion as an intuition of God as the source of all unity. Whenever a person has a sense of the ultimate fundamental oneness of all things, said Schleiermacher, this God-consciousness was an inner perception of God's unifying presence. Recall also that in a rather turn-the-tables move, Schleiermacher argued that science itself has its roots in God-consciousness, in the experience of ultimate Wholeness. Science expected to find that all of nature's patterns form a reliable intelligible unity, that it all fit together.

Schleiermacher applied this perspective to oppose belief in miracles. He faced the awkward fact that most ordinary Christians had beliefs much like those of what Hume called the barbarous nations about supernatural agents at work, even though Christians at least placed a single God in the top position in the universe. It was precisely in those cultures where scientific knowledge about nature was weakest that belief in miracle-like powers seemed strongest, said Schleiermacher. In those same cultures, he claimed, the intuition of the Whole, of a single God, was also weak or absent. Belief in miracles implied there was no ultimate unity but only a bits-and-pieces universe in which supernatural interventions by God mingled with natural events without final coherence. Belief in miracles was a belief that God, whose truest nature was to be the source of unity, would supposedly go against that unity. Every belief in the interruption of nature's patterns by a supernatural power was therefore an anti-religious belief, as Schleiermacher defined true religion.

> Where . . . a conception of miracles is commonly found, namely, in conditions where there is least knowledge of nature, there, too, the fundamental feeling [of God-consciousness] appears to be weakest and most ineffectual. . . . It follows from this that the most perfect representation of omnipotence would be a view of the world which made no use of such an idea.[12]

Like many deists, Schleiermacher reinterpreted biblical events in non-miraculous ways. The incarnation of God in Jesus was not the descent of a supernatural being into human history. The doctrine should instead be understood as a way of expressing recognition that of all the people of history Jesus had the greatest God-consciousness, and was therefore the one in whom the human was united most closely to God.[13] Because of his high degree of God-consciousness, Jesus should be accepted as the truest guide to full and genuine religiousness. Schleiermacher then translated other miracle stories into symbols that were not literally true. Did Jesus really cast out demons from people in Galilee? No, answers Schleiermacher; these exorcisms are just symbolic of the transformation in life that people underwent because of their encounter with Jesus. Similarly, belief in a life after death should be thought of as a symbol of human confidence that the meaning of our lives is somehow ultimately vindicated, rather than as the continued existence of a spiritual soul after death.[14]

Schleiermacher's miracle-free version of Christianity came to be called "liberal theology." It became very influential. It is the theology which fundamentalists will later explicitly reject as a subversion of true Christianity.

Twentieth-century liberal thought

By the early 20th century there were odd theological combinations of liberal thought with more traditional language about miracles. Theologians were struggling to be both traditional yet also "scientific."

An influential position known as Neo-orthodoxy, stemmed from the writings of a famous Swiss theologian, Karl Barth. (A current form is the "radical orthodoxy" described in an earlier chapter.) Barth's ideas often seemed to be traditionally supernaturalistic in that he asserted the centuries-old doctrine that true faith was the product of God's grace, and that God gave this grace to those whomever God chose. This faith does not need rational justification. It needs only to be affirmed and lived. Yet his way of stating these and other traditional doctrines was rather liberal, in the sense of a Christianity without miracles. His belief in "eternal life," for example, does not quite affirm traditional belief in an individual life beyond the grave but instead echoes Schleiermacher:

> What is the meaning of the Christian hope . . .? A life after death? An event apart from death? A tiny soul which, like a butterfly, flutters away above the grave and is still preserved somewhere, in order to live on immortally? That was how the heathen looked on the life after death. But that is not the Christian hope. . . . Resurrection means not the continuation of this life, but life's completion.[15]

Similarly, in the late 1930s the German scripture scholar and theologian Rudolph Bultmann gave wide currency to the expression "demythologize." Recall that the word "demythologize" stands for any attempt to reinterpret religious tradition in such a way as to exclude divine interruptions of the lawful course of nature. In this sense the ancient Stoics demythologized when they declared that Zeus was not a being who acted irregularly but was actually the everlastingly reliable divine Logos within the universe. Similarly the deists who wished to do without miracles were all engaged in demythologizing many traditional religious beliefs. Bultmann agreed, precisely because he believed the universe which science describes was bare of such interventions.[16] If there is a story in the Bible that tells of a miraculous act in which the laws of nature are suspended or exceeded by some divine activity, the contemporary Christian is to understand that this is only a mythological way of speaking that was appropriate for people of long ago.[17] Contemporary educated people are supposed to know better.

Many liberal theologians in the 20th century still struggle to reconcile the method and findings of modern science with traditional religious beliefs. They often transform traditional beliefs about the miraculous intervention of God, into human modes of expressing a general faith that there is a deep-down presence of God in everything, everyone, and every event. This God is not such as to be a busybody, as Minucius Felix long ago put it, but the incomprehensible Ultimate about which the human person can say only enough to affirm generally that this God is the grounds for human confidence that life is ultimately meaningful.

Divine agency and 20th century science

Religious philosophers speak of "divine agency" to label the way God might act in the world, as an agent (a doer) causing events. Belief in God as creator-sustainer of the universe is the most basic instance of belief in divine agency. God does one big act, the single and ongoing miracle of the existence of the universe (definition of miracle #4). Traditional Christian belief has also included a notion of divine Providence. This says that God includes everything that will ever happen in a single plan and purpose. But the usual question about miracles is whether there are other and more specific ways in which God is an agent, intervening here or there in history and human life.

Religious philosophers have coined the phrase "special divine action" (SDA) as part of an analysis of possible divine interventions.[18] An SDA could as easily just be called a miracle (though some Christians argue that the name "miracle" should belong only to SDAs which are also publicly wondrous and religiously meaningful). Those who speak of SDA, however, seem to want a special language to reinforce the impression that they are trying to reconcile belief in divine interventions with modern science, rather than rely simply on the traditional belief that God can do whatever God wants.

Various SDA theories share two common goals. The first is to avoid a complete determinism in the universe. Cosmological naturalism might imply a universe in which every event that would ever take place is completely pre-determined by the natural chain of cause-and-effect. If some God-like intelligence could understand all aspects of all events in the universe at one point in time, it would be possible in theory for that intelligence to then be able to predict every subsequent event in the universe.

The second goal of those thinking about SDA is to not violate the physical law of the conservation of matter and energy. Belief in divine interventions seems to imply that God is adding divine activity to the already existing activity of the universe. This constitutes an addition of energy. If God were to intervene in very small ways, of course, the additional energy might not be enough to even be detectable. Nonetheless, several Christian theologians and philosophers who are also well versed in science have sought to avoid postulating any additions of divine energy to the universe even while maintaining that there is a real and additional special divine agency. Three different pathways or modes of action have been suggested by religious writers.

Quantum indeterminacy provides one possible path. A "quantum" is the name given by Max Planck in 1900 to a discrete amount of energy that is the equivalent of a single photon, emitted by an electron under certain circumstances. Armed with this little piece of information, physicists investigated the characteristics of electrons and their behavior around a nucleus. The combination of a nucleus and one or more electrons buzzing around the nucleus constitute an atom. On the subatomic or "quantum" level the electron is very odd. It seems to occupy simultaneously a whole range of positions around the nucleus rather than being in just one place at a time. If anyone tries to measure the electron, however, to determine its position more precisely, the state of being in many places "collapses" into one particular state and location. Prior to that collapse, a physicist can only speak of indeterminate probabilities, meaning that the state which occurs at the collapse cannot be predicted. (Arguments raged for some decades over whether this was just a limitation on the ability of science to do the measurements, or whether the electron itself was truly indeterminate, so that even if one could measure it without making it collapse it would still not be in any one determinate place. The predominant interpretation in physics now says the electron's state is truly indeterminate in itself. What this means remains foggy.)

Quantum physics may leave open a tiny door for interventions which do not add energy, and which would not even look at all like interventions. God could work within the atoms on the quantum level, somehow making the collapses, when they occur, to go in one direction, so to speak, rather than another. If God were to do this in the appropriate several billion atoms at the same time, they might then collectively behave so as to bring about something extremely unusual, so unusual it would be a kind of miracle, even though the collapses themselves were going to happen in one way or another even without divine intervention.

Chaos theory provides a second path for adding SDA to the otherwise closed system of nature. Imagine that a storm system is brewing over the southwest U.S., across Texas and Oklahoma. The combination of jet stream flow, humidity, heat, wind patterns, and topography is contributing to the formation of a certain area of clouds, of winds that could turn into tornados, of rain that could be heavy enough to cause floods. Natural laws are at work in this seemingly chaotic combination. It is not truly just chaos. Nonetheless the level of complexity is such that a tiny difference could amplify. Perhaps a large truck drives down a road when the conditions are right and the vortex of air it creates behind itself sets off a sequence of events which produce a tornado near a town where it would not have otherwise formed. The truck moved down that road at that precise moment, though, because the driver had slowed earlier to avoid running over a jackrabbit, which happened to be at that spot because it had stopped to try to get rid of a flea. That single flea thus could be blamed, in a way, for a tornado, which in turn would have lots of other effects. Now substitute some tiny action by God—an SDA—touching the systems of events in the universe in extremely tiny ways, with divine foreknowledge of the results that will emerge from these tiny touches. God would then be adding so small an amount of energy to the universe that it need not count for much.

In fact, as theologian-physicist John Polkinghorne proposes, perhaps God makes the tiny touch by adding information on the quantum level.[19] This is the third path suggested by which God might engage in an SDA, by adding information from the top-down. The expression "top-down" represents the kind of influence human consciousness seems to have on the human body. Say to yourself, "I think I will stand up," and your thoughts make your body go through the motions of standing up. Thoughts are very powerful influences, yet they feel as though they only arrange how things happen, rather than adding energy to the universe. Thoughts are also a kind of information—an encoding of ideas or images. Codes are arrangements of energy, rather than additions of energy, the argument goes.

Some theologians and philosophers even speak of a divine presence as a kind of cosmic information field. Every event in the universe happens within the scope of a flow of divine ideas or values. The theology known as "process thought" uses this model. It is part of the whole truth about the natural world, in this theology, that there is a divine persuasion at work, calling all events to better possibilities, yet in the end leaving all events some degree of freedom. Every event has an aspect of divine action, without a determinism that eliminates freedom.

Challenges to SDA ideas

A number of objections have been made to such ways of opening the universe to SDA. One of them is that God would still be adding energy to the universe, even if in a form so subtle as to be undetectable. God would be doing something the universe would not have done on its own. Nudging electrons or influencing fleas still adds energy. Any act of adding information would be an act, an energy event which arranges electrons according to a certain code.

Second, this is no longer a full methodological naturalism. It opens the door to supernaturalism within science precisely because it is using scientific theories—about quantum states, chaos analysis, information theory—to do theological work. It declares that the universe should not be treated as entirely natural. Because the points of divine intervention are so small, the interventions generally would be invisible. Ironically, one of the traditional values of supposed miracles is to give evidence of God. Invisible actions would not constitute evidence. Such miracles would look just like entirely natural events. Divine activity then becomes an unnecessary hypothesis to account for events, which is not the goal of the religious interest in SDAs.

Third, skeptics look at the efforts to make SDAs compatible with science with incredulity. Straining so hard to find some tiny room for God to intervene makes the whole process seem a bit strange. Why not just admit that the old image of an anthropomorphic Being who freely interrupts or adds to the forces of nature indeed should be demythologized, as Bultmann urged. Accept at least a full cosmological naturalism, these skeptics would say—or admit to a metaphysical naturalism and get over belief in God, others might add.

Finally, an objection can come from a traditional religious perspective rather than a scientific one. God seems seriously restricted by having to work only on a quantum level or by tiny touches; that is not the traditional notion of an all-powerful God acting in history and human life. The effort to reconcile religious belief with science leads the theologian to restrict how God may be portrayed as acting.

Fundamentalism and miracles

Whether religion without miracles is adequate for people is a significant question. There is reason to think that liberal religion has less appeal to a great many people than miracle-filled religion. Liberal religion deprives people of a sense that there is a God who is actively present in a person's life, able to intervene at least in some even secret way, to offer help and strength and more. It also seems to be severely at odds with the many miracles in scripture.

When the movement known as "fundamentalism" first took form in the early 20th century in the U.S. it defined itself precisely as opponents of various kinds of liberal theology. Where Schleiermacher and others demythologized the Bible, the fundamentalists took the Bible literally. The Bible said that Jesus worked miracles, so liberal theology is wrong. The Bible says God raised Jesus from the dead, so liberal theology is wrong. If Jesus was not in fact raised from the dead, says the Apostle Paul in his first letter to the Christians at Corinth, then their faith is in vain. Conflict about miracles is a prime instance where religion and science are clearly in very uneasy tension. On this topic there is no neat distinction between a science which studies only nature and religion which focuses on values. Both science and religion make claims about what is factually effective or what factually happens in the world.

This chapter has described a long history of tension between the expectation of a rational natural order, and a sense that God acts specially in history outside of or beyond that natural order. The tension has not disappeared. Those who favor science are prone to emphasize the regularity and reliability of the natural order. At the same time many religious people remain frustrated by this attempt to banish God's special activities. This conflict will appear again in chapters here on biological evolution. To get to this topic, however, we first need to consider the platform, as it were, on which biological evolution took place. This is cosmic evolution.

For further reading

Burns, R. M., *The Great Debate on Miracles: From Joseph Glanvill to David Hume*. (Lewisburg: Bucknell University Press, 1981).

Geisler, Norman L., *Miracles and the Modern Mind: A Defense of Biblical Miracles* (Grand Rapids: Baker Book House, 1992). Primarily a defense of miracles in the Bible, including Jesus' miracle of healing and the resurrection, with a rebuttal of Hume.

Larmer, Robert A., ed., *Questions of Miracle* (Montreal: McGill Queen's University Press, 1996). A defense of belief in miracles.

Tracy, Thomas F., ed., *The God Who Acts: Philosophical and Theological Explorations* (University Park, PA: Penn State University Press, 1994). A more difficult set of arguments.

Part Five
Cosmic Evolution: how did we get here?

Varieties of Universes 11

The previous chapter focused on the question of whether there is a God who intervenes in nature and history to bring about that which would not occur by natural causes alone. The chapters of Part Five will focus on theories about the nature of the cosmos as a whole, whether the cosmos has the sort of basic intelligibility that would justify the naturalism of science, the human place in that cosmos, and what the order of the universe might imply about its source or design.

The current scientific description of the universe implies quite different things to different observers. To metaphysical naturalists it seems clear that the universe is all that is, was, or will be, as Carl Sagan once put it, and that it runs entirely by mindless natural patterns and forces. There is no sign of a Creator or Providential Orderer; there is no evidence for any plan or purpose to the universe.

Christian theologians, on the other hand, have long declared that the Bible and nature constitute two different "books" through which a person can know about God. The book of nature can be read and interpreted just as the books of the Bible can be. From the viewpoint of a person who already believes in God as Creator of the universe, the whole story of the universe is an answer to the question of what God is doing. God is doing the universe. Both methodological naturalism and cosmic naturalism are compatible with this view. (Recall that only metaphysical naturalism says no God exists.)

Ancient universes

A culture's concept of the universe goes hand-in-hand with its concept of the realm of the supernatural. A primitive hunter-gatherer culture typically lives in a relatively small universe, not too much larger than the distances the tribal bands actually travel. We have seen that such tribal cultures believe that there are many spirit-beings, especially the spirits of the dead. But they rarely have a concept of a spirit-being large enough to deserve the name "god" (even though some writers refer to these spirits as "gods"). They have many origin stories, of where humans came from or why we die. The stories are not integrated with each other, though. So there is no overall unity to their picture of their universe.

More economically developed cultures based on animal herding or agriculture tend to have hereditary rulers, a separate class of the powerful who rule others. People of these cultures also then begin to believe in gods, who rule over spirits and people just as kings rule over their subjects. Agricultural societies live in a much larger universe. These are cultures which trade with other cultures, as well as go to war with them. They know from all this travel and interaction with others that the universe is fairly large. Their mythical tales of the gods are told against this larger background. The myths sometimes tell of even cosmic events, including the formation of the whole cosmos out of some primordial material by some divine beings.

One name for these agricultural polytheistic societies is "archaic." It is typical of archaic cultures that the universe in which they live is not fully a cosmos. The word "cosmos" is Greek for a reality that is well-ordered or arranged in some sort of overall unity. (*Kosmein* = to put in order; "cosmetic" comes from it.) As Chapter 6 notes, an archaic universe is a mixture of order and disorder. Because there are gods, there is some order to nature. The sun god rides through the sky every day; the moon goddess has her regular rotation. The goddess of the crops does her job each year, the two gods of fertility engage in sex with each other each year to begin the fertility cycle again. Yet the gods also represent a fair amount of disorder. They battle among themselves. Out of petty emotions they set people against people or drive a king to do stupid things and cause chaos in the land. They send sudden storms, earthquakes, volcanic eruptions, droughts, all in unpredictable ways. There is order in the archaic universe, but only partial order. This order is also largely unreliable.

Previous chapters have indicated that only with the arrival of the great "classical" stage of culture, as in China, India, and Greece in the 6th century B.C. or so, is reality perceived as a full cosmos, with a deep-down all-embracing order. This is bold thought. The world still looks disordered. For reasons unknown to us, the intellectual elite in various major cultural centers nonetheless decided to hunt for an overall intelligibility—a final unity to all things—in spite of a seeming lack of complete order.

The universe and time

There are three major views of the relation of the universe and time. In some ancient philosophical theories the universe had always existed following the same patterns and maintaining the same basic order everlastingly. Today it would be called a "steady state" universe. Plato and Aristotle favored this view. Some modern cosmologists who speak of "multiverses"—an endless collection and sequence of universes like ours—treat the sum of all these universes, or at least the basic conditions that give rise to these universes, as always existing.

Other theories postulated a cyclical process, in which the universe arose out of some primordial conditions but would then collapse, as it were, back to those conditions and then begin the cycle again. This was the position of the Stoics. Divine fire, the Logos, would form a wonderfully designed universe, which would eventually collapse back into basic fire, at which point, the Logos would form the universe anew. The religions of India also developed a cyclical notion of the history of the universe. In one somewhat artificial version, the creator God Brahma brings the universe into order, Vishnu maintains its order, then Shiva the Destroyer wipes it out. Then the cycle would begin again. Buddhism has had versions of this. In Taoism the process of nature goes through lesser cycles like the seasons of the year and some longer cycles also, but the balance of Yin and Yang always places limits on the process, returning things to balance eventually. Modern physics has entertained a similar idea. This universe seems to have arisen from a "Big Bang" some 13.7 billion years ago and, for all we know, could collapse in a Big Crunch many billions of years from now.

A third theory viewed the history of the universe as a linear process of a few thousand years, with a beginning, a pre-ordained order of development, and a point of completion or fulfillment. This view was originally common to the religions of the West, even though it did not fit with ancient philosophies. (If we change the thousands of years to many billions, it may fit with current cosmology.)

The Western linear view seems to have its origins in Persian Zoroastrianism, as early as around the 11th century BCE. The universe began from an act of Creation by Ahura Mazda, the divine Wise Lord, who created a universe of goodness and at first ruled it completely. But there also existed Ahriman, the Evil One, father of lies. He despised goodness and set about seducing spirits and humans to follow the path of evil. This created a twelve-thousand-year conflict between those who adhered to Ahura Mazda's ways of goodness and those who followed Ahriman. This long conflict would conclude in a great battle that would destroy the earth. The forces of good would be triumphant in the end, so much so that after 3,000 years of purification in flame even the evil people and demons would have been cleansed completely and would be able to join the angels and saints, so to speak, in paradise.

Chapter 6 here alludes to a transforming event in Judaic history: In the 6th century BCE leading Judeans were taken into exile in Babylon. Before long the Persians conquered the Babylonians and moved into the city, bringing Zoroastrian religion with them. Out of this exile period, came the Judaic belief that Yahweh, the God of Israel, was the single God of the whole universe. Sometime after this Judaism came to accept a linear story to that universe. This story appears in the form of apocalyptic literature, beginning with parts of the Book of Daniel, ca. 165 BCE. Such literature describes a divine plan for history, culminating in the overthrow of the present world order and the establishment of a Kingdom of God centered in Jerusalem. (It is called apocalyptic because the last book of the Christian New Testament, is named in Greek, Apocalypse, meaning "Revelation." This book is entirely about what has come to be known as the end of the world, though it really tells about the transformation of this world into the Kingdom of God.)

Christianity adopted apocalypticism. Jesus' own language seems to reflect apocalyptic beliefs, as in Matthew 24 or Mark 13. The Book of Revelation predicted that after the final battle between the Beast (scholars can only make guesses about the identity of this Beast) and Christ and the angels, God would establish a new sky and earth and the rule of Christ. "There will be no more tears," says the Book of Revelation.

Apocalyptic literature presupposed that the universe was not very old and would not last much longer in its present state. Mesopotamia and Egypt were the oldest city-cultures then known in the West. The Egyptians could trace their major dynasties back to the Old Kingdom prior to 3000 B.C. Jews and Christians were sure that the world was older than that, because the stories in Genesis of creation up to the time of Noah and the flood took many generations of men who lived from 700 to 800 years before they died. But even by this estimate the world was what we would think of as rather young. By the 1st century A.D. Christians could reckon the world to be maybe even more than 5,000 years old (the Jews made it to be younger than that). Some early Christians adopted the idea that the God who created in 6 days would also plan for 6,000 years of history before the end "A thousand years is but a day in the eyes of the Lord," says Psalm 90 in the Hebrew Scriptures. Thus the 6 days of creation would be followed by 6 days of 1,000 years each, until the end times. Presumably the new universe to follow upon the destruction of this one will itself be everlasting. Linearity would then seem to come to an end.

In tune with the universe

A purpose behind many ancient and modern philosophies, as well as imbedded in most religions, is to determine how life should be lived. Both the goal of life and the means to achieve that goal are part of philosophy and theology. The picture they give of who we are, of the world we live in, of the highest values, and of possible outcomes, constitutes a framework for life.

Recall that Epicureans followed the opinion of 5th century BCE Greek atomists, who said that all events are part of the movement of atoms in space, following basic laws of nature ("necessity") and the random flow and bumping of atoms ("chance"). This was a basically stable process, with random variations occurring against the everlasting backdrop of the interplay of chance and necessity. In this universe a person's life had no special meaning. The wise person would learn to seek the legitimate pleasures of life in moderation, the joys of friends and family, of helping others, and then accept calmly the death that comes to all.

Recall also that the Stoics disagreed with the Epicureans, mainly in rejecting "chance." All things are governed by the divine *Logos*. This single divine reality governs everything. There is no "chance." All things are meaningful parts of the divine rational order. People should learn the attitude of acceptance toward the divine order. This will give them peace of mind. The true Stoic complains of nothing, for all is in accordance with the divine rational order. Internal equanimity is the philosopher's goal.

In China, Taoism also proposed a form of life based on the patterns of nature. To a Taoist, the way of nature could be capitalized (if written in a language with capital letters), as the Way, the way of nature in fact. Confucians and Mohists and other ancient philosophers in China tried to construct theories of the best social and political order. Taoists resisted these as grandiose plans. Their recommendation was simple, and could easily fit with Epicurean philosophy of how to live. Learn to accept what is natural; go with the flow of nature. The everlasting Tao of nature balances all things out in the long run. Spring flows into summer, which fades into autumn. Out of autumn winter arrives, but to be followed again by spring. Birth leads to vigor, which fades into age and ends up in death, but leaving new births behind to continue the cycle. Accept this flow also, says the Taoist, if you seek to be at peace.

The many views of the universe can be confusing. These views, however, give us an appreciation of how difficult it has been for the human race to figure out just what kind of universe we live in, as well as what style of life is most appropriate in that universe. Religions have adopted one or another model, depending, it seems, on their own cultural context. To press home the point that it has not been at all easy to determine what the universe is like, here is a larger list of possibilities. The brief descriptions do not provide adequate explanations for each picture of the universe. Only a few of them will be explained more fully in the pages to follow. The list is intended just to jog the mind into recognizing how difficult it might be to settle on the correct picture of the universe. The length of this list makes it all the more impressive that modern science has good grounds for saying that only one or two of them are close to being correct.

An incomplete list of models of the cosmos

1. A universe of basic inner essences (tree, star, dog, water), each of which is unchangingly true to its own nature as the source of nature's reliability, and each of which has its own inner goal-directedness to act in its own way. (Aristotle)

2. A universe of geometric and harmonized essences that make up the macrocosmic order of the overall universe, which exist all together in microcosmic complexity in each human person, thereby making the person locus for controlling these forces through "natural magic." (Neoplatonism)

3. A universe in which most events are due to "secondary" (i.e., natural) causes, but in which there are also divine supernatural interventions to produce effects which natural causes alone would not have produced. (Supernaturalism, whether strong or occasional)

4. A universe which divine beings invisibly manipulate things the way any person can, but with immensely greater power, by intimate knowledge of nature, thereby producing whatever these beings want. (Polytheisms)

5. A universe in which permanent inner essences do not exist, so that one can only try to identify external reliable patterns such as the pattern we call gravity or characteristics such as solidity, and then see how these basic externals in fact interact, perhaps describing these external patterns mathematically for maximum precision. (Empiricism)

6. A universe of two major components: matter—the passive atoms physically kept in motion somehow (by God? by "inertia"?) which collectively constitute all physical reality including all animals and the human body; and spirit—immortal and purely spiritual (non-material) rational souls. (17th century mechanistic philosophy)

7. A universe in which inert physical matter is organized into life-patterns by the presence of various non-material but fully natural "subtle spirits," which make inert matter operate in a certain way. (Vitalism)

8. A fully material and evolving universe, which has within itself sufficient energy to account for all activities in the universe, including all life and even human consciousness and rationality as part of the material process. (Contemporary naturalism)

9. A universe in which only mind is really real, with all seeming materiality only a false way of perceiving things, or perhaps a temporary process that mind itself is undergoing. ("Idealism")

10. A self-contained evolving universe in which the development of sequential levels of responsiveness and consciousness are due to a divine element that is part of the matrix of the universe and is nurturing this development in hidden ways. (Whitehead and "process theology.")

11. An ephemeral universe of change which is not the really real but is a shadow alternative to the unchanging realm of true Being and Truth. (Hindu thought)

12. A universe that is divine, in some sense of the word. Perhaps the universe is alive and thinking itself into its many forms. Perhaps the universe is not alive and thinking but as the source of all the many things and patterns and processes of the cosmos is worthy of ultimate reverence.

The human place in the hierarchy of being

Another Hellenic set of ideas about the universe had a lasting influence in the West. The multiple forms of life, plants and animals, suggested to the ancient Greeks that the universe contained a full range of the possible forms of life, each fitting into its appropriate niche, and all of them ranked one above the other in a hierarchical scale. Arthur Lovejoy referred to it in the title of his book on the topic as *The Great Chain of Being*.[1] This perspective dominated European thought until the age of Copernicus.

According to this view, the lowest aspect of reality was simple materiality—basic earth was the most evident form of it. The earth in turn gave birth to higher elements. Copper and silver and gold and gems were "generated" and developed in the earth like embryos developed in living beings.[2] Also generated by earth were the crudest forms of life like moss and maggots. For Jews and Christians this implied that not all life had to have been created by God in the beginning, a truly interesting belief in light of current religious claims that the first appearance of life requires divine intervention. (Perhaps one could think of the emergence of moss and maggots from dirt as a form of working out Augustine's "seminal reasons" which God had planted in creation.)

From these lowly forms the hierarchical arrangement of beings mounted upwards, reaching its highest physical form in humans. We have seen that earth, water, air, and fire were the four basic elements that composed all material things. Some thought that the heavens were made of air and the stars and sun of fire. Aristotle speculated that the heavenly bodies might be made of a fifth basic element, a perfect and shiny sky element. Aristotle argued that the highest aspect of nature was a Prime Mover encompassing the heavenly spheres, keeping them rotating. Aristotle called the heavens perfect and the earth flawed and messy. In the late Middle Ages his cosmology would come to have a dominant influence because the authority of Aristotle was enormous in the minds of medieval philosophers.

We have also seen briefly in Chapter 6, about the nature and existence of God, that in the philosophy of Aristotle's teacher, Plato, beyond the heavenly beings (such as angels in the Christian version), the single Ultimate was not the Prime Mover but the One, the supreme unity in comparison to which we can be aware of multiplicity. This One was also the Good, the ultimate source of goodness in the universe. In Plato's conception of things, the One/Good, as well as other "higher" realities, were not merely perfect but also utterly different from the physical or material. Material reality was changeable and therefore corruptible, because whatever can change can fall apart or rot. Opposite that is spirit, a form of existence that is incorruptible and therefore naturally immortal, including the human soul. This division of all reality into two very different basic types, matter and spirit, is called "dualism." (It is not the only kind of dualism. Other dualities exist—part vs. whole, male vs. female, etc.)

As the intellectual standards declined in the ancient world (ca. 200 CE and later), a theory which claimed it had been revealed through a mystical source, or had a prophecy or sign to uphold it, or was a special revelation from a god, could garner as much esteem as one that tried to follow a more rational method. Then as now, a theory which felt emotionally right to people or offered a kind of wish-fulfillment had a good chance of being accepted. A theory could also gain status if it could claim that it represented the wisdom of one of the great minds of the past. Thus a system of ideas that could call itself "Platonic" added the authority of the name of Plato to it.

By the 3rd century CE a result was the popularity of a grand theory known as Neoplatonism. It borrowed ideas from Plato, appropriating the prestige of his name. It described the universe as the great "chain of being" in which everything was as it should be. In the 3rd century CE it was as popular among the educated as Christianity, though Christianity would soon surpass it, especially after the emperor Constantine legitimized Christian belief and practice in the 4th century CE and made it the norm in the empire.

The Neoplatonists built upon Plato's division between the physical body, the source of limitation and corruption; and the spiritual soul, the seat of intellect, which belonged by its nature to a heavenly (sky) sort of existence. This made the human person the meeting point of the two major aspects of the entire universe, the material and the spiritual. The human person, said later Platonists, was a microcosm of the macrocosmic order. What took place within a person reflected the whole universe. This implied that what a person did might also produce cosmic influences. This provided the basis for belief in a kind of "natural magic," which was treated by some as the highest "science."

In the 16th century, attempts to harness the power of this natural magic were as common as attempts to develop a new science based on mathematics and measuring. In the early 17th century Neoplatonism was still alive and well. Scholars avidly read works attributed to Hermes Trismegistus—thrice-great Hermes—which supposedly had been inspired by an Egyptian God who was actually the same as the Greek god Hermes. This text was reputed to be older than Moses, and was thought to contain genuine instructions about natural magic. The text was in fact composed in the 2nd or 3rd century CE as a Neoplatonist tract. Its contents were supposed to be secret knowledge, hidden from ordinary people, until it had finally been translated from the ancient Greek. Not only had the information contained therein been hidden or "occult," but the natural magic forces which it described were also hidden in nature. Many aspired to learn to control those occult forces and become a magus, a master of magical powers.

Many Neoplatonist ideas are alive and well today in what we call New Age thought, perhaps also a somewhat religious set of ideas. Some New Age proponents create love potions and cast spells. New Age thought often includes belief in extra-sensory perception or ESP. This is a collective name for unusual powers of the mind such as telepathy (mind-reading), telekinesis (moving objects by mind power alone), and clairvoyance (ability to "see" events at a distance or in the future).[3] The study of these powers is called "parapsychology" because the abilities are sometimes categorized as paranormal ("para" means along-side of and therefore different from the normal). Whether or not these really are "religious" in some sense, they are not scientific.

Seventeenth-century options

At the time of the beginnings of modern science, it was not yet clear what model of the universe would win out. The 17th century was the time of Galileo (1564–1642) and Johannes Kepler (1571–1630), the great astronomer. Kepler did believe in certain natural magical powers. In particular he believed in astrology. But his own studies and mathematical skills slowly moved him in the direction which Galileo had taken, which was to treat the stuff of the universe not as something full of natural magical forces but as matter in motion, able to be measured mathematically. Galileo was on the track toward the "corpuscular" interpretation of the universe, the idea of the ancient Epicurean atomists that all things in the end were composed of tiny uncuttable particles, a theory shared by many. At the same time, Aristotle's science was still predominant among the more traditional philosophers of nature. The Catholic Church especially favored Aristotle, partly because scholastic theology, the theology which stemmed from Aquinas and other great thinkers of the 13th century, had adopted much of Aristotle's natural philosophy (science) in creating an up-to-date theology for the times.

We have advanced a long way since the 17th century. Subsequent chapters will tell more of the history of the development of cosmology and biology. In the end it turned out that the semi-Epicurean corpuscularism was closest to describing how the universe in fact does work. But that theory was not adequate either. The 17th century had no idea of the extreme complexity of the universe on atomic, molecular, and cellular levels.

How do we know there are not other weird or mysterious or even mystical aspects of the universe about which modern science has no clue? We can dream up all sorts of universes, whether one of the dozen listed earlier in this chapter or several more. The success of modern science nonetheless stands in contrast to the lack of success of any of the other methods at giving us some truth-claims that test out well in practice.

The next chapter will take us further along the journey through 20th century understandings of the cosmos and their impact on religious thought. For that, the chapter will have to back up a bit and start with the situation at the time of Galileo.

For further reading

Brown, Neville, *Engaging the Cosmos: Astronomy, Philosophy, and Faith* (Brighton: Sussex Academic Press, 2006). This begins with ancient Mesopotamian ideas and includes even Japanese traditions.

Edis, Taner, *Science and Nonbelief* (Westport, CT: Greenwood Press, 2006). It includes chapters on the history of the relation of science and spiritualism as well as the history of naturalism.

Freeman, Charles, *The Closing of the Western Mind: The Rise of Faith and the Fall of Reason* (New York: Vintage Books, 2002). A story of the demise of Hellenistic rationality and the descent into the early medieval dark ages.

McGrath, Alister E., *The Order of Things: Explorations in Scientific Theology* (Hoboken: Wiley-Blackwell, 2006). A set of essays on many aspects of developments in religion and science since the beginning of the Enlightenment.

Cosmic Order 12

It has been around 400 years since Galileo began to argue in favor of the Copernican theory that the sun was the center of the universe. We would say, of course, that the sun is the center of only our solar system. But Copernicus' view was a radical change from the previous geocentric view, which placed the earth at the center of the entire universe.

Since Galileo's time the general picture of the universe has kept on changing. By the end of this chapter we will have arrived at a universe far, far different from Galileo's. The history is worth recounting because each step along the way had religious implications. Religious responses changed over time, however, so that the story of the last few centuries provides a look at some interesting alternative responses by religion to scientific theories about the cosmos. The next chapter will complete this review with a look at contemporary arguments about what the universe might or might not indicate about belief in God.

Astronomy from Ptolemy to Galileo

Galileo was put under house arrest by the Roman Inquisition in 1633. His crime was to have rejected Ptolemaic geocentric (earth-centered) astronomy and to have supported the heliocentric (sun-centered) theory of Copernicus instead. The roots of this story go back all the way to the ancient Babylonians who kept excellent records of the movement of the stars and planets, good enough to enable the ancient Greek philosopher Thales to predict an eclipse of the sun in the 7th century BCE. These records were also put to use by a man named Hipparchus in the 2nd century BCE to construct a detailed time table of the heavens and a picture of the universe to go with it, one that placed the earth at the center of the universe.

These ancient astronomers were also aware, though, of the possibility that the earth revolved around the sun. A century before Hipparchus, an astronomer named Aristarchus (320–250 BCE) had proposed heliocentrism as a way to make sense of some of the evidence. (They would have used the word "phenomena" or "appearances" instead of "evidence.") But this would also mean that day and night were caused by the earth revolving on its axis once every 24 hours, rather than by the sun flying around the earth. Another 2nd century BCE Alexandrian, named Eratosthenes, figured the approximate circumference of the earth at about 25,000 miles, very close to right. So it was clear that the earth would have a surface speed of more than 1,000 miles an hour at the equator in the Anglo mode of measuring.

Early in the 20th century there were predictions that if automobiles ever traveled faster than 60 miles an hour it would be impossible to breathe at that speed. So it is not surprising that the rate of 1,000 mi/hr did not strike ancient astronomers as a reasonable possibility. They discussed problems of centrifugal force throwing objects right off the earth, of articles dropped from heights being left behind as the earth whirled around, of air movements and great winds.

An equally serious objection to the claim the earth went around the sun was the apparent lack of parallax of the stars (see Figure 12.1). If the earth circled the sun, any given star should *appear* to shift its position between January and July, for example, unless it was extremely farther away than the 16th century thought possible.

To see parallax in operation, close one eye and hold your thumb out in front of you, covering some object at a distance from you. Then without moving your thumb, open the closed eye and shut the other eye, but keep looking at the same object. It will shift about an inch and a half—the distance between your two eyes. In its orbit around the sun, the earth shifts over 180 million miles. So nearby stars should seem to shift

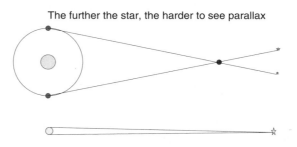

Figure 12.1 Parallax.

positions somewhat between Winter and Summer. In the 17th century, however, no one could find any parallax at all.

By the 2nd century CE an astronomer working in Alexandria named Ptolemy, the family name of the general of Alexander's army who took over Egypt after Alexander's death, tried to assemble all the previous work about the skies into one coherent package. It took him many volumes to do this. Muslims later named this the Almagest—the Great [work].

Ptolemy placed all the stars in a single "heaven," a single orbit, we would say, perhaps embedded on a crystalline (and transparent) sphere holding all the stars; after all, the stars all move together as though fixed in relation to one another. Planets move separately from each other and from the stars and therefore each had to have its own "heaven" to move in; perhaps each heaven was another crystalline sphere, some speculated.

Hipparchus and the others had done very good work at collating precise information. This information could be used to predict exactly where each of the heavenly bodies would be at any time of the year, for years in advance. Astronomers could predict both solar and lunar eclipses quite well, and could make out star charts to guide sailors. But the astronomers could not figure out just why and how it all worked out so well. What they were seeking was a *theory*. They had the "laws" of heaven, in the sense of knowing the *patterns* of movement. But they could not construct a mental picture of how the universe was constructed that made full sense of the details of their information. Ptolemy decided explicitly to settle just for "saving the appearances."

The phrase "saving the appearances" stands for preserving the evidence in the sense of not going against the evidence. The evidence was the detailed information that had been gathered since the days of the Babylonians. It was fairly good and accurate information. So the basic rule of Ptolemy was to make sure that no theory was constructed that conflicted with the evidence. Ptolemy noted there were two major competing systems, both of which fit with at least a lot of the evidence, the geocentric system and the heliocentric. Ptolemy chose the geocentric because it seemed simpler to him.[1]

According to the received wisdom of those times, especially the opinions of the great Aristotle (4th century BCE), the heavenly realms were free from the messy imperfections of earth, where things bumped into each other constantly and eventually fell apart. The heavens were changeless realms of stately circular motion which endlessly returned the planets and stars back to their proper positions. The great heavy and decay-filled earth was at the center of this universe.

Nonetheless, there were problems with this Ptolemaic picture of the skies. First, the planets had the disconcerting habit of seeming to move backwards in their orbits at predictable intervals. In the Copernican system it is easy to explain this. Because the earth is closer to the sun it travels faster than the outer planets. If it did not it would slowly spiral down into the sun. This means that at certain points in its orbit the earth passes Mars, Jupiter, and Saturn. From the viewpoint of the earth they momentarily appear to go backwards as the earth passes in front of them. But as the earth keeps going round the sun the outer planets will appear to resume their forward course.

A second oddity in the ancient system is why Mercury and Venus always remain near the sun. In the Ptolemaic system there is no explanation for this. In the Copernican system the inner planets always stay near the sun because they have small orbits quite near the sun.

As a third problem, the moon, planets, and sun did not behave well. The long-term data gathered over centuries made it appear that not only were the orbits not perfectly centered on the earth, but the orbits were not even perfectly circular. (Not even the Copernican system accounted for all of this very well; it took Kepler to make fuller sense out of it in works published from 1609–1619.) Because of all these problems, Ptolemy had handed on his own system as a theoretical construction that was not necessarily the truth. He knew this well. It "saved the appearances," but there were many unanswered questions.

The Muslims inherited the Ptolemaic system when they conquered much of the Byzantine Empire, including Egypt and Alexandria. Europe received the Muslim knowledge, beginning in the 11th century, and were able to use it to fill out their small knowledge of astronomy from other texts. From the 12th century on, people continued to do astronomy and astrology as best they could, using excellent information from the Almagest. They learned new methods of mathematics, including the highly suspicious Arabic way of enumerating and calculating, using what we still call "Arabic numerals," instead of the familiar Roman numerals.[2]

The well-known breakthrough came with the work of Nicholai Copernicus, the Polish astronomer. Those were difficult times in Europe. In 1517, Luther had opened divisions in Christendom that had violent political implications. New ideas clouded the horizon within which the people of Europe had lived their lives, making everyone unsure of where things were going and whom to follow. Copernicus' seemingly new theory on the movement of the planets therefore felt threatening.

Copernicus (1473–1543) read a version of the Almagest and was exposed to the heliocentric theory of Aristarchus, but now had better mathematical techniques for analyzing things along with some observations of his own. By the early 16th century he had worked out much of a heliocentric theory. He did not manage to get his great work *De Revolutionibus Orbium Coelestium* published until 1543, the year of his death. The publisher, Andreas Osiander, added a preface which tried to take the sting out of the theory by saying that it need not be taken as truth but only as a more convenient way to organize the data for practical uses like navigation and astrology, that it was only an attempt to "save the appearances" without claiming it was actually true. (Osiander did not sign the preface, leaving the impression that this disclaimer was Copernicus'.) Galileo and others came to think that it was indeed true, as had Copernicus himself.

Biblical and Christian beliefs

By this time there had been more than 1,000 years of Christian use of the Ptolemaic system. It is odd that many 16th century people felt that Ptolemy's system fit with the Bible. The universe of the Hebrew Bible includes a flat earth sitting on four pillars with a hard firmament overhead to hold back the waters of chaos. Here are some relevant texts.

> Genesis 1:6 "Let there be a vault [firmament, dome] in the waters to divide the waters in two." (The word in Hebrew is like the word for a bowl.)
> Psalm 75:3. "The earth and all who dwell in it melt; It is I who have firmly set its pillars."
> 1 Samuel 2:8 "For the pillars of the earth are the LORD'S, And He set the world on them."
> Job 37:18 "Can you help him [God] spread the vault of heaven, or temper that mirror of cast metal?" (A sky like a hard metal dome)
> Job 38:4-6 "What supports its [the earth's] pillars at their base?"

There were also biblical lines that seemed to indicate that the sun had literally stood still in the sky, as in the book of Joshua, or that God could make it move backwards in the sky, as in the second book of Kings. These lines could fit either with the flat earth of the Bible, over which the sun moved under the dome of the firmament, or with a spherical earth in the center of the universe with the sun revolving around it, as in the Ptolemaic version. They did not fit well with a sun stationary at the center of things.

> Joshua 10:12-13 (In a battle against five Amorite kings, Joshua prays to Yahweh to prolong the day to give time for the Israelites to conquer the kings fully)
> "Sun, stand still over Gibeon, and, moon, over the Vale of Aijalon.
> The sun stood still and the moon halted, till the people had vengeance on the enemies.
> The sun stood still at noon. There was never a day like that before or since."
> 2 Kings 20:8-11 (Hezekiah, king of Judah, is sick and going to die. Yahweh announces a cure through the prophet Isaiah. Hezekiah doubts and asks for a sign from God. Isaiah asks Hezekiah which sign would be more convincing to him, for his shadow to lengthen ten steps, as it normally does, or go backwards ten steps. Hezekiah says it is harder for it to go backwards.)
> "The prophet Isaiah then called on Yahweh, who made the shadow go back ten steps on the steps of Ahaz." [A staircase built by Ahaz?]

In spite of the sayings in the Hebrew Scriptures presupposing a flat earth under a hard dome, many educated Jews and Christians of later centuries nonetheless adopted the Ptolemaic view, because this is what the best science seemed to require. Some early Christians had at first thought it a dangerous innovation to go against the clear words of the Bible. Augustine tried to dodge the issue somewhat as he struggled with the conflict between the biblical view and Ptolemy's geocentrism. In words quoted later by Galileo in his letter to the Grand Duchess, Augustine describes two views of heaven, the sky, as a solid object of some sort, containing the earth in its center or covering it:

> What is it to me whether heaven, like a sphere, surrounds the earth on all sides as a mass balanced in the center of the universe, or whether like a dish it merely covers and overcasts the earth?

After Augustine's time, most learned Christians accepted Ptolemy's view. They adopted Ptolemaic astronomy so thoroughly, in fact, that by the time of Copernicus many Christians no longer recognized Ptolemy's theory as an idea imported from Greek science into their religious tradition. If they could first abandon the Bible for Ptolemy, it would not seem to be difficult to abandon Ptolemy for Copernicus. But tradition is difficult to change.

The disturbing new view of the heavens

The story of Galileo's part in the Copernican controversy is fairly well known. As a leading natural philosopher (scientist) of the 16th and early 17th century he led the way in producing not only new scientific conclusions, as about the pendulum and the rate of acceleration of falling bodies, but also in developing a better scientific method. Galileo acknowledged the value of logical clarity and coherence. He frequently used the expression "necessary demonstration," meaning logical analysis through a syllogism.

Perhaps more important was his insistence that necessary demonstration had to be attached to careful "sense experience." Recall that the 14th century nominalists had declared that because God could make any kind of universe God wanted, the only way to tell what sort universe exists is to go look, to get empirical evidence. Galileo agreed. He was a university professor of mathematics. When he looked he could also measure, and the precision of measurement and analysis that mathematics made possible was a major factor in his success. Precise measurement yielded clear and consistent evidence. No matter how persuasively logical a theory was to the mind, it was still necessary to make sure the theory fit the *evidence* very exactly, and that the evidence was described to others who could then do their own checking. In this conviction modern science was born. It was still in its infancy with much to learn. But philosophical speculation alone would no longer be enough to determine truth.

For a variety of reasons Galileo found the Copernican refurbishment of Aristarchus's sun-centered universe more plausible than the Ptolemaic system. He worked out the mathematics concerning the tendency of a spinning earth to throw things off the planet, and showed that the force of gravity that made things fall was very much stronger than the centrifugal force due to the earth's spin. Even at the equator's 1,000 mile/hr speed, objects would stay quite nicely on the earth's surface.

Galileo could not answer a different problem about gravity, though. In the four elements theory of the universe, with the earth at the center, material objects fell to the earth because the planet earth was at the center of the universe. The natural place for the element earth was at this center The fact that objects even fell down deep wells was evidence that material objects seek to get as close to the center as possible. If the earth was not the center of the universe, however, then some different explanation was needed as to why objects fell to its surface anyway, as it raced around the sun in its orbit.

We associate the idea of gravity with Newton. The fact of "heaviness" (*gravitas* in Latin) was an old idea. Newton's accomplishment was to conceptualize gravity as a special force characteristic of every physical body, and to work out the precise mathematical statements that could connect earthly gravity with the force that held the moon in orbit around the earth and the planets in orbit around the sun. This solved Galileo's problem with gravity.

It is often said that people of the 16th century rejected Copernicus' theory because it made the home of the human race no longer the center of things. That is partly true. But in the Ptolemaic system the imperfect earth was also closest to hell, which was right under people's feet in the hot regions of the underground. It was hell, in fact, that was at the universe's exact center. The earth itself was placed at the center of the universe also because the element earth is the lowest of the four elements, the least energetic, and the least noble. The heavenly realm above remained perfect, as Aristotle had insisted; because of original sin, though, this central earth was not merely lowly but the realm of terrible imperfection. The words of the 16th century essayist Michel de Montaigne are a good indicator of the status of the earth as he describes humans and their condition:

> This creature feels and sees that it is lodged here amid the mire and filth of the world, fast bound and riveted to the worst, the most lifeless and debased part of the universe, on the lowest story of the lodging and the farthest removed from the celestial vaul.[3]

Placing the earth in the sky, therefore, promoted it to a higher "heavenly" locale, though the heavens themselves were now of uncertain status.

Very troubling to most people of the times was the way the (seemingly) new heliocentric theory upset the neat hierarchical order of the great chain of being. From hell's fires up to a hard earthly surface and then up to the heavenly bodies in the sky and finally all the way out to God's throne, an ordered pattern from lowest to highest kept everything in its appropriate place. Above the fallen realm of sin on earth, it was supposedly a fully perfect order, as the planets moved majestically in circles to create a cosmic music of the spheres.

Then in 1609 Kepler announced that the orbits of planets were not circles at all. Using precise astronomical observations made by his one-time employer, Tycho Brahe, Kepler showed that the orbits were elliptical. He also established that the planets had the disconcerting habit of speeding up a bit as they approached the part of their orbit that was closest to the sun and slowing down as they moved away from the sun. At about the same time, Galileo's telescope made it clear that the surface of the moon was mottled and bumpy and that the sun had dark blotches on it. There was no perfection in the skies. The tidy and relatively small Ptolemaic universe had been an orderly homey place. This was not true of the new vast and messy universe.

In the early 17th century the social and political order, daily ethics, economic practices, and family order were united with the religious portrait of the great hierarchical chain of being. To disturb any part of this scheme was to upset all the other parts. It was horrendous enough that the social-religious order of Europe had been shaken apart by the Protestant Reformation. Now the philosophers were shaking up the physical universe itself. Two pieces of poetry are frequently quoted to show how disturbed people felt in the 17th century about the new ideas. Both assume a clear hierarchical ordering of all of reality. The first is from Shakespeare. By the word "degree" he refers to steps in the great hierarchical ladder of being, which includes family, social, political, and ecclesiastical order also.

> When the planets
> In evil mixture to disorder wander,
> What plagues and what portents, what mutiny
> What raging of the sea, shaking of earth,
> Commotion in the winds, frights changes horrors,
> Divert and crack, rend and deracinate
> The unity and married calm of states
> Quite from their fixture. Oh when degree is shak'd
> Which is the ladder to all high designs,
> The enterprise is sick. How could communities,
> Degree in schools and brotherhoods in cities,
> Peaceful commerce from dividable shores,
> The primogenitive and due of birth,
> Prerogative of age, crowns, sceptres, laurels,
> But by degree stand in authentic place?
> Take but degree away, untune that string,
> And hark, what discord follows. Each thing meets
> In mere oppugnancy. The bound waters
> Should lift their bosoms higher than the shores
> And make a sop of all this solid globe:
> Strength should be lord to imbecility,
> And the rude son should strike his father dead . . . .[4]

From the distance of the 21ˢᵗ century we can see that what Shakespeare worried about could eventually be handled by new theories. Theories of democracy and individual political rights, of capitalism in economics, and of separation of church and state, would arise in the 17ᵗʰ and 18ᵗʰ centuries to explain how to make social order coherent and intelligible again after the breakdown of the old order, the old "degrees." Intellectual revolutions as thorough-going as this do not come about easily or quickly. But the development of science as we know it now was contributing to this revolution with inexorable force.

Deism and a new skepticism

One of the things that made possible a revolution of social, economic, and religious ideas was deism. It was able to put in place a new sense of coherent cosmic order, and would hold things together until people could absorb some of the implications of the new science in their lives. The universe seen through the eyes of an 18ᵗʰ century deist was still a well-ordered universe. On the basis of the marvelous mathematical laws of nature developed by the new science, the deists constructed their arguments for God's existence by comparing the patterns of the universe with the mechanical regularities of a clock. Nicholas of Oresme in the 14ᵗʰ century, Boyle in the 17ᵗʰ century, and Paley in the 19ᵗʰ century used this analogy to prove that the universe could no more have arrived at such marvelous order by accident than a watch could assemble itself by chance. Here are Boyle's own words about the universe.

> It is like a rare clock, such as may be that at *Strasburgh*, where all things are so skillfully contrived, that the engine being once set a moving, all things proceed, according to the artificer's first design, and the motions of the little statues, that at such hours performs these or those things, do not require, like those of puppets, the peculiar interposing of the artificer, or any intelligent agent employed by him, but perform their functions upon particular occasions, by virtue of the general and primitive contrivance of the whole engine.[5]

But even as deism began, the scientist-mathematician-philosopher Blaise Pascal (1623–1662) was writing what became his *Pensées*, at a point in his life where he had become religiously very devout. He felt deeply bothered by the results of the new science:

> [Section 229] This is what I see and what troubles me. I look on all sides, and I see only darkness everywhere. Nature presents to me nothing which is not a matter of doubt and concern. If I saw nothing there which revealed a Divinity, I would come to a negative conclusion; if I saw everywhere the signs of a Creator, I would remain peacefully in faith. But, seeing too much to deny and too little to be sure, I am in a state to be pitied; wherefore I have a hundred times wished that if a God maintains Nature, she should testify to Him unequivocally, and that, if the signs she gives are deceptive, she should suppress them altogether; that she

should say everything or nothing, that I might see which cause I ought to follow. Whereas in my present state, ignorant of what I am or of what I ought to do, I know neither my condition nor my duty.[6]

Nineteenth-century physics later helped undermine belief in a well-ordered universe through the notion of entropy. Entropy is the one-directional tendency of all forms of energy (in the long run in an open system) to dissipate. Whatever organization or order exists, it all tends eventually to break down into undifferentiated energy. The entire universe tends to fade into cosmic boredom, the "heat death" of everything, as it has been called (actually, an eventual complete chilling out of everything). Such considerations inspired Feuerbach and other skeptics. By the end of the 19th century many a philosophically minded person was proclaiming the ultimate aimlessness of everything as part of a universal tendency to triviality and death. Sartre would echo this in the 20th century.

Meanwhile the astronomers continued to search the skies. In 1838 Friedrich Bessel finally established a clear parallax measurement for a star, 61 Cygni, about 11 light years from earth (and actually a binary star—2 orange-red dwarf stars). To get a sense of how far this is in miles, multiple 6,457 by one trillion (a thousand billion). The universe was now terrifyingly larger than even the 17th century had feared.

An expanding universe

It was not until the 20th century, however, that it became clear that some of the stars in the sky were not mere stars but were entire galaxies. Through the crisp air of Flagstaff, Arizona, the 24-inch reflector at the Lowell Observatory showed the astronomer V. M. Slipher that some blurs of light in the sky were actually entire galaxies of stars. The universe had just become even more enormous.

Slipher was also the first to identify a "red shift" in the light coming from many galaxies. This red shift is the Doppler effect, first described by Christian Doppler in Germany in 1842 as it applied to light; others applied it to sound. You have heard a Doppler effect if you have ever seen an auto race. With a roar the cars approach where you are sitting. As the cars pass by the roar suddenly drops down a tone or two, not in volume but in pitch. The cause of this odd effect is that as the cars are moving toward you they are catching up a small bit with the sound waves they are emitting toward you. This "compresses" the waves, making them higher pitched to you than they otherwise would be. As they pass they are then racing away from the sound waves that are coming to you from them. This stretches out the sound waves making them lower pitched to you.

The same effect appeared with many galaxies Slipher observed. The stars should have been emitting about the same wave lengths of light as we see in our own galaxy, varying with the size of the star. Instead the light from almost all of the galaxies were "lower-pitched" than they should have been. The light was shifted toward the red end of the light spectrum. This would make sense only if all those galaxies were moving away from us. In every direction Slipher looked, the universe seemed to be receding.

In the 1920s the astronomers Edwin Hubble and Milton Humason, using the new 100-inch reflector of the Wilson Observatory near Los Angeles, confirmed that a large number of stars in the sky were entire galaxies of stars. They studied more than 40 galaxies and discovered that red shift was greatest for those galaxies that were further away. These galaxies were racing away from earth faster than closer galaxies. The universe was apparently expanding outward.

A standard image to aid in grasping what an expanding universe looks like is to think of a large balloon with little spots all over its surface. As the balloon fills up with air the skin of the balloon stretches. As this happens, every spot on the surface of the balloon moves away from every other spot. The universe seems to be expanding in the same way, but in 3 dimensions not just 2 (or 4 if we include time).

By roughly calculating the rate of expansion and making also a rough estimate of the size of the universe, astronomers could work backwards in time, to establish when the whole universe had started its expansion. Even in the early 20th century it was clear that the universe was billions of years old. Some thought as much as 20 billion, though the current estimate at the beginning of the 21st century is just under 14 billion. In any case, this put the long history of humankind on earth into cosmic perspective. Not only are humans lost in space, so to speak, but lost in time also.

For further reading

Asimov, Isaac, *The Universe: From Flat Earth to Quasar* (New York: Avon Books, 1966). A dated book, but still a great read. The history of astronomy from the ancient Babylonians on.

Greenstein, George, *The Symbiotic Universe: Life and Mind in the Cosmos* (New York: William Morrow and Company, Inc., 1988). Popular, but raises good questions and issues.

Hetherington, Norriss S., ed., *Cosmology: Historical, Literary, Philosophical, Religious and Scientific Perspectives* (New York: Garland, 1993). The subtitle says it all.

Kuhn, Thomas S., *The Copernican Revolution: The Astronomy in the Development of Western Thought* (Cambridge: Harvard University Press, 1957). Excellent summary of much of the history but with an odd "social construction" approach. Kuhn keeps overlooking or side-stepping the important role the evidence played.

13 Religious Interpretations of the Cosmos

To repeat, the knowable universe contains roughly one hundred billion galaxies. Pause and reflect on that number. Then add that the average galaxy has roughly one hundred billion stars. To say we live in an enormous universe is an understatement.

Compare the size of the knowable universe to standard images of God. The God portrayed by more anthropomorphic images can be dwarfed by the universe. It is difficult to imagine that God is in charge of each and every event on this single planet Earth, whether by actively creating each event as in Muslim theology, or by having planned and/or overseeing every one of those events as in most Christian and Judaic theologies. Picturing an anthropomorphic God as creator and guide of billions of galaxies, each with billions of stars, stretches the image of God mightily. The God of Aquinas, the Infinite and changeless Ultimate cause of all existence might be more easily affirmed as the source of this entire immense universe. This notion, however, is not as religiously useful for many people.

Those who write on God and the cosmos have a number of different ways to bring the two together. The usual goal is to do this without violating either the science or the religious tradition which these writers hold. There are perhaps four main ways in which this has been done. The first is to mysticize the cosmos in rather general terms. This is common among many scientists with a somewhat generic Protestant orientation. A second way is to mysticize the cosmos in much greater detail. Teilhard de Chardin and others followed this path. Teilhard was a Jesuit priest. There are a few books by conservative or reformed Jews who do something similar, nonetheless I will call this second main way of uniting notions of God with knowledge of the universe the Teilhardian approach. The strong anthropic principle (SAP) is the third way. Process theology is the fourth. We can look at each of these in turn. First, though, an outline of what science now tells us about cosmic evolution will set the context for interpretations of that evolution.

A brief history of the universe

The universe seems to have begun about 13.7 billion years ago in a "big bang," an unimaginably large explosion of energy, which has been expanding ever since. Within a fraction of a second after the Big Bang (see "A Quick History" below here for more details) the four basic forces of the universe had separated out of the original undifferentiated energy–gravity, the strong force, the electromagnetic force, and the weak force. By this time quarks had also appeared, the building blocks of protons and neutrons, which make up the nuclei of atoms. When the universe had cooled enough, stable atoms could form, from the simplest hydrogen, with one proton and one electron, to deuterium, which is hydrogen with a proton and neutron in the nucleus, to the more complex helium, whose nucleus is usually composed of two protons and two neutrons.

As the universe whirled about, still expanding and still cooling, great clouds of hydrogen and helium (and a touch of lithium) coalesced and, eventually, after about 3 billion years, because gravity pulled segments of the clouds into large dense concentrations, out of those clouds stars began to burn. The fuel at first was mainly hydrogen. When a large enough mass of it condenses under the force of gravity the center of the mass begins to undergo a process of atomic fusion, in which the electrons are stripped away and the nuclei are slammed together with such speed that they form more helium.

Some stars are modest in size, like the earth's sun. They burn slowly and last many billions of years. Some are huge, much larger than the sun. They go through cycles of burning up (fusing) most of their hydrogen and helium. At a certain point, some of their material expands rapidly out into space, but their cores collapse inward. In this collapse the vast amounts of helium and heavier elements that have formed also crunch together even more densely than in the first stage of the star's life and through further fusion form heavier elements like carbon and oxygen and silicon. Enormously large stars repeat again the process of outward expansion and inward collapse to form much heavier elements like iron and nickel. Such a star may even expand and collapse once again. This time the shock wave emitted from the collapse of the iron core will hurtle outward, slamming into elements in the parts already expanding outward more slowly. The shock wave will be strong enough to force some of those elements to form the heaviest of all atoms such as gold and uranium.

Some of those elements, after millions or even billions of years drifting in space, fall into orbit around another star. Gravity would have to gradually pull together this material and slowly produce a planetary core and mantle to support a surface zone. After a time much of the heavy debris in orbit around the star would be swept up by newly forming planets. It would no longer crash steadily onto the new planets. After sufficient cooling, one such planet might develop life.

About one-third of the earth is composed of iron, mostly in the two layers of the core. The core is surrounded by the mantle, composed of a number of elements, averaging out to a density less than that of the core. On top of the mantle rests a very thin crust, much of it composed of compounds of silicon, ranging from 5 to 30 kilometers in thickness, on an earth that is some 6,400 kilometers in diameter. All these earth materials were first created in the fusion process of massive stars. Without that long history, neither our planet nor we would exist.

The earth itself was formed only about 4.5 billion years ago, over 9 billion years after the Big Bang. About 3.5 billion years ago the first life forms appeared on this planet, over 10 billion years after the Big Bang. It would be very interesting to know how many other planets exist in the knowable universe with conditions adequate for life, and to know how long ago the first of those planets formed. Perhaps it does not always take 10 billion or more years before the conditions are right somewhere or another for life. It would seem to take at least 5 billion, however, and perhaps a few billion more as in the case of our planet.

A timeline of the universe

THE BIG BANG: Some 14 billion years ago everything in the known universe was an infinitely dense and hot point that exploded with unimaginable violence. The four forces of nature that now govern the universe—gravity, electromagnetism, and the strong and weak forces—had not yet come into existence out of the primal energy. Energy and matter were undifferentiated.

BY 10^{-43} SECOND: The universe had cooled to 100 million trillion trillion degrees. Gravity became a distinct force; "matter" was an indistinguishable soup of intensely energetic collisions.

AFTER A MERE 10^{-34} SECOND: The temperature had dropped to a billion billion billion degrees—cool enough for the first particle-matter to coalesce. Quarks, the building blocks of protons and neutrons emerged, as did electrons and similar particles, in the form of both matter and antimatter. The strong force, which holds protons and neutrons together, split off. Three distinct forces—gravity, the strong force, and the electroweak force—began running the show.

BY 10^{-10} SECOND: The electroweak force split into the electromagnetic and weak forces. From that moment on, the four forces together began shaping the universe.

AT 10^{-5} SECOND: The universe had cooled to a trillion degrees. Quarks could stick together to form stable protons and neutrons. Antiquarks formed antiprotons. For every 10 billion particles of antimatter, the universe contained 10 billion and 1 bits of matter. In the dense soup, flecks of antimatter and matter collided, annihilating each other in a flash of photons, leaving only a fraction of the original mass of the universe.

ONE SECOND AFTER THE BIG BANG: the now sluggish neutrons and protons slammed into each other, stuck together, and formed the nuclei of helium, lithium, and heavy forms of hydrogen. After this brief instant in time, the temperature fell below a billion degrees and the density of the ever-expanding universe was too low for such nuclei-forming collisions to occur again. (Billions of years would pass before stars forged helium into heavier elements such as carbon and oxygen.)

WHEN THE UNIVERSE WAS 300,000 YEARS OLD: and 3,000 degrees hot, nuclei captured electrons as they whizzed past and formed the first atoms. The photons that the electrons had once interacted with began to streak the universe with light.

AFTER 1 BILLION YEARS OR SO: The pull of gravity caused atoms to coalesce into clouds of gas. Galaxies formed as the nascent clouds continued to swirl, perhaps around bits of very dense but undetectable "dark matter." In another billion years the galaxies began to group together into superclusters and gigantic structures—bubbles of space with walls of thousands of galactic clouds.

AFTER 3 BILLION YEARS: Stars formed in the clouds and began to shine. Earth and our solar system formed 9 billions years after the Big Bang. After basking for another billion years in the light of our star, our planet sprouted its first traces of life. Life on earth appeared after 10 billion years of cosmic development.

Religious skeptics examine this history and conclude that there is no evidence of either a plan or a purpose. For billions of years mindless sequences of events happened finally to spin off, accidentally as it seems, a rare planet like earth which could give rise to a tortuous evolution of life. In fact, look too closely at details of the universe and it will look not merely unplanned but generally unfriendly to life. Asteroids have wiped out a wide swath of life on earth at times. Out in the larger cosmos galaxies collide pulling each other to shreds. Neutron stars, stars so incredibly dense that one of them a few miles wide has a gravitational pull that drags large objects in at a speed that causes a collision so violent that gamma rays radiate out over vast distances, which would wipe out any life that might happen to exist anywhere in the neighborhood.

In the face of these claims Bultmann's response remains possible—the great "nevertheless." No matter if science says the universe is ultimately aimless, lacking any ultimate meaning and thereby threatening every limited attempt at finding meaning. Bultmann says "nevertheless" he will have the courage to believe. Kierkegaard's earlier response was along the same lines; the knight of faith will leap into the chasm, trusting as Abraham trusted when asked to sacrifice his son.

There are other religious responses, however, which seek a greater reconciliation between religion and science. We can look here at the four types listed earlier, one at a time.

A mysticized cosmos

In 1995 Paul Davies won the annual Templeton Prize in religion and science, worth well over a million dollars, so he is a useful example of thinkers who offer at least vaguely religious perspectives on the cosmos as a whole. In varying degrees they try to describe a larger and more general religious sensibility which fits with the picture of the universe provided by science, though the specifics of their positions sometimes vary greatly from each other.

Davies has high aspirations. In the preface to his book, *God and the New Physics* (1983) he claims that science is better than religion at providing a path to God. By this he means that 20th century cosmology offers a way to answer some of the most basic and general questions about the nature, order, and purpose of the universe. His answer is a bit thin, though. Where the old deists found detailed evidence of a Designer in the static intricate order of things, particularly of complex life forms, Davies finds only hints of some larger plan and purpose.

Davies slowly offers descriptions of the universe intended to evoke awe in the reader. Yet he does not argue that this is a religious experience upon which a person might ground religious faith. He raises too many problems for religious faith. On the one hand, for example, Davies suggests that the mathematical intelligibility of the universe can be taken as an emanation from the mind of God. Davies balances this, however, with the question of the increasing entropy of the entire universe. As all energy dissipates into an increasingly random distribution over the next few billion years, is the power of the mind of God thus evaporating; is the mind of God itself doomed to eventual dissolution?

This clearly is a very odd question for a Jew or Christian or Muslim. For these theistic religions the "mind" of God shares in God's eternity. Throughout the book Davies similarly balances suggestions of how physics might tell us something about God, with questions that then challenge the religious possibilities that Davies first finds implicit in that physics. The overall effect of the book, is to leave the reader with a set of haunting hints that God and the divine purpose for the universe lie hiding just beneath the surface of the naturalism by which physics properly operates. I call this a vaguely "mysticized" approach to the cosmos.

The same can be said of Stuart Kauffman's view. In his book *Reinventing the Sacred* (2008), Kauffman says we do not need a supernatural God who created the world. But we can treat the endless creativity of nature itself as a sacred force. He contrasts his approach with reductionism, claiming that reductionism overlooks the marvelous power of nature to produce ever greater levels of complexity. He is of course not alone in this observation. Reducing events to their simpler causes does not pay adequate attention to the ongoing *emergence* in the universe of higher complexity. Kauffman adds, however, a deep sense of awe at this process of emerging complexity, treating its creativity as though it were divine. This sounds close to pantheism, the view that nature as a whole is God, and vice versa. In the end he mysticizes the cosmos a bit, without quite making it divine, and without making it clear just what causes this emergence of complexity.

The Teilhardian approach

Pere Pierre Teilhard de Chardin, S. J. (of the Society of Jesus—the Jesuits) is a long enough name that he is most often referred to simply as "Teilhard." He died in 1955 at the age of 74 after a productive life as a paleontologist. During his lifetime his Catholic Church was firmly dualist, sharply dividing the spiritual from the material, and thinking of material existence, at least in this current world, as a fallen state. His Church affirmed with the book of Genesis that God made the material world good. After that happy beginning, however, sin entered the world and only the eventual transformation by God of the physical universe into something more glorious will overcome the corrupting influence of that sin upon our material existence. Meanwhile, even while promising a bodily resurrection in the end, the Catholic Church scorned materialism in two forms—metaphysical naturalism which says only the material universe exists, and moral materialism which seeks to find fulfillment in material possessions and powers.

Teilhard very early developed a radically different sense of the physical universe. He interpreted the universe through a framework of cosmic evolution, and then tried to match this up with his Christian faith. During his lifetime his religious superiors and the Roman Catholic authorities were generally opposed to his work, arguing that his prior allegiance to a scheme of cosmic evolution led him to a distorted form of Catholic faith. He was not allowed to publish any of his various books and articles on this topic. They got into print only after his death, when his sister had control of his papers.

His most famous work, *Le Phénomène Humain* (1955), appeared in English in 1959 as *The Phenomenon of Man*. That same year the Vatican issued a warning that bishops should discourage Catholics from reading it. This warning was reaffirmed in 1981. The book has since appeared in a new translation in 1999, now titled *The Human Phenomenon*. It uses unusual language to express a sweeping scientific and then religious vision of cosmic history, of the human place in that history, and the ultimate goal of that history.[1]

Teilhard asks his readers to look at the universe from new angles. Two things stand out for him. One is that there is a "within" to things. In human beings it is our marvelous complex and self-reflecting consciousness. Other mammals possess a consciousness also, just a less complex form of it. Even the simplest life-forms, down even to an ameba, have an inner complexity adequate to allow the life-form to respond to stimuli from the outside world. Teilhard claims that science tends to overlook this "within," but that he himself is not being unscientific by calling attention to it. This inner dimension is part of the natural world and therefore science should include the inner dimension in its descriptions of reality. Teilhard argues that matter itself has this power of inwardness implicit in it.

The second thing that stands out for Teilhard helps to explain the first thing. This is the "law of complexification," as he calls it. This law has a number of specific aspects. First is the tendency of material reality to scatter and differentiate. From the primordial Big Bang onward, differentiation has been the rule. From raw energy came the four basic forces and eventually different types of material particles. From the first, however, forms of convergence also took place, in which the differentiated forces and particles interacted or united to form more complex realities. Quarks unite to form protons and neutrons, which in turn unite with each other and eventually with electrons to form atoms. Diverse types of atoms unite to form compounds like water and carbon dioxide, and so on. Later writers will call this process "emergence."

The cosmos crossed a major threshold when some of those diverse compounds formed so complex a unity that life appeared for the first time. When life appears the "within" aspect of the material universe becomes more evident. Life is active response to the environment. Life itself leads on to more explicit forms of consciousness until it arrives at human consciousness, another major threshold crossed. The "interiority" present all along in the history of the universe has achieved its greatest manifestation in us reflectively self-conscious humans, so far as we know.

Teilhard focuses on the human home, the planet earth. He calls it the geosphere, on which there now floats a thin biosphere. In and on this biosphere for the last tens of thousands of years a "noosphere" has been developing. "*Nous*" is the ancient Greek word for mind. The name "noosphere" points to the fact of humankind spreading out across the planet. Teilhard also refers to this stage as "hominization," signifying the spread and development of human consciousness across the face of the earth.

The cosmic law of complexification has not stopped with the appearance of human consciousness, Teilhard claims. First humans differentiated, making the planet home to thousands of cultures and languages. In many places convergence took over once again. The great civilizations of the world represent the unification of different peoples into larger social, economic, and political order. Differentiation thereby increased also, with the appearance of social classes and division of labor into different types of work. Out of these differences rose ideals of social convergence, in the United Nations' Universal Declaration of Human Rights, for example, and of economic convergence, as in the process of globalization occurring now. Teilhard today would have celebrated the internet as the newest form of international convergent hominization.

Differentiation and convergence on an ever-higher level of complexity has been the ongoing law of the cosmos, says Teilhard. There is no reason why we should expect it to stop now. The convergence of human consciousness can be expected to cross another threshold eventually, even if we cannot yet imagine what it will be like. Complexification has always meant rising to another level of consciousness, however, another expansion of the "within" of things into a more fully explicit state. So we should expect that also will be the human future. More "conscientization" will be the outcome. The future will be "hyper-personal"—some sort of state beyond the personal.

So far Teilhard claims this description of cosmic evolution remains fully within the boundaries of science's naturalism. It describes what in fact has happened, according to the evident long-term pattern of differentiation and convergence into greater complexity, which in turn manifests higher consciousness, and extrapolates more of the same to come.

Teilhard's analysis then takes an explicitly religious and somewhat poetic turn. Convergence into complexity manifests a "tendency to unite," he says. In humans this tendency achieves its highest and most meaningful form in love. As with consciousness in general, however, the tendency to unite which we call love has been a tendency in all things, albeit on a simpler level. The "within" of things has apparently always contained not just the potential for higher and higher consciousness but for greater and greater forms of unity. We can say then that the force driving the universe from within is love—or at least what we call love in its human form.

Teilhard turns to his own religious tradition to make further sense of this process. "God is love" says the first Epistle of John in the New Testament (4:8). The God who creates and propels and guides the universe has embedded in the universe a kind of divine love as its driving force, Teilhard declares. John's Gospel begins by speaking of the divine Word (*logos*), through whom all things are made. This divine consciousness lies within the universe guiding it. Even more specifically connected to Christ, the Letter to the Colossians by Paul speaks of Christ as "the first-born of all creation" and as the one in whom "all things hold together" (1:15, 17). All things therefore are a mode of the presence and power of God, not only in a very general sense but specifically in those elements of consciousness and love which have been the goal of the universe up until now.

This is not the final goal, Teilhard says again. Hyper-personalization awaits the human race as a whole. A point of total convergence has yet to arrive. God is Alpha and Omega, says the book of the Apocalypse. As Alpha God is the beginning and basis of all things; as Omega God is the fulfillment of all things. Religiously speaking, eventual total convergence will be the Omega Point. The purpose of cosmic history, therefore, has been for the cosmos to return to union with God through human consciousness, when that consciousness achieves the unity with God promised as eternal life.

There is much more to Teilhard's vision, some of it arising from his Jesuit training in mysticism and the practice of "finding God in all things," some of it perhaps adjusted to fit the demands of Catholic doctrine of the mid-20th century. This short sketch, nonetheless, captures some of the flavor of a highly mysticized but also detailed interpretation of cosmic history.

Teilhard's vision is clearly not a metaphysical naturalism; belief in a Creator is central to it. The vision is closer to a cosmological naturalism, in which God has planned, created, and sustains the entire universe in a single miraculous act of creation, drawing it forward somehow to a point of fulfillment. Teilhard writes as though the long cosmic process of development did not need any interventions by God. Given the beliefs of the Catholic Church of those days, to which he strove to remain faithful, he might have settled for a bare methodological naturalism, still leaving room for miracles. In his overall thought, however, miracles would be quite unimportant. To find God no one need look for divine interventions. Teilhard views the entire cosmos as shouting out the presence and purposes of God.

Critics of Teilhard's vision will often grant him the right to be awed by cosmic history, including the history of life on this planet. Carl Sagan, for example, shares in this sense of awe even though he does this as a metaphysical naturalist. Teilhard crosses over into poetic excess, perhaps, when he declares that "love" is the driving force of the development of the universe. But it seems clear to the skeptics that when Teilhard attributes all this to a divine power and presence, that Teilhard is simply applying his prior religious faith to science's view of the universe. The skeptics, of course, do not share that faith.

The anthropic principles

Teilhard began with belief in God and with several specific aspects of that belief, such as that God is love. Many an atheist, however, has judged Teilhard's vision to be just a poetic attempt to cover over the aimlessness of the cosmos with blankets of comforting images. With much greater attention to extremely specific scientific details about the universe, some thinkers have responded by striving to make a scientific case that there had to have been a Designer of the universe who made the universe such that something like human life was bound to appear. This does not differ from Teilhard's basic notions substantially, but it adds a stronger argument for believing in a Planner-Creator God. The argument is called the strong anthropic principle (SAP).[2] It is a form of deism, but applied to an evolving rather than a static universe.

"*Anthropos*" is the Greek word for human person. The strong anthropic principle says that the universe seems to be set up exactly right to eventually produce intelligent life, like humans. A more precisely accurate name for this argument would be to call it "the argument from fine tuning." Others have called it the "goldilocks" argument, named after the fairy tale character who rejected things that were too big or too small, too hot or too cold, too soft or too hard, and was satisfied only when she found things that were just right. The universe, says the anthropic principle, seems to have been fine tuned so that things are just right for the long process of cosmic and biological evolution that leads to the emergence of intelligent life like us humans.

There is a weak anthropic principle (WAP). The fact that we humans are here and able to ask questions about the universe is obvious evidence that the order of this universe can give rise to and support human life. If the universe had not been such as to allow us to exist, then we would not be here to ask anything about it. The universe we encounter is necessarily human-friendly, to that extent. SAP analysis goes further to find multiple ways in which the universe had to be very precisely tuned to make humans possible at all. So many fine-tunings exist, says the SAP, that they could not all have appeared and converged by chance alone to make a human-friendly universe. A little background concerning the universe is needed to understand the arguments offered in favor of the SAP.

The four basic forces in the universe, as indicated earlier are (1) the electromagnetic force, which manifests itself in electricity, magnetism, and light; (2) gravity, a relatively feeble force were it not a characteristic of every object in the universe with mass; (3) the strong force, which binds together the protons and neutrons in the nucleus of an atom; and (4) the weak force, which affects the quarks of which protons and neutrons are composed. According to the SAP it turns out that each one of these forces has the very precise strength that would allow the multi-billion-year processes to take place that include the evolution of stars and planets and thus produce the conditions for life to be possible. Each of the forces must individually be within certain fairly limited parameters as well as interact with each other very precisely to produce such a universe. Together they create the time span needed, first for galactic clouds to form, then for stars to be born in those clouds, then for the sequence of expansions and collapses which produce heavier elements needed for planets to form and for the complex compounds out of which life might arise. With all this in place even more billions of years must pass for life to appear and gradually develop the level of complexity of conscious beings.

The core of the SAP argument is that many things must have been exactly right— finely tuned—for all this to occur, starting with the precise strength of the four basic forces of nature. Had gravity been a small percentage weaker, the original hydrogen and helium would have expanded outward so quickly as to never form the galactic clouds that give birth to stars. Without some massive stars, no heavier elements would form, and no planets or life would even have been possible. If the force of gravity had been a small percentage stronger it would have been strong enough to make the universe collapse into a big crunch in less than a billion years. So no stars would have had time to form, nor would life have time to evolve. The sun and planet earth and life in general would never have been possible.

The other three basic forces also need such fine tuning. If the weak force were too weak, no protons or neutrons would have formed. If it were too strong very odd protons and neutrons would probably form—or none at all. If electromagnetism were off just a little bit either way, the electromagnetic bonds between atoms would not make possible the complex combinations that contribute to life, such as amino acids. The box just below points out that the strong force, which holds protons and neutrons together in elements more complex than simple hydrogen, had to be tuned just right also. The list of fine-tunings is a very long one, and carries a reader deep into fine complexities of physics and chemistry.

Here is a brief sample of a very specific and somewhat difficult analysis of a single basic force in the universe and how finely tuned it has had to be. It is difficult to understand, especially because of language such as "10E+18." Other paragraphs are even more obscure. Do not worry if this paragraph is unclear to you; it only illustrates the extent to which an argument for SAP attends to very precise details.

The *nuclear strong force*, too, must be neither over-strong nor over-weak for stars to operate life-encouragingly. "As small an increase as 2%" in its strength "would block the formation of protons out of quarks," preventing the existence even of hydrogen atoms,[35] let alone others. If this argument fails then the same small increase could still spell disaster by binding protons into diprotons: all hydrogen would now become helium early in the Bang[36] and stars would burn by the strong interaction[37] which, as noted above, proceeds 10E+18 times faster than the weak interaction which controls our sun. A yet tinier increase, perhaps of 1%, would so change nuclear resonance levels that almost all carbon would be burned to oxygen.[38] A somewhat greater increase, of about 10%, would again ruin stellar carbon synthesis, this time changing resonance levels so that there would be little burning beyond carbon's predecessor, helium.[39] One a trifle greater than this would lead to "nuclei of almost unlimited size,"[40] even small bodies becoming "mini neutron stars."[41] All which is true despite the very short range of the strong force. Were it long-range then the universe would be "wound down into a single blob."[42]

This passage is from a much longer essay by John Leslie at
http://www.origins.org/articles/leslie_prerequisiteslife.html

See Leslie's book, Universes *(Routledge, 1989), chs. 2 & 3 for more detail.*

(Though the complex paragraph above appears on the Origins site, a set of pages devoted to promoting Intelligent Design arguments, this particular article is by a person whose overall analysis of SAP is very cautious and competent, as in his book Universes *(NY: Routledge, 1989). For a description of many specific "fine tunings" see chapters 2 & 3 of* Universes.*)*

Another set of finely tuned conditions make this particular planet a safe home for life to develop over 4.5 billion years from the planet's primordial beginnings to us. Our planet is marvelously well situated, far enough from the sun not to be crisped, close enough to keep most of its water in a liquid state. Its tilt assures that different parts of the globe receive good doses of warming at different seasons, so the zone for life to develop is large. The moon has enough gravitational drag on the planet so as to keep it from wobbling about. A severe case of wobbles would condemn too many areas to long periods of overheating alternating with long periods of freeze. The giant planets Jupiter and Saturn sweep up enough debris from the solar system that this planet is no longer bombarded constantly by meteors, but allow a few through, to upset the order of life on the planet and send the evolutionary process off in new directions occasionally, one of which directions produced us. The outer core of the planet, made of iron, generates an electromagnetic field around the earth that protects life from excessive solar radiation. The list of planetary conditions supportive of life is quite long. At times a person will include the "just right" conditions of the planet earth as part of an SAP argument.[3]

This is much weaker, however, than it may at first seem. In a galaxy with a hundred billion stars, and with a hundred billion other galaxies each with their own stars, it is not surprising that at least one planet would win the cosmic lottery and be just right for the evolution of life to our stage of complexity. For even a few such planets to exist there *need* not be any original Designer. Of course, there still *could* have been one who created galaxies such that the odds would favor an earth-like planet or two. Such wonderful planetary conditions, nonetheless, provide evidence for only a weak anthropic principle.

The main force of the SAP therefore lies not in the special qualities of planet earth but in the finely tuned factors that make any stars and planets at all possible in the first place. If our universe is the only universe that has existed, say SAP proponents, it would be extraordinarily unlikely that all these factors would converge to produce a "just right" goldilocks set of conditions that make human life possible and perhaps some sort

174 Understanding Religion and Science

of intelligent life probable or even inevitable. This is so enormously unlikely, says the SAP, that it is evidence that the universe was designed by a cosmic Intelligence.

Conundrums still abound. We have no way, at least not at present, of getting behind the four basic forces of nature to see why these forces emerged and at precisely the strength they actually have. We can ask, without being able to answer, whether there is something about the original raw energy of the universe that forces it to collapse partly into those forces at their actual strength. If physicists ever manage to connect up all aspects of the universe, from quarks (and whatever composes them) and quantum conditions, all the way to gravity and everything in between in one coherent theory, perhaps that will provide more answers. Perhaps.

Skeptical responses to the SAP

Scientists who are skeptical about the SAP have speculated there may be multiple universes, even an endless number of different universes, each with different basic laws. The word "multiverse" has been coined to label this position. If true, then the odds increase that at least one of these universes would happen to have the fine-tuning that would lead to intelligent life. If not, if this is the only universe that exists, then it would be much more plausible to argue that the universe was deliberately fine tuned by some supra-cosmic Intelligence to produce *anthropos*—if not precisely us humans, nonetheless some intelligent form of life. At this point it is difficult to say whether this is the only universe that has existed. No one has seen or experienced other universes, nor is there even indirect evidence of other universes. So their existence is highly speculative.

The speculation includes several possibilities. One is that a whole universe such as ours can arise from a fluctuation of the quantum vacuum. The nature of this quantum vacuum is also somewhat speculative; how it might come to fluctuate is also. If it sounds like getting something from nearly nothing, speculation proposes that this near-nothingness exploded out into complexity in such a way that the sum of all the matter and forces of the universe is zero (or something like that). An instance of this would be matter and anti-matter, each annihilating the other back to near-nothingness when they meet.

Others have argued that there may be an infinite sequence of universes, each of which collapses upon itself in a Big Crunch with all its energy and matter then emerging on "the other side," whatever that might be, in a Big Bang of a new universe (or brand new state of the stuff of a single cyclical universe). Stephen Hawking, the famous physicist, has recently undercut this possibility by claiming that a black hole can eventually release its content, back into the universe from which it came. At the same time the expansion of this universe seems to be increasing, not decreasing. An increase in the rate of expansion implies that the universe will spend all its energy into the infinite rather than collapse in a Big Crunch.

Further speculation has it that every time a quantum state of an electron resolves itself into this position or that mass, the alternative possibility also exists—and thereby generates a different universe. Given the innumerable—literally innumerable–such quantum events, there would have to be innumerable universes being generated at any moment. This speculation seems even more bizarre than others. It is not important here to sort all these speculations out. The purpose of describing a few of them is to make clear that there are a great number of possibilities, all of them speculative—i.e., very uncertain.[4] Their main impact so far, is to allow skeptics a way around the SAP argument by the notion of multiverses.

Skepticism about the SAP argument for the existence of a Designer may be based on the notion of God or Designer a person has. Some like Richard Dawkins, find any notion of God highly implausible because the word "God" implies to them an anthropomorphic agent who intervenes in history and nature.[5] Such skeptics think that both the demands of rationality and the success of science in closing the gaps where people used to find God show that no such God exists. So they resist the idea of a supra-cosmic Designer God as well.

Theologians claim it is more accurate to think of God as the Uncaused Cause, perfectly simple and changeless. Whatever produced the universe—whether a quantum vacuum fluctuation or some mysterious energy or something else—still produced what we must at least think of as a universe quite precisely tuned for eventually producing conscious life. The theologians might ask, why it is not legitimate to think of this as "what everyone calls God," on the grounds it did what a Creator would do, if there were one? Even in fact what a Designer would do, if there were one? (Later we will see that some today who argue for a Designer also argue this Designer operates through interventions in nature, through miracles.)

God and the universe in process theology

First came "process *philosophy*," mentioned earlier in Chapter 6. Though its founder, Alfred North Whitehead, devoted a few pages to the idea of God, he did not develop this idea very thoroughly. Then came a small flurry of process *theologies*. The version promoted by Charles Hartshorne has proved the most fruitful for most people. The description which follows is based mainly on Hartshorne's ideas with a few simplifications.[6]

There is no use asking questions about why there is a universe at all, says Hartshorne. Such metaphysical questions are unanswerable. Accept the fact of the universe and worry only about how it operates and what must be true for it to operate that way.

Following Whitehead, Hartshorne asserted that the basic stuff of which the universe is made are tiny events or "actual occasions," by which he meant points of energy-happenings. This is what atoms consist of—complex points of energy. The universe is not static; its basic nature is to be in process, with every event occurring and then immediately fading into another event, instant by instant.

Each little event has two aspects to it. One is the passive aspect, of being affected by other events. The other aspect is active; it is the response the event makes to the influence of other events. These active responses can even be called "free" in the limited sense that any event can respond to outside influence in a variety of ways, not just a single way.

Whitehead used Teilhardian-like language for some of this (both of them were influenced by previous philosophers). Each event's passive aspect can be called its material aspect (or physical "pole"); and each event's active aspect can be called its mental aspect (or, again mental "pole"). Just as for Teilhard, the ability of anything to respond actively to its environment is a "within," an interiority that blossoms eventually into consciousness in animals and into self-aware consciousness in humans.

The universe has been evolving ever great levels of complexity, says Whitehead, still in step with Teilhard on this point. Why is that so? Whitehead and Hartshorne argue that there must be some force that draws the moments of the universe toward the sort of balanced complexities one finds in higher organisms and in whole ecologies. Whitehead says that this force produces the sort of balanced but dynamic order we call beauty. But Whitehead also says explicitly that this force apparently is not a coercive force, because the order and complexity that contribute to beauty mix everywhere with a degree of breakdown or stagnation. The universe contains both good and bad. This is a sign of the "freedom" which every event possesses.

Process theology therefore looks for a cosmic influence that has certain attributes. First it must contain within itself in some way or another some ideal standards of order and complexity, of consciousness and beauty. Second, it must be able to exert some sort of pressure on the universe to get it to adopt degrees of order, complexity, consciousness, and beauty. Third, because of the incompleteness of this ordered complexity, the basic force must allow the moments of the universe some real freedom to say yes or no to the possibilities which the force seeks to make real. So the force must restrain itself to *luring* or calling to the moments of the universe, providing goals ("initial aims") for each event to achieve as its own next best possibility.

Hartshorne expands upon Whitehead's original ideas about God to translate this process philosophy into a full theology. "God" is the name for the cosmic force which has been luring the pieces of the universe into an order that includes ever-greater complexity, consciousness, and beauty. The eternal aspect of God is the changeless set of ideals which somehow lie within this force. The eternal side is God's unchanging personality, so to speak. God is not, however, entirely eternal. This personality belongs to a cosmic Self which is active in the world. Its action consists of luring every event to live up to its next best possibilities. So the whole universe is contained within the scope of the activity of God. The word for this is "panentheism"—all-IN-God-ism. The universe itself is not divine. That would be "pantheism"—all-God-ism. God does contain the whole universe, nonetheless, within the scope of the divine ideals and action.

This provides an interesting answer to the question of whether God intervenes in the world. The answer is a sweeping affirmative. God intervenes at every moment and everywhere by luring, calling, tempting, inviting every single event to its next best possibility. This God also acts upon every person as a set of events, always calling or inviting every person to their next best possibility. Interestingly, however, this constant intervention occurs on so subtle a level as to be invisible, except in the long-term effects of order, consciousness, and so on.

Process theology has become quite popular in the U.S. among those in the field of religion and science who want to reconcile religion and science. It allows a much more specific analysis of the interaction between God and the world than mysticized science approaches. It also provides a defense against one of the most troubling problems of theism, known traditionally as "the problem of evil." As noted earlier, it would be clearer to call this the problem of suffering. The problem again is this: if one conceives of God as perfect intelligence (omniscient) and also, as is traditional, as perfectly good and perfectly powerful (omnipotent), why do so many people, including little children, suffer from disease, debilities, disasters, and death? Process theology answers that God is not coercive but persuasive. God allows all of creation some degree of freedom. The price of freedom is often pain. God is always at work nonetheless calling creation to a better form.

Islamic tradition might applaud process thought for coming closer to the truth. Muslim occasionalism, as the chapter defining miracles pointed out, says that God's will is the cause of every event that takes place in the universe. Process thought, however, grants to all the actual occasions of the universe a greater degree of independence than Islamic theology. In Islam even the free choices a person makes are caused by God. (This presents special theological problems. Those who choose to do evil thereby end up in hell. If God's will has directed those choices, argued some medieval Muslim philosophers, it is not fair that a person goes to hell. These philosophers eventually lost the argument. Stricter Muslim thinkers refused to restrict the range of God's will at all.)

Among current religious writers John Haught has produced what may be the most eloquent extension of Whiteheadian ideas about the cosmos, joining to it the more specifically Christian vision of Teilhard. Haught proposes that an adequate religious interpretation of the universe must embrace both cosmic and biological evolution and find in all of this a divine influence that calls everything to an ultimate fulfillment. He asserts that "the cosmos is embraced by an incomprehensible divine mystery that promises an eternal significance and unimagined coherence to the sequence of happenings that make up evolution and our lives within it."[7]

Haught gets more specific by using somewhat more anthropomorphic language about God. God has created a universe to be free in its development. Where the skeptic sees aimless randomness in cosmic history, Haught envisions God tenderly luring all of reality toward an increase of diversity, complexity, and beauty, but always leaving that reality free in its development. The universe's own experiments with possibilities for the future take place within the context of a cosmic aim provided by God.

Haught does not try to prove God's existence and guidance of the universe, though he finds clues of the divine activity in the development of mind and meaning over cosmic time. Haught's main goal is to argue that a metaphysical naturalism is much too limiting an understanding of reality, and that an adequate cosmic view must dig deeper than scientific naturalism.

Conclusion

Four types of cosmic visions have appeared in this chapter—mysticized cosmos, Teilhardian, the SAP analysis, and Process thought. These do not exhaust the possibilities, as was said at the beginning. Haught's use of more than one of them to create his own synthesis illustrates this also. The many possible universes listed in Chapter 11 indicate some other options available. The four discussed here represent a sampling of some major alternatives, ones commonly promoted today by those seeking to reconcile religion and science's view of the cosmos.

Metaphysical naturalists, however, look at the same cosmic history, and at what seems to be a deep degree of randomness in cosmic evolution, and continue to wonder how religious people can live comfortably with the story of the cosmos. Not even the SAP seems to give the skeptics pause. This may be because invoking a divine cause of anything sits poorly with naturalism. The skeptics are metaphysical naturalists.

Cosmic evolution is the background for biological evolution. A fully naturalistic interpretation of the history of life presents an additional challenges to religious belief, as well as opportunities for religious thinkers to reinterpret those beliefs in a new context. The next three chapters will review biological aspects of the cosmic story.

For further reading

Barrow, John D., *Theories of Everything: The Quest for Ultimate Explanation* (Oxford: Clarendon Press, 1991). Dense but intelligible description of theories of the universe.

Sagan, Carl, *Cosmos* (New York: Random House, 1980 and 2002). The script of the well-known television series. A gentle but firm atheism with an awed metaphysical naturalism.

Schroder, Gerald L., *Genesis and the Big Bang: The Discovery of Harmony between Modern Science and the Bible* (New York: Bantam, 1990). Schroeder uses traditional Judaic interpretations of the Hebrew Scriptures and adds some scientific twists of his own.

Weinberg, Stephen, *Dreams of a Final Theory: The Scientist's Search for the Ultimate Laws of Nature* (New York: Vintage, 1994). A few chapters here promote metaphysical naturalism, though not by that full name.

Part Six
Biological Evolution: how did we get here?

Basic Theories of Evolution 14

The origin of the theory

William Paley's 1802 final edition of his *Natural Theology* was required reading at Cambridge University for some years, including when Darwin later attended. Darwin learned it well. This work was, perhaps, the last great exposition of an argument from design based on what we might call the "old" universe. This was the universe of the Bible, created about 6,000 years earlier. The Bible seemed fairly clear on the age of the earth. If one could accurately date, say, the year of the death of Alexander the Great (323 BCE), or King David (967? BCE), then it would be possible to use genealogies in Genesis to count backwards to the appearance of Adam. Church of England Archbishop Ussher did precisely that, concluding around 1650 that God created the universe in 4004 BCE, beginning on the evening of October 23, a Sunday of course—the first day of the week.

The Archbishop would have agreed that in the previous five thousand six hundred and some years the universe had remained basically the same, except for at least two major events. The first was "the Fall," also called by Western Christianity "Original Sin."

This was an act of disobedience by the first humans, a rebellion against God's instructions not to eat of the tree of the knowledge of good and evil. As the Western Christian tradition developed, especially under the influence of Augustine, this disobedience was blamed for disrupting enormously not only the relation between humans and God but also the order of nature in general, thereby accounting for natural disasters.

The second great event was the universal flood recounted in the book of Genesis. Although Noah and the other seven people on the great ark saved two of every "kind" of unclean animal and seven of every "kind" of clean (legitimate to eat) animal, all other land-based life on the planet was temporarily wiped out (vegetation apparently sprang back up again when the waters receded). The sloshing of the waters, pouring down through the flood gates of the firmament (the sky-dome), and erupting upwards from the watery underground depths, accounted for the many seashells embedded in rocks on mountaintops.

In spite of these two disruptions of nature, God's basic creation remained the same. The same grasses and other plants created on the third day nourished animals and birds and people created on the sixth day. After the flood God also allowed carnivorous life styles for humans and for many animals. Most importantly, the basic structures of every "kind" remained as God had first created them. Paley could presume that the life forms around him in the world were relatively unchanged since their origin. Paley only needed to show, he thought, that these forms were so marvelously constructed as to be a clear sign that they were the result of deliberate design and not the result of accident.

Paley's argument was a powerful one. Many are familiar with the general opening argument. If a person stumbles across a rock, the rock will appear to be just a random object. But if a person stumbles across a watch, even a brief inspection makes it clear that the watch was designed for a purpose. It is not just that a watch is complex. A thunderstorm is complex also; but it does not give the appearance of having been designed for a purpose. It is the orderly and intricate arrangement of the parts of a watch and their very regular interaction that cries out "deliberate design." Play with the watch and see how moving one part makes another move, how a whole sequence of motions follow up the first, in the same order each time. Even if the watch is imperfect or is broken, even if in fact the person has never seen a watch before, says Paley, the orderly and intricate arrangement of the parts and their effect on one another still says "design."

Only two short chapters at the beginning of *Natural Theology* make this general argument. The entire rest of the book provides specifics to illustrate the extent to which the natural world has thousands of such watches, each one evidently constructed intelligently to carry out some purpose. Paley discusses a variety of plants of different types and their complex structure that allows the plants to grow, thrive, adapt to changes in the environment, and reproduce. He does the same with a large number of animals, noting the wonderful construction of eyes and knees and heart, and so on. He considers the many forms of insects, each with complex organs and structures to enable them to survive, eat, avoid enemies, and reproduce. The ability of spiders to construct their webs is a true marvel all by itself. How does this tiny arachnid with no brain to speak of, know how to create such webs? Example after example fill the pages of Paley's book.

But even as Paley refined his ideas, evolutionary ideas were afoot in Great Britain and Europe, ideas about the cosmos, about the geology of the earth, about life forms, and even about culture.

Pre-Darwinian ideas of forms of evolutionary change

Speculation about an evolving cosmos extends back at least to the philosopher Descartes, who explored the idea of cosmic evolution in his *Principles of Philosophy* in the early 17th century, though he concluded that any cosmic process of change had proceeded mechanically up to the present stable, no longer evolving order of things. In 1755 Immanuel Kant had gone further, offering more arguments and extending his speculation into rather wild realms of thought for the time in his *Universal Natural History and Theory of the Heavens*. Laplace's later work, mentioned briefly earlier here, was a continuation of this line. All of them offered descriptions of a cosmic evolution—or at least of the solar system.[1]

Others began to find evidence to justify evolutionary theories about the surface of the earth. The geologists of the 18th and earliest 19th centuries had mostly resisted theories about a long period of geological evolution. Neither were they much impressed by speculations concerning cosmic evolution. Instead they were mostly people raised to accept the Bible and the traditional interpretation that God had created the world much as it is now. They could account for many strange formations on earth by supposing that the great flood of Noah's time was not the only large catastrophe. The Bible could not contain an account of every event that had ever occurred; it would take much too long a book to do this. But a great number may have occurred, if God so chose. That could include lesser catastrophes such as the destruction by God of the ancient cities of Sodom and Gomorrah.

This way of interpreting the earth's history was known as "catastrophism." A key issue in this position was, however, not so much the bare fact of catastrophes, but the belief that these catastrophes had been caused by divine intervention within a time span of only a few thousand years. Traditional geologists believed that the biblical account of the history of the whole world was at least approximately correct, so that the estimate made by Archbishop Ussher that the earth was created in 4004 B.C. was plausible to them.[2]

The idea that the earth itself, however, had also undergone a very long process of change, a kind of geological evolution, could make sense of all sorts of evidence that had been accumulating, from the sea shells on mountains, to the layering of rock as seen in ravines and coal mines and on mountainsides and along oceans, as well as the layering of different kinds of fossils in those strata of rock, to the remnants left behind in various layers along the paths of glaciers, to observation of present-day erosion and the laying down of sediment and the activity of volcanoes.

By 1795 James Hutton was able to assemble a vast range of data in favor of "uniformitarianism." This was the theory that the current condition of the earth was not the result of a few past catastrophes like Noah's flood. It was instead the product of long uniform processes of the same kind that were still occurring, to build up mountains and erode them down again, to send up volcano after volcano to spread large fields of lava upon previous fields of lava, to gradually lay down silt deposits in rivers and oceans. Because of Hutton's careful analysis of geological strata in his 1795 work, *Theory of the Earth*, he has been called the discoverer of "deep time," the many millions of years, as they thought, of earth history. Building on this, Charles Lyell (1797–1875) confirmed Hutton's uniformitarianism with his 3-volume (1830–1833) *Principles of Geology*, read by Charles Darwin during his voyages aboard the H. M. S. *Beagle*.

The name uniformitarianism is a bit misleading. The uniform process of nature, after all, can produce many catastrophes. This word nonetheless identified the position of those who interpreted the geological evidence as signs of an extremely long process operating by natural causes. (Seashells on mountains were thought to be due to the rising and falling of continents, bobbing up and down in place over long eons.)

In the 18th century there were theories of the evolution of culture also. The voyages to strange lands and peoples that had been going on since the end of the 15th century had brought a confusion of information about tribal life. The discovery of the new world and its inhabitants evoked worried discussions about human nature. As long as Europeans had contact mainly with complex literate civilizations like Islam or had knowledge of major cultures along the silk route, the Europeans could suppose that people fit into a limited range of behavior. The book of Genesis says that the second son of Adam and Eve, Cain, who killed his brother Abel, found a wife in the city. City-life therefore must somehow have been part of the original condition of humans. The other part included farms, large and small, and even some very primitive forest life by people whose life-style had apparently degenerated into simple hunting and gathering.

But suddenly from the East Indies, Africa, and especially the Americas it was clear that human beings were more various in thoughts and beliefs and morals and government and worship than had been dreamed of. Most importantly, it looked as though a primitive hunting and gathering life was extremely common across wide swathes of North and South America. New theories of the evolution of culture tried to make sense of all of this.[3]

Jean Jacques Rousseau (1712–1778) claimed that humans developed from a state of savagery to one of civilization, though Rousseau had mixed emotions about which of these two was better ("savagery" meant life in the wild, not wildly irrational or vicious). The late 18th century Scottish Enlightenment saw a number of interrelated theories by

David Hume, Adam Smith, and others about stages of cultural evolution from savagery to their contemporary scientific times.[4] After another century of scientific developments, the intellectuals of the late 19th century had reason to perceive progress in history; they considered themselves and their accomplishments to be the high point of cultural evolution. They were interested in identifying the major stages of that evolution.

It is not at all surprising that in the midst of all the 18th century evolutionary theories of the cosmos, the earth, and society, there were also various theories of biological evolution. A hundred years before Darwin, a French mathematician-astronomer named Maupertuis (1698–1757) had speculated on whether the species on the earth now, could have descended from earlier species, through a process something like natural selection. He was trying to make sense of fossils of animals which no longer existed, but which were similar in important ways to animals which did exist in his time. Was there a relation between a mastodon and elephants; what about the saber-tooth tiger and current-day tigers? Maupertuis concluded that evolution of one kind of tiger from another earlier kind was theoretically possible, but of course it had not happened.

A significant contribution to early evolutionary thought appeared in 1796, more than a dozen years before Darwin's birth, written by his grandfather, Erasmus Darwin. He was a bit bolder than Maupertuis. His book, *Zoonomia*, proposed there indeed had been a very long and progressive biological evolutionary process.

The most important evolutionist of the early 19th century was Jean Baptiste Lamarck (1744–1829).[5] In a work entitled *Philosophie Zoologique* (1809), he argued that evolution took place through the acquiring of new characteristics through the life experiences of the organism, characteristics that were then passed on to the next generation. A giraffe which stretched its neck to reach leaves high on a tree would acquire a longer neck, and would pass on the slightly elongated neck to the next generation. If the next-generation giraffe stretched just a bit further, it would hand on a yet longer neck. Unfortunately for Lamarck's theory, there was a fair amount of evidence against this. (After 2,000 or more years of circumcision of all Jewish males, this change is still not passed on to the next generation.) Yet for those persuaded that there had been an evolutionary process, it was necessary to find some theory or another to explain how it had happened. In the absence of a competing theory, Lamarck's was supported by many, including atheists or skeptics who liked the naturalism of Lamark's explanation—no divine intervention is required to account for a sequence of development.

Though many religious people rejected theories of geological evolution on the grounds that the Bible told a different story, early geological theories were nonetheless not intrinsically unreligious. It looked as though there had been mass extinctions of species every so often. At points in the geological strata, entire groups of fossils that had been abundant would suddenly disappear. A few layers would then show relatively fewer fossils of any kind for a time; then higher layers would show a great increase in the diversity and number of fossils, many of them from new species. An opinion favored by many was that God, for God's own inscrutable purposes, had wiped out most life at various times, and then created new life forms. The evidence of mass extinctions and then the appearance of multiple new species served as extra reason to see God's hand in nature. Louis Agassiz, an anti-evolutionary naturalist, supported a view that the 60 to 100 various mass destructions of old life-forms and the appearance of new ones were God's work: "Here again the intervention of the Creator is displayed in the most striking manner, in every stage of the history of the world."[6]

The five largest mass extinction events

1. Cretaceous-Tertiary (K/T), ca. 65 mya (million years ago). Dinosaurs were among those wiped out. About 50% of all biological species disappear from the subsequent geologic strata.
2. Triassic-Jurassic, ca. 200 mya. About 20% of all marine families (and up to 50% of all marine genera) go extinct, as well as many land life forms.
3. Permian-Triassic, ca. 251 mya, the largest extinction of all, 'the Great Dying." This included the disappearance of 53% of marine families, 84% of marine genera, about 96% of all marine species, and an estimated 70% of land species (including plants, insects, and vertebrate animals).
4. Devonian-Carboniferous "transition," ca. 360 mya, but with many extinctions in this general period occurring over 20 mya, during which time about 70% of all species disappeared.
5. Ordovician-Silurian, ca. 440 mya, with two major extinction periods. Close to 50% of marine genera died out.

The causes of these major extinctions are not clear. Some evidence favors the theory of Walter and Luis Alvarez and colleagues, that the K/T extinction was caused by an asteroid about 6 miles thick. It crashed to earth near the Yucatan Peninsula, throwing up vast amounts of water and earth, setting fires which clouded over the atmosphere. This caused the death of much plant life, on which large herbivorous dinosaurs depended, which in turn were the food source for carnivorous dinosaurs. (Mounds of rotting dinosaur carcasses, however, might feed a lot of tiny early mammals for a long time.) While it is clear that an asteroid did hit at that time, it may have only been the coup de grace, on top of other climatic changes. Paleontologists still struggle to account for extinction events, larger and smaller. It appears that there is a drop in sea levels associated with many or even most extinctions. An ice age would contribute to this. One theory, for example, proposes that Gondwana, the super-sized aggregate of what would later be entire continents, drifted over the area of the South Pole, where a huge ice cap built up draining water from the seas. Periods of extraordinary volcanic activity could also cloud the skies around the earth, blotting out the sun long enough to initiate an ice age. The Deccan Flats in central India are a remnant of closely paced vast volcanic explosions. Siberia has similar flats. In any case, extinctions large and small make the whole evolutionary process at least appear to be highly random and careless about life. Asteroids, volcanic eruptions, drifting continents, and such have made life's development on this planet take many strange twists. In the long run, it is not just the more fit which survive; it is also the more lucky.

As the reality of the evolution of the earth and perhaps of the solar system sank in, philosophers found a number of ways to picture a divine presence in it. In 1844 Robert Chambers, in his *Vestiges of the Natural History of Creation*, provided careful arguments to claim the long process of biological evolution was divinely guided. His intent was to argue against the atheistic use of Lamark's ideas and therefore to defend religion.[7] He ended it with a mild disclaimer about the compatibility of his ideas with religion, saying only that we do not yet know enough to see how the relation of religion and evolutionary science will work out. To many Victorians this was still too radical, too unbiblical. Chambers was aware this might be the case; he published his work anonymously. His authorship was not made public until after his death. The uproar it caused made Darwin hesitant about publishing his own theory.

Purpose in evolution

Some who were skeptical about traditional religious doctrines nonetheless perceived a patterned purposefulness to nature. Thus in England Herbert Spencer's (1820–1903) evolutionism was quasi-religious. He claimed that the whole universe was evolving, physically, biologically, and socially; and that this process of evolution was producing an ever-higher moral sentiment. He argued that religious beliefs, especially religious moral sensibilities, are products of "the religious sentiment." This arose out of the process of evolution and should therefore be treated as evolution's purpose.[8]

Herbert Spencer had published an early version of his theory of social evolution before Darwin's *The Origin of Species*. He joyfully accepted Darwin's theory as an implicit support of his own claim that societies evolve from primitive to advanced, through competition among ideas and social forms, with the rule being: "survival of the fittest." (This was Spencer's phrase originally, not Darwin's, used by Darwin eventually in a later edition of *The Origin of Species*.) Spencer's ideas were a reflection of 19th century capitalism. He believed that the pain and misery experienced by the poor, the abused laborers in the new factories, the backward cultures of the world, were part of a grand evolutionary scheme of nature, which by weeding out the less fit would automatically produce better results in the long run. Totally free competition, however rough it might be in the short run, would create a wealthier, healthier, happier world eventually. Spencer's theory eventually became known as "Social Darwinism."

A German biologist named Ernst Haeckel (1834–1919) illustrates the thoroughly materialistic way in which scientific perspectives of the 19th century often interpreted evolution, human life, and the nature and place of religion. He was a materialist in the sense that he disbelieved in any supernatural or spiritual substance. The stuff of the universe (what we today might call matter-energy) was all that is. Yet at the same time Haeckel was impressed with the power of thought. He concluded that mind or psyche or power-to-sense-and-know, to give it a complex title, was an aspect of matter.

We humans are entirely natural and material; and that includes our consciousness. "Consciousness, thought, and speculation . . . [are] functions of the ganglionic cells of the cortex of the brain."[9] What we call soul is a natural phenomenon, not a supernatural or "spiritual" one in the Cartesian or traditional dualistic interpretation, which sees matter and spirit as two different kinds of things.

Haeckel went beyond offering these ideas as science. He proposed that they be part of a *natural* religion, a kind of evolutionary-progressive religiousness in which the name God stood not for any supernatural reality, but only for the basic substance of the universe, accorded almost divine respect for its power to give rise to evolution and to thought. It was a monistic religion—i.e., one without the dualism of matter and spirit.

Haeckel rejected all belief in the supernatural as superstitious, thought that the influence of religious leaders on government was quite harmful, and claimed that Christianity's traditional otherworldliness was bad. At the same time he believed that the ethical teachings of the Christian and other traditions had much in it that was valuable. Human beings should live by an ethic of love of neighbor and also love of self. People should learn to be sympathetic to one another and even to animals. The family is important and must be supported, though the old idea that women are subordinate or inferior to men is harmful and must be eliminated. According to Haeckel, all of this can be learned from the evolution of the natural world. The process is deeply meaningful, directed toward higher values. Knowledge and acceptance of this natural order is true religion. Here is almost a deist's attitude again, only now shifted from a static to an evolving universe and, more importantly, become pantheistic, no longer distinguishing God from the cosmos.

Thus in Darwin's day there were various models of cosmic and biological evolution in competition. These many names and positions are important to historians. It is enough for here, though, to use them just to provide a richer sense of the place of Darwin's theory of evolution in the religious context of the time.

The Darwinian revolution

Darwin published *The Origin of Species* in 1859, defending his theory of how biological evolution had taken place, a theory that he had arrived at almost 20 years earlier. As is often the case, it was not the ingenuity of the theory that counted; others had similar theories before him. His general theory was already in the air in the writings of Adam Smith and Thomas Malthus, from whom Alfred Russell Wallace also picked it up later than Darwin. What was needed was the painstaking work of assembling all the relevant evidence and showing how it all fit together.

The Origin of Species is a sweeping review of information about the distribution of various life-forms on the planet. Much of this information he had gathered first-hand, through his five-year travels around the world on the H. M. S. *Beagle* as an amateur "naturalist" (anyone who studied nature in detail). Some he developed later in England, working on mistletoe and barnacles and worms. Much of it was gleaned from countless reports of other naturalists from various parts of the world. He had many volumes worth of material, and hoped to be able to publish these volumes one by one, because the theory he had slowly developed represented what for those times was still a controversial "naturalism" (here meaning the supposition that only natural causes should be used to explain aspects of nature).

Darwin was compelled to publish his theory in 1859 (he had already circulated a brief version of it in 1844), because Alfred Wallace was about to publish his own version. Feeling rushed, Darwin took pains to indicate that the single volume of 1859 was only an abstract of the information he had, and that he would have liked to publish a fuller explanation and defense of this theory.

Darwin's theory has four major aspects. The first is the reaffirmation of the general belief that evolution occurred: "descent with modification." This line summarizes the conclusion that present-day species are modified descendants of earlier organisms. The next three aspects of Darwin's theory constitute his explanation of *how* this descent-with-modification occurred. The first of these aspects is the raw fact of "superfecundity." Every species has more offspring than will survive, sometime many more. The second aspect is the fact of a natural and somewhat random (unplanned) variation among offspring in a species, especially through sexual reproduction. The third is that there is another seemingly unplanned process of selection of which offspring will survive and which not. This selection occurs most frequently through the struggle for survival. The offspring which die before they can reproduce will not pass on any of their variant characteristics. Darwin later noted that the selection process also includes sexual selection, wherein some males fail to mate, because they were rejected by a female or out-competed by another male. In either case this was a "natural selection" that determined what the next generation would be like.

The overall process is random to a great extent, yet is also "lawful." The variations in the offspring were at each stage just variations on a current species, not a wildly creative process producing utterly new forms of life in a single step. The process is also "lawful" in that there is a severe weeding out of possible life-forms by the environment and the competition for survival and reproduction. Environmental factors place clear limits on what life-forms can survive well and reproduce. Whatever the random variations that happen to occur in any species, in the long run the environmental conditions will support some and kill off others. The result is that surviving species are well adapted to the environment, adapted in thousands, even millions, of very specific ways through a process of what seemed to Darwin to have been a process of well over half a billion years.[10]

The Chicken or the Egg?

Darwin's theory of evolution answers in favor of the egg.

LAMARCK'S THEORY: The chicken adapts to its environment. If its food is on rocky ground, for example, a constant pecking at this hard ground will produce a tougher beak. This change in the chicken will then be passed on to its offspring. So the change in the chicken leads to a new kind of chick, one with a harder beak, that develops in the egg.

DARWIN'S THEORY: No matter how tough a chicken's beak gets that will not produce chicks with harder beaks. (Just as no matter how often the tails are lopped off a certain species of dog, the pups are nonetheless born with full-length tails.) But no offspring is identical to its parents. There is natural variation among offspring (even in non-sexual reproduction some variations appear occasionally). So the egg comes first: a variation in a species appears in the offspring.

CONFUSION OF LANGUAGE: Evolutionists unfortunately sometimes speak of "adaptation" as the mechanism of evolution. By this they mean only that those variants that happen to be better adapted to the environment in which they live will have a better chance at surviving to reproduce and pass on their particular genetic pattern: "reproductive success." Evolutionists do *not* mean that the individual living organisms adapt to their environment, like the individual chicken might adapt to hard ground by developing a hard beak.

CONFUSION OF IDEAS: A major misunderstanding about the evolutionary process is the idea that one species gradually changes until it turns into another species. The evidence indicates that when a new species appears it may usually do so while the old species continues. A new species is an off-shoot *from* the old species, not a transformation of the entire old species.

Darwin's theory supported what many called a "mechanistic" model of reality and others called "materialism." It sustained the scientist's search for naturalist explanations of things rather than supernaturalist ones. It added to the impression that the physical forces at work in the universe could account not just for cosmic and geological processes but also for the development of life-forms and even human beings. The inner workings of living things and how they manage to transmit their basic nature to their offspring was still unknown. But if the evolution of life in the broad sense could be explained as the workings of natural patterns, just as the formation of geological strata and the orbits of the planets could be, then it would seem that everything, life included, could be reduced to "mechanical" or materialist explanations.

A universe in flux

An important implication of Darwin's theory was that it completed the picture of a universe in constant development. The cosmos, the earth, society, and now biological life all share in an endless process of change. This was as disturbing to the 19th century British traditionalists as the loss of "degree" or hierarchy was to Shakespeare's audience.

Darwin's theory abolished the notion of the fixity of species. From before the time of Aristotle, in Greek philosophy as well as in Hebrew (and later Christian) religious thought, it had been assumed or argued that there were basic essences or natures that accounted for why there were dogs and tomatoes and monkeys and people. Plato and Aristotle believed that a dog was a dog because a dog had a dog's nature. But does dogginess necessarily remain the same down through the millennia, regardless of historical change?

The contemporary viewpoint, derived partly from Darwin's theory, is that the name we give a species is just a convenience; and in the long run a temporary convenience. "Dog" is not a changeless nature. The human mind can learn to think of dogginess in a certain way that can be preserved in books and films for centuries or more, giving an kind of artificial permanence to dogginess. But there is no pure essence of dogginess written in heaven that a set of animals will continue to reflect. The current descendants of wolves might all go extinct, but first give rise to a different kind of canine that will go by the name of dog, though we would not be tempted to call it that if we saw it today.

If the human person is also a product of the evolution of the cosmos, then perhaps the same is true of human beings as of dogs. Homo habilis (tool-using human) existed two million years ago, as much like a chimpanzee in form as like homo sapiens, yet human enough to make tools and probably also to use language.[11] Homo erectus was surveying the territory about one million years ago, with a larger brain than homo habilis. Slope-browed Neanderthals roamed and hunted one hundred thousand years ago, only to be replaced (outbred? outhunted? integrated through breeding with other hominids?) by Cro-Magnon or "modern" humans by around thirty thousand years ago. We are descendants of these round-foreheaded, large-brained modern humans. Our descendants in a million more years may be quite unlike us (if we do not become extinct before then).

Every biological thing on the planet, from a virus so relatively simple it probably does not deserve the name "living," to the most complex organisms we know of, ourselves, is a story of "descent with modification." Two paleontologists, Stephen J. Gould and Niles Eldridge, challenged some evolutionary biology by claiming that the descent was a bumpy one, with jerks and jumps here and there in the line of modifications.[12] They call this "punctuated equilibrium." It actually names what Darwin had already noted, that fossils indicate that some species could remain unchanged (in equilibrium) for millions of years, but then suddenly variants could appear (the punctuation), especially after periods of mass extinction. Arguments over this are part of an intramural battle among evolutionists, people who nonetheless all agree that each species is a variation on former species, and that all together are variants on a basic DNA code active within the nucleus of each cell of every living being.

Whether through punctuation or gradual process, each life-form is a transitory moment, a temporary expression of an ongoing process of change, with each moment blending into the next. The process is very slow. Our ancestors can be forgiven for fail-ing to notice it and thinking instead that the basic life-forms are somehow fixed and immutable and forever distinct from one another.

If this is true, then every life-form, just like every temporary feature on the planet and every temporary form of the solar system and galaxy and universe, is one more passing way in which the basic stuff of the universe can exist. All things that are around us now, ourselves as well, are variant ways that matter-energy, as we now think of it, can take shape before moving into new shapes. And if everything is a temporary shape taken by matter-energy, then in a sense everything is just one thing: matter-energy, operating according to the basic physical natural laws of the universe, out of which increasingly complex forms have often emerged.

Disagreements with Darwinism

In addition to the traditional Christian criticisms of evolution, which the next chapter will take up, there were two other and closely related kinds of major disagreements with Darwin's theory of just how evolution took place. One was the belief of Spencer, Haeckel, and others, that there was an inner purposefulness to evolution; the other that each life process had to have some inner vital spirit, like a soul, guiding its individual development and growth.

As we have seen, Spencer claimed there was a special direction to evolution, a kind of invisible hand at work (echoing Adam Smith's image of a capitalist economy). Henri Bergson later promoted a vaguely similar set of ideas in France. Hegelian and other Romantic interpretations of nature did not disappear from Germany. These theories represent ongoing support for models of the evolving universe in which there was a pur-poseful order, perhaps even one planned by a Creator.[13] Fortunately, we do not need to review each of them; it is enough to see that belief in purposefulness was wide-spread.

Darwin, on the contrary, included a double randomness as part of his theory. Both the variations among offspring and the effect of the environment "selecting" among those offspring did not seem to represent any purpose to Darwin. The strange sequence of the fossils, the odd geographical distribution of many species, and in particular the many periods of extinction, great and smaller, seemed quite unplanned to Darwin.

The other major disagreement with Darwin's theory was the conviction that there were too many aspects of life processes that Darwin's mindless mechanistic theory could not explain. It was one thing to accept that an already existing animal could give birth to a near copy of itself. Reproduction was obvious. Those who called themselves "vitalists" insisted that it was something else to show how the mindless cells of an embryo know how to develop into a well-functioning organism, or how this little copy had within it the power to guide wounded tissue to heal itself or, in the case of the sala-mander, to produce an entire new tail. The vitalist Hans Driesch could still argue in

1914 that "The regeneration of the salamander confutes, as is well known, the orthodox Darwinism of Darwin's followers . . . ."[14] Driesch concluded that "The whole life-process is in no way the result of physico-chemical events, but rather controls them." Not just "descent" but an additional guiding vital principle (a life-force) was needed to explain the whole range of life activities, Driesch claimed; so Darwin's model of a purposeless mechanical universe was not adequate.

Social construction of reality?

Those today who still object to Darwinian theory have sometimes taken refuge in the position of social constructivism. They argue that all scientific theories are products of certain social conditions. We have seen that some argue that Darwinism is a product of 19th century capitalist theory, that Darwin's theory succeeded because the theory supports what a capitalist society wanted and wants to believe. Survival of the fittest; free competition to weed out the weak or inferior—these fit with the rugged capitalist individualism.

But the second objection to Darwinism just cited, a form of vitalism, makes it clear that among scientists there were still various competing models of reality. There were other lingering ideas of a Neoplatonist or Aristotelian model and method. In Germany "idealistic morphology" became popular in the early 20th century.[15] According to this theory, each species represents a changeless type or essence. The implication of Darwin's theory that natures are in flux, changing over time, did not fit with this viewpoint.

The method of the morphologists was not the method of science. The morphologists claimed that the fundamental way to grasp these natures was through insight or intuition of the inner essences of things, rather than through a slow empirical accumulation of descriptions of their characteristics and behavior. The position was also a kind of vitalism in the minds of its adherents, who sought to grasp the basic types of life in order to know and influence the life-forces that dwelt in living beings and gave them their "type-form" of life.

Darwin's theory, on the other hand, has continued to fit well with a very wide range of different kinds of relevant evidence, which keeps on pouring in. Paleontologists continue to identify new fossil species. Their location in the geological strata fits with the general evolutionary picture of the development of life on this planet, from invertebrates to vertebrates such as fish, from fish to amphibians and then to reptiles, and so on. A number of new transitional forms have been identified. These include the tiktaalik from about 375 mya, a fish of sorts, but with forward limbs and a movable neck, as though it were close to an amphibian. Two transitional forms between a land mammal and a whale have been identified, classified as forms of "ambulocetus" or "walking whale," from around 40 mya.

Tiktaalik also anchors an interesting aspect of vertebrates with limbs. It is a lobed-finned fish, which means that its fins had an internal bone structure that is still common. Each of four fins show one bone connected directly to the main body. At the end of this single bone a two-bone structure emerges. Then a collection of bones extends further out ending in a number of digits like fingers or toes. All mammals today have this "homologous" structure, including us humans (check out the structure of your own arms and legs), as though we have a common ancestry, perhaps extending back to tiktaalik or other lobe-finned fish. In various families of organisms such homologous features suggest common ancestry. (Extra evidence such as relations in DNA forms is needed to determine the degree of common ancestry, because some structures are only "analogous" to each other—structure similar in form or function but which are not due to common descent.)

As knowledge developed of the structure of chromosomes and then genes and then finally DNA, everything continued to fit well with the general Darwinian theory of variation on what already exists followed by natural selection. Mitochondrial DNA in fact—the genetic makeup of the tiny energy-factories in each eukaryotic (cells with nuclei) cell—enables biologists to track back in time the probable sequence of mutations in any genetic line, all in concert with what one would expect if the Darwinian model is basically correct.

After close to 150 years of testing Darwin's basic theory, with many specific additions and changes to aspects of it, the lines of evidence have continued to converge in favor of the theory. All along the way the theory might have been "falsified" by some line of evidence that simply would not fit with it. But as is the case with science in general, there is now very strong reason to say "so far, so good," and to argue that it would be truly unreasonable to reject the theory.

For further reading

Desmond, Adrian, and James Moore, *Darwin: The Life of a Tormented Evolutionist* (New York: Warner Books, 1991), provides a good biography of Darwin.

Fortey, Richard, *Life: A Natural History of the First Four Billion Years of Life on Earth* (New York: Alfred A. Knopf, 1998), goes back about 3.5 billion years, and tells the story of life since then quite clearly with extensive references to specific fossil findings.

Larson, Edward J., *Evolution: The Remarkable History of a Scientific Theory* (New York: Modern Library, 2006), very clearly written.

Evolution and Christianity 15

Darwin's theory has held a number of challenges for traditional religious thought. Here is a quick list of implications of Darwin's theory that many Christians have found threatening. Some of them also bother Orthodox Jews and traditionalist Muslims.

1. It suggests the Bible errs about the age of the earth and the origin of species.
2. It makes the sequence of life on earth, including the many mass extinction events, look unplanned.
3. The process of life is a brutal process, "red in tooth and claw."
4. Human beings turn out to be just advanced ape-types, not embodied spiritual souls, each specially created by God.
5. Materialism looks more plausible; science edges closer to metaphysical naturalism.

The five challenges to religious belief

The challenge to the reliability of the Bible

Darwin's theory did not really add much to the list of challenges to biblical authority. By the 1830s, Hutton and Lyell had already established that the earth was probably many millions of years old (they did not yet have the evidence that would extend that age into a few billion years), whereas the Bible seemed to allow for not much more than

6,000 years. Hutton's uniformitarianism appeared to call into doubt the prior belief that there had been a single great flood in Noah's time. (The Qur'an tells a much less specific story about creation and its date, so Muslims do not have the same potential problem as Jews and Christians.)

In 1857, 2 years before Darwin published *The Origin of Species*, Phillip Henry Gosse published a rather intricately argued work entitled *Omphalos*. This Greek word means "navel," referring to the belly button. The purpose of the book was to show that God might have created the universe to appear to be incredibly ancient when in fact it was relatively young. Gosse's pivotal question was whether the first man and woman, freshly created by God rather than born of human parents, had navels—*omphaloi*. His ingenious answer was that, yes, God would create them with navels because humans had navels. Little Cain and Abel and Seth, their first three children, after all, could otherwise be rather troubled that they had this little puckered button in their tummies whereas mommy and daddy did not. So Adam and Eve would look as though they had a longer life history than in fact they did.

Consider the trees in the Garden of Eden, Gosse continued. We know there were at least two of them, the tree of the knowledge of good and evil and the tree of life. Did these trees have rings? Well, yes, said Gosse—that is what gives a tree its structure. The trees would not have stood unless they had been created to look as though they had been growing for many years. What about the ground out of which the trees grew? That too would have to have the kind of complex layers that develop only over thousands of years. So God inevitably had to create the earth in a form that would make it look as though it were at least a great many thousand years old. In fact some particular materials, like the chalk that forms the great white cliffs of Dover, would have to look as though millions of years of development had passed. On and on Gosse analyzes aspects of nature and makes the same basic argument: when God created the world God naturally created it as a functioning world, in which many aspects of it would look as though they had taken enormous time—deep time—to develop.

This argument was not greeted with great enthusiasm by its intended audience, those educated people who were no longer taking the Bible literally. This may have been partly because of the troublesome fossils which people kept digging up, including gigantic life-forms, many of which were no longer found anywhere on earth. In 1841 Sir Richard Owen coined a new term for some of them—"dinosaurs" or terror-lizards. Perhaps such beasts had perished because Noah's ark could not contain them all. But then why had God created them in the first place? Furthermore, the Bible seems to say that Noah had taken aboard the ark one pair of *every* unclean animal (pigs, for example), and seven pair of *every* clean animal. Many of the extinct species fit the category of "clean," able to be offered as sacrifice to God, because like cattle, for example, they chewed their cud and did not have cloven feet. Why was the mastodon left off the ark, if presumably elephants were boarded? Mastodon and elephant could both have been accommodated, after all, if Noah took on board only very young ones. Clearly it would also have taken Adam a very long time to name all the animals, as the second chapter of Genesis says. These worries sound odd now to many a 21st century person, but they were live issues at the time.

Though Darwin's theory still strikes 21st century fundamentalist Christians as alarmingly unbiblical, he should not be given the main credit (or blame) for challenging the Bible in his own time. The reliability of the Bible had already been challenged by the approach known as the "higher criticism," though the name "historical-critical method" is more informative. As early as the 16th century Europeans had been developing techniques for examining historical documents "critically"—that is, not to take them at face value but rather to ask critical questions, such as whether the sources were fully trustworthy, whether other records were available against which the accuracy and reliability of the documents could be checked, whether there were anachronisms in content or language which pointed to a different time of composition than the documents claimed, and so on.

The Book of Daniel, for example, set in the Babylon of the 6th century BCE, includes predictions of the future, revealed to Daniel in a dream, about subsequent kings or rulers. But the predictions include many mistakes and are not very detailed, until they concern events in the 2nd century BCE in the area of present-day Syria and Palestine. No other text written prior to the 2nd century BCE makes any reference to the Book of Daniel. For this and other reasons, including vocabulary, this text or a major portion of it appears to have been written around 165 or so BCE. The writer wanted to give his ideas extra weight, it seems, by making them marvelous visions of the future rather than just contemporary opinions.

The effect of applying this historical-critical approach to the Bible was to treat it like any other humanly produced document, perhaps subject to error. A set of seven essays published as the book *Essays and Reviews* only a few months after the publication of Darwin's *Origin of Species,* included one by the clergyman and noted classicist Benjamin Jowett on the topic of interpreting scripture. He promoted the historical-critical method. Another of the seven clergymen contributing to this volume, Baden Powell, used an argument like Schleiermacher's to argue against miracles. Traditionalist Anglicans sought heresy charges against the seven. The uproar over this book actually obscured arguments going on over Darwin's work. (Ironically, one of the seven went on to become Archbishop of Canterbury, the leading bishop of the Anglican Church.)

A seemingly unplanned process

Jewish, Christian, and Muslim theologies have traditionally said that God rules all aspects of the universe so that nothing happens purely by chance. Not a sparrow falls to the ground, says Matthew's gospel, except in accord with God's will. Even the hairs of our heads are numbered, this passage continues (Mt: 10:29–31). God knows the future free choices each person will make, says traditional doctrine. Islam agrees strongly through its occasionalism.

Darwin's theory introduces a degree of randomness. The variation among offspring is not entirely random, as was noted. Chickens beget chickens, and Rhode Island Red chickens beget Rhode Island Red chickens. Nonetheless, even the best attempts at breeding in Darwin's day could be difficult; there was a degree of unpredictability about whether fast horses would produce only fast offspring, or short-legged dogs would give birth only to short-legged dogs. We know now that the somewhat random shuffling of DNA alleles (parallel genes) is a source of variation, with a degree of unpredictability to it.

Natural selection also has an apparent randomness built into it. Characteristics of an organism that make it well adapted to its environment may become handicaps if the environment changes. The polar bear is well suited to moving on the ice cap of the arctic, diving into the ocean at times, hunting for seals to eat. Now the polar ice cap is melting. The formerly well-adapted polar bear is ill adapted to its new environment. During the centuries from around 950 to 1250 Europe enjoyed a warm period, during which more land was opened to cultivation, more food was produced, and the human population expanded. Then in the early 14th century cold and rainy weather struck. Often crops rotted in the fields. The period from 1315 to 1317 has been called the time of "universal famine" in Europe. Now there were too many people for the amount of food and up to 10% of the population died.

Odd relations among species make things look unplanned. The penguins of the Galapagos Islands do not appear well designed for life so far from the Antarctic, though as semi-aquatic birds in a context without predators to offer much threat, they are adequately adapted to survive. Blind fish in underground caves with vestigial eyes do not appear to have been designed for life in the dark; they look instead more like awkward variants of surface level fish. Invasive species sometimes push out older ones. This makes it clear the older species were not maximally adapted as though designed for their environment. Instead their form and function was just good enough to survive until a somewhat better adapted species showed up.

The many mass extinctions or "wipe-outs" in the fossil sequence made the long-term history of life on this planet also look rather random. In addition to the five major extinction events identified earlier there were numerous other such events, some worldwide, many local, and a great many individual cases of extinction. People could question whether God was really in charge of a history in which species and genera and families developed, only to be wiped out, 99% of them never to be seen again.

The brutality of nature

The chapter here on atheism noted the long-standing problem of evil. The traditional problem of evil was intensified, however, by new knowledge of nature and its long history. Darwin described, for example, a certain wasp which lays its eggs in caterpillars.

When the eggs hatch, the larvae begin to eat the caterpillar from the inside out, leaving the vital organs to the last so that the caterpillar remains alive while the larvae are devouring it from within. Paley had seen this as a sign of God's wonderful design, providing such a good healthy start in life for the wasp larvae. Darwin doubted that the caterpillar would agree with this assessment.

The history of extinctions worked on people's minds. It bothered Tennyson, for example. His poem, "In Memoriam," completed in 1849, was written to commemorate the life and mourn the death of his good friend, Arthur Henry Hallam. Tennyson struggles to find meaning in life, in the face not only of the death of his friend, but in light of what the geological record seemed to indicate. This was 10 years before Darwin published his theory. Tennyson declares that nature cares about species even though individuals die, but then reminds himself of the evidence found in cliffs of the extinctions of whole species. Nature is brutal. Is this what an all-good God would create, he asks? Here are some of Tennyson's lines.

> Oh yet we trust that somehow good
> Will be the final goal of ill,
> To pangs of nature, sins of will,
> Defects of doubt, and taints of blood;
>
> That nothing walks with aimless feet;
> That not one life shall be destroy'd,
> Or cast as rubbish to the void,
> When God hath made the pile complete;
>
> That not a worm is cloven in vain;
> That not a moth with vain desire
> Is shrivell'd in a fruitless fire,
> Or but subserves another's gain.
>
> Behold, we know not anything;
> I can but trust that good shall fall
> At last—far off—at last, to all,
> And every winter change to spring.

But meaningfulness eludes him as he considers the kind of information on which Darwin will dwell also, the evidence in rocks and cliffs of species now long extinct:

> Are God and Nature then at strife,
> That Nature lends such evil dreams?
> So careful of the type she seems,
> So careless of the single life . . . .

> * * * *

> 'So careful of the type?' but no.
> From scarped cliff and quarried stone

> She cries, 'A thousand types are gone:
> I care for nothing, all shall go.'

* * * *

Tennyson thinks of us as needing to trust in divine love but confronting brutalities of nature that seem to cry out that such trust is unwarranted:

> Who trusted God was love indeed
> And love Creation's final law—
> Tho' Nature, red in tooth and claw
> With ravine, shriek'd against his creed . . . .

The status of the human person

By 1871 Darwin was ready to take the plunge into a topic he had tiptoed around in earlier work, whether human beings are an exception to the general claim that the species now on the earth were descended with modification from earlier species. If humans are not an exception, then the clearest candidates for the human ancestral line are the primates, the great apes. Many felt it somehow demeaning to belong in the same family with apes, one of the lower animals.

The religious objections were more specific. First of all, there is the problem with biblical inerrancy again. Genesis 1 and 2 each declare that God made the first man and woman at the beginning. In Genesis 1 God makes the man and the woman together, in the divine "image and likeness," on the sixth day of creation. In Genesis 2 God first makes the man out of dirt, then makes the animals, and then the woman out of a rib of the man. The two stories are a bit hard to reconcile with each other. Nonetheless, the Bible has God specially creating humans, not making them evolve out of some lower creature.

Oddly, descending from lower animals was less of an issue in Darwin's time than it has become today among fundamentalist Christians. In Darwin's time some religious people argued that the human body might well have evolved out of some ape-like predecessor. God could have used the process of evolution to prepare the bodies of the first humans. At the proper time God would then have infused those bodies with human souls. Because common religious belief said human souls are intrinsically "spiritual" (non-material) they are quite different from the physical body produced by evolution. The soul has the power of intellect and free choice; the soul as a non-physical reality is naturally immortal. Therefore, the Christian could conclude, the soul makes humans higher in quality and significance than any other beings on earth.

Fundamentalist Christians in the 20th and 21st centuries, however, disagree. They fear that those who now propose physical descent of the human from ape-like ancestral stock are abandoning belief in a spiritual soul, as we will see later. That has serious implications, the fundamentalists argue, even for here and now.

Muslim scholars have their own worries about human origins. The Qur'an declares that God made humans specially. Here is a translation of one of the relevant passages:

> Behold! thy Lord said to the angels: "I am about to create man, from sounding clay, from mud moulded into shape; When I have fashioned him (in due proportion) and breathed into him of My spirit, fall ye down in obeisance Unto him." (The Noble Quran, 15:28–29)

A relatively liberal Muslim scholar, Nuh Ha Min Keller, accepts much of evolutionary theory, arguing though that it is more like a plausible hypothesis than a firm truth. But he insists on two points. One was made earlier here, that God directly causes every event. The other, that humans have special dignity because they were made directly by God out of clay and the divine breath.[1]

Naturalism

Tim LaHaye, co-author of the well-known *Left Behind* series of novels, declares that the theory of evolution is at the root of many evils. He calls the theory of evolution anti-Christian because it is a major support for atheistic and materialistic humanism. Its challenge to the Bible and to belief in a Provident God are clearly atheistic. When atheism liberates people from God it glorifies the human. Humanism is a double doctrine, says LaHaye, and doubly wrong. It declares first of all that the primary goal of humans is to take care of themselves and each other in this material world; and second that the means to accomplish this is to trust in human abilities.[2] This sets up worldly happiness as a primary goal. It also fails to recognize the fallen nature of humans because of original sin. A disastrous effect of evolutionary theory is to turn the human person into an animal, bereft of an immortal soul. Once we can conclude we are only animals, says LaHaye, we can behave like animals. Promiscuity, abortion, pornography, and homosexuality are all then justifiable, he declares.[3]

The Reverend Ken Ham, a fundamentalist writer and pastor currently at the anti-evolutionary Institute for Creation Research in San Diego, sponsor of the Creation Museum in Northern Kentucky, and editor of the creationist journal *Answers in Genesis*, agrees with LaHaye's moral concerns:

> Over the last hundred years, people who were not Christians readily accepted evolution, as it is a belief system that purports to explain the world without God. Humans are simply a result of chance. That is, no one owns you—you own yourself! This means that you are under obligation to no one. As this view became established in society, people started to ask questions such as—If evolution is true, and there is no God who is Creator, why are there

laws about marriage? Why are there laws against deviant sexual behavior? Why are there laws at all?[4]

Materialism and humanism flow naturally also from evolutionary theory, the religious critics argue, because that theory accepts only natural causes as explanations for events in the world. Once a person gets used to looking exclusively for what is part of material nature, only a small step separates the person from metaphysical naturalism, the assumption that the material universe of nature is all that exists. By squeezing God out of the story of the origin of life and of basic life-forms, by forgetting that humans are special creatures of God made in the divine image with a spiritual soul specially implanted in each person by God directly, life is nothing but material nature alone. In the next chapter we will see that the Intelligent Design proponents oppose naturalism strongly, attacking "The naturalistic dream of turning science into applied materialist philosophy . . . ." as William Dembski puts it.[5] (The next chapter will feature his ideas.) As we have seen, Muslims reject naturalism even more strongly, on the grounds that supposedly natural events are in fact what God directly wills.

Creationism

There are two types of religious responses to evolutionary theory, depending on which threats seem most ominous. As we have just seen, many 19th century religious believers were able to accept evolution provided only that special room was left for God to implant a spiritual soul. A second concern was to reaffirm belief that God has a purposeful plan for the universe as a whole. Even though the course of evolution on this planet tends to look somewhat confused and unplanned, nonetheless, various religious writers include biological evolution as part of their cosmic religious vision. Paul Davies, Teilhard de Chardin, Alfred North Whitehead, and John Haught are examples.

The other major type of response by theists to evolutionary theory has been called creationism, in both an older version, known as Young Earth Creationism (YEC) and a newer version known as Intelligent Design (ID). The language here misleads. Anyone who believes that this universe is indeed a creation by God could be called a "creationist." Nonetheless, in the 20th century fundamentalists appropriated the word to use it for "young-earth" creationism. This is based firmly on biblical literalism, the conviction that every phrase in the Bible, revealed by God, is somehow the literal truth. This form of creationism begins with a belief that the whole earth is only about 6,000 years old, as the Bible seems to indicate; hence the name "young earth creationism."

There is also what one critic calls the "new" creationism, to make things even more confusing. This is the label that the philosopher Robert Pennock pins on the proponents of "Intelligent Design" or "ID."[6] This expression also misleads. Anyone who believes that God designed this whole universe could claim belief in intelligent design. A deist or any religious person who holds to cosmological naturalism could be called a creationist. When you see the phrase "Intelligent Design" in capital letters, however, or just "ID," that indicates the position of those who are really proposing more than intelligent design of the universe; they argue that there some sort of intelligent designer must have *intervened* in the world. It would take many pages to do justice to either the old or new creationism, but something does need to be said here on each of them. Because the "New Creationism" of "Intelligent Design" has a strong movement behind it, and because it constantly promotes its perspective for inclusion in the classroom, it deserves a chapter to itself, the chapter following this one.

Young earth creationism

Old-fashioned creationism, so to speak, is young earth creationism. (We can pass over in silence those who are still flat-earthers.) Young-earth creationists (hereafter just "creationists") assert that God made the world in 6 days, resting on the seventh (Gen. l:1–2:4a; also Gen. 2:4b-3:25). During this period God made all the basic "kinds" (as the King James translation expresses it) of vegetation and water inhabitants and birds and land animals, and finally the man and the woman who are the ancestors of the human race. Furthermore God destroyed all animal life on the planet during the great flood of Noah's time except for the animals which Noah and his family took aboard the ark with them (Gen.6:5–9:17), so that all animals alive today are descendants of these sea-farers.

Creationists claim that their analysis is rational and scientific, though some acknowledge that this is just to help unbelievers see the truth, not to rely on their human reason instead of on God's revelation. A major goal behind calling creationism scientific is to try to get it into science classes in the schools as an alternative theory to Darwinism.

Whatever the motive or justification, creationists offer three kinds of arguments: (1) that evolutionary theory leaves unexplained or deals badly with a number of facts, (2) that evolutionary theory turns out to be unsubstantiated faith in naturalism rather than science, and (3) that creationists have a better alternative interpretation of the evidence.[7] Because the Institute for Creation Research has been publishing these arguments for many years, creationist tracts tend to repeat them.

There are many *facts*, the creationists first of all claim, that the theory of evolution does not account for well at all. A living cell is so incredibly complex a form of life processes and pieces that it is clearly impossible for a living cell to evolve by chance out of non-living matter. The odds are so strongly against the possibility that it is not merely a matter of billions to one but of astronomically higher odds. So it is reasonable and even necessary to suppose that only God's intervention could produce life.

Other fallacies abound, say the creationists, often agreeing on a common list: Paleontologists measure the age of fossils by determining what geological strata the fossils come from and the geologists determine the age of the strata by the fossils. This is circular. Radioactive dating procedures used to determine the age of strata of the earth are unreliable. Moreover, the geological strata are not neatly laid out to read time's record from them; instead they are broken and sometimes upside down from neighboring strata. Individual aspects of various species could not have evolved. The bombardier beetle which sprays its enemies with acid could not have evolved acid-production gradually before having a good means to get rid of the acid or it would have dissolved its innards in acid. Whales could not have evolved from land-dwelling mammals, as evolutionists think, because if the nose passages had to move from the front as they are on a cow to the top of the whale as they now are, then the poor inter-mediate form of the animal as it evolved from cow to whale would have drowned from rain dropping in its nose on land or from inhaling sea-water in the ocean. The scien-tific fact of entropy—that all isolated systems tend to increasing disorder—goes contrary to the idea that this world could have had an increasingly ordered progres-sion of life-forms during the past three billion years. It would take something like a life-forming power to pull matter into complex order contrary to its natural tendency to disorder.

Most important of all, say the creationists, there are serious gaps in the fossil record, with no direct evidence of a gradual transition from one species to another as Darwin expected, and there are no instances of anyone seeing the evolution of one species from another taking place. The "missing link" problem is not just about transitions from apes to humans, it is a problem for evolution in general. If Darwin were right, then there would be extremely numerous transitional forms from one species to another, as evolu-tion proceeded step by step. Darwin's theory says there should not only be a sequence of forms such as from fish to amphibian or amphibian to lizard. There should also be many intermediates, say, from early forms of fish to later forms, to semi-amphibious fish to semi-fish-like amphibians, and so on. They claim we do not have fossils that show such step-by-step developments.

In addition to all these problems with facts, creationists have a problem with the very nature of evolutionary theory as *scientific*. Science works by experimentation and observation of events, creationists claim. Evolutionists cannot experiment on the events of past millennia, nor can they observe those events. Evolution is therefore just a the-ory, not science. It is in fact a kind of faith, an unproven and unprovable vision of how things might be which denies that God or any other supernatural agent might be responsible for events and claims instead that only natural causes are real.[8] It is a mate-rialist and naturalist faith, in that it supposes rather than proves that all physical events have natural material causes. Like Hume, evolutionists presume that miracles do not happen and therefore can never be invoked to explain anything about the world.

Finally, the creationists offer an alternative explanation for the evidence that evolutionists point to, the evidence of fossils and geological layers and similarities among animal species. In the beginning, say the creationists citing scripture, God made all the basic "kinds" of animals, as the King James Version of the English Bible has it. God made them apparently according to an economical pattern with a few basic elements God chose to use over and over again, such as giving all mammals four appendages (showing up as flippers, say, in some sea mammals). This explains homologous features.

The fact that a single God made all the basic kinds also explains adequately why many animals seem to have a family resemblance among themselves. There may well have been a partial evolution—a "micro-evolution"—of many species from a single "kind" of animal aboard Noah's ark. An original wolf-type on the ark might be ancestral to all current wolves, dogs, and coyotes, for example. But this is not the macroevolution of one entire kind out of another kind, as Darwinians claim.

The many layers of fossils and geological strata can be explained by the flood which Noah survived, a flood sent by divine intervention. A flood which drowned the world would leave many fossils. Rock and dirt and clay would settle at different rates, leaving different kinds of layers, each with it own typical fossils, because the rate of death and of settling would also vary for different animals with different swimming abilities and with different specific gravities.[9] YEC advocates are now taking tour groups into the Grand Canyon to point out evidence that the Canyon was produced by a single major flood rather than millions of years of erosion.[10] In the extreme a few still propose the answer suggested by Edmund Gosse in his booklet *Omphalos*, that God made the universe as we now see it *to look as though* it had evolved over many billions of years when in fact God made it only about 6,000 years ago.

The creationist literature repeats these same challenges over and over again. As the final backup argument, Ken Ham's Creation Museum in northern Kentucky repeats in many places along the walls, that there are two distinct starting points for arriving at conclusions about evolution. One of them is prideful and fallible human rationality. The other is God's revelation. It should not be surprising that those who trust in human reason instead of God's word go seriously wrong.

Responses to young earth creationism

A person exposed only to such creationist literature can be excused for having serious doubts about evolution.[11] But in spite of the vigor of creationist attacks, these criticisms of evolutionary thought are only superficially competent. The creationist literature passes over, whether intentionally or through ignorance, a vast amount of relevant information. Even an introductory college textbook in biology or geology provides sufficient information to shatter the creationist analyses.

As the previous chapter mentioned, for example, the paleontologists are actually doing fairly well at discovering more transitional forms like tiktaalik and ambulocetus; and archeopteryx probably does represent the kind of transition that might have led from reptiles to birds.

Multiple forms of radiometric dating exist, to provide more than one check on the age of rocks or fossils. Even without this more precise method of dating geologic strata, a relative history, of what layers came early or later relative to each other, supports the conclusions that the earth is truly ancient, requiring at least hundreds of millions of year of development.

As to the scientific nature of evolutionary theory, both astronomy and geology also do much of their work out of a laboratory. All three of these contain ideas that are falsifiable by new evidence. This is true also of creationist beliefs; repeatedly they have been falsified by relevant evidence of geological transformations over billions of years and the sequential appearance of various life-forms. (The issue of whether life could evolve out of non-life will come up again in the next chapter.)

Darwin defended his theory against the apparent lack of extensive transitional forms in the fossil record by noting that a very tiny proportion of any life-forms would be fossilized. This hit and miss process would not readily fill in gaps. To that we can add that any variant characteristic in an organism would not easily lead to new species. Most genetic variants get swallowed up in the larger genetic pool of species members. There is a "reversion to the mean," a return to an average distribution of characteristics. A new species would more readily appear if a few members of a group with unusual characteristic were cut off from breeding with the larger group. In that smaller group the unusual would have a better chance of becoming usual for that group and lead to a new species. But then the older and newer species would also be separated and a bit less likely to appear in a single fossil sequence. Moreover, the time of greatest change in populations occur during and after the periods of mass extinctions. After some catastrophe such as climate change has opened up many new niches for variant life forms there seems to usually have been an explosion of new developments, happening so quickly geologically speaking, that the sequence of forms would not at least look very gradual to our eyes.

We could extend analysis and argument about the evidence for evolution. That evidence is extensive enough, however, that several chapters would be needed to sample it adequately. The endnotes and books listed here for further reading will have to carry that weight.

Most creationists seem to first presume that the Bible must be literally true in a historical sense, which carries with it a conviction that the theory of evolution simply cannot be correct. So no matter how poor the creationist science, if it attacks the theory of evolution it feels legitimate. Although it is not their intent to do so, they discredit religion in the eyes of many science-minded people. When Richard Dawkins attacks religion, he seems to have their style of thought and faith firmly in view.

For further reading

Evolution and religion

McCalla, Arthur, *The Creationist Debate: The Encounter between the Bible and the Historical Mind* (New York: T & T Clark, 2006). An excellent and readable review.

Numbers, Ronald L., *The Creationists: The Evolution of Scientific Creationism* (Berkeley: University of California Press, 1992). A clear telling of the story of the sub-title.

Ruse, Michael, *The Creation-Evolution Struggle* (Cambridge, MA: Harvard University Press, 2006) interprets this struggle as the outcome of two different responses to the loss of traditional faith in Victorian times, one a conversion to naturalism, the other a turn to fundamentalism.

Young earth creationism: those in favor of it

Heinze, Thomas F., *The Creation vs. Evolution Handbook* (Grand Rapids: Baker Book House, 1972). An evolution-refuter's handbook saying vestigial organs and radiocarbon dating and many other things are not good evidence for evolution.

Morris, Henry M., *The Scientific Case for Creation* (San Diego: Institute for Creation Research, 1977). One of the early leaders of the "scientific creationism" movement. This book represents the general position and evidence and analysis normally brought to bear.

Young earth creationism: those against it

Godfrey, Laurie R. ed., *Scientists Confront Creationism* (New York: W. W. Norton, 1983). An excellent selection of articles on aspects of science related to the creationists' claims.

Isaak, Mark, *The Counter-Creationism Handbook* (Westport, CT: Greenwood Press, 2005). Provides detailed information and analysis about evolution and its evidence, addressing directly many of the creationists' main arguments.

Prothero, Donald R., *Evolution: What the Fossils Say and Why It Matters* (New York: Columbia University Press, 2007). With useful illustrations by Carl Buell.

16 The New Creationism: Intelligent Design

The previous chapter noted that, strictly speaking, the current proponents of Intelligent Design should probably not be called creationists.[1] The name "Intelligent Design" could denote deism, which proposes that the universe is the work of an Intelligent Designer. Deists say that God planned, created, and sustains the universe but no longer intervenes. ID rhetoric often obscures, however, their claim that the design had to have been carried out by direct *interventions*. A more accurate name for their position therefore would be "Intelligent Intervention." Nonetheless, William Dembski, one of the leading theoreticians of the ID movement, chose the name Intelligent Design. The name has become embedded in current arguments.

The ID proponents share a few ideas with the young earth creationism described in the previous chapter. They argue that the appearance of at least the very first life on this planet is so incredibly improbable it could not possibly have happened without intelligent intervention of some sort. Most ID proponents also argue that there is inadequate evidence for evolution because of a lack of intermediate forms. This makes it reasonable to conclude, they imply, that an intelligent agent intervened to produce each major new type of life on earth. Most ID proponents differ from the young earth creationists in that they accept the great age of the cosmos and the earth. They accept the geological evidence that there has been a long sequence of life-forms that have appeared and gone extinct over many millions of years.

To leave room for divine interventions the Intelligent Design advocates reject naturalism entirely, including methodological naturalism. Dembski uses strong language: "Naturalism is the disease. Intelligent design is the cure. Intelligent design is a two-pronged approach for eradicating naturalism."[2] Dembski complains about Schleiermacher's rejection of miracles in 1799. Schleiermacher said nature is a closed system without miraculous interventions, says Dembski. Here is Dembski's response:

> I submit that there is no system of nature. . . . The very conception of a system of nature already presupposes that the world is a self-contained system of natural causes. In other words, Schleiermacher's system of nature presupposed naturalism from the start.[3]

Dembski is challenging Schleiermacher in much the same way that Geisler challenged Hume's ideas, on the grounds that these two skeptics about miracles ended up in a full naturalism precisely because naturalism was their premise from the start.

Dembski is usually cautious about promoting belief in miracles, perhaps because the ID movement wants their position taught in school science classes, where religious beliefs are out of bounds. But occasionally he shows his concern to protect belief in miracles. When he complains that science-minded people support naturalism and protest against invoking divine intervention, he attributes this protest to the scientists' desire for maximum intelligibility in nature: "Invariably the reason for such protests is the fear that miracles will undo the intelligibility of the world." He claims that "The positivistic push for comprehensive rational knowledge, however, has been intense these last few centuries." Then he asks, "Is intelligibility worth purchasing at the expense of miracles?"[4] His answer to the last question is clearly "no."

Philip E. Johnson also promotes the ID movement. He is an expert on criminal law procedures, which he taught as a faculty member of the Law School at the University of California in Berkeley. He published *Darwin on Trial* in 1991 to attack evolution in particular, and *Reason in the Balance* in 1995 to attack naturalism in all its forms.[5] To some extent he shares the arguments of earlier anti-evolutionists, reformulating the various reasons given by young earth creationists that the theory of evolution lacks adequate evidence. His many books against evolution merit attention because he is so unrelenting in his attacks. He conceives of his role as one who will gradually drive a wedge between sound religious belief, as he understands it, and the empty naturalism of modern science.

Dembski and Intelligent Design

Dembski is the person who has done the most to make the new interventionism a social force. He applies to the task his two Ph.D.s, one in mathematics and the other in philosophy.[6] He uses his knowledge of mathematics to calculate the odds against something as complex as a single living cell coming into existence by a series of chance arrangements among various simple compounds like methane and ammonia. The young earth creationists had done this also, but they never engaged in an analysis as elaborate as Dembski's.

Dembski defines certain states of affairs as "complexly specified information" (CSI). By this he means not merely complex realities. The ecological balance of a small pond is extremely complex. But that complexity comes about through an unplanned interplay of the various forms of life in the pond, in interaction with the soil, weather, and other conditions. CSI is better represented by something like the DNA molecule, which is structured in accordance with very specific *information*. The DNA molecule is not merely highly complex; it is also complex in the way coded instructions in a computer are complex, or the way an encyclopedia description of how to build an internal combustion engine is complex. We immediately recognize that the informed complexity of an encyclopedia has to be the result of intelligence. The DNA molecule has enough well-ordered information in it to instruct a single fertilized cell how to start and carry through the extraordinarily complex process of producing an entire organism. Therefore it must have been designed also, says Dembski.

In basic form this is Paley's old argument. The highly functional complexities of a mammal's eye or the parts of the reproductive system of mistletoe work together in too purposeful a manner to have occurred by chance alone. Dembski, however, adds an extra layer of sophisticated analysis to the argument, partly just to establish the need for a designer and partly to argue that the designer intervenes.

There would seem to be at least three forms of intervention needed, according to Dembski. The first would be to create the first instance of life on earth. The second would be to create humans, extremely unusual in the complexity of their central nervous system and the DNA required to produce it. The third, never directly stated but nonetheless often implied in any form of ID which rejects evolution, or at least macroevolution, is to specially create each of the major *kinds* of life on earth in sequential batches as indicated by the fossil sequence.

Dembski's design filter

There are only three ways events can occur, Dembski argues. One of them is by "necessity." Here Dembski is borrowing the ancient Epicurean word for the laws of nature. The second is by chance, or accident. The third is by design. Dembski offers a "design filter" to identify where design—meaning an intelligent intervention—must have occurred.[7] When you see some CSI first ask if natural laws alone could have produced it. One of the basic laws of nature is entropy—things fall apart. At the very least, the laws of natural are boringly repetitive rather than creative. It is this repetitiveness that constitutes the reliability of the laws of nature. They are unbending. That is why we can call them "laws" of nature. So they cannot produce CSI, Dembski argues.

When you have eliminated natural laws as the cause of CSI, you can then look to the second possibility, that it might have come about by chance. But chance alone just causes chaos. Some complexity can be created by the intersection of natural laws and chance such as the weather. But the weather does not get increasingly complex in the specified, information-guided way a single living cell does. A weather system does not represent CSI.

It is in rejecting chance as the mechanism to produce CSI that Dembski gets very complex himself. He addresses the possibility that on this planet, with billions upon billions of chemical events taking place daily, even the very highly improbable might nonetheless finally occur.

One answer was suggested by the Miller-Urey experiment in the early 1950s at the University of Chicago. Stanley Miller, a graduate student directed by Harold Urey, set up an apparatus to recreate what were thought to have been the conditions on earth a few billion years ago, including hydrogen, water, methane, and ammonia, which are pervasive on the earth. Miller used electrical jolts to simulate the effect of ultraviolet light or lightning. By the end of a week of operation, Miller and Urey found that various "organic" compounds had formed, including a significant percentage of amino acids, of which proteins are made, as well as some of the building blocks of nucleic acids (the components of DNA). With millions of years of such conditions, would it be possible that at least once, some of these proteins and acids would form the first self-replicating compound? If so, this is how life could have evolved by natural processes alone.

Miller and Urey were probably incorrect about some aspects of the environment at the time of the first appearance of life. They may have applied electrical charges more continuously than might have been the case. On the other hand Joan Oró (or spelled Juan Oró; he is male but Catalan), using only a couple compounds in a wet solution produced not only many amino acids, but among them adenine—one of the four building blocks of DNA. For that matter, up to 90 different kinds of amino acids were found in a meteorite that landed in Australia in 1969. It is apparently not difficult for amino acids to form and survive even in as unfriendly an environment as outer space.

None of these acids produced in the Miller-Urey or the Oró experiments were nearly as complex as DNA and RNA, the nucleic acids that compose genes or carry information to create proteins. So the products of these experiments were still a long way from any form of life. It has also been over half a century since Miller-Urey experiments, and in spite of extensive further experimentation in many contexts no one has succeeded in creating life in a test tube. Nonetheless, a variety of other proposals have been made about how life originated without intelligent intervention needed.

Dembski is not surprised that no one has really figured out the whole story yet. From the relatively simple amino acid compounds produced by nature to the enormous complexity of DNA is an overwhelmingly large jump. One could as easily hope, to use a common example, that a pile of somewhat complex components could assemble into a functional jumbo jet when tossed about by a tornado. Dembski does not rest with the mere assertion that the CSI of DNA is highly improbable. He takes it upon himself to mathematically figure the odds of it happening. He concludes that the odds are in the range of the impossible. To be in the range of the impossible is not to be absolutely impossible. But it is to be so improbable that it is not at all reasonable to suppose that it could happen by chance. Only a prior bias toward naturalism, toward belief that nature is a closed system, Dembski argues, could lead scientists to rely on chance as the explanation for such CSI. The CSI of life, therefore, cannot reasonably be ascribed to either necessity or chance.

The flaw in the argument

Those who criticize ID argue that it consistently overlooks the core of the theory of evolution, which is natural selection. This is a fourth possible source of complexity, in addition to chance, necessity, or design. The process of evolution is in fact precisely a combination of chance and necessity filtered by natural selection.

Dembski does not take this option seriously as a way to account for the *origin* of life. Natural selection is a principle in biology, he says. It does not apply to the states when there is no life for it to work on. That conclusion is not correct, however. Natural selection is constantly at work on any results of the interaction of nature's laws and chance. It sorts out the results: those that are more stable and better suited to survive, more often do survive. We call those that can survive more readily "better adapted" to features of their environment. When the environment of the earliest stages of the universe cooled down sufficiently, for example, electrons were able to stay in stable orbits around nuclei. Of all the multiple forms of interactions of forces and different quarks that appeared right after the Big Bang, only a very few of the more complex combinations produced turned out to be highly stable. We call these forms hydrogen and helium (and a bit of lithium).

On earth some 3.7 mya ago, any complex amino acid chain which appeared spontaneously, might survive longer than other chains, depending on their structure in their environment. If over many millions of years a single chain, out of multiple trillions produced each day by chance, necessity, and the "selection" imposed by the environment, should end up with the ability to self-replicate, that is sufficient to set in motion all subsequent forms of natural selection on the replications of that chain. Eventually one descendant of that original chain may be so complex as to be called living.

We have no way of knowing whether this is the way life began. Nonetheless, even the most improbable may occur eventually at least once. We also have no way of knowing whether something like this may have happened once or a million times. But the theory of natural selection shows at least how it is possible that life could both originate and develop without a designer. Darwin's theory is powerful.[8]

A special related problem the ID scenario presents to the average biologist would be the number of interventions needed to get the variety of life on earth without evolution. Biology divides organisms into Domains (3 of them), kingdoms (6), phyla (more than 35), classes (a few hundred), orders (hundreds in each class), families (many hundreds in each order), genera (many hundreds again), and species. Biologists have named somewhere around 1.8 million species, and new ones continue to be found.

A common creationist argument has been that there may have been significant microevolution but no macroevolution. The evidence of gradual steps from one "kind" to another is missing, says Phillip Johnson, for example. The ID proponents have in common with the Young Earth Creationists that they rarely address the relevant evidence, in this case concerning the number of "kinds" there have been.

The idea of microevolution proposes that many species arise from a parent stock, perhaps a genus containing many species, or perhaps even a family containing many genera and species. Perhaps one basic "kind" such as the wolf, might constitute the genus for dogs and coyotes. Or perhaps the inclusive "kind" could be pushed back to the level of the family out of which various lupine and canine genera have developed.

Over 600 chordate families have been identified. These are organisms with a vertebrate or something like a spine. It then does not include the many orders of molluscs and insects and hundreds of other orders, each of these orders containing numerous families.[9] If each of the different "kinds" had to be produced through some sort of intelligent intervention, and produced in the sequence in which they first appear in the fossil record, then intelligent intervention took place many thousands of times over a very long time. The same sequence of life-forms, of course, includes such a large number of mass extinctions that well over 90% of all families have disappeared from the earth.

A theologian might be as challenged by this picture as a biologist. Theologically, God is said to have infinite power. Producing endless new families of life-forms, wiping many of them out along the way, over many millions of years should certainly be within the competence of such power. The God of a universe of a hundred billions galaxies, each with many billions of stars, would nonetheless have been terribly busy on this one tiny planet for over three billion years. Theologically speaking, this suggests a very odd image of divine activity. The ancient Stoics would have recognized this God as the busy tinkerer of which they complained.

The ID proponents never directly say that God had to intervene anywhere near this often. If the design process requires only a very few interventions, on the other hand, that would imply that the rest of the sequence of the development of life on the planet must have come about by a natural process, something that would have to be very much like evolution. If natural evolution can accomplish the vast majority of biological developments, reliance on a few divine interventions may be easier to imagine. But if evolution can take care of all the rest of the development, it would be reasonable to suppose it could take care of all development. The notion of intelligent interventions becomes unnecessary as a hypothesis to account for the variety and sequence of life-forms on the planet.

Michael Behe and *Darwin's Black Box*

In addition to Dembski's theoretical arguments about the odds of CSI happening without an intervening designer, the biochemist Michael Behe, in his book *Darwin's Black Box* (1996 and 2003), claims that he has identified some concrete instance of kinds of complexity that fulfill the requirements to be CSI. He calls them "irreducibly complex" processes or structures. Among the ID proponents Behe is alone so far in offering what might count as genuine empirical evidence. For this reason it is instructive to consider his arguments at some length.

He uses a mousetrap to illustrate what he means by irreducible complexity. A mousetrap is an arrangement of parts all designed to work together to achieve a certain goal. A mousetrap has a base, to which is attached a framework with a spring, a bait-holder, a release trigger, and a metal bar which, when released, snaps across the mouse to kill or imprison it. Remove any single one of those parts, and there is no longer a functioning mousetrap. It is irreducibly complex. It could not have evolved piece by piece, starting with a base, and then adding a spring. Such a contraption would not function. Even if a bait-holder were added, it still would not function. Adding the release trigger still would not be enough. All the parts must be assembled at once; they cannot slowly evolve by natural selection. The mousetrap clearly had to have been designed, says Behe.

Behe has identified four or five different biochemical structures or processes that he says show exactly this kind of irreducible complexity. Behe does a good job of making complex biochemistry rather clear in his book, describing the cascade of events that go into blood clotting or the very complex mechanism of the flagellum of certain paramecia. By describing how all the numerous parts of these mechanisms must all work together, he intends to show that these are irreducibly complex. He further claims that there is no literature in the biochemistry journals that shows how such complexity could have come about by a step-by-step process of natural selection.

Behe has many critics. Other biochemists have provided information showing how it is at least possible for these supposedly irreducible structures to have evolved step-by-step. The major element in their analysis is the long-standing set of observations that in the evolutionary process old parts of the DNA genetic code can be adapted to new uses. This is particularly true because there is often a duplication of some part of the code, so that two different sites on the code could carry out the same function. When that happens one of these two parts can change without harm to the organism. The change can sometimes perform a new function that works for the organism.

There is a lot of "junk" in the genetic code, available now and then to take on new functions. A newly adapted part of the code can also take over for an older part that does not quite work as well, and which eventually disappears. At that point the new part has become essential, part of an irreducible complexity. But once upon a time it was not essential; it evolved into that function.

The sharpest critique of Behe's arguments comes from those who point to very specific information in the biochemistry journals that does in fact show how some irreducible complexities like the flagellum structure could have come about step-by-step. There are flagella now functioning that do so with fewer parts or different parts than the ones Behe says are essential for any functioning flagellum. It is not hard to see how a new part could be added to improve the function a bit, and old parts drop away.

Kenneth Miller is one of Behe's major critics.[10] Miller is also a biochemist (and like Behe also a Catholic). He too points to many articles which describe possible step-by-step paths of the evolution of current "irreducible" structures out of slightly earlier less efficient structures. Miller also attacks Behe's illustration of the mousetrap. He shows how a mousetrap could "evolve" from a tie-clip (a spring clip) to a better tie-clip to a poor mousetrap to a better one. Or, to begin from the other end, Miller ingeniously describes how you can remove this part or that from a mousetrap and still have a functioning though poorer mousetrap. The little square wood base of the normal simple mousetrap turns out not to be essential. The other parts could simply be nailed to the floor. This produces an inferior mousetrap because it is nailed to one spot and cannot be moved. But it is a functioning mousetrap.

Behe could note that illustrations cannot always be perfect. His use of the mousetrap to illustrate his basic claim about clotting cascades and paramecia flagella may be an imperfect illustration, as Miller shows it to be. But on the other hand Behe originally thought the mousetrap was irreducibly complex because he did not have the imagination to see how it could evolve step-by-step. He likewise overlooks possible steps for the evolution of the other examples of irreducible complexity which he provides.

Without realizing it, Behe was using an "argument from ignorance." On the surface his argument says that certain structures simply could not have been caused by natural causes. But in reality it is an argument that says *I do not see* any way this could have been caused by natural causes. What a scientist tends to do in such a case is to take this as a challenge to discover how it could have a natural cause, something that science can study and learn from. This is the point of using at least methodological naturalism in science.

Behe fights on

Behe has a second book entitled *The Edges of Evolution*, in which he takes a somewhat different approach to argue that the theory of evolution is not adequate. Unlike most other ID proponents, he concedes that the "modern synthesis" of Darwin's ideas is basically accurate. Behe says more than once that the evidence has become even stronger in favor of the general idea of "descent with modification," the claim that all life on the planet shares a common ancestry. Behe has found, however, another genetic problem which, he argues, makes it highly reasonable to suppose that at least some genetic changes had to have been under intelligent guidance.[11] Because these are specific changes, they seem to require specific interventions by some intelligent agent. (If the agent is God, of course, we would call such interventions miracles. But Behe is cautious in his language.)

Behe addresses the issue of what is known among evolutionists as co-evolution. One form it takes is sometimes called an "arms race." This theory says to imagine that long-ago ancestors of the gazelle were not so swift as modern gazelles. They needed to be only swift enough to normally be able to escape the long-ago ancestors of cheetahs. But the slower cheetahs did not get to eat as often as the faster cheetahs. So the faster cheetahs more often survived long enough to pass on some of their greater talent for speed to the next generation. This is turn meant that the slower gazelles were now much more likely to get eaten, leaving the faster gazelles to survive more often and to pass on their extra swiftness to their offspring. Gazelle and cheetah alike gained more speed through this process of co-evolution.

Evolution proceeds because there are variations among the offspring, variation on which natural selection can work. More than one source of variation exists. Sexual reproduction is a major source (or the swapping of genetic material that sometimes goes on among the simplest cells, which do not reproduce sexually). Genetic mutation is another. This comes in its own variety of forms. Both sources of change are limited, Behe stresses.

Sexual reproduction has to work with limited material. The genetic code cannot just call up changes that would be helpful. Generally speaking, variations are just variations of what already exists. Genetic mutations may sometimes provide a useful change. But such genetic changes are more often harmful than beneficial. Even when a change does provide some advantage it may do so at a high cost.

Most significant, says Behe, when we look at the story of actual organisms it is striking how poor they are at participating in their relevant arms race. His prime example is the bacterium which causes malaria, *P. falciparum*. The bacterium infects red blood cells and uses the material there to multiply and produce copies of itself. The new copies destroy the cell, spread out into the blood stream, infect many new blood cells, and repeat the multiplication, destruction, and further invasion.

Malaria has shown great success at evolving into forms which are resistant to various antibiotic drugs. For quite some time quinine could inhibit malaria. Then a simpler drug, chloroquine, produced in the laboratory, also worked very well. But there are roughly a trillion malarial cells (10^{12}) in a single sick person, and at any given time there are as many as a million people (10^6) who have malaria. In effect, every day there are something like a quintillion (using a U.S.-style numerical name) living malarial cells (10^{18}).

As with playing the lottery, Behe notes, winning a jackpot becomes almost inevitable if you buy enough tickets. A quintillion tickets every day is quite a few. It is hardly surprising therefore that here and there a malarial cell has a single mutation that confers immunity or at least strong resistance to a given drug. Because that cell will not be killed by the antibiotic normally used, it will live to make copies of itself and before long will become rather common. Malaria has in fact become resistant to a wide range of drugs.

But all along a different mutation in humans has resisted malaria in an entirely different way. We see this mutation most readily in its extreme form, when both parents carry it and pass on a double dose of this mutation to one or more of their offspring. Then the effects of this mutation appear as sickle cell anemia, a disease which distorts the shape of red blood cells into a sickle form. In this shape the cells can bunch up in tight points in the capillaries, cause great pain and even lead to an early death.

It was long a puzzle why the death rate produced by sickle cell anemia did not rather quickly weed this trait out of the gene pool. Research finally showed, however, that the effect of a single copy of the gene which produces sickle cells protects the red blood cells in more than one way from malaria. An evolutionary mutation, therefore, turned out to be another step in an arms race between the human genome and the genome of the malarial cell.

Behe points out two significant aspects of this change, though. First, the mutation falls far short of the ideal. On the average, in populations where most people carry the gene, it protects two out of every four of their children—the two who carry one copy of the sickle cell gene. But on the average it also leaves one child without any particular resistance to malaria and another child with sickle cell anemia. The second significant aspect is that the sickle cell trait, unlike recently invented antibiotics, has been around for hundreds of years. Behe's pointedly asks then why the malarial parasite has not evolved a defense against the sickle cell trait. It has quintillion opportunities every day, after all, to luck out and have a mutation that would counterbalance the effect of sickle cells.

Behe offers a rather detailed description of what mutations might compensate for or overcome the resistance to malaria that sickle cells provide. One path, he argues, would be a pair of complementary mutations. Unfortunately to get the right pair of mutations is extremely more difficult than to produce a single useful mutation. The best evidence for this is that in spite of a quintillion opportunities each day, those two mutations have not appeared, Behe notes. Even in theory the odds of not just one but two mutations, which in turn must complement each other, are extremely high odds.

In general then, Behe argues, it is not reasonable to expect that unplanned or undesigned mutations can be positively creative enough to produce complexly organized biological systems. This is particularly true in populations which are far smaller than those of bacteria. Once there were only a few million hominids. It is contrary to reason and evidence, Behe concludes, to suppose that the collection of mutations in the hominid genome which has produced the modern human, for example, could be the result of chance, particularly in any case where two or more complementary changes are needed—perhaps to produce the ability to aim and throw rocks, or create the first stages of speech. The same is true of any other highly complex organisms on this planet. It is by far more reasonable to suppose that some intelligent agent has acted to provide positive creative steps in evolution.

The limits to success

Critics of *The Edges of Evolution* have attacked Behe's argument at several points, most of them scientific. Behe's analysis of the pair of mutations needed argues that we should not be surprised this set of mutations has not taken place because the odds are so strongly against those precise two mutations occurring together.

That the malarial bacterium has not evolved a way around the sickle cell defense need not be all that surprising. It is precisely an unplanned or undirected evolutionary process that produces rather random results. It also looks as though the human DNA is actually gradually drifting in the direction of greater resistance to malaria, as certain kinds of hemoglobin which destroy or inhibit the malarial bacterium are becoming more common in areas infested with malaria. Natural selection is at work again. Those with more of the anti-malarial hemoglobin in their veins are more likely to survive, reproduce, and pass on the anti-malarial blood types.

There are two interesting and awkward theological implications to Behe's argument. The first of these Behe acknowledges head on: his argument entails the conclusion that malaria was deliberately designed through an intervention by whomever or whatever has been doing the designing of the universe. The malaria bacterium *P. falciparum* manifests precisely the kind of complex organization that Behe argues cannot be the result of Darwinian random variation and selection alone.[12]

Behe asks why a designer would do this? Is the designer a demon? "Are viruses and parasites part of some brilliant as-yet-unappreciated economy of nature, or do they reflect the bungling of an incompetent, fallible designer?" Behe asks, and then responds that we do not know. But we should not duck out on this problem because it makes us feel uneasy. If Darwinian evolution is inadequate to explain malaria, we should face up to that, Behe insists. The ordinary theist, however, may be excused for feeling seriously uneasy with the notion that a designer who may be God has deliberately intervened to produce the ills of humankind. U.S. fundamentalists such as Pat Robertson have claimed that many disasters and diseases are God's punishments for sin. The theological difficulty with their case is making sense of why God would punish not merely the guilty but the innocent, such as the millions of children who die every year of malaria.

A second theological problem appears in the picture of the intelligent designer Behe invokes. He is clear that intelligent design does not necessarily entail that "the transcendent God" is that designer.[13] That takes philosophical or theological arguments, Behe says (a point worth remembering when discussing whether ID has a place in the classroom). The process of life on this planet has been chaotic enough to fit just as well with the idea of the Raëlians—that space aliens seeded life on this planet and have been tinkering with it for millions of years. They needed the long stretch of time because they were learning as they go, making many mistakes along the way. This could also account for various mass extinctions.

On the other hand, if Behe himself, for personal religious reasons, is willing to identify the intelligent designer (intervener) as God, this God seems rather inexpert. This point is made, ironically, by another ID proponent named Cornelius G. Hunter. His main purpose is to complain that proponents of evolution actually engage in theological reasoning. Therefore evolution should be kept out of science classrooms because it relies on religious arguments.[14] Here is Hunter's argument. Evolutionists note, says Hunter, that countless species have thrived for millions of years but then have been wiped out by changes in climate or by some natural disaster, many of them seeming to have left no descendants at all. Undirected natural process would make sense of this. The evolutionists ask "Would an Omniscient Designer do things this way?" It seems not, the evolutionists argue. The DNA package has a great many hitchhiker genes, along for the ride but doing little. A random process of evolution would explain this. Would a Divine Designer do things this way? It seems not, say the evolutionists.

Furthermore, many organisms do not seem well designed in the first place. Humans share in the limited mammalian eye, whose neurons from the cells in the retina run across the top of those cells, obscuring vision. The eyes of raptors (hawks, eagles) are much better "designed." The human spinal cord is an awkward and trouble-prone adaptation of a vertebrate structure that works well for quadrupeds and even knuckle walkers like chimpanzees. The human appendix contributes relatively little but can kill a person if it becomes infected. An undirected evolutionary process would produce results like this.

To ask whether a Designer would do things like this, Hunter insists, is to ask theological questions, not biological. If evolutionary theory is built upon metaphysics or theology, then it should be excluded from science classrooms. Ironically, Hunter's discussion of the theologizing done by evolutionists elaborates a great amount of the evidence that makes evolution look like a purely natural and undirected process, or as Behe's argument implies, the work of a rather ill-skilled agent.

The main story of evolution, say critics of Behe and ID in general, is that evolution is as Hunter describes it, not a combination of brilliantly appropriate design and ordinary deficiencies. The evolutionary process produces make-shift forms, orderly enough for the most part to survive and reproduce but none of them perfect. There is nothing left over that requires an intelligent intervener. Nature is beautiful to us, awesome in grandeur, often inspiring in detail. But all of it, every piece of it, at least *appears* to be part of the process Darwin described—variation acted upon by a somewhat brutal process of natural selection over a few billion years, that wipes out countless species in a seemingly random way and "selects" by far the majority of all offspring for an early and perhaps painful death. If an intelligent intervener is at work amid all this, the evidence does not suggest this designer is very competent, as God is supposed to be. If the designer is God, in fact, it is a God who shows less competence than even the "everyday" God described earlier here. It is a God who has made a universe such that it requires constant tinkering.

An evolutionary form of deism, of course, could still say that God planned the universe in such a way that a natural process of evolution would eventually take place. Behe examines this possibility seriously, but insists that evolution without extra intelligence guidance is still not enough.

To conclude, neither Dembski's nor Johnson's nor Behe's many books have managed to raise good evidence for doubting that the theory of evolution can account for the whole history of life on earth. There are many unsolved questions, of course, in the study of evolution, just as there are in any field of science. But the range of converging evidence of a sequence of life forms in the fossil record, homologous structures like the bones of vertebrate limbs, patterns of DNA, geographical distribution of related life forms, is extremely strong. Add the observations that Hunter makes about the process looking rather unguided, and there is good reason to accept the theory of evolution as adequate to account for the life-forms on this planet.

Good reason, that is, unless a person has a form of religious faith that conflicts with evolution. Although Young Earth Creationist opponents of evolution often cite what they perceive to be its bad moral effects, the main concern of the ID proponents is miracles. Biblical religion, as Johnson calls it, demands belief in divine interventions.[15] This sort of biblical religion cannot be comfortable with cosmological naturalism, with an eternal and changeless God who plans, creates, and sustains in a single changeless act. They even reject methodological naturalism (Behe excepted) as not only the beginning of a slippery slope into a fuller naturalism, but as a deliberate exclusion of the most important kind of events, divine interventions.

Intelligent Design and the schools

In the U.S. a great deal of money (much of it from the Discovery Institute of Seattle) and energy and publicity has been going into efforts to get schools to require that biology classes "teach the controversy" between the ID proponents and mainstream biology. President George W. Bush agreed that "teaching the controversy" would be right. A majority of U.S. citizens also agree. Americans tend to like to be fair about things; it seems only fair to teach both sides of a controversy.

The actual situation in school districts is a bit more complex. Not all high school biology teachers are really that familiar with the large range of evidences for the reality of "descent with modification" as the source of the many life-forms on this planet. Some are fundamentalists who are antagonistic to evolutionary theory in the first place. It is easy to suspect that teaching the controversy will turn out to be teaching the supposed failings of evolutionary theory and the brilliant insights of Intelligent Design arguments.

Other high school teachers who are well versed in evolutionary theory and the evidence for it, will be in an awkward position if they are told to "teach the controversy." Some high school biology teachers have minimized discussion of evolution in the classroom, to avoid upsetting fundamentalist parents. Others simply describe the theory, giving some examples, without doing a full review of all the relevant evidence for evolution. If these teachers have to "teach the controversy" it would mean that they would now have to present the evidence concerning evolution and also about ID. If they do this competently they will end up showing the students that the evidence for evolution is very strong, and that the weak points ID proponents claim to see in the theory tend not to be very significant. A thorough examination of the evidence and arguments for Intelligent Design theory will also show that ID is scientifically rather weak. By entering into such analyses the teacher is treading upon the religious sensibilities of many of the students and their parents. Most teachers do not want to be put in that position. They would prefer to teach only what most biologists claim is valid evolutionary science, and to leave further philosophical arguments, with their possible religious implications, entirely aside.

The ID group found 100 Ph.D.s in science to sign a statement that the theory of evolution is flawed, to use this statement as evidence that there really is a scientific controversy over evolution. Many of these signers are not evolutionary biologists, though some are. Some of the biologists said when interviewed later, however, that they supported the general theory of evolution but are bothered by the incompleteness of this or that minor aspect of the theory. The National Center for Science Education (NCSE) promptly asked how many scientists would sign a contrary statement, one supporting evolution. There were too many responses. So NCSE decided they would sign up only those named Steve or Stephanie (or Estaban or Etienne), in honor of Stephen J. Gould who had just died. The NCSE estimates that 1% of the U.S. population are named Steve or such. In April 2007, a biologist name Steve Russell was the 800th person to sign the statement .[16] If the NCSE estimate is correct, there are as many as 800,000 scientists who support evolution, though not all of them are evolutionary biologists. So all in all the "controversy" to be taught is a political or religious controversy, not a scientific one.

An ironic result of the ongoing attempts by ID and creationists in general to attack the teaching of evolution in the schools, is to heighten the tension between religion and science. Those dedicated to good science see many people attacking it in the name of religion. Those favoring a creationist position come to see modern science as an enemy. The recent extreme, perhaps, can be found in the words of Ben Stein, an actor who is also the narrator of a documentary video of sorts, entitled "Expelled." The main target of the video is Darwinism; it is a defense of four people who the video claims lost their jobs or positions because they favored Intelligent Design over evolution. In a notorious TV interview with the evangelical pastor Paul Crouch (part 5 of the interview), Stein attributes the holocaust to Darwinism. His summary conclusion: "Science leads you to kill people." This is rhetorical overkill, one presumes, and should not be taken as the stance of Intelligent Design advocates. It nonetheless symbolizes a deep religious antagonism to scientific naturalism.

Another topic that can produce similar tension is human nature. The theory of evolution is often taken to say that humans are fully products of material evolution, lacking the spiritual soul which religious tradition has made a central doctrine. Now neurological studies support the materialist position. That is the topic of the next chapters.

For further reading

Intelligent Design proponents (in addition to those in the endnotes)

Dembski, William, ed., *Mere Creation: Science, Faith & Intelligent Design* (Downers Grove, IL: InterVarsity Press, 1998), articles by many different supports of ID.

Johnson, Phillip E., *Defeating Darwinism by Opening Minds* (Downers Grove, IL: InterVarsity Press, 1997), a short introduction to Johnson's arguments and style.

Intelligent Design opponents (in addition to sources in the endnotes, especially Miller)

Haught, John, *God after Darwin: A Theology of Evolution* (Boulder: Westview Press, 2000). Also see his *Is Nature Enough* (New York: Cambridge University Press, 2006) in which he excoriates metaphysical naturalism, which he calls "scientific naturalism" unfortunately.

Pennock, Robert, ed., *Intelligent Design Creationism and Its Critics: Philosophical, Theological, and Scientific Perspectives* (New York: MIT Press, 2001). Philosophers, theologians, and scientists contribute to this critical analysis of ID.

Some URLs

To get a sense of the complexity of the enormous number of branching families of organisms, go to the *Tree of Life* at http://tolweb.org/tree/phylogeny.html

Pros and cons on Dembski can be found at http://www.nctimes.com/~mark/bibl_science/dembski.htm

National Center for Science Education has numerous links to those critical of Dembski's analyses. http://www.ncseweb.org

Dembski's main sponsor can be found at http://www.discovery.org/csrc

Jonathan Well's book, *Icons of Evolution: Why Much of What We Teach about Evolution Is Wrong*, has been popular among ID proponents. For a chapter by chapter critique try, http://www.talkorigins.org/faqs/wells or http://ncse.com/creationism/analysis/icons-evolution

For criticism of Wells: http://www.ncseweb.org

For a quick but older critique of Behe: http://bostonreview.mit.edu/br21.6/orr.html

Part Seven
Human Nature: who are we?

The Soul Tradition 17

The human soul should be safe from science, it would seem. In Christianity and among at least some Jewish and Muslim scholars, the soul has been defined as a spiritual reality. In popular usage the meaning of "spiritual" varies. When people refer to the spiritual side of life, they often mean to refer vaguely to the moral aspect or the aspect that seeks meaning and love and hope, or just to religious concerns, whatever they may be. Science has little to say about the "spiritual" in this sense, except perhaps through psychological studies of how people think about such things.

In Western theology and philosophy, spiritual has a more precise meaning. It refers to a non-physical reality, one outside the laws and patterns and actions of the natural world. Because science follows a methodological naturalism, the spiritual in this sense is outside of the scope of science. Science today nonetheless challenges belief in a non-physical soul in a variety of ways. But first, a history of traditional ideas about the soul will help define the word more precisely—or indicate three or four possible meanings of the word. We can start out by speaking of the soul as the inner self, and gradually see what this inner self has been thought to be like.

> ## Some notions of the inner self—a sampling
>
> Select whichever of these is closest to your conception of the soul. If none of them suits you entirely, briefly amend one of them to make it work for you.
>
> 1. "Soul" is just a poetic word to stand for the set of inner thoughts and feelings a person has. These thoughts and feelings are entirely products of brain processes. (Scientific naturalism)
> 2. It is a ghostlike reality which survives the death of the body, perhaps to last for a long time or perhaps to slowly fade away. (Primitive and other cultures)
> 3. It is a non-physical being that dwells in various physical bodies, one after the other. After the death of one body it is reincarnated in another. In between incarnations it may exist on a spiritual plane. (Theosophy)
> 4. It is a non-physical reality which cannot die, but needs to be part of a body-soul person to be complete. So after death it still needs to be rejoined to a body to be a full self. (Scholasticism)
> 5. It is a non-physical reality which cannot die. It is therefore immortal by its nature. It eventually will live a purely spiritual (non-physical) existence, as in a purely spiritual heaven of some sort. (Platonist)
> 6. The inner self of a person is part of an infinite divine Soul. Eventually the person may dissolve back into this Soul and never have to live individually again. (Hindu)
> 7. There is no real self. The inner "self" is just a collection of attachments to existence and various aspects of life. (Buddhist)

The notion of the soul in Christian and Judaic tradition

The Judaic and Christian idea of a spiritual soul as the inner self goes back to traditions which precede Christianity. The history of belief in a soul is, in fact, quite complex. Two major strands contributed to the formation of Judaic and early Christian notions of the soul. The first is the development in Judaism during Hellenistic times of belief in a resurrection from the dead and a new life.[1] The second is the set of alternatives present in Hellenic philosophy, especially the Platonist belief, in a non-physical soul which leaves the body behind at death.

Early Judaic notions of the soul

Judaic ideas about the inner self and what happens to it at death varied over time. The Book of Exodus is clear that God will reward those who keep the covenant with God, but the rewards mentioned are all in this life—health, victory over enemies, fertility for crops, livestock, and people. Life after death is at most sleeping in Sheol, a condition in which nothing at all happens.

It would not have been surprising, perhaps, had Judaism eventually picked up Egyptian hopes for a physical life after this one. The pyramids stocked physical things needed by the Pharaohs in their next life, food and wine and a barge for sailing the Nile. As the centuries passed in Egypt, eventually not only the Pharaoh but any good person might hope to receive a second life. But it looks as though two other cultures rather than the Egyptian had most influence on Judaic thought.

The first was the Persian culture and its Zoroastrianism, which we looked at briefly in Chapter 11. This tradition promised a physical resurrection of the dead, into a garden (paradise) or into the purifying flames of the pit, which would burn away all evil from the person and make him or her worthy of paradise also. Some Zoroastrian texts do refer to a kind of soul which survives the body, but nonetheless promises that at a final time of judgment a whole person, what we might call body-and-soul, will live again.

We have seen that many leaders of the Judeans were in exile in Babylon when Persia conquered this territory in the later 6th century BCE. Many Jews in fact remained in Babylon for centuries, exchanging ideas with the Jews who had been allowed by the Persians to return to Jerusalem. This provided long-lasting exposure to Zoroastrian thought.

The second major cultural influence was Hellenistic. This is the name for the cosmopolitan culture which spread over the entire Eastern Mediterranean from even before the time of the conquests by Alexander the Great in the late 4th century BCE. When Alexander defeated the Persians, Greek culture came to overshadow the lingering influence of Persian culture.

Greek philosophies offered more than one set of thoughts on the inner self. Note again that we call these thoughts philosophy, but the Greeks did not distinguish between philosophy (the love of wisdom or knowledge), and what we would call science. The goal of philosophy was knowledge of anything and everything. Carefully argued Greek ideas about the inner self were attempts to do the equivalent of psychology. This is a point to return to.

The Greek philosopher Socrates (469–399) presents an argument in more than one of the dialogues written by Plato, in favor of the notion of an inner self which belongs to a non-physical realm and which is trapped temporarily in a body. Because this inner self is not physical it does not decay and fall apart as physical things do. By its nature it does not die; it possesses a natural immortality. No god has to provide a life after death for this inner self.

At death, the soul has a tendency to find another body. A person who dies is likely to be reincarnated into physical existence again. A philosopher who contemplates eternal truths and value will fortunately be able to escape the body for good. It will dwell in the non-physical realm of perfection to which it naturally belongs. To Plato it would be a terrible thing to have a physical resurrection of the sort that Zoroastrians promise.

Being physical is the source of all the many evils which afflict people, such as illness, hunger, pain, debility, not to mention lice and terrible odors.

Of the many other philosophical positions, it is worth mentioning the Epicurean teaching again. According to Epicurus, everything that exists is made up of material atoms moving in space. Whatever the inner self might be, it too is made up of material atoms. At death the atoms of the person begin to fall apart. Life and thought go immediately; the body as a whole slowly decays. That is the end of the person entirely.

In addition to the two philosophies of the inner self, Platonist (and a similar Aristotelian) and Epicurean, popular Hellenistic culture provided another important source of ideas. Ghostly selves of the dead often appeared in dreams to people. In the Iliad, for example, from the 8th century BCE, Achilles sees his dead companion Patroclus in a dream and takes this to be a real appearance of his friend. Patroclus reminds Achilles that he has not been properly buried. Without burial Patroclus will not be able to enter Hades and find rest—a boring rest, to be sure, but a state better than having to roam the land without rest. This boring afterlife was thought to be the end state for most people. A rare hero, especially one like Hercules whose father was the god Zeus, might earn enough fame and honor in life to be invited to join the gods in a blessed life after death. Even the Roman emperors eventually wanted to be declared gods after their death. If official rituals took place in their honor, with sacrifices and praise, then they too could dwell in this happy condition.

There are disputes about which of these four approaches (Zoroastrian, Epicurean, Platonic, and popular Hellenic) had the greater influence in Judaism in the centuries before the beginning of Christianity. Ecclesiastes, a piece of scripture usually dated to around the 3rd century BCE, seems to take the Epicurean view, perhaps because this is closest to the most traditional Judaic belief that there is no real life after death. Ecclesiastes (also called Qohaleth) expresses this poignantly:

> [T]he fate of humans and the fate of animals is the same; as one dies, so dies the other. They all have the same breath, and humans have no advantage over the animals; for all is vanity. All go to one place; all are from the dust, and all turn to dust again. Who knows whether the human spirit goes upward and the spirit of animals goes downward to the earth? (3:19–21)

The last line of this passage shows that the author has heard of the idea that at death the human spirit might ascend to a better existence. Perhaps the author had heard of the Zoroastrian garden or of Plato's spiritual soul or of both. But his response is that we do not know the answer.

Lines from earlier Jewish writings sometimes seem to promise resurrection from the dead. Passages in the writings of the prophets Ezekial and in Isaiah, from around the late 6th century BCE, speak of clothing the bones of the dead with new flesh and new life. Scripture scholars today, however, tend to think of such statements as promises that the Jewish people in Exile in Babylon and elsewhere will be allowed to create the

Judean nation again, rather than as promises of individual physical resurrection from the dead. In the Book of Daniel, however, usually dated to around 165 BCE, there is what appears to be an explicit promise of physical resurrection, saying that "many of those who sleep in the dust of the earth shall awake, some to everlasting life, and some to shame and everlasting contempt" (12:2). This may echo the Zoroastrian linear view of history, ending in a resurrection into a paradise.

By the time of Jesus, then, Jews differed among themselves about what happens at death. Generally the Sadducees, the priestly-family aristocrats of those times, rejected the idea of a life after death. They were traditionalists on this point; Moses (the Pentateuch or Torah or Law) did not offer any life after death. Generally, the Pharisees, those who were scribes and scholars, had adopted belief in resurrection, with the Book of Daniel as part of their justification for this. Ordinary Jews, on the other hand, may have shared in the common human belief, sustained also by popular forms of Hellenistic culture, that our inner selves, called "psyches" in Greek, are inherently ghost-like and may have some sort of continued existence after our deaths.

Earliest Christian notions of the soul

What did the earliest Christians believe? Jesus promised that the Kingdom of God was near, that a messianic "Son of Man" would come with power in clouds with the angels— lines that echo parts of the Book of Daniel—to establish the kingdom of God. And it is Daniel who speaks of those now "asleep in the dust"—i.e., who are dead—who will be raised to new life.

But Jesus also speaks in a way that might imply that those who have died nonetheless still survive as real selves. In Matthew's Gospel, for example, Jesus admonishes his listeners not to be afraid of those who kill the body but cannot kill the soul (10:28); the Greek word for soul here is *psyche*. As often happens, interpreting what Jesus might have meant is difficult. This is an account in which the Aramaic language which Jesus spoke has been translated into Greek. What a Greek-speaker might mean by this word is not necessarily what an Aramaic speaker might have intended. Nor can we know how those listening to Jesus understood this word. The people to whom Jesus spoke were probably unfamiliar with philosophical categories and used to the more popular notion of a ghostly inner self.[2]

A somewhat clearer idea of earliest Christian beliefs appears in a passage in which the Apostle Paul is defining for the Christians of Corinth what they ought to hold concerning life after death. Paul has heard that the Christians have been told there is no physical resurrection of the person after death. None of the Greek schools of philosophy would accept the idea of a physical resurrection, and Platonists would actively reject the idea of having to live again in the corrupting embrace of physical matter.

Christianity, however, was based on belief in a resurrection from the dead. Paul insists on physical resurrection on the grounds that Jesus' physical resurrection is precisely what provides confidence that others will have a new life also. But what then of the Platonists' complaint about physical existence? Paul provides an intriguing, though not fully clear, response:

> [N]ot all flesh is alike, but there is one kind for humans, another for animals, another for birds, and another for fish. There are celestial bodies and there are terrestrial bodies; but the glory of the celestial is one, and the glory of the terrestrial is another . . . . So it is with the resurrection of the dead. What is sown is perishable, what is raised is imperishable. It is sown in dishonor, it is raised in glory. It is sown in weakness, it is raised in power. It is sown a physical body, it is raised a spiritual body. If there is a physical body, there is also a spiritual body. (I Cor.15:39–40, 42–44)

There are perhaps two oddities in this text, one more obvious than the other. The more obvious is the notion of a "spiritual" body. A clue to the meaning lies in the Greek, *soma pneumatikon*. *Soma* is a body; *pneumatikon* originally meant airy or breath-like. A common meaning of "spirit" in many languages is tied to the notion of the breath of life. While we breathe, we live; cease to breathe, cease to have this spirit, and we die. Paul offers a special kind of breath-body, one that is not corruptible like earthly things but incorruptible like the changeless yet physical beings in the heavens called sun and moon and stars. So Paul neatly solves the challenge from Platonism. Christians should indeed look forward to a physical resurrection, not into the sort of corruptible body which the Platonists disdain, but into an incorruptible body of celestial glory. For Paul the whole person is a bodily being; the type of body will change through resurrection.

The second oddity is covered up by translation. The expression "physical body" in the same sentence, sometimes translated as "natural body," is an attempt to put into English the Greek phrase "soma psychikon." The adjectival form of psyche is used not to indicate soul but the natural or physical body. This shifts the meaning of psyche away from the purely spiritual (non-physical). It is reasonable to conclude, then, that this early Christian notion of the inner self or psyche did not reflect a Platonist belief in a non-physical soul.

In earliest Christianity expectation of resurrection into a new body was colored by an another expectation, that the Kingdom of God would arrive soon in power. In Paul's first letter to the Thessalonians he praises them because they serve God, as they "wait for his Son from heaven, whom he raised from the dead, Jesus, who delivers us from the wrath to come" (I Thess. 1.10). Many people have died waiting for Jesus; they are "asleep." Paul wants to comfort those whose loved ones have died. He tells them:

> For the Lord himself will descend from heaven with a cry of command, with the archangel's call, and with the sound of the trumpet of God. And the dead in Christ will rise first; then we who are alive, who are left, shall be caught up together with them in the clouds to meet the Lord in the air; and so we shall always be with the Lord. (I Thess. 4:15–17)[3]

No mention is made of re-uniting souls with bodies. Paul writes as though the whole person will be raised from the dead, and soon. But a few generations passed and the Lord had not yet come. So speculation increased about what happened to the "dead in Christ" until the coming of the Kingdom. Only later did Christian literature begin to speculate about the "souls" of the dead awaiting resurrection.[4]

A generally safe conclusion about earliest Christian ideas of the soul, then, would be that this inner self or psyche was an aspect of the whole bodily person. Resurrection from the dead offered hope that the entire person, asleep in the dust, would be raised to a new life in a new kind of body.[5]

Ideas on the soul in later Christian tradition

Judaic and Muslim traditions on the soul begin often with reference to lines in Genesis or in Surah 15 of the Qur'an, which say that God molded the first human out of dust or clay and then breathed into it the breath of life. Neither Jews nor Muslims, however, have a single interpretation of this that all are supposed to agree on. Christians did eventually develop a single dominant interpretation, though the path of its development was complex and confusing.

This is evident in the ideas of one of the earliest Christian theologians, Irenaeus, whom we already encountered in a chapter on miracles. Following a division proposed by Plato, Irenaeus divided the person into three parts, body or flesh (sarx), soul (psyche), and spirit (pneuma). The psyche accounted for inner emotions, as is appropriate for a physical soul, whereas the spirit accounted for intellectual thought and free choices.[6] This tri-partite division became common among many early Christian thinkers, including those associated with Alexandria in Egypt, the locale of the great library and a center of Platonist thought. But a simpler division of the person into just two parts, body and soul, gained ground as time went on.

Augustine on the soul

A clear marker of this shift appears by the time of Augustine of Hippo, who adopted a Platonic (Neoplatonist, to be exact) notion of the soul as a purely non-physical self dwelling in a body.[7] The Platonist desire to escape materiality entirely clashed with Christian belief in a physical resurrection, so Christianity could not accept an unqualified Platonism. But it could work with a modified version in which a person was not just the person's soul but instead was a body-and-soul composite, a physical body, and a purely spiritual soul united in a person.

In Augustine's work *The Literal Meaning of Genesis*, for example, he chews over various notions of the soul and how it relates to the body.[8] He struggles in particular to decide where souls come from. Perhaps, as the Neoplatonists thought, individual souls pre-exist earthly life as pure spirits which have flowed out from the World Soul and then descend to their bodies at the appropriate time. Or, adapting a Stoic idea, maybe they exist in the "causal reasons" which God planted in the universe at the beginning, out of which the many things in the world eventually emerge by natural processes? In that case souls would evolve out of the material universe at the time and in the way God had pre-established (a rather interesting possibility—that soul will evolve out of matter). Or perhaps God specially breathed the very first human soul into Adam, and out of Adam and Eve soul itself is passed on through reproduction. Or it could even be that God creates every new soul individually. Augustine could not provide firm answers, though he tended to favor special creation of each soul by God. This made it easier to suppose that the soul was purely spiritual and not somehow passed on by the physical act of reproduction.

Aquinas on the soul

Fast forward then to the 13th century. Beginning in about 1100 CE Europeans were inheriting and responding to sophisticated Muslim philosophy on many topics, including the soul. Many works of Aristotle had been translated into Arabic and became the focus of intense philosophical study. In general, Aquinas supported Augustine's notion of physical body joined to a spiritual soul, but used Aristotle's categories to nail the idea down more precisely.

Aristotle had argued that every living thing had a "soul" in a broad sense of that term—a *psyche*.[9] Plants have vegetative souls, empowering them to grow and reproduce. Animals have sensate souls, empowering them to grow and reproduce, and also to move about and have sensations and images in their "minds." Humans have intellective souls, empowering them to grow, reproduce, move about, have sensations and images—and also to think reflectively, to have an intellect.

The distinctive intellectual abilities of humans go beyond that of other animals. To think, for Aristotle as for Plato before him, was to be able to have what is often summed up in the phrase "self-transcendence." Do not take this in any mystical sense. It simply means that in our minds we humans can stand back from our current experiences and think about them. We can attend to what we sense or feel or imagine right now, and then compare it consciously to past occasions or compare it in our minds to potential future occasions. By being able to mentally step back from (or rise above, transcend) the immediate moment, we can evaluate our situation and make some choices. So the power of conscious intellection is also the power to make choices. "Intellect and free will" are the words often used to identify those inner abilities that are peculiarly human. These are what make humans more than just a different sort of ape, or at least make humans a very special sort of primate.

A 20th century expert on languages, Derek Bickerton, provides language to label the difference between reflective human thought and the thought of other animals.[10] All animals share an ability for what Bickerton calls "online" thinking. This consists of awareness of current states of external and internal reality, through sensations of things and events around the organism as well as of internal states such as hunger or pain. Only humans show a powerful ability for "offline" thinking, which is to be able deliberately to picture in the mind things that happened in the past, might be happening at a distance, or may happen in the future. Offline thinking can create worlds in the mind, portray universes that have never existed, devise improbable scenarios in imagination. This includes an ability to imagine oneself in some of those other scenarios, and then to think about how we might react, what our values or hopes or fears would lead us to do, and thereby rehearse a kind of alternative life for ourselves. Offline thinking is what philosophers and theologians point to when they speak of "intellection."

Aquinas agreed with Plato—and with the theory that Augustine had preferred—that the power of intellection was an ability to mentally transcend the world of matter, to contemplate abstract qualities like perfect truth and justice, or even mathematical ideas like a perfect circle. Therefore the human soul was not like the material souls of plants and animals; it was non-physical, a spiritual reality. An interesting aspect of the truly non-physical is that it is not bound by time and space, as physical realities are. Having no spatial dimensions it could join the infinite number of angels dancing on the head of a pin without creating any crowding; at least it could if it were free of the body.

With all this in mind Aquinas was able to construct a version of human identity and the inner human self. We humans are composed of body and soul, just as Plato said. The soul of itself is a spiritual reality, which is also therefore free and immortal. But the soul's nature is to be the empowering aspect of the whole person. It is unnatural for the human soul to be without body. That is why full salvation is not simply the ongoing life of the immortal soul, but must include a resurrection into a new body-soul existence. Aquinas' position came to be accepted in Western Christianity and is not significantly different from Eastern Christian views.

The non-material soul as ancient science

To repeat, the ancient philosophy which produced the idea of a non-material soul might best be seen as ancient science. This becomes clear through a comparison of ancient and modern theories. Aristotle's science explained the living activities of plant life by vegetative souls, animal life by sensate souls, and human life and thought by intellective souls. Modern biology offers a different account of how living things operate, relying on biochemistry and physiology to explain life activities. Neoplatonism explained the order of the cosmos as a hierarchy of being emanating downward from the One all the way down to dirt. Today the scientific story of cosmic evolution begins with the energy of the Big Bang, moves to the emergence of the four basic forces of the universe, the formation of particles, then atoms, then stellar furnaces churning out heavier elements, then complex compounds, and then at least on this planet the evolution of life. In Neoplatonic physics and biology (though the latter name had not been coined yet) soul-power emanating from the One, given order by the Nous and passed on by the World Soul, provided the motive power and the goal-orientation to the patterns of the cosmos. In modern science the emergence of the DNA information code, developed over billions of years of variation and natural selection, now accounts for the life processes and their apparent goal-directed behavior.

Christians adopted the old theories as the best science of their times, adapting them to fit basic Christian beliefs. What we could call "scientific" aspects of ideas about the soul took different forms in medieval theology. A major question in astronomy, for example, was whether the motion of the planets meant they also had souls.[11] Similarly, Aquinas finds it natural to discuss how powers of sensation are acts of a complex body made up of all four of the basic elements.[12]

This is not our science, but it is clearly an attempt at a philosophy which seeks what current science still seeks—to know how the forces and elements of the world operate. The question now is how far religious thinkers might extricate key ideas about the inner self from these ancient frameworks and reinterpret them in light of discoveries of modern science. Jewish, Christian, and Muslim religious leaders have an option of responding to the new scientific understandings positively, abandoning elements of ancient Greek science where necessary. They also have the option of holding on to ancient science.

The working out of the Copernican crisis offers clues of how this might work. Christians had adopted the Ptolemaic earth-centered astronomy and treated it as though it were part of revelation. Here again are the words from the decree of the Roman Inquisition on Galileo's Copernican heliocentrism: It "is absurd and false philosophically, and formally heretical because it is expressly contrary to the Holy Scripture." They said this even though Galileo had made the point that the astronomy of the Bible was different from the Ptolemaic view which the Inquisitors defended.[13] Time has proven Galileo correct, however, to try to extricate astronomy from ancient Greek science. It may now prove equally correct to extricate notions of the inner self from ancient Greek science.

There is a significant difference between the two cases. The Ptolemaic astronomy could eventually be shown by empirical evidence to be false. No empirical evidence can count against the existence of a non-material soul. No matter how much modern science interprets mental states as fully natural brain processes, it could still be possible there is also an invisibly operating, non-material soul hiding beneath these material processes.

Vitalism provides a better point of comparison. Chapter 14 noted that one source of opposition to Darwin's theory came from a form of vitalism, belief that something like soul-force had to be at work in the universe. In the 19th and early 20th century some vitalists were willing to concede that perhaps the old concept of soul was not quite correct. Many life processes, nonetheless, vitalists declared, could not be explained unless there was some sort of force guiding those processes. Polyps and starfish cannot generate new limbs by blind mechanical processes alone. The mindless cells of an embryo cannot know how to grow into the right types and move to the right places. Clearly, some goal-directed vital (living) force had to be involved, they insisted.

Vitalism, like belief in a spiritual soul, cannot be disproved. Vital powers might be at work in ways that cannot be detected. But vitalism has become an unnecessary hypothesis. Knowledge of DNA and RNA, of the biochemistry of embryonic development and of clotting and healing mechanisms of the body, has made vitalism simply a useless theory. The long-standing belief in a non-physical soul is suffering the same fate at the hands of modern science. As brain studies advance, the notion that there is a non-physical soul to account for human intellectual abilities may look more and more like a forlorn holdout from the days when the world was full of animating principles called souls. A look at such studies and related evidence can help determine what is more probably correct. That is the work of the next chapter.

For further reading

Crabbe, James C. M., ed., *From Soul to Self* (New York: Routledge, 1999). A history with contributions from eight different writers.

Martin, Raymond, and Barresi, John, *The Rise and Fall of Soul and Self: An Intellectual History of Personal Identity* (New York: Columbia University Press, 2006). A history of Western ideas beginning with ancient Greece and running through contemporary neurophysiology.

McGraw, John J., *Brain and Belief: An Exploration of the Human Soul* (Del Mar, CA: Aegis Press, 2004). Segments on the history of ideas, on physiology, and on basic human issues.

Science on the Mind

If there is a non-physical soul, exempt from the laws of nature, then it is also exempt from scientific scrutiny. Current science nonetheless, in accord with its naturalism, is looking at the inner activities traditionally associated with a spiritual soul and finding ways to interpret those activities as processes of the physical brain. Relevant evidence about human cognition and the inner self comes from paleontology, anthropology, developmental psychology, evolutionary psychology (sociobiology of humans), and neurological studies. These contribute increasingly precise and thorough understanding about the possible developmental history of the human mind over the last few million years. This and the following chapter will take up some of the scientific discoveries relevant to understanding the mind and inner self.

The history of the human mind

We can start with our evolutionary cousins, the chimpanzees. They can recognize themselves in mirrors, engage in what appears to be deliberately political and also deceptive behavior (not necessarily two different kinds of behaviors, of course), and use a few simple tools as well as teach others how to use those tools. Probably the smartest chimp known to date is a bonobo or pygmy chimp named Kanzi. He grew up watching his mother being taught a kind of symbol-language by Sue Savage-Rumbaugh and others, and turned out to be a truly excellent if accidental student. Kanzi is the Aristotle of the bonobos. He can recognize and respond to 200 different spoken words, and can manipulate numerous physical symbols in two-word sentences. Both self-awareness and an ability to learn a form of communication well beyond basic chimpanzee vocal signals, are signs of a fairly complex animal intelligence. This is nonetheless far from human "intellection."[1] A three-year-old human child uses both language and tools in exceedingly more complex ways than even a well-trained and mature chimpanzee, and the human child has only just begun a long history of personal cognitive development.

Analyses of the degree of divergence between chimps and humans of DNA in mitochondrial cells, tiny "organelles" which live within the larger cells of all multi-celled organisms (and all cells with nuclei), make it probable that there was a common ancestor of chimpanzees and humans around five million years ago. Over the last three or four million years diverging series of hominids walked the earth. Over the same period the evidence also supports a concomitant development in intellectual abilities.

Paleontology and tools

Particularly striking is the series of stone tools associated with hominid fossils. The best estimate of human ancestry still traces it back to any of a variety of australopithecines (southern apes). The transition from ape to what should be called pre-human or "hominid" is unclear. It would take extensive further fossil finds to get more confidence in estimating which species descended from which. In any case, the dividing line between ape and early hominid is a bit arbitrary. Paleontologists look for fossil skulls which would hold a larger brain, including diminishment of the concavities at the temple area which in the australopithecines was needed for anchoring very large muscles attached to the jaw for chewing tough food. They look for bones of the wrist and hand which provide greater dexterity. They look also for hip and leg bones which show signs of incipient or full bipedalism, especially if this is confirmed by a hole in the bottom of the skull for the spinal cord rather than closer to the rear of the skull as it is for knuckle-walkers like chimpanzees. The point at which enough of these characteristics are so prominent that we should start speaking of hominids instead of apes is partly a matter of convenience.

It is clear that a number of hominids began to make tools around 2.2 mya (million years ago), earning the name "homo habilis" or handy hominid. Their tools were simple stone axes, found in the Oldewan gorge in Eastern Africa, chipped on one side to make a sharp edge. Physical anthropologists spent months practicing stone chipping to make sure the axes they found were deliberately made and not merely accidentally broken rock. They still practice the art of chipping different kinds of rock to learn from this how much care in the selection of the rock, how much skill and care in chipping, and how much awareness of diverse uses went into this or that tool.[2] About 1.7 mya, more complex stone tools, chipped on two sides to create finer edges, appeared in the vicinity of fossils of homo ergaster and homo erectus, hominids with larger brains than homo habilis. Some evidence suggests these hominids had learned to use fire, perhaps for cooking or just for warmth, as much as 1.5 millions years ago also. (It is not clear when they might have learned to make fires themselves rather than just to preserve burning embers of naturally occurring fires.)

By around 200 kya (thousand years ago, using "kilo" to represent thousand) and up to 40 kya, both Neanderthals and an early "homo sapiens" were making a wider variety of better crafted stone tools, including axes, scrapers, and cutters. Both of these species of humans had much larger cranial capacity than homo erectus. More recently yet, by the upper paleolithic era (beginning around 40 kya) modern homo sapiens was producing an even greater variety of stone tools—awls, needles, scoopers, and other carefully crafted tools for specific purposes appear. The Neanderthals were using such tools themselves, though the variety of tools varies with the location. The Neanderthals disappear from the fossil record about 30 kya. Perhaps their intelligence, as good as it was, was too limited to allow them to compete with modern homo sapiens.

Through more than two million years, then, the evidence indicates that brain cases enlarged even as tool making got more sophisticated. The evidence points strongly to a gradual development of intelligence, from that possessed by the earliest hominid down to modern humans.

Language use

Studies about language provide further relevant information relevant to the evolutionary development of the brain. Humans are born with innate tendencies that conduce to learning language. Even during the first year of life children will attend longer to vowel sounds that are part of the language they hear from their parents than they do to foreign vowels sounds. When a variety of vowel sounds are played in the presence of an American child, for example, the child ignores umlauted vowels but attends to each of the varieties of "u" or "o" sounds used by the child's parents. During the second year of life the child works very hard to try out different sounds, adjusting them to approximate parental speech. During the third year the child is putting together words in patterned ways, creating sentences the child has never heard before, using a grammatical logic simpler than real languages tend to be (creating a past tense by adding "-ed" as in "Mama buyed me a toy"). During this and the next few years the child shows an astounding ability to learn new vocabulary. Out of this process eventually comes the adult's ability to use language to describe, persuade, analyze, and argue, all "intellectual" skills. The brain is apparently programmed to proceed through this learning sequence, if the overall environment provides the means for this.

ere are interesting speculative reconstructions of the sequence of brain develop-
, from proto-chimps to us, that led to this set of linguistic abilities.[3] Occasionally
hominid skull fragment has interior impressions suggesting that the areas of the
involving speech in humans today were already partly developed toward ability
for speech. The pathway for the nerves from brain to tongue increases in size over time,
perhaps as speech increases. Some evidence identifies a shift in the larynx to a lower
place in the throat than in apes, toward the position that aids in the formation of more
precise language sounds.[4] Whether any of these reconstructions are adequate, they
share in the general hypothesis that the human biological structures that make language possible developed over millions of years.

Genetic changes are selected (survive and spread) when they confer some advantage
for the survival and reproduction of the genes that carry those changes. There is always
a cost to brain functioning, especially in us humans. Cat and dog brains use about 5%
of the metabolic energy of these animals; monkeys and apes about 10%. But 20% of
human metabolism is devoted to brain maintenance and functioning.[5] In all these animals brain mass is only about 2% of the mass of the whole organism. In terms of energy
used, human brains are expensive to maintain. Each evolutionary step along the way, as
the brain placed more and more demands on the resources available to the whole body,
it must also have been paying its way by conferring extra means for survival.

Language in particular may have been very helpful, for shared planning, agreement
on who is to hunt or gather food, discussing how to deal with an enemy. It is reasonable
to suppose that the development of language, from the original limited vocalizations of
early apes through to current human language ability, had to proceed step-by-step, with
each step representing greater linguistic "intelligence" than before. Each step is what
Dembski could call a further development of CSI—complexly specified information,
arising, however, from evolutionary development rather than requiring a series of
interventions. A plausible hypothesis arising from all this is that the power of thought
we humans now enjoy did not suddenly appear about 70,000 years ago or later, when
fully modern humans first existed,[6] but that such thought is the product of a long physiological evolutionary development.

Nothing logically forbids the alternative hypothesis first proposed in the 19th century,
that all these developmental steps were preparing a brain with excess capacity not yet
used in intellection, a brain that someday would work with a newly created spiritual
soul in the first truly intellective activity. A religious person could then maintain that
God began to create human souls only when the brain was fully ready to allow at least
some truly human beings to engage in such thought.

Yet there are difficulties with this. First, energy-expensive brains that were not yet
employed as fully as they would be later when they had spiritual souls guiding them,
should have put the carriers of these brains at a disadvantage so that such brains would
tend to be weeded out by natural selection. Second, how should we think of Neanderthals and other pre-humans? Homo erectus and later hominids used their larger brains

for cognitive skills beyond that of apes or chimpanzees. If this high intelligence could slowly emerge from material evolution, what is there to say that the next step, fully human mentition (thought processes), did not? Neanderthals were able to think and plan better than any other animal on the planet, until Cro-magnons (we) came along, as their complex tools show. They used tools, cooked with fire, and perhaps even had some verbal communication. Does this imply a hominid soul of a lesser kind? Or that no soul is needed to get at least very close to modern intellectual ability? It seems to be the simpler hypothesis to imagine that the human powers of thought and choice evolved as part of brain evolution.

Neurophysiology

Information from paleontology converges with the results of brain studies. We can too easily overlook the range of activities of the human brain. It takes a very unusual brain to use language as humans do, for example, and not just because it took millions of years for these various now-innate abilities to evolve. MRI (magnetic resonance imaging) and other devices provide means for adding greatly to our knowledge about the brain. They can track the complex interacting brain processes that go into an ordinary conversation. In Broca's area of the brain (like other so-called areas, not entirely a discrete section), we somehow select words out of long-term memory to express our ideas, activate other parts of the brain to help put the words in grammatical order, and almost simultaneously, it seems, use motor segments of the brain to coordinate precise motions of the lips, tongue, jaw, larynx, pharynx, and diaphragm. Even as we do all this we employ an adjoining area (Warnicke's) to monitor our speech, making almost instant adjustments in our word choice, pronunciation, volume, sometimes in response to the information our eyes are providing us about how our ideas are being received. The brain can do an enormously complex amount of work, most of which we are not consciously aware of.

Materialists of the 18th century were already looking to brain activities to explain human powers of thought. Some of their conclusions did not hold up at all well. A long tradition of "physiognomy," for example, asserted that a person's physical makeup indicated something of the person's personality. At the end of the 18th century Franz Joseph Gall in Vienna proposed that the various bumps and dents of the human skull indicated something about a person's intellectual and moral tendencies. In 1815 Thomas Forster coined the term "phrenology" for this. Phrenology was soon called quackery by critics in Great Britain and much of Europe. But it remained popular enough that in the U.S. in 1901 Henry Lavery and Frank White produced a "psychograph" to measure a person's head very precisely and spit out a set of numbers to categorize personality and abilities. To have one's personality read off by this machine became very popular.

Unfortunately, it was indeed quackery. Careful comparative studies failed to confirm the claims being made by phrenologists. On the other hand, the idea that different parts of the brain might have different mental functions has turned out to be quite true. Which means that phrenology was and is quackery not because it was entirely wrong, but because practitioners did not have adequate evidence at all for the many claims they made. A tendency to favor a materialist interpretation of human thinking was not enough to sustain phrenology. Without adequate evidence a popular theory is still not good science.

A rather famous injury gave a strong clue about the brain. Phineas Gage was a foreman on a railway crew in Vermont.[7] He was a reliable worker who lived an orderly life in general. In 1848 he made an error in tamping down some blasting powder in a hole in a rock to split it. The powder ignited with the tamping rod still in the hole. The three-foot long tamping iron, about an inch and a quarter in diameter, shot straight up into Gage's left cheek, drove right through the top of his head, and landed about 30 yards away. Not all the specific damage to the brain is known, but at least part of the frontal lobes were lost. Somehow Gage managed to survive this accident and after a recovery period went back to work. His personality was markedly different, however. He was no longer steady and reliable; in fact he was emotionally erratic.

Only in recent years has Phineas Gage's change in personality been accounted for. The pre-frontal lobes, the parts of the brain right behind the forehead, carry out the work of careful and complex reflection on our own behavior. These parts, when fully developed, are in strong contact with emotion centers in the mid-brain and can balance out emotional impulses by reflecting on potential consequences of acting on or restraining those impulses. The frontal cortex was part of the damaged section of Gage's brain.

Interestingly, as the brain develops over the early part of a person's life, the brain gradually carries out its final developmental processes by working from the back to the front, establishing new neural connections, but also weeding out unused connections, apparently to make the brain work more efficiently.[8] The brain does not finish the development of the frontal areas until last, around the age of 20 or later, so rational control of emotional impulses can be more difficult prior to that age. If there is also a non-physical soul at work in a person, it would seem to be significantly constrained by the slow development of the brain. On the other hand a long process of brain development, from conception to age 20 or later, would account even for the gradual development of the higher intellectual processes once attributed to a spiritual (non-physical) soul. Such a soul again becomes an unnecessary hypothesis.

Other studies of the relation between brain processes and specific mental abilities have accumulated over the last century and a half. In 1862 Dr. Paul Broca of France connected a patient's loss of ability to speak with a brain lesion in an area of the left side of the brain we still call "Broca's area," mentioned above. Karl Wernicke identified another area in 1874 connected in this case with disruption of the ability to understand spoken language. Studies of relations between the activities of various parts of the brain and forms of cognition increased steadily throughout the 20th century and, with the help of modern imaging techniques are increasing.[9]

The inner self

Disputes arise especially over the nature of the inner self, the "I," which each of us experiences herself or himself to be. We have seen that this has been the object of a vast range of philosophical speculations and arguments, beginning in the West with Plato (or Socrates) and stretching down through the 20th century in the works of various philosophers.

A major argument focuses on whether there must be a single central "self" amidst all the workings of the brain, which monitors—both consciously and perhaps also unconsciously—experiences, reflections, and choices. Some approaches to this question borrow comparisons from discussions about how a computer might be made intelligent. Engineers are very far from achieving that, but in the course of working on the problem have learned a great deal. The human mind works differently from computers. Most computers usually work by sheer speed of computation along single paths. Some computing activity, though, can be divided up into distinct tasks which can be done in parallel. Human minds work by an awesomely greater complexity of interconnections along many paths simultaneously. Speculations about how to build an intelligent computer usually propose that intelligence requires multiple interacting processors such as the brain already possesses.

The vivid visual images we have of the world, for example, are created in us by a set of distinct neural columns in our occipital lobes at the back of the cortex. One set of neurons responds to major differences in light or dark, another to specific linear boundaries, another to motion, another to certain colors. All of these columns of neurons are connected in turn to another set of neurons which integrate these various aspects of what we see into a single image. Here there is a hierarchy of functions, with one "higher" integrating processor, as it were, making use of the distinct contributions of "lower" processors dedicated to specialized tasks, and doing it all at dazzling speed.

The earlier description of the interaction of multiple sections of the brain in speech is a clue that the brain in general has a great number of different "processors." With that observation in place, it is then possible to formulate better the question of a single inner self. This becomes the question of whether among the many processors there is a physical locale or a functioning unity of some cells that is the master processor, coordinating many of the rest of the processors.

Such a central processor would not need to coordinate all brain activities. The reticular formation in the brain stem controls a great number of regular body processes, including sleep, without the need for any conscious thought at all. It has an impact on the autonomic nervous system running through the torso, which also operates with no need for any central self to control it, in regulating the functions of many organs. Most brain activities are not subjectively (able to be experienced consciously) available at all. The inner self, though, does seem to be experienced subjectively—we experience ourselves thinking and choosing.

Philosophers have long used introspection to determine what the inner self is like. But magnetic resonance imaging sometimes gives us a different picture than introspection provides. The brain tells us we feel a prick on our hand at the same time we see the needle applied to our hand, when in fact there is a lag in the time it takes the brain to register the feeling. Without our knowing it, the brain reconciles sensory input so it "makes sense." A fairly well-localized part of the brain involved in making decisions shows activity a split second before a person is conscious of making the decision. It is as though the brain decides things prior to our consciousness; then we experience the decisions as though we just consciously decided them. In these cases the subjective self is told things by the brain, as it were, rather than telling the brain what to do.[10]

Such simple brain activities may be poor guides to the more abstract and complex forms of reasoning and perhaps also to the strong human sense of self-aware free choice?[11] One school of thought favors attributing these types of inner experience to a central processor function in the brain. This has the advantage of establishing a single inner self. It also matches our experience of being able to say that "I" think or do or choose certain things. Introspection—thinking about our mental processes—seems to support this.

It gets rather complicated, however. Sometimes our thoughts themselves feel like they are "me," as when we are happily anticipating a party that is about to begin. But sometimes we observe ourselves being happy in anticipation. We can say to ourselves "Wow, I am really happy thinking about this party." If I am aware of myself as happy, I am observing myself. But who is the "I," who is doing this observing? Is it the same "I" that is happily anticipating, or is it an observer "I"? Are there then two layers of "I," a second "I" who is aware of the first "I" happily anticipating? It gets worse. If these questions make sense so far, if you have been thinking about the observer "I," then there is an "I" that is aware of an observer "I" that is aware of an "I" that is happily anticipating.

The alternative to the single inner self model is to suspect that the many modules or processors of the brain are like a committee, one whose members have worked together for many years and by custom defer to each others' expertise.[12] When serious reflection is needed, let the frontal lobes take over; when it is time to play tennis, let the motor sections have priority. In any case, as with any committee, every member may have some input in such a way that at the end it is not really possible to say which member did this or that, which member did more or less, and so on. Self-awareness may be a kind of internal sequential 'conversation' that parts of the brain carry on with each other very quickly.[13]

Whether this is sufficient to provide a single "self" remains the question. It may be the philosopher Leslie Dewart is on an insightful track when he adds that it takes language to create explicit self-consciousness. Unless we learn to employ language in specifically self-referential ways by getting familiar with the ideas of "I" and "me," a clear sense of selfhood does not develop.[14] The hungry two-year-old Allison who says "Allison wants a cookie" has identified herself by the name others have given her. It will take more language experience before she learns to identify herself as an "I" who wants a cookie.

Developmental psychology

Little Allison's development is part of a longer-term development of mental skills, which are themselves apparently dependent on an ongoing physical development of the brain. Between the age of 3 and 4 a significant new ability appears, called "theory of mind" by developmental psychologists. As is often the case, this label is not as helpful as it ought to be. It stands for the emerging awareness that other people have minds that can be different from that of the child. A psychologist shows a candy box to Billy, age 3, and asks Billy what is in the box. Billy responds, "candy"? The psychologist opens the box and shows Billy it is full of pencils, undoubtedly a big disappointment to Billy. Then Sally enters the room and the psychologist asks Billy what Sally will think the box contains. Billy says "pencils." That, after all, is what the box contains. Why would Sally say anything else? A four-year-old put in Billy's position—let's call her Judy—would respond "candy," knowing full well that will be the reasonable and hopeful guess Sally will make.

As the brain continues to develop physically, sometime between the age of 6 and 8 most children will have left behind their invisible friends for good and will realize that Santa Claus is a fiction. Around the age of 11, the brain will develop further and before long the adolescent will find it possible to learn basic algebra, as well as become tormented by thoughts of how others think of the adolescent: I see you seeing me, and it concerns me what you think of me. Around the age of 20 the frontal lobes finally finish most of their development and take over their role of thinking things through somewhat rationally and trying to control the emotional responses of the mid-brain. These developmental stages toward sharper and more complex mental abilities look as though they depend on brain development. A spiritual soul would not undergo such material development. (The sequence of neurological development probably plays a role in the development of the stages of faith which James Fowler identifies, as in Chapter 1.)

Split brain studies

There are other mental oddities that fit better with the supposition that mind is what the brain does. We know, for example, that the right side of the brain, normally lacking its own language centers, does not have *conscious* awareness of information which it is in fact receiving and processing accurately from the senses. This became evident in the study of some people whose corpus collosum, a thick connecter between the left and right sides of the brain, was surgically severed to prevent severe epileptic seizures.

Objects in the left visual field are seen by the right side of the brain (images passing through the lens of the eyeball are inverted and reversed side-to-side). Likewise, objects in the right visual field are seen by the left side of the brain. The corpus collosum keeps the two sides of the brain in close contact with each other, so the difference between right and left brain is normally not evident. Severing the corpus collosum creates a different situation. The left side of the brain can no longer be informed by the right side, and vice versa. If an image is flashed quickly in the left visual field, faster than the eyes can turn to bring that image to the center, the image registers only in the right side of the brain. A person who is then asked what she or he saw invariably cannot say. The person lacks conscious knowledge of the image.

Oddly, however, the person does know non-consciously. When give a choice between two other objects, say a hammer and a spoon, the person chooses the object that would go best with the image. An image of a nail evokes the response "hammer." An image of a bowl of soup evokes the response "spoon." The person responding will nonetheless insist that the response is just a guess, usually making up some explanation.[15]

On the other hand, an image which is flashed in the right visual field, traveling therefore to the left side of the brain, can be identified explicitly by the person with the split corpus collosum. The left side of the brain contains Broca's area and other areas which normally facilitate speech. This seems to mean that it is precisely language that gives us the ability to have an "I" who is consciously aware of what we experience. It would be odd if a self-aware spiritual soul could receive information through only part of the brain. It would not be odd for a physical brain to have such a limitation. It would be odd for a spiritual soul not to have an awareness of itself as an "I" unless the physical brain articulates this.

The endnotes in this chapter provide leads to some of the many books which summarize the result of brain studies over the last century or so. They describe scientific explorations which have taught us a great deal about the inner self and our minds. The goal of science, of course, is to keep on learning, with every new piece of information opening doors to more. None of the contents of this chapter disprove the existence of a non-physical (immaterial) intellective soul. Yet taken together these studies support the naturalistic supposition that reflective intellection and self-awareness are processes which evolved over time and which the brain can carry out without need of any further source of intellective power. That is the situation that the traditional belief in a spiritual soul now faces.

For further reading

For an excellent but brief set of pages on the development of tool use concomitant with hominid evolution, including increasing brain size, dispersion across continents, etc., see http://www.handprint.com/LS/ANC/stones.html

Feinberg, Todd M., *Altered Egos: How the Brain Creates the Self* (New York: Oxford University Press, 2001). This surveys arguments by philosophers and neurophysiologists.

Gazzaniga, Michael S., *The Mind's Past* (Berkeley: University of California Press, 1998) provides a summary by a pioneer and expert in brain studies.

The Freedom of a Material Soul

This chapter will be more speculative than previous chapters. Science is still learning a great deal about human consciousness and brain operations. The analyses of several problems are necessarily sketchy and tentative. Those analyses can nonetheless at least open up some possibilities for working with the tension between modern neuroscience and basic human issues related to the tradition of the soul. The most basic problem is this: if human thought and choices are all carried out by a material brain, the word "soul" becomes only poetic, a metaphoric label for the inner self, or for an inner life of thoughts and feelings and commitments. Even this metaphoric "soul" may appear to be threatened by reductionistic materialism.

A full-fledged materialism implies that all events are fully determined by natural causes. This makes the entire universe "deterministic," including even the activities of the material brain. All thoughts, aspirations, poetry, commitments, acts of love, noble choices, are therefore phenomena produced by the material workings of a brain which is determined by various natural causes to engage in such thoughts and choices. Soul and free will seem to evaporate.

> There is no more potent source of anxiety about free will than the image of the physical sciences engulfing our every deed, good or bad, in the acid broth of causal explanation, nibbling away at the soul until there is nothing left to praise or blame, to honor, respect, or love.[1]

These words of Daniel Dennett in his *Freedom Evolves* capture the double issue of human freedom. One side is the question of free will and human responsibility for their choices. Belief in inner human freedom is belief that people can be responsible for their choices and therefore be deserving of praise or blame for what they do. The other side is human dignity. If our decisions are made for us by a chain of natural material causes, not only have we lost freedom but also a sense of special worth. Reductionism appears to win.

Reductionism, as described earlier, is an essential part of science. One can "reduce" gold, for example, to the sub-atomic particles of which it is made and the nuclear and electromagnetic forces which hold those particles together. In one sense that is easy to do. An atom of gold is composed of 79 protons, the same number of electrons arranged in six "shells," and enough neutrons to bring the atomic weight up to almost 197. The protons and neutrons are held together in the nucleus by the strong force; the electrons surround the nucleus in a certain way because of known characteristics of the electro-magnetic force.

This accurate reductionist account is nonetheless also seriously inadequate. An emergentist view is also required. What counts is the particular interrelational arrange-ment of protons, neutrons, and electrons of gold. This arrangement is not just a gather-ing of particles; it is a particular structured pattern bonded into a stable unity, which produces characteristics unique to gold—the malleability and ductility, the shine and color, its particular conductivity. This arrangement is analogous to a code, an ordering of bits of the atom to produce a certain outcome. The arrangement is thus a kind of "information."

Gold is rather simple, of course—a single element. The power of interrelational structure among atomic particles to produce the element gold is exceeded enormously by the power of interrelational structure among elements—oxygen, carbon, nitrogen, hydrogen, and phosphorus, especially, to form chains of compounds whose order pro-duces life activities. Some chains of compounds eventually developed differentiations and levels of interaction that constitute cells. Cells eventually achieved a set of stable interrelated activities that constitute multi-celled organisms. Each of these steps is a higher level of information. Each level of information produces more complex activi-ties. Each one of these higher levels of information has emerged from prior lower levels. Again, complexly specified information (CSI) increases step-by-step, with new proper-ties emerging at each level. (Dembski's description of CSI turns out again to be quite useful, but without requiring anything more than a very long process of variation and natural selection to account for it.)

A great variety of emergentist positions on the human mind exist. Here is a sampling to make that point. Keith Ward agrees that the soul emerges from the evolution of mat-ter. He supports a "soft materialism," as he calls it, which proposes that what emerges from matter might yet be more than material. Richard Swinburne also concludes that the soul is a product of the material evolution of the universe, but he claims that soul has become so distinct from matter that only a new sort of body-mind dualism adequately describes the nature of this evolved soul. William Hasker proposes that the human mind is a "soul-field" generated by the brain, analogous to a magnetic field generated by a magnet, both fields real and distinct from what generates them. He is concerned to assert that this "soul-field" can exert "downward causation" on the physical brain in order to escape determinism.[2] Obviously, there is no agreement among those seeking to defend the mind/soul against reductionism.

In response to such positions, some neurophysicists do happily proclaim themselves reductionists. The noted neurophysicist Paul Churchland, for example, offers what he himself calls a "reductionist" account of the inner self or mind, reducing mental activities to brain operations.[3] He says he seeks an entirely naturalistic or "physicalist" account of mind operations. He wants to focus on these complexities as natural processes, unhindered by old claims that some aspects of mind are not due to regular natural process but to a non-physicalist (spiritual) force called "soul."

Churchland's language is misleading. He thinks his choice must be between belief in a spiritual soul of some sort and scientific reductionism. A third more emergentist and historically minded approach exists to describe inner freedom. To discuss this we first need more background.

The complexity frontier

In us humans billions of brain cells interconnect and interact over trillions of synapses. No matter how powerful and informative the results of MRI and other studies, they will be able to provide only a relatively rough map of the brain terrain. Neurophysiology will continue to show which parts of the brain, and which connections in those parts, act with what strength, for different kinds of thought and emotion. But a map is not the actual complex territory.

Consider a comparison. A biologist can study what is going on in a 40-acre parcel of land. The number and kinds of trees can be counted; the same is true of bushes and grasses and ivies. Molds and fungi add to the complexity. The biologist can also give a good estimate of the number of ant hills or dens, the types of ants in each, and can approximate the number of ants of each kind. Badgers and beetles and birds can be noted and categorized; the life habits of each invites further study. Soil analysis will reveal the amount of clay or loam and its acidity, the worms at work, and the kinds of bacteria which predominate.

But all this will still only be partial knowledge of the many aspects of this piece of ecological complexity. Even if this knowledge were much more thorough, mapping all these elements still does not indicate what is going on at any given moment in the 40 acres nor what precisely will occur the next day. Which ants will war on which others? What fledglings will fall out of the nest, and of these which will be found and killed by some predator? Will the robin eat the spider under the fourth elm tree before the spider's web traps a flying insect? Endless such questions can arise.

Freeman Dyson has called this the "complexity frontier" of science, an ever-receding complexity horizon.[4] Although neurophysiology will continue to learn a great deal about the brain and its processes, those processes involve synaptic connections inter-acting in extraordinarily complex patterns. The full specific activities of the brain will remain beyond the complexity frontier.

The activity and results of the DNA code in a single cell is already an achievement of nature exceedingly far beyond what ancient science even guessed at when they tried to explain life activities in general. The activities of the human brain surpass that of a cell by many orders of magnitude. In humans the full set of informational codes of ele-ments, compounds, cells, multi-cellular life, and neural cell interaction with trillions of potential interconnections are beyond computation except in the most superficial and general way. It is not surprising that the ancients thought they would have to invoke some sort of animating spirit to explain life, and a special immaterial soul to explain cognition.

As the previous chapter indicated, there is an alternative model now available, well-grounded in highly specific and complex information, of mind as activities of the brain (and the central nervous system in general). This model describes conscious thoughts and choices as sets of activities carried out by the brain, under the influence of the human genetic code, as well as the influence of the individual learning that the code makes possible, and also the influence of thousands of years of cultural developments handed on from generation to generation on how to do intellection in various ways. Take note of the many levels of natural causes at work here—DNA guides the develop-ment of the human organism, including the ability of the organism to learn new things through personal experience, learning which in turn depends upon the development of culture with all its specific language codes, physical tools, cognitive tools (like writing and highly abstract mathematical methods).

Layers of the self

A still deeper examination of the levels of causes behind even a single idea or choice will aid greatly in discussing the nature of the inner self, of mind or "soul," and the abil-ity of that self to make conscious choices. We can divide those causes into the standard two categories of nature and nurture.

Nature

Proponents of evolutionary psychology (sociobiology applied to humans) make some interesting claims about innate human tendencies. The starting point of sociobiology is the long-standing observation that all organisms are guided in their behavior not just by learning but also by inherited tendencies, including even the tendency to learn.

Instinctive behavior is strong evidence that genes can dictate how organisms behave. Lone spiders know how to spin well-structured webs; among most vertebrates strong sexual interest arises at a certain stage of physiological development; cats tend to avoid home when a new cat is born there. In some cases the compulsive nature of instinct stands out more starkly. A trap-door spider catches an insect, takes it to the edge of its little den in the ground and leaves the insect at the edge, goes into the den to check it out, and then returns to the insect to drag it into the den for dinner. Biologists explored this behavior by quickly moving the insect a short distance away when the spider darted in to check the den. Upon emerging the spider traveled to retrieve the insect and drag it back to the edge of the den again. It then checked the den out again before coming back to drag the insect into the den. The biologists repeatedly moved the insect a short way from the den. The spider continued to retrieve it but then leave it again at the edge of the den in order to check out the den. The spider apparently could not take the insect directly into the well-checked den; the insect had to first be left at the exact side of the den. Instinct ruled; the genes were in full control.

The logic of survival of the fittest would seem to say that it would always be those genes which promote the most thoroughly selfish behavior that get passed along. A lioness with genes that tell the lioness to grab the most food, even at the expense of others in the pride, stays healthy and survives to pass on genes that dictate such selfishness. A lion whose genes tell it to grab the most food it can and also to mate with as many females as possible will pass on its grabbing and mating genes more often. Selfish behavior, therefore, ought to flourish and grow. There could even be a special bonus for a free-loader, a lioness who tended not to engage in the dangerous effort of bringing down an animal but who then would grab all the meat for herself possible. This would be true also of the lion who was a "sneaky Pete," who did not engage in the tiring and often dangerous fighting with other males for the chance to mate. A sneaky Pete would wait for the stronger males to be distracted by fighting among themselves for access to the females. Pete could then sneak in some matings with less effort and more safety.

One of the beginnings of sociobiology was the observation that in spite of the logic of survival of the fittest, there was a significant amount of altruistic behavior in many animal groups.[5] Altruism, strictly defined, is not just cooperative behavior—I'll scratch your back if you'll scratch mine. Altruism is a willingness to help another even at personal cost beyond any gain. The bird which sounds the alarm at the sight of a hawk calls attention to itself and can be in greater danger. A bird which quietly hides at the sight of a hawk will more likely survive, as the hawk gets adequately fed by killing a bird not in hiding. A particularly notable case are honey bees. When a bee stings, its stinger get ripped out from its bottom lobe to remain in the victim and continue to release its poison. This increases the effectiveness of the defense of the hive. But each bee which stings also then dies. It cannot pass on its genes to sting to protect the hive. That poses the question of how that genetic tendency survives.

It was the social insects such as bees that provided the path to the answer that became sociobiology. Each bee that dies in defense of the hive is also dying in defense of copies of its own genes. Each hive consists of the offspring of the same queen and up to a dozen mates, who themselves are probably related to the queen. So the genetic makeup of all the bees in the hive is very similar. The genes that die after a bee loses its stinger are assuring that copies of these genes survive in others. So the gene remains "selfish" even in sacrificing a copy of itself, because that act helps assures that copies of itself live on.

The analysis gets more complicated when applied to most other organisms which reproduce sexually, but the basic idea remains the same. The bird that gives the hawk warning cry to its flock is probably alerting related birds with many copies of the same alarm-giving gene. So the gene is still being successfully "selfish" by aiding the survival of copies of itself. (The word "selfish" is meant only metaphorically; genes do not think, have goals, etc. As genetic characteristics vary through mutation and other processes, some genetic shift will happen accidentally to guide the organism to protect copies of itself by protecting kin. That variant gene will then more likely spread by being more often protected by kin.)

"Kin favoritism" is one of the favorite topics of evolutionary psychology. The math is relatively simple. Any person's full sibling will share, on average, 50% of the person's genes. A person's first cousin will, on average, share about 16% of the person's genes. It would be to a gene's long-term advantage if it prompted its carrier to fight to the death to save three or more full siblings, because those siblings carry copies of that gene. The copy in the self-sacrificing carrier would be lost, of course. But the kin-favoritism gene copies would be saved. It would also be to a gene's advantage were its carrier willing to make that sacrifice for nine or more first cousins. Anyone living as part of an extended clan would share many genes with others in the clan, including the gene for kin-favoritism.

This, at least, makes sense out of one of the great traps humans are often caught in, the tendency to defend the clan or the tribe by engaging in cycles of revenge. If a bear clan member kills your cousin, your aunt and uncle expect you to join in the search for revenge. The clan chiefs—we sometimes call them warlords—who fight in Iraq, Afghanistan, and Somalia today, are echoing the behavior of the Scotch and Irish, and before that the English and Germans, the Chinese and Japanese, and so on. This holds among many of the drug gangs today. One of the most difficult tasks in forming a state is getting people to turn over the job of revenge to the state and its law system. Where the state is weak blood feuds among clans or tribes will be normal. Blame it on the genes.

Nurture

On the other hand a hopeful sign in human history appears in the many techniques societies have invented to ward off blood feuds. The Cheyenne and Sioux did it by rules that banished a killer from the tribe. The killer could return eventually if the relatives of the dead person agreed, perhaps after some years, and usually with some special gift from the family of the banished killer. In other cultures the desire for revenge was quieted by rules that stipulate what blood money must or could be paid in recompense for a death.

We poor humans, then, are not left to the mercy of our genes alone. We can create customs or rules or laws which regulate our genetic inclinations. We can change clan competition into peaceful (usually) support for local sport teams. We can establish rules of marriage to put boundaries around competition for mates and establish parental responsibilities as much as possible. Parents can teach their children the values of mutual tolerance, or teach them that every person, not just kin, deserves basic respect and protection. Such rules develop over the centuries, even over the millennia.

We are normally too little aware of our dependency on cultural development about how we use our brains and respond to innate tendencies. We do not normally recognize, for example, that literacy is a powerful but rather unnatural human activity. It takes years of training and practice to communicate clearly in writing or print. That is a major reason high school graduates still must take more courses in "composition" when they arrive at college. Twelve previous years of practice turn out not to have been enough to use this special tool very well, because literacy places heavy demands on a person. A good writer has to imagine how the words and their order will give a clear understanding to even an absent reader who has no chance to ask questions of the writer. This in turn trains the writer to try to develop more insight into how others think and use language. Literacy also makes it possible to formulate complex and difficult sequences of ideas, checking them for overall coherence.

Literacy is just one example of the enormous range of human cultural products which affect thoughts and values. Globalization demonstrates this repeatedly. Small farmers in developing countries use a cell phone to find out what price they can get for which crop. Ambitious but deprived women in patriarchal cultures find they can get small loans to set up their own business. But globalization is only the current edge of historical cultural development that began among humans up to 70,000 years ago. That long process contributes mightily to the ability of brains to think thoughts and choose values that otherwise would have remained outside the horizon of what anyone could think or do.

Each person also has a unique personal history, a long set of experiences with reality, especially and emphatically with other people, which shape a person's thoughts and decisions. Parents, relatives, friends, the neighborhood, the society, religion, formal education, and today extensive communications media contribute endlessly and relentlessly to the shape of the inner self. Behind each decision a person makes, therefore, lies a deep range of influences. The formation of every individual personality derives from more than 10,000 years of cultural development described here earlier, from primitive preliterate hunting and gathering animism, to more complex societies with hereditary rules and worship of gods, to arguments about a single Ultimate which provides underlying rational order to the universe. We are normally only dimly aware of the wide and thick range of economic, political, social, familial, philosophical, and religious ideas and forces we have inherited from those 10,000 years of culture. The combination of brain complexity, personal history, and cultural resources produce a mind that can be aware of the infinite horizon described in the chapters on God, and at the same time of skeptical questions about the infinite described in the chapter on atheism. That same mind is self-transcending in the sense of being able to think about self, with an awareness of a wide range of possibilities and values. This gives us the power to consciously choose how we act.

Inner freedom

With this background in place, about the complexity frontier and the layers of the self, we can look at the notion of an inner human freedom available to a fully natural, brain-generated, inner self. A central question is how this can be done without succumbing to a total determinism.

Attempts to save the concept of free will usually propose only two alternatives. One is the possibility favored by many theologians and philosophers that there is some non-determined causality exerted by the will in making a genuinely free choice. This possibility, however, affirms free will as a cause that itself in some aspect is uncaused (undetermined). This is a awkward position, not only for a naturalistic science which seeks natural causes for everything, but for Western theology also. That tradition has said that God is the sole uncaused cause of everything else. Having a will which operates uncaused is hard to make sense of in any framework. It raises the further question also of how a person directs the will to choose in a given way. A person can say, "Well, I just decide what I want," but then is left with no further understanding. On the other hand, to try to develop "will power" or strengthen the will is precisely an attempt to make the will something caused, determined, developed, strengthened. It is then no longer treated as an uncaused power.

The second alternative denies free will and offers a fully reductionistic determinism. Because our choices are made by our brains, which are entirely physical, all of our thoughts and choices are therefore fully determined by the ordinary laws of cause and effect of material reality. This might seem to eliminate genuine freedom altogether. Our inner experience of making choices would then not be free at all, even though it feels free. If so, this could eliminate a basis for holding people responsible for their choices.

("Epiphenominalism" is a name given to the rather extreme position which claims that the brain does all the work of thought and choice on a non-conscious deterministic level which creates conscious thoughts and choices as surface by-products. Thoughts and choices are phenomena—events—which occur upon [*epi* in Greek] the surface of the brain like foam floating on top of ocean waves.)

Chaos and quantum indeterminacy as sources of freedom?

Faced with this awkward pair of choices, theologians and philosophers have sometimes sought room for free will in two aspects of nature which seem to escape from full material determinism. They hope to find room for human freedom in the same two aspects of the physical universe that some have used to leave room in the universe for God to intervene.

One is the element of "chaos." Chaos theory, as it is called, emphasizes two aspects of nature. One aspect is the order hidden in what seems disorderly. The sawtooth ridge of a mountain range seems random. There appears to be more chaos than order in the jagged outline. Yet the laws of physics are still at work. The mountain range cannot rise too high without its weight making that part of the continental plate sag or even melt. The melting temperature is determined by the composition of the rock in the plate. The same is true of a major storm. The wind and water flow in seeming chaos, yet they too follow laws of physics. Air pressure varies with the water content; temperature determines how much energy the storm contains. Natural determinism is at work even in what appears simply chaotic.

The other aspect of chaos theory is the unpredictability of complex systems, an unpredictability which suggests an escape from full determinism. A famous illustration of this is the image of a butterfly's wing setting in motion a tiny air current, which contributes then to a diversion of a breeze, which in turn alters the flow of a jet stream slightly, which in its turn leads to a major storm on the other side of the world. (The flea on the rabbit in the road in front of the truck in Chapter 10 would be a comparable cause.)

It would be more accurate, however, to see "chaos" not as an instance of indeterminacy but as another instance of the complexity frontier or horizon. Chaos theorists do not deny cause-and-effect determinism here; they only note that the variable long-term effects of multitudinous small events are far too complex to predict. So chaos theory does not really provide a way to carve out room for non-determined action, such as free will is thought to be.

The other instance where strict determinism does in fact fail is on the sub-atomic quantum level, where only statistical probability rules and not deterministic cause-and-effect. We have seen that quantum indeterminacy is a strange concept. It says there are states of electrons which are neither clearly located nor have determinate mass. Their location and/or mass does not gel, as it were, until some form of energy hits them. The resulting location and mass cannot be fully predicted. The outcome of an energy hit can be estimated only statistically, what is likely to happen. This eliminates full determinism in favor of a degree of randomness. But if free will exists only as a function of quantum indeterminacy, then it is not the conscious choosing which the idea of free will seeks to save. Quantum indeterminacy does not save free will either.

Inner freedom as conscious choosing

Fortunately, between the concepts of free will and mindless determinism, there is a third way of thinking about freedom. It builds upon a very traditional idea in philosophy, one that goes back to at least the late Middle Ages. Thomistic scholasticism did quite well without the notion of free will for centuries. Aquinas proposed instead that we do make free *choices*. This sounds like mere word play, but the change in words can call attention to a shift in interpretation. According to scholastic philosophers like Aquinas the will is *determined* (controlled) by its nature to seek whatever the intellect presents to it as the good. The intellect, as it reflects on things, decides where the good lies and where it does not.[6] It is the responsibility of every person to seek to understand clearly what is good and what is not—to develop an "informed conscience" in the traditional language. This focuses on the historical reality of a person's life and choices, on the long process through which a person learns to reflect on what should be considered good or bad.

Most philosophers bypass this learning process. They focus on individual decisions and create descriptions of those decisions which place conscious choice in charge of the process. Philosophers such as Ward, Swinburne, and Hasker mentioned earlier, reject what they call a "bottom-up" approach, which portrays consciousness as entirely caused by non-conscious and fully determined brain-states. Instead they seek a "top-down" description of thought and choice by supposing that a spiritual or semi-spiritual soul emerges from brain activity. The Christian philosopher Nancy Murphy firmly promotes a "physicalist" (materialist) notion of mind and consciousness, but she wants to be sure that the mind is at least partly in charge, not just controlled by unthinking physical brain processes. So she also claims that the brain produces a superior "mind," which then exerts a top-down influence on the workings of the body, including brain functions.

Neither the top-down nor the bottom-up images, in fact, represent the reality of brain states and human thought and choice. Both are vertical images. It would be truer to the historical nature of existence to use a "horizontal" image, to represent the ongoing influence of sequences of past states of self-reflective consciousness on subsequent states of the brain. Every state of human self-consciousness is part of a stream of consciousness, a changing stream in which events (experiences, thoughts, decisions) upstream determine something of the path of thoughts downstream. When we think about what seems to be our current thinking, we are actually thinking about what we have just done in the previous minutes or seconds. The thoughts we had then, the conscious choices we made then, affect what we think next.

The causal flow from past to present and to future states of consciousness is highly complex, because the upstream sequence of ideas and values is so long. Prior to any single decision lies a fountain of personal experiences. Prior to those experiences flows the river of culture into a person's life out of the thousands of years that culture has been developing. The dreams, hopes, fears, analyses, judgments, and critical reflection of many hundreds of generations converge in each of our lives by a thousand different routes.

Chaos theory applies here also. There are natural limits or determinants on what each of us learns. We can only learn what a human mind, perhaps aided by books and computers and other media, is able to learn. We cannot sense quarks directly; we cannot plot the trajectory of space satellites on our own; we cannot leap complex equations at a single bound. We also have various tendencies built into us by genetic programs, tendencies which limit or empower us. But within such limits the capacity of the human mind is otherwise—well, unlimited. We do have something like an openness to an ever-receding horizon of possibilities.

To repeat: most of what the mind does is not conscious. We noted that the brain keeps the autonomic nervous system running, for example. This keeps our innards operating as they should, without our awareness (except when things go wrong). Similarly, when we are prompted to identify ourselves by typing in our mother's "maiden" name, our brain somehow pulls that name up out of storage into consciousness without us knowing or even experiencing what the brain is doing to accomplish this. We carry on oral arguments without being able to sense the operations of Broca's area, Warnicke's area, the relevant motor control areas of tongue, lips, and larynx, yet they are all highly involved in the process. These are only a few of a thousand activities our brain performs for us, without us experiencing the actual neural activity as such.

When we make choices we think we first consciously choose, and that choice is then carried out by our brains. Interestingly, it may be the other way around, as the previous chapter noted. The psychologist Benjamin Libet tell us that a non-conscious activity first takes place in the part of the brain whose activity signals that decisions are being made.[7] This non-conscious activity occurs as much as a half second before there is activity in the part of the brain where people consciously make decisions. Should we therefore conclude that non-conscious brain activity and not conscious choice determines what we do or think? Perhaps so, but we should not stop there. We should not forget that any non-conscious activity is itself preceded by prior brain activity, some of it conscious. It is not the single moment of reflection or choice that should be the object of analysis when thinking about making conscious choices. It should be the stream of various states of consciousness and unconsciousness. Those elements of conscious thought in the stream of brain activities give us the possibility of exercising conscious responsibility for our choices.

External freedom vs. inner freedom

Two types of "freedom" characterize human choices and activity. They differ significantly. When we want to talk about a human ability to choose in a way that makes us responsible for our choices, inner freedom counts.

We have a kind of "outer" or external freedom when we are not coerced to act in a certain way. The coercion can be mild, in the form of persuasive efforts by parents or teachers or neighbors. It can be very strong, as when someone holds us at gunpoint or physically ties us up. It can be somewhere in between as when civil and criminal laws threaten us with punishment for certain acts. When no coercion at all exists, we can say we are free, free to do whatever we want. At that point we may then happily surrender to impulse or habit, without thought for the consequences. We are then free only in the sense a dog off the leash is free or a bear roaming the woods. Ironically, surrender to impulse or unthinking habit is actually a loss of inner freedom, a loss of the kind of thought and choice that makes us able to be responsible for our acts.

Two notions of human freedom

1. External Freedom—from restraint or coercion
   Freedom from external constraint keeping a person from doing what she or he wants.
   Political freedom is part of this, to be free from government or military controls.
   There are many possible external constraints, such as threats from bullies or street gangs, demands made by parents or teachers, or outright physical coercion.

2. Internal Freedom—making conscious responsible choices
   The ability to make conscious choices includes the following:
   1. Awareness of the situation one is in
   2. Recognition of the possibility of thinking and choosing about the situation
   3. Reflection on possible outcomes of different choices or actions
   4. Possession of certain basic values that seem worth achieving
   5. Use of those values to judge which outcomes are good or bad
   6. Possession of the habit of trying to seek the good and avoid the bad
   7. The act of consciously choosing a path of action to achieve what one thinks is good or avoid what one thinks is bad
   8. Possessing other habits needed to overcome obstacles to seeking the good and avoiding the bad, such as patience, persistence, willingness to accept some personal loss.

The word "autonomy" is sometimes used as a synonym for "freedom," but that word has its own ambiguities. A child's autonomy is to get to do what the child feels like, even without any conscious reflection and with little sense of responsibility—beyond a desire not to get caught doing something for which the child will be punished in some way. To an adolescent, autonomy means being left free by parents, teachers, and others, to do what the adolescent feels like. The adolescent may define "responsible" as a synonym for obedience, because adults seem to think that a person is irresponsible every time the person does not follow orders. The autonomy of a responsible adult, an adult who has the habit of reflecting before choosing, in the light of basic values, is the fullest human autonomy. It is this ability and this habit that makes a person able to be genuinely responsible for her or his own choices and actions.

Notice that this inner human freedom and responsibility does not require a "free will" that has an uncaused aspect. This sort of freedom is caused or determined by conscious thought in the light of values learned. We all live in a kinder world to the extent people make conscious decisions guided by values like honesty, compassion, and justice.

In any given situation the process of inner reflection and choice will not normally be this carefully deliberate. The eight steps listed under "Internal Freedom" in the chart would be rather burdensome if a person had to go through them carefully one at a time. Ordinarily each of us is carried along by habit. It matters then which habits we have chosen to adopt—yes, chosen. There are many such instances, of course, in which a person does carefully go through such steps. Deciding on a career, whether to buy a house and which house in particular, marriage, raising children, all may propel a person to work hard at each one of those steps. We exercise our capacity of conscious reflection and choice to different degrees in different situations.

A lost analogy and a disenchanted universe

We have seen that with many theologians speaking about God's influence on the world an analogy between human choices and divine influence has been popular. From at least the time of C. S. Lewis, in his book *Miracles*, the possibility of divine intervention in the physical world has been compared to the influence of a human mind on the body.[8] While none of the theologians claimed to be certain just how the mind worked on the body, it seemed clear enough to them that it did. Every time a person reflects carefully and consciously on what to do next and then does it, could be an instance of this sort of action.

As long as the mind was also thought to be the activity of a spiritual soul, not a physical reality, the analogy had a certain positive force. A spiritual soul is not part of material nature; neither is God. If humans make choices and act in the world by the power of a spiritual—non-material—soul, may not God do the same? If the mind is the processes of a physical brain, however, the analogy disappears. In any person the effect of mind upon body is an effect of material processes on material processes or things, not the effect of the immaterial on the material.

More generally, the supposition that the entire person, mind and body, is a physical whole, not a dualistic combination of matter and spirit, tends to divide up the whole universe differently than has been common in much of Western religion. Popular religious imagination tends to divide all things into the material and the spiritual, placing souls, angels, demons, and God on the spiritual side of things. Belief in a spiritual human soul makes belief in angels and demons more plausible. On the other hand, belief that the human inner self is what the material brain processes produce makes belief in spiritual beings like angels and devils more odd. If even the human mind is physical processes then the whole universe can be understood as a pattern of material cause and effect.

This in turn may make it easier to adopt a full cosmological naturalism. In that case the major division a religious person might then make would simply be between "creation"—the whole matter-energy universe still developing including human persons—and the Uncreated, God. The universe now empty of the many spiritual souls, might also be empty of demons and angels. The world would be "disenchanted," except to the extent a religious person could still see it as the ongoing presence of God as the origin and sustaining power of it all. If the whole universe is material, of course, that may be a step closer to supposing that metaphysical naturalism is the truest picture of things.

Life after death

Traditional religious doctrine about life after death might still seem to stand in the way of abandoning belief in a spiritual soul which is immortal by its nature. This notion is common not just to much of Western religions, but also to religions of India and perhaps some forms of Eastern Buddhism. Most hunting-gathering cultures take for granted at least some form of continuing life after the end of regular existence. Belief in an inner spiritual self is so common that it too may be close to innate.

On the other hand, Jews, Christians, and Muslims alike have insisted that the new life they expect after death is not purely spiritual. As Chapter 17 noted, according to these religious traditions, the final state is to be a resurrected bodily existence. On these grounds the Christian Orthodox churches still usually forbid cremation of the body. The belief that renewed physical life is part of life after death seems to require a special act of God, to "raise" or create a new bodily existence. If religious tradition requires a special act of God for a full life after death, the same tradition can say that God can do this without having to rely on a naturally immortal soul. Belief in that kind of soul, after all, was rejected by the very earliest Christian writer, Paul.

The belief that the inner self is produced by brain processes nonetheless makes it easier to agree with the ancient Epicureans as well as with current-day American Humanists, that because at death the brain dies, the whole human person dies, including the inner self. As science continues to follow its course of naturalism, explaining even thought processes as brain activities, life after death may increasingly lose plausibility. Scientific naturalism still has many challenges for religious tradition.

For further reading

On the evolution of the human mind

Byrne, Richard, *The Thinking Ape: Evolutionary Origins of Intelligence* (New York: Oxford University Press, 1995).

Griffin, Donald R., *Animal Minds* (Chicago: University of Chicago Press, 1994).

Malik, Kenan, *Man, Beast, and Zombie: What Science Can and Cannot Tell us about Human Nature* (New Brunswick: Rutgers University Press, 2000) insists that we humans have "extended" minds, meaning that it is social interaction that enables us to speak and think.

Arguments about materialism and the soul

Wallace, B. Alan, *The Taboo of Subjectivity: Toward a New Science of Consciousness* (NY: Oxford University Press, 200). Does not fear materialism.

Ward, Keith, *Defending the Soul* (Chatham, NY: OneWorld, 1992), warns against materialism.

Sociobiology

Axelrod, Robert, *The Evolution of Cooperation* (New York: Basic Books, 1984). A slim book to show how cooperation with others is an evolutionarily stable strategy.

Clayton, Philip and Effrey Schloss, eds., *Evolution and Ethics: Human Morality in Biological and Religious Perspective* (Grand Rapids: Eerdmans, 2004). Many articles by experts on "evolutionary ethics."

Cultural evolution

Barnes, Michael Horace, *Stage of Thought: The Co-Evolution of Religious Thought and Science* (New York: Oxford University Press, 2000). An analysis of cultural developments over the last 10,000 years in China, India, and the West, using Piaget's categories of intellectual development.

Diamond, Jared, *Guns, Germs, and Steel: The Fates of Human Societies* (New York: Norton, 1997).

Gellner, Ernest, *Plough, Sword, and Book: The Structure of Human History* (New York: Blackwell, 1995).

Epilogue
20 Religion and Science: Conflicting Commitments

Those who study religion and science are familiar with such names as Ian Barbour, John Polkinghorne, and Arthur Peacocke, all of who manage to be both well-qualified physicists and also theologians or religious philosophers.[1] Francis Collins, the person who successfully led a scientific team to decode DNA, argues for religious belief, including even the rational possibility of miracles, in his book, *The Language of God*. He and other religious scientists usually seek to show that their religious belief can be made compatible with their science. If they first have personal reasons for religious belief, then they match it with what the evidence tells science about the world. The same is true of religious or philosophical thinkers comfortable with any naturalism which is not atheistic, which could include John Haught and Alister McGrath.

For many, nonetheless, religious commitment and scientific rationality and its naturalism are foes. Recent years have seen the publication of a variety of books attacking religion in the name of scientific rationality, as Chapter 7 indicated. The purpose of this chapter is to speculate on the reasons for the differences between the rationalistic skeptics and their religious critics. It will focus not on those who reconcile religion and science comfortably, but on those who do not.

Two basic commitments

An argument from an essay by the 19th century philosopher William K. Clifford (1845–1879) on the ethics of belief appeals to many science-minded skeptics. Here are his words:

> A shipowner was about to send to sea an emigrant-ship. He knew that she was old, and not overwell built at the first; that she had seen many seas and climes, and often had needed

repairs. Doubts had been suggested to him that possibly she was not seaworthy. These doubts preyed upon his mind, and made him unhappy; he thought that perhaps he ought to have her thoroughly overhauled and refitted, even though this should put him at great expense. Before the ship sailed, however, he succeeded in overcoming these melancholy reflections. He said to himself that she had gone safely through so many voyages and weathered so many storms that it was idle to suppose she would not come safely home from this trip also. He would put his trust in Providence, which could hardly fail to protect all these unhappy families that were leaving their fatherland to seek for better times elsewhere. He would dismiss from his mind all ungenerous suspicions about the honesty of builders and contractors. In such ways he acquired a sincere and comfortable conviction that his vessel was thoroughly safe and seaworthy; he watched her departure with a light heart, and benevolent wishes for the success of the exiles in their strange new home that was to be; and he got his insurance-money when she went down in mid-ocean and told no tales.

What shall we say of him? Surely this, that he was verily guilty of the death of those men. It is admitted that he did sincerely believe in the soundness of his ship; but the sincerity of his conviction can in no wise help him, because *he had no right to believe on such evidence as was before him.* He had acquired his belief not by honestly earning it in patient investigation, but by stifling his doubts. And although in the end he may have felt so sure about it that he could not think otherwise, yet inasmuch as he had knowingly and willingly worked himself into that frame of mind, he must be held responsible for it.[2]

Clifford's essay may have been inspired by his own experience of shipwreck on the coast of Sicily in 1870, on a ship hired to carry a group to observe an eclipse. Seven years later he steadfastly opposed the idea that faith could substitute for evidence as a basis for belief. In this same essay he famously declared, "It is wrong always, everywhere, and for anyone, to believe anything upon insufficient evidence."

Scientists are often inclined to agree with Clifford. A commitment to scientific rationality is a commitment to abide by the method of science, on the reasonable grounds that this method has worked extremely well for figuring out how the universe factually operates. Ideally, science speaks confidently about its conclusions only when it has sufficient evidence to justify that confidence. That is why geologists long rejected Wegener's theory of moving continents, and why physicists are still skeptical about cold fusion.

Unlike scientific conclusions, most religious beliefs cannot be checked against empirical evidence. While some like Schleiermacher have argued for an underlying core experience shared by all religions, in fact divergent historical and cultural factors play a large role in religious beliefs. Hindus in India, Muslims in Egypt, and Catholics in Brazil differ on a number of major truth-claims, and there seems to be no way of judging which of these, if any, have a rightful claim to be considered more accurate than the others. These factors provide reasons for the person strongly committed to rationality to be skeptical of religious beliefs.

We have seen that those committed to a religious perspective offer their own justifications. Human reason is fallible; the truth-claims of science are able to change. So science itself does not provide a fully reliable source of truth. Trusting in revelation or tradition may provide a secure reference point for making sense of life. Further, religion offers more than just truth-claims. It offers also community and an identity built on sacred values. Religion faces the basic evils in life and offers some form of salvation. It tells a whole story that binds all these factors together in a meaningful and guiding unity. Religion can inspire a person to look beyond personal interests and develop compassion for others. To many, such arguments seem to justify making the commitment to a religious tradition more basic than the commitment to scientific rationality.

A more basic difference among people

Other areas of human inquiry exhibit similar choices between two differing commitments. The noted psychologist Jerome Bruner claims to have evidence of two distinct types of mentality. One of these he calls a logico-scientific mode of thought. Like science and many philosophies, it searches for the regular and reliable patterns or forces which account for the messy particulars of the world. His description of this mode of thought may partly explain why not everyone finds it appealing. It

> seeks to transcend the particular by higher and higher reaching for abstraction, and in the end disclaims in principle any explanatory value at all where the particular is concerned. There is a heartlessness to logic: one goes where one's premises and conclusions and observation take one, give or take some of the blindnesses that even logicians are prone to.

Contrast that with the other type of mentality, which Bruner calls "narrative." This mentality makes sense out of life and provides direction for the future by telling stories, especially about people and their needs, desires, intentions, and how these work themselves out in the complexities of life.

These two distinct modes of thought can be found across time and across cultural boundaries. In ancient Greece Plato divided previous thinkers into the *theologoi*, those who speculated on mysterious things, and the *physiologoi*, those who attended mainly to empirical evidence about nature. An instance of the first might be Pythagoras, whose interest in mathematical order was more mystical than practical. The latter is typified by Xenophanes, who was skeptical about the existence of gods, and wanted to rely entirely on physical evidence for his opinions. This division was important also in ancient India. While the religious schools discussed ultimates, as in the Upanishads, the empirical Carvaka school was as skeptical as Hume would be many centuries later.[3] In the late Middle Ages the Aristotelians loved rational analysis of how God, logically speaking, would have acted in creating the world. In response the nominalists insisted God did not have to follow human rationality. The European Enlightenment celebrated scientific rationality; the Romantics who followed sometimes complained with Keats that scientific rationality was unweaving the rainbow.

To help clarify the distinction between these two types of thought, we can look at a current form of this division as it appears in academic anthropology. A fierce argument has been going on for some time between those who favor "scientific" anthropology and those who favor "interpretive" anthropology. Scientific anthropologists, sometimes called "rationalists," seek to find general patterns in human behavior across cultures. Interpretive anthropologists are wary of cross-cultural comparisons. They prefer to restrict themselves to creating "thick"—i.e., detailed and usually sympathetic—descriptions of individual cultures, evaluating each culture only in terms that members of that culture would accept as valid. If a tribal group insists that some of its members can foresee the future through what we might call magical methods, or that other of its members can turn themselves into a certain animal, the interpretive anthropologists' attitude is usually one of respect for such beliefs. They would refrain from using foreign scientific or rationalistic criteria to evaluate them. The noted 20th century anthropologist Edward Evans-Pritchard, for example, complains about anthropologists who dismiss belief in magic and spirits because their own culture has taught them to be skeptical.[4]

Good reasons exist for caution about comparisons between or among cultures. Outsiders may find it very difficult to understand well a culture other than their own, so analyses should be cautious. In the past, judgments about the unworthiness of some cultures helped to justify colonialism, oppression, and even slavery. The scientific anthropologist normally agrees that local cultures which wish to resist and maintain their own identify should have their wishes respected.

The scientific anthropologists are nonetheless not as respectful of beliefs about magic and spirits and animal transformation. It is not scientific, of course, to overlook potentially relevant data. Perhaps some tribe members have unusual skills in predicting future outcomes or in imitating certain animals, which lead to exaggerated claims about the abilities in question. In the end, though, the scientific anthropologist is comfortable calling some beliefs mistaken as truth-claims (though perhaps symbolically significant to the people), labeling them factually false, and doing so by using scientific criteria which may be foreign to the culture under study.

The interpretive anthropologist is more likely to subscribe to some degree of cultural relativism. Each culture has its own history and therefore its own form. Outside criteria like the method of science should not be imposed upon another culture. Even to compare truly different cultures to each other risks imposing foreign universal categories on a local way of life. This is something to avoid, the interpretive anthropologist usually claims.[5]

The interpretive anthropologist does not fully succeed at this and cannot. To understand a culture a person must understand patterns in that culture, patterns of authority or power, patterns of family formation, patterns of food-gathering or production, patterns of magic and dealing with spirits, patterns of singing and dancing and arguing and playing games and fighting. Many of them inevitably are patterns which appear in some form in every culture, or at least in various cultures around the world. Humans share the same DNA, with whatever innate inclinations that might include. Humans all face common tasks—as part of parent-child relations, relation to kin, dealing with strangers, finding and distributing food and water, dividing up work assignments, dancing and singing—the list could be a very long one.[6] Cross-cultural similarities should be expected. It is odd that the interpretive anthropologists resist adding to their appreciative study and interpretation this further goal of learning more of what humans might share or at least so it seems to the scientific anthropologist.

Layers of differences

Other differences among people may also echo the difference between the religious and the scientific commitments. Consider the many things that fascinate the imagination today—astrology, UFOs, witchcraft, ESP, gems with power to affect both psychological mood and physical health, homeopathic medicine. The journal *The Skeptical Inquirer* has provided many years of analytical reports on deeply held beliefs of this sort that seem impervious to challenge from the evidence.

The stage magician who calls himself "The Amazing Randi" (James Randi, mentioned in Chapter 10) set up a foundation in charge of a one million dollar offer to anyone who could prove the existence, under scientifically controlled conditions, of such things as dousing, bending spoons or moving them with the mind, mind-reading, and other paranormal phenomena. The conditions had to be agreed upon by both the James Randi Educational Foundation representatives and the person who took up the challenge to show the Foundation her or his ability. This assured that the challenger agreed that the conditions were fair. *The Skeptical Inquirer* repeated Randi's offer in some form or another almost every issue for some years. Very few accepted the offer and tried to demonstrate a special skill or talent. None succeeded.

Nonetheless, large proportions of the U.S. citizenry continue to find these ideas plausible and appealing, often providing elaborate justification for their position.[7] Here is the conclusion of a rather "scientific" anthropologist, James Lett, based on his survey of much of the paranormal literature:

> [M]ost paranormalists come ultimately to the conclusion that there must be something wrong with the epistemological principles of science. While they express this conviction with varying degrees of sophistication, most parapsychologists and pseudoscientists share a common viewpoint: they see themselves as isolated, embattled crusaders for truth, courageously undermining an entrenched scientific establishment that is conservative, close-minded, and culture-bound.[8]

This is the same view that Intelligent Design supporters have of their own status. In the strange documentary "Expelled," the narrator, Ben Klein, tells the story of supposedly noble individuals, fighting for the truth, but facing rejection or even expulsion from their jobs because of a close-minded pro-evolution establishment.[9]

Why this strong and lasting difference among people? The British anthropologist Robin Dunbar offers one possibility as to why many people may be slow to commit themselves to a scientific approach about truth-claims. Our brains, says Dunbar, developed for over one hundred thousand years or more in contexts where snap judgments were necessary, where anthropomorphizing saved one's life, and where the ability to concoct good stories was valuable both for entertainment and for planning. "The human mind was not designed as a rational scientific mind." says Dunbar. "In a very real sense, we have to work against our natural instincts."[10] I suspect he is correct, at least for many people. (Interestingly, this correlates with Barrett's claim in Chapter 7, that atheism is also unnatural, that the human mind naturally anthropomorphizes forces of nature, and finds human-like agents at work everywhere.)

Western educational systems promote some degree of rational analysis, as in algebra and physics classes in secondary schools. For some students this training works well; for others it does not, and for reasons that are not always clear. This difference could account for anthropology's two schools and for the difference between those who believe in paranormal powers and those who do not. But it does not explain where the differences come from in the first place. It is not just a matter of the level of education. Interpretive anthropologists, after all, generally have doctoral degrees from reputable universities.

Religion and thought styles

Given the contrasts between different modes of thought or different commitments, it is not always clear where to put religion. For decades the *Journal for the Scientific Study of Religion* has been publishing studies to see what typifies religious belief. The answer generally depends on what sort of religiousness is involved. Is it strongly committed or weakly? Does it expect divine intervention or not? Is it correlated with anxiety or courage or happiness or any of a number of personal characteristics?

The answer about where to put religion may lie in analyzing the style of religion involved. Science has a single basic method, whereas even within Christianity there are different ways of having faith, different types of doctrines about divine activity, and therefore different ways of responding to the various kinds of naturalism. Similar differences exist in Judaism and Islam. There is one scientific culture with a commitment to a certain kind of rational method, and a wide variety of religious cultures.

Chapter 2 quickly summarized James Fowler's descriptions about different types of faith. That list described one of the earliest stages, the "intuitive-projective" mode of thought that we all seem to share up to the ages of 6 or 7. This is a mode of thought in which we have a strong tendency to personify realities and hold firmly to whatever vivid images take up residence in our minds. Brian Wenegrat tells the story of a four-year-old boy who experienced his first earthquake.[11] He quickly decided that "earthquake" was the name of a giant who lived in the earth and shook things up. No matter how his parents explained what an earthquake is, the boy stuck to his notion of the giant. This story amuses us. Yet many adults are also convinced that a variety of happenings must be the work of conscious beings. Conspiracy theories illustrate this well. The collapse of the World Trade Center towers on 9/11 has spurred a whole theory that the Bush administration planted explosives in the buildings to make them fall, to provide more impetus for going to war in Iraq. AIDS was created by a racist government to attack Black people, and the various moon landings were all faked in a studio on earth, say two other theories.[12]

Most religions seem much more restrained in their claims about how the world works, but perhaps only because we are used to most religious truth-claims. The Unification Church claims that Jesus saved human souls by his death on the cross but did not save the human body because he failed to get married. The Church of Scientology says we humans are actually all Thetans from far away in the cosmos, now trapped in these limited bodies on earth. These may strike the average person as comparable to belief in the earthquake giant or that the moon landings were faked. To the science-minded skeptic, however, most traditional religious beliefs are just as fantastic.

Fowlers stages nonetheless suggest successively more sophisticated modes of religious belief. The "catechism faith" that arrives with concrete operational thought—memorizing specific truths on the authority of a leader or scripture—is usually less wildly imaginative than the ideas of a five-year-old or a conspiracy theory fan. Narrative faith—seeking a more comprehensive and coherent story to guide and inspire—constitutes a fairly normal adult mode of thought, as Bruner indicates, though it first appears in adolescence. Theological faith—seeking to make what one believes internally coherent and at least compatible with evidence, using a formal operational thought style—comes closer yet to the sort of rationality science promotes. Critical or "conjunctive" faith finally rests in the hope for or commitment to belief that life is ultimately purposeful because the transcendent mystery every human can encounter is in some sense what the word "God" stands for. This sort of faith should not, it would seem, trouble the science-minded skeptic at all.

On the other hand, for many who are deeply religious, critical faith is scarcely religious faith at all. To them it is certainly not true Christian or Jewish or Muslim faith, which clearly affirm special and wondrous acts in history by a personal God. Some 19th century skeptics thought that as good education spread religious belief would decline. This became known as the "secularization" thesis. That has happened to some extent among scientists, as the chapters on atheism indicated. It has also happened in Europe. In spite of predictions in the 1960s, however, that secularity—a lack of religion—was inevitably on the increase, that has not been evident in the U.S. Nor is it apparent that religion is in decline in the world in general.

Perhaps one more source may provide clues about the source of the differences among people on religion. Jonathan Haidt, a psychologist at the University of Virginia, outlines five basic values which guide people: compassion, justice, community, authority, and boundaries.[13] Those who are most liberal in their politics and religion emphasize compassion and justice over the other values. One should promote justice everywhere, not just within one's own community; compassion for others can legitimize acting against authority; boundaries between groups, such as differences in clothing, food preparation, family rules are significant but subordinate to compassion and justice. Those who are more conservative in their politics and religion give approximately equal weight to all five values. In some cases, at least, boundaries prevent being open to others who are too different; authority must be maintained even if as a consequence some otherwise unnecessary injustice results. Unfortunately, Haidt does not claim to understand why people treat these five values differently.

A value that does not show up on Haidt's chart is a commitment to rationality. This commitment has its own tradition and community in the West. Commitment to the scientific method also has what could be called an ethical aspect. The ethic of science requires submitting conclusions and evidence to the criticism of others. Those others do not get to reject conclusions on the grounds that they do not like them, or that they are offensive to their community or challenge their authorities, but only on the grounds that there are flaws or inadequacies in the formation and testing of the hypotheses involved. A person who chooses not to submit hypotheses to the hard test of evidence, or who chooses not to allow all others to critically evaluate the conclusions the person arrives at or defends, is also choosing to stand outside of science.

The fact that a commitment to such rationality does not appear as one of the basic values which guide people may indicate that dedicated rationality is a learned value, not something natural to people. Yet formal schooling usually includes training in such rationality. So it is not clear why this training succeeds in leading only some, not all, to make the commitment. We seem unable to say much more than different types of minds are at work.

Fowler and Haidt are only two of the great number of those who investigate differences among religious people and between religious and skeptical people. As Chapter 2 indicated, many a religious person is likely to say all such analyses are irrelevant. Religious tradition judges people by their virtue and devotion, not by secular measures dreamed up by psychologists. Not all religious people would agree with this assessment, of course (recall the many forms "faith" can take). Polkinghorne, Barbour, and Haught and others like them accept science and rationality in their theology and religious philosophy.

So the question lingers why some people submit happily to the requirements of the scientific method while others resist. To the person who cherishes rationality highly, the question seems silly. To live life by non-rational norms seems, well, irrational. Many people who value rationality highly see religion as non-rational and even offensive to rationality in its willingness to have faith in some things for which there is inadequate evidence, and to praise such non-rational faith as though it were legitimate or good. To the person who cherishes a religious tradition (or wishes to protect other cultures or promote belief in paranormal powers) too much rationality violates traditions and values which have highly important places in a person's life, or violates the dignities of other cultures, or impedes the pursuit of something beyond the seemingly cold realms of normal science.

To make it all the more complicated, the philosopher Michael Ruse even detects a certain hidden secular religion in some scientists. From the time of Darwin onward, Ruse argues, the anti-evolutionists took their position most often in order to defend traditional religion, biblical beliefs, notions of divine providence. The evolutionists themselves, however, in Ruse's account exhibit a certain devotion that extends beyond empirical investigations and the testing of hypotheses. In particular Ruse finds a certain "post-millennialism" in a great deal of writings grounded in an evolutionary framework.[14]

Millennialism is the belief in the establishment of the Kingdom of God on earth, as described in the Book of Revelation of the Christian New Testament. Judaism often entertains a similar belief in a future Messianic Age. Islam has a similar belief about the End of the World as we know it and a last judgment. Most devout believers expect this state to arive in the future. Their position can be called "pre-millennial." Among liberal Christians in the 19th century belief in human progress prompted a revision in the traditional belief. Perhaps, said some Christians, the Kingdom of God has already begun. Perhaps it is present in the many points of human progress. Perhaps it has been arriving all along through the progressive and purposeful patterns of evolution. If the millennium has already begun to develop, then we live after—post—at least part of the millennial process.

Ruse points to 19th century thinkers like Herbert Spencer in England and Ernst Haeckel in Germany, whom we saw in an earlier chapter, as representatives of a quasi-secular form of post-millennialism. In the 20th century, Julian Huxley, grandson of Darwin's bulldog Thomas Huxley, promoted this view, along with several other non-religious thinkers. In this case, even the scientists thus seem to need a "narrative," a larger story guided by values and goals.

Most of the time, the differences described here between those devoted more to scientific rationality and those devoted more to a religious tradition do not cause much harm. Both sides can often join in the same projects at work, raise their children together, celebrate life's blessings and commiserate with each other over life's sufferings.[15] The state of religious tensions in the world, however, make plain that this mutual tolerance, this sharing of life in spite of some basic differences, is itself a commitment, not an inevitable part of life. In the West, the European Enlightenment of the 17th and 18th centuries promoted the ideals of common and basic human rights. In India some of the Mughal Emperors promoted tolerance between Muslims and Hindus and

Christians. Similar stories can be told about periods of the Persian empires and the Chinese. Unfortunately stories can also be told of narrow intolerance in the name of God or tradition, in locales around the world and through time. Scientific rationality has usually had a difficult time in such eras.

Tension between many religious-minded people and those devoted to scientific rationality will continue. Religion will adapt to some conclusions of science nonetheless, as happened in the movement from a biblical flat earth to a Greek global earth, and from the Ptolemaic geocentric theory to the heliocentric interpretation. Today the theory of evolution remains contentious, but evidence continues to pour in, just as it has in the last two centuries. Even most of those who object to aspects of scientific rationality in the name of faith will, in the long run, probably accede to good and extensive evidence. Unless, of course, civilizations of the world enter a new dark age. Let us enter a prayer—whether a secular or religious one—that we do not.

Notes

Introduction

1. Stanley Jaki, *Cosmos and Creator* (Edinburgh: Scottish Academic Press, 1980). Harold Nebelsick, *Theology and Science in Mutual Modification* (New York: Oxford University Press, 1981). Rodney Stark, *For the Glory of God: How Monotheism Led to Reformation, Science, Witch-Hunts, and the End of Slavery* (Princeton: Princeton University Press, 2003).
2. Similar models appear in Ian Barbour, *Religion in an Age of Science* (San Francisco: Harper & Row, 1990) and John Haught, *Science and Religion: From Conflict to Conversation* (New York: Paulist Press, 1995).
3. Stephen J. Gould, *Rocks of Ages* (New York: Ballantine, 1999), promoted the idea that science handles truth-claims about the universe; religion deals with values. Gould called these two NOMA—non-overlapping "magisteria" (areas of teaching authority).
4. Richard Dawkins, *The God Delusion* (New York: Mariner Books, 2006) is his most recent and most aggressive attack on religion. See also his *The Ancestor's Tale, The Blind Watchmaker, Climbing Mount Improbable, Unweaving the Rainbow*, and *A Devil's Chaplain*. Victor J. Stenger says belief in God has flunked as a working hypothesis, in *The Failed Hypothesis: How Science Shows that God Does Not Exist* (New York: Prometheus Books, 2008).
5. Christopher Hitchens, *God Is Not Great: How Religions Poison Everything* (New York: Twelve, 2007) argues this vehemently, as is evident from the title of Ch. 2, "Religion Kills."
6. Recently an archeologist reported finding an early Chinese form of writing from around 8,000 years ago. This would be truly startling. We can only wait further analysis of the relevant findings.
7. Princeton: Princeton University Press, 1955.

Chapter 1

1. http://en.wikipedia.org/wiki/Letter_to_Grand_Duchess_Christina contains the whole text.
2. Taken from a translation of the decree as it appears in Janelle Rohr, *Science and Religion: Opposing Viewpoints* (St. Paul, MN: Greenhaven Press, 1988), pp. 23–28, whose source for the decree was Karl Von Gebler, *Galileo Galilei and the Roman Curia* (Merrick, NY: Richwood Publishing Co., 1879), no pages given.
3. Robert Wuthnow, *Meaning and Moral Order: Explorations in Cultural Analysis* (Berkeley: University of California Press, 1987), pp. 187–190.
4. Susan Kwilecki, "A Scientific Approach to Religious Development: Proposals and a Case Illustration," *The Journal for the Scientific Study of Religion*, 27/3, Sep., 1988, 307–325.

Chapter 2

1. Two others are famous for giving their own version of this argument. In a 1910 work, Rudolph Otto declared that religious faith is based on a prior inner awareness of an awesome and fascinating Mystery, in his *The Idea of the Holy* (New York: Oxford University Press, 1958). In the U.S. Mircea Eliade taught generations of students at the University of Chicago that religion is based on an "experience of the sacred" which perceives the sacred to be a unique dimension, quite different from the profane or non-religious. See his *The Sacred and the Profane: The Nature of Religion* (New York: Harcourt Brace, 1959).
2. John F. Haught, *God and the New Atheism: A Critical Response to Dawkins, Harris, and Hitchens* (Louisville: Westminster John Knox Press, 2008), p. 60.

Chapter 3

1. For example, see William Dembski, *Intelligent Design: The Bridge between Science and Theology* (Downers Grove, IL: InterVarsity Press, 1999), p. 202, "naturalism is the disease" for which Intelligent Design is the cure; or Phillip Johnson, *Reason in the Balance: The Case against Naturalism in Science, Law, and Education* (Downers Grove, IL: InterVarsity Press, 1995).
2. John F. Haught, *Is Nature Enough: Meaning and Truth in the Age of Science* (New York: Cambridge University Press, 2006).

Chapter 4

1. Some 20th century critics said Eddington's equipment would not have been able to make the measurement as precisely as was required, and suggested that Eddington's support for Einstein may have led him to find the result he was looking for. In any case, the case for Einstein's theory does not rest on this single test. As always, the theory has had to survive many such tests.
2. A. Hrobjartsson and P. C. Gotzsche "Is the Placebo Powerless? An Analysis of Clinical Trials Comparing Placebo with No Treatment," *New England Journal of Medicine,* 2001; 344:1594–1602, claims the placebo effect does not exist. Most studies say it does.
3. Based on: Bruce V. Lewenstein, "Cold Fusion and Hot History," 135–163, *Osiris,* Vol. #7, 1992 *Science after '40* [i.e., 1940], edited by Arnold Thackray. In addition to *The Cold Fusion Times,* the online journal *Infinite Energy* summarizes and/or has links to papers and reports on many attempts at creating usable fusion energy.

Chapter 5

1. Bryan Appleyard, *Understanding the Present: Science & the Soul of Modern Man* (New York: Doubleday, 1992), p. 9.
2. Paul R. Gross and Norman Levitt, *Higher Superstition: The Academic Left and Its Quarrels with Science* (Baltimore: Johns Hopkins, 1994) provide a biting critique of the postmodern approach to science.
3. The situation is more confusing if the word "modern" is applied to art and architecture. In that case the "modern" is the break from classical art which began with impressionism and expressionism in the 19th century and appeared later in 20th century square-angled architecture.

4. Michael Ruse, *Mystery of Mysteries: Is Evolution a Social Construction?* (Cambridge, MA: Harvard University Press, 1999) explores this in great detail, using just evolutionary theory as an example.

5. Social constructivism goes back to Pyrrho of Elis, who went to India with Alexander the Great and was startled along the way at the differences of beliefs and customs in different cultures. His ideas gave rise to a philosophical school of skepticism. He may have learned this skepticism from a prior school of thought in India.

6. George A. Lindbeck, *The Nature of Doctrine: Religion and Theology in a Postliberal Age* (Philadelphia: Westminster Press, 1984). See pp. 32 to 35 for the various phrases and sentences quoted in this paragraph, pp. 67 and 80 for his dealing with beliefs in the resurrection of Jesus as a miraculous event, and p. 80 for his assertion that doctrines "affirm nothing about extra-linguistic or extra-human reality."

7. Steve Fuller, for example, in his *Philosophy of Science and Its Discontents* (Boulder: Westview Press, 1989), 4–5, claims all knowledge exists only in linguistic-social practices, which vary from culture to culture. He concludes that the content of science cannot be preserved unchanged across cultures.

8. Thomas Kuhn, *The Structure of Scientific Revolutions* (Chicago: The University of Chicago Press, 1970). This is the second edition, which includes Kuhn's response to critics.

9. Thomas Kuhn, *The Essential Tension* (Chicago: The University of Chicago Press, 1977), pp. 321–322.

10. For more on this check out http://en.wikipedia.org/wiki/Chakra

11. R. Barker Bausell, *Snake Oil Science: The Truth About Complementary and Alternative Medicine* (New York: Oxford University Press, 2007), provides an excellent review of various ways in which alternative medicines, including those based on ancient beliefs, have failed to show effectiveness beyond that of ordinary placebos.

12. See Douglas L. Medin and Scott Atran, eds., *Folkbiology* (Cambridge, MA: MIT Press, 1999).

13. Richard G. Olson, *Science and Religion: From Copernicus to Darwin* (Baltimore: Johns Hopkins Press, 2004), pp. 39–42.

Chapter 6

1. See Mark S. Smith, *The Early History of God: Yahweh and the Other Deities in Ancient Israel* (Grand Rapids: William B. Eerdmans, 2002, 2nd ed; or Robert Gnuse, *No Other Gods: Emergent Monotheism in Israel* (Sheffield, England: Sheffield Academic Press, 1997).

2. *Proslogion*, taken from *St. Anselm's Basic Writings*, S. N. Deane, tran. (LaSalle, IL: Open Court 1903), pp. 1–10

3. Jared Diamond, *Guns, Germs, and Steel: The Fates of Human Societies* (New York: W. W. Norton, 2005) (1999) explores the particulars of exchanges between East and West and everything in between.

4. David Ray Griffin, *Religion and Scientific Naturalism: Overcoming the Conflicts* (Albany: SUNY Press, 2000), is a well-known process theologian who argues this.

Chapter 7

1. For a summary of an initial survey in the early 20th century and then the follow-up survey at the end of that century, see the journal *Nature*, Vol. 394 (1998), 313.

2. The first person to use such a phrase may have been Henry Drummond *The Ascent of Man*, (New York: James Pott & Co. Publishers, 1894), p. 333, though the idea itself is an old one.

3. Victor J. Stenger, *God, the Failed Hypothesis: How Science Shows that God Does Not Exist* (Amherst, NY: Prometheus, 2008).

4. Feuerbach, Ludwig, *The Essence of Christianity* (New York: Harper & Row, 1957), p. 33. This is George Eliot's (Marian Evans) translation of 1854.

5. Sigmund Freud, *The Future of an Illusion* (New York: Doubleday Anchor, 1955, [1927]), pp. 22, 24.

6. Richard Dawkins, *The God Delusion* (New York: Houghton Mifflin, 2006) is his most recent full attack.

7. Both of the statements come from Richard Dawkins, "The Improbability of God," *Free Inquiry* [Journal of the Council on Secular Humanism] Vol. 18, #3. Summer, 1998.

8. John F. Haught, *God and the New Atheism: A Critical Response to Dawkins, Harris, and Hitchens* (Louisville: Westminster John Knox, 2008), pp. 21–24.

9. Justin L. Barrett, *Why Would Anyone Believe in God?* (New York: Altamira Press, 2004).

10. Andrew Newberg, Eugene D'Aquili, and Vince Rause, *Why God Won't Go Away: Brain Science and the Biology of Belief* (New York: Ballantine, 2001), p. 172.

Chapter 8

1. The distinction between preternatural and supernatural deeds was maintained as late as the 17th century. Stuart Clark, "The Scientific Status of Demonology," pp. 351–369, in Brian Vickers, ed., *Occult and Scientific Mentalities in the Renaissance* (Cambridge University Press, 1984).

2. Ruth Harris, *Lourdes: Body and Spirit in the Secular Age* (New York: Penguin, 1999).

3. Glenn McGee and Arthur Kaplan, "Playing with God: Prayer is Not a Prescription" 2007. *The American Journal of Bioethics* 7/12:1.

4. Seth M. Asser and Rita Swan, "Child Fatalities from Religion-Motivated Medical Neglect," *Pediatrics*, 101/4, April, 1998, 625–629.

Chapter 9

1. Irenaeus, *Against Heresies*, Bk ii, Ch. 28.2 in *The Writing of Irenaeus*, Vol. I; Vol. V of the Ante-Nicene Christian Library (Edinburgh: T & T Clark, 1868), pp. 220–221.

2. This echoes, I believe, something said by Chesterton or Belloc; I do not have the source.

3. *On the Trinity*, III. 5, trans., Stephen King, *Fathers of the Church*, Vol. 45 (Washington, DC: Catholic University of America Press, 1963), p. 106.

4. Jules M. Brady, S. J., "St. Augustine's Theory of Seminal Reasons," *The New Scholasticism*, Vol. 38, 1964, pp. 141–158.

5. *De Genesi*, Bk. VI, Ch. 18, p. 199.

6. *City of God*, 770–771; Bk XXI, sect. 5.

7. *The Enchiridion*, tran. Albert C. Outler (Philadelphia: Westminster Press, 1955). Ch. IX. See also Ch. XVI in which Augustine declares that there is no need to know the cause of earthquakes but only the causes of good and evil.

8. My sole source on this work is an unpublished 1982 dissertation by Carol Susan Anderson, *Divine Governance, Miracles, and Laws of Nature in the Early Middle Ages* (Ann Arbor: University of Michigan Dissertation Services, a copy printed in 2000).

9. Steven J. Dick, *Plurality of Worlds: The Origins of the Extra-Terrestrial Life Debate from Democritus to Kant* (New York: Cambridge University Press, 1982), pp. 31–32, notes the history of this question from its mention in Lombard's *Sentences*, "whether God is able to make the world better than he has made it." Aquinas approved: "Given the things which actually exist, the universe cannot be better" in *S.T.* I.25.6 ad 3.

10. Francis Oakley, *Omnipotence, Covenant, and Order*, pp. 41–65. (Ithaca, NY: Cornell UP, 1984)

11. See Alister McGrath, *The Intellectual Origins of the European Reformation* (Oxford: Basil Blackwell, 1987), "Nominalism: The Problem of Definition," pp. 70–75.

12. See Edward Grant, "Science and Theology in the Middle Ages," in Ronald Numbers and David Lindberg, *God and Nature* (Berkeley: University of California, 1986), pp. 49–75, for a survey of 12th–13th century thought including various kinds of nominalism and their effects.

Chapter 10

1. Keith Thomas, *Religion and the Decline of Magic: Studies in Popular Belief in Sixteenth and Seventeenth Century England* (London: Weidenfeld & Nicolson, 1971), pp. 638–639.

2. See H. R. Trevor-Rops, *The European Witch-Craze of the Sixteenth and Seventeenth Centuries and Other Essays* (New York: Harper Torchbooks, 1969); and Norman Cohn, *Europe's Inner Demons: An Inquiry Inspired by the Great Witch-Hunt* (New York: New American Library Meridian Book, 1975).

3. As in E. Graham Waring, ed., *Deism & Natural Religion: A Source Book* (New York: F. Ungar, 1967), pp. 8–12.

4. Ibid., pp. 49–51.

5. As noted by Richard Westfall, "The Rise of Science and the Decline of Orthodox Christianity" in Lindberg and Numbers, *God and Nature*, p. 227.

6. Ibid., pp. 66–81.

7. Ibid., pp. 145–152.

8. Andrew Janiak, ed., *Isaac Newton's Philosophical Writings* (New York: Cambridge University Press, 2004) "The World or Treatise on Light," Ch. 7, Vol. I, pp. 92–97.

9. See Robert J. Richards, *Darwin and the Emergence of Evolutionary Theories of Mind and Behavior* (Chicago: University of Chicago, 1987), p. 337.

10. Collins, C. John, *The God of Miracles: An Exegetical Examination of God's Action in the World* (Wheaton, IL: Crossway Books, 2000). This Evangelical defense of supernatural interventions, rejects both "occasionalism" and "providentialism."

11. Norman L. Geisler , *Miracles and the Modern Mind: A Defense of Biblical Miracles* (Grand Rapids: Baker Book House, 1992).

12. Friedrich Schleiermacher, *The Christian Faith* (Edinburgh: T. & T. Clark, 1928; 2nd German ed.), pp. 178–184.

13. Ibid., pp. 374, 385–390.

14. Ibid., pp. 703–707.

15. Karl Barth, *Dogmatics in Outline* (New York: Harper and Row, 1959), p. 154.

16. Rudolph Bultmann's *Jesus Christ and Mythology* (New York: Scribner's, 1958), pp. 18, 32–44.

17. Ibid. See Ch. 5, *Jesus Christ and Mythology*, "The Meaning of God as Acting."

18. Nicholas Saunders, *Divine Action and Modern Science* (New York: Cambridge University Press, 2002) is notable for using this language.

19. John C. Polkinghorne, *Science and Providence: God's Interaction with the World* (West Conshohocken, PA: Templeton Foundation Press, 2005 [originally SPCK, 1989]), pp. 35–39.

Chapter 11

1. Arthur O. Lovejoy, *The Great Chain of Being: A Study of the History of an Idea* (New York: Harper, 1960).

2. William R. Newman, *Promethean Ambitions: Alchemy and the Quest to Perfect Nature* (University of Chicago Press, 2004) describes the hope of alchemists to speed up the natural process of generating precious metals, to turn lead into gold.

3. See David Ray Griffin, *Religion and Scientific Naturalism: Overcoming the Conflicts* (Albany: SUNY, 2000) for a modern attempt to justify belief in such powers and to call them fully natural.

Chapter 12

1. Marshall Clagett, *Greek Science in Antiquity* (Freeport, NY: Books for Libraries Press, 1955), Ch. 7 "Greek Astronomy," p. 94. Or see William P. Wightman, *The Growth of Scientific Ideas* (New Haven: Yale, 1951), 29–43, for the history of "The Geometry of the Heavens" (Ch. IV), from before Plato to the 13th century.

2. A. C. Crombie, *Medieval and Early Modern Science*, Vol. II (Garden City, NJ: Doubleday Anchor Book, revised, 1959), 166–220 offers a review of the ideas, criticisms, and problems in the Ptolemaic system in the work of Europeans from 1475.

3. From the "Apology for Raimond Sebond" in *The Essays of Michel de Montaigne,* tran. George B. Ives (New York: Heritage Press, 1946), Vol. I, Bk 2, p. 598. For more on this topic see Dennis R. Danielson, "The Great Copernican Cliché," *American Journal of Physics*, 69/10, Oct. 2001, 1029–1035.

4. William Shakespeare, *Troilus and Cressida*, I, 3. These words, written in 1602, show that even Copernicus' 1543 views were upsetting. Kepler and Galileo would soon make the skies even messier.

5. "A Free Inquiry," section I, in Robert Boyle, *The Works*, Thomas Birch, ed. (Hildescheim: George Ohms, 1965), Vol. V, p. 163.

6. Blaise Pascal's *Pensées* or *Thoughts*, trans W. F. Trotter (New York: P. F. Collier, 1910), p. 82.

Chapter 13

1. Or to taste the mystical flavor of Teilhard's thought, see his *The Divine Milieu* (Mahwah, NJ: Paulist Press, 2007).

2. Brandon Carter coined this name in a 1973 address, "Large Number Coincidences and the Anthropic Principle in Cosmology." *IAU Symposium 63: Confrontation of Cosmological Theories with Observational Data* (Dordrecht: Reidel, 1974), pp. 291–298. John D. Barrow and Frank J. Tipler, *The Anthropic Cosmological Principle* (Oxford University Press, 1986) offer one of the more thorough descriptions of aspects of the universe that would support SAP.

3. Jay W. Richards, "Why Are We Here: Accident or Purpose?" pp. 131–152, in H. Wayne House, ed., *Intelligent Design 101* (Grand Rapids: Kregel, 2008), provides more details of this argument, pp. 138–146.

4. Martin Rees, *Before the Beginning: Our Universe and Others* (New York: Basic Books, 1998) gives one account. Lee Smolin, *The Life of the Cosmos* (New York: Oxford University Press, 1997) gives a somewhat different version. Both books contain a lot of the words "may," "could," "would," and so forth, signs of the speculative nature of the ideas presented.

5. Richard Dawkins, *The God Delusion*, pp. 99–118, on the SAP.

6. Joseph Bracken, S. J., is one of the most productively creative of process theologians, in such works as *The Divine Matrix: Creativity as Link between East and West* (New York: Orbis Books, 1995), and *The One in the Many: A Contemporary Reconstruction of the God-World Relationship* (Grand Rapids: Eerdmans, 2001).

7. John F. Haught, *God after Darwin: A Theology of Evolution* (Boulder, CO: Westview Press, 2000), p. 122. Also see his *Deeper than Darwin: The Prospect for Religion in the Age of Evolution* (Boulder, CO: Westview Press, 2004), and *Is Nature Enough? Meaning and Truth in the Age of Science* (New York: Cambridge University Press, 2006).

Chapter 14

1. Davis A. Young, *The Biblical Flood: A Case Study of the Church's Response to Extrabiblical Evidence* (Grand Rapids: Eerdmans, 1995), recounts the history of the accumulation and evaluation of relevant evidence.

2. See James Peacock and Thomas Kirsch, *The Human Direction: An Evolutionary Approach to Social and Cultural Anthropology* (New York: Appleton-Century-Crofts, 1970).

3. See Ronald L. Meek, *Social Science and the Ignoble Savage* (New York: Cambridge University Press, 1976).

4. Roger Hahn, "Laplace & the Mechanistic Universe," in David C. Lindberg and Ronald L. Numbers, *God and Nature* (Berkeley: University of California Press, 1986), pp. 265–266.

5. His full name is Jean Baptiste Pierre Antoine de Monet, Chevalier Lamarck.

6. In his *Essay on Classification* (Cambridge, MA: Belknap Press, Harvard University Press, 1962; originally 1857/1859), pp. 103–104. John Hedley Brooke, *Science and Religion: Some Historical Perspectives* (New York: Cambridge University Press, 1991), pp. 194, 253–254. Chs. VI, VII, and VIII provide a history of various ways in which religious thinkers opted for one model or another in response to new evidence concerning geology and fossils.

7. See John Durant, "Darwinism and Divinity: A Century of Debate," pp. 9–39; in John Durant, ed., *Darwinism and Divinity: Essays on Evolution and Religious Belief* (New York: Basil Blackwell, 1985).

8. Herbert Spencer, *First Principles* (London: A. L. Burt Home Library, 4th ed., 1880), pp. 11–13.

9. Quoted in *The Encyclopedia of Philosophy* by Rollo Handy, Vol. III, p. 400. [The reference is to *The Riddle of the Universe*, but no page is given.]

10. Buffon's 18th century estimate of the age of the earth was about 130,000 years. Lord Kelvin rejected Darwin's theory on the basis of his own calculation of the earth's age (by the rate of cooling of the earth) at about 50 million years, too short a time for the gradual process Darwin portrayed, as Darwin agreed. See Stephen Toulmin and Jane Goodfield, *The Discovery of Time* (Chicago: University of Chicago, 1965), pp. 141, 222.

11. Richard E. Leakey and Roger Lewin, *People of the Lake: Mankind and its Beginnings* (Garden City, NY: Doubleday, 1978), espec. Ch. 12, pp. 251–282. Precise analyses are available in Paul Mellars and Chris Stringer, eds, *The Human Revolution: Behavioral and Biological Perspectives on the Origin of Modern Humans* (Princeton, NJ: Princeton University Press, 1989). On language origins in this volume see Philip Lieberman, "The Origins of Some Aspects of Human Language and Cognition," pp. 391–412. On the evolution of the human ability to think, see Richard D. Alexander, "Evolution of the Human Psyche," pp. 455–513. Merlin Donald, *The Origins of the Modern Mind* (Cambridge, MA: Harvard University Press, 1992), provides an excellent review in his early chapters.

12. See Ronald W. Clark, *The Survival of Charles Darwin* (New York: Random House, 1984) for a summary. Richard Dawkins argues this position is not basically different from the 20th century Neo-Darwinian synthesis, but only highlights the bursts of change followed by periods of stasis. *The Blind Watchmaker* (New York: Norton, 1986), in Ch. 9, "Puncturing Punctuationalism," pp. 223–252.

13. See Robert J. Richards, *Darwin and the Emergence of Evolutionary Theories of Mind and Behavior* (Chicago: University of Chicago Press, 1987), Ch. 8 on religious responses. For example George Romanes argued in 1873 that God guided evolution in hidden ways (though Romanes later abandoned this position), pp. 337–342, 543–544.

14. Hans Driesch, *History and Theory of Vitalism*, tran. C. K. Ogden (London: Macmillan, 1914), 138. Driesch conceded that traditional belief in Aristotelian-types souls might no longer be plausible, even while he continued to defend his own "neovitalism." For a summary of its later fate see Michael Horace Barnes, *Stages*

of Thought: The Co-Evolution of Religious Thought and Science (New York: Oxford University Press, 2000), pp. 163–168.

15. Worlf-Ernst Reif, "Evolutionary Theory in German Paleontology," in Marjorie Grene, ed., *Dimensions of Darwinism* (Cambridge, MA: Cambridge University Press, 1983), pp. 173–203.

Chapter 15

1. See http://www.masud.co.uk/ISLAM/nuh/evolve.htm for his letter to Suleman Ali, July 14, 1995.

2. See, for example, Tim LeHaye, *The Battle for the Mind* (Old Tappen, NJ: Fleming H. Revell Co, 1980). For a more recent and stronger statement, see Tim LaHaye and David Noebel, *Mind Seige: The Battle for Truth in the New Millennium* (London: Thomas Nelson, 2001/2003).

3. Not just Protestant fundamentalists take this position. A look at the website of Phyllis Schafly, a Catholic, at http://www.eagleforum.org/column/2004/dec04/04-12-29.html shows that she shares Lahayes's conclusions.

4. http://www.answersingenesis.org/creation/v6/i2/creationII.asp. As of May 9, 2008.

5. William Dembski, *Intelligent Design: The Bridge between Science and Theology* (Downers Grove, IL: InterVarsity Press, 1999), 120.

6. Robert T. Pennock, *Tower of Babel: The Evidence against the New Creationism* (Cambridge, MA: MIT Press, 2000).

7. Some typical creationist sources: Richard B. Bliss, Gary E. Parker, and Duane T. Gish, *Fossils: Key to the Present* (Creation-Life Publishing, 1980); M. Bowden, *The Rise of the Evolution Fraud* (Creation-Life Publishers, 1982), Robert E. Kofahl, *Handy Dandy Evolution Refuter* (Beta Books, 1980). For updating on creationist claims use the Answers in Genesis website at www.AnswersinGenesis.org

8. John N. Moore, *Questions and Answers on Creation and Evolution* (Grand Rapids: Baker Book House, 1980) is a good example.

9. Henry Morris deserves the credit for promoting this version of creationism. See his *Evolution and the Modern Christian* (Grand Rapids: Baker Book House, 1967) or *The Twilight of Evolution* (Grand Rapids: Baker Book House, 1982).

10. Tom Vail: *Grand Canyon: A Different View* (Green Forest, AZ: Master Books, 2003), is one of the books illustrating this interpretation.

11. For a list, with criticisms, of a good number of creationist books see Stan Weinberg, ed., *Reviews of Thirty-One Creationist Books* (San Francisco: National Center for Science Education, 1984).

Chapter 16

1. The name was given to them by Robert Pennock in his book criticizing them, *Tower of Bable: The Evidence against the New Creationism* (A Bradford Book) (Cambridge, MA: MIT Press, 1999).

2. William Dembski, *Intelligent Design: The Bridge between Science and Theology* (Downers Grove, IL: InterVarsity Press, 1999), 120.

3. Ibid., p. 63.

4. Ibid., pp. 67–68. But on pp. 86–89, Dembski insists that an intelligent intervener need not do miracles.

5. An excellent book to show Johnson's overall strategy is his *The Wedge of Truth: Splitting the Foundations of Naturalism* (Downers Grover, IL: InterVarsity Press, 2000).

6. Dembski publishes a lot, such as the more recent *No Free Lunch: Why Specified Complexity Cannot Be Purchased without Intelligence* (NY: Rowman and Littlefield, 2002).

7. William A. Dembski, *The Design Inference: Eliminating Chance Through Small Probabilities* (New York: Cambridge University Press, 1998).

8. Daniel Dennett, *Darwin's Dangerous Idea: Evolution and the Meanings of Life* (New York: Simon & Schuster, 1995) is an excellent review of the implications and applications of the theory.

9. For an exhausting illustration of the numbers of classes, orders, families go to the website http://tolweb.org The "tol" in the website name stands for "tree of life."

10. Kenneth R. Miller, *Finding Darwin's God: A Scientist's Search for Common Ground between God and Evolution* (New York: HarperCollins, 1999). For further information see www.millerandlevine.com/km/evol

11. Michael Behe, *The Edge of Evolution: The Search for the Limits of Darwinism* (New York: Simon & Schuster, 2007).

12. Behe, Op. Cit., pp. 237–238.

13. Ibid., p. 229.

14. Cornelius G. Hunter, *Darwin's God: Evolution and the Problem of Evil* (Grand Rapids: Brazos Press, 2001). Hunter has a Ph.D. in biophysics.

15. Phillip E. Johnson, *Reason in the Balance: The Case against Naturalism in Science, Law, and Education* (Downers Grove, IL: InterVarsity Press, 1995), pp. 48–49.

16. Consult http://www.ncseweb.org to locate more recent information on Project Steve.

Chapter 17

1. David Kraemer, *The Meanings of Death in Rabbinic Judaism* (New York: Routledge, 2000), and Neil Gillman, *The Death of Death: Resurrection and Immortality in Jewish Thought* (Woodstock, VT: Jewish Lights Publishing, 1997).

2. John W. Cooper, *Body, Soul, and Life Everlasting: Biblical Anthropology and the Monism-Dualism Debate* (Grand Rapids: Eerdmans, 1989), a review of relevant biblical texts and common beliefs in the 1st century.

3. This passage translated into Latin uses the word "*rapti*" for "caught up." This guided some English translations to use the word "rapture" as a translation of the original Greek. This is the rapture which precedes 7 years of tribulation before the end, in the interpretation of evangelical Christians. For a full version, see the novel *Left Behind*.

4. Caroline Walker Bynum, *The Resurrection of the Body in Western Christianity, 200–1336* (New York: Columbia University Press, 1995) tells of the continuing Christian concern about how bodies would be resurrected. Even in the Middle Ages, she claims, Christians thought of the person not as a soul but as a whole person.

5. Nancey Murphy, *Bodies and Souls, or Spirited Bodies?* (Cambridge University Press, 2006), especially pp. 16–22, offers another set of arguments that the soul is an aspect of the whole person, not a separable non-physical reality.

6. See Paul S. McDonald, *History of the Concept of Mind* (Burlington, VT: Ashgate, 2003), pp. 124–129.

7. Ronnie J. Rombs, *St. Augustine and the Fall of the Soul: Beyond O'Connell and His Critics* (Washington, DC: Catholic University of America Press, 2006) provides a detailed analysis of Augustine's changing ideas on the soul.

8. Saint Augustine, *The Literal Meaning of Genesis*, tran. John Hammond Taylor, S. J. (Ramsey, NJ: Newman Press, 1982), Vol. II, #42 in the Ancient Christian Writers Series. Books 7, pp. 3–31, and 10, pp. 96–132, chews over these possibilities at some length.

9. Philosophy majors should go to this site for a more exact rendition of Aristotle's ideas on the soul: http://faculty.washington.edu/smcohen/320/psyche.htm

10. Derek Bickerton, *Language and Human Behavior* (Seattle: University of Washington Press, 1995).

11. Edward Grant, *Planets, Stars, and Orbs: The Medieval Cosmos, 1200–1687* (NY: Cambridge University Press, 1995), pp. 474–487, 545–547.

12. As in *Summa Theologica*, I, 75, 5, obj. 2 and ad 2.

13. John Brooke and Geoffrey Cantor make this point in passing in *Reconstructing Nature: The Engagement of Science and Religion* (Edinburgh: T & T Clark, 1998), p. 110.

Chapter 18

1. George Page, *Inside the Animal Mind: A Groundbreaking Exploration of Animal Intelligence* (New York: Broadway, 2001).

2. R. Foley, "Hominid Species and Stone Tool Assemblages," *Antiquity*, 1987, Vol. 6, 380–392. Steven Mithen, *Prehistory of the Mind: The Cognitive Origins of Art, Religion, and Science* (London: Thames & Hudson, 1996), has summaries with illustrations of stages of hominid brain and tool-use development, pp. 24–27 and passim.

3. Two excellent reviews and analysis of relevant data from the variety of scientific fields that bear on language are these two psychologists: Michael C. Corballis, *The Lopsided Ape: Evolution of the Generative Mind* (New York: Oxford University Press, 1991); and Merlin Donald, *The Origins of the Modern Mind: Three Stages in the Evolution of Culture and Cognition* (Cambridge, MA: Harvard University Press, 1991).

4. Philip Lieberman, "The Origins of Some Aspects of Human Language and Cognition" reviews fossils and comparative studies of primate vocalization. In Paul Mellar and Chris Stringer, eds, *The Human Revolution: Behavioral and Biological Perspectives on the Origin of Modern Humans* (Princeton: Princeton University Press, 1989), pp. 391–414.

5. Drubach, Daniel, *The Brain Explained* (New Jersey: Prentice-Hall, 2000).

6. The estimates tend to change. Anatomically modern human were around by 70 kya, but around 35–40 kya there was apparently a new burst of creativity, visible in body decorations, cave art, musical instruments and new tools. But stay alert for more recent information.

7. Antonio Demasio, *Descartes' Error: Emotion, Reason, and the Human Brain* (New York: Vintages, 1995) is one of many accounts of Gage's experience, as well as other informative information about brain functions.

8. Gerald M. Edelman, *Neural Darwinism. The Theory of Neuronal Group Selection* (New York: Basic Books, 1987).

9. Numerous sources are available on the history of discoveries about the brain. An interesting place to begin is Gordon M. Shepherd, *Creating Modern Neuroscience: The Revolutionary 1950s* (New York: Oxford University Press, 2009).

10. Rita Carter, *Mapping the Mind* (Berkeley: University of California Press, 1999), has much of the same information as other books mentioned on brain studies, but focuses a bit more on recent results from brain scans.

11. There are uncertainties about the plasticity of the brain in developing patterns of interaction in early life and after trauma to the brain in later life. With proper stimulation the brain seems able to rewire itself to compensate for damages to this area or that.

12. Philip N. Johnson-Laird, *The Computer and the Mind: An Introduction to Cognitive Science* (Cambridge, MA: Harvard University Press, 1988), supports the single inner self model. Or see Steven Pinker, *How the Mind Works* (New York: W. W. Norton, 1997).

13. Steven Mithen, *Prehistory of the Mind: The Cognitive Origins of Art, Religion, and Science* (London: Thames and Hudson, 1996), proposes a "cognitive fluidity" among the various "modules" of the mind/brain.

14. Leslie Dewart, *Evolution and Consciousness* (Toronto: University of Toronto Press, 1989).

15. An excellent and clear summary can be found in "Spheres of Influence" by noted psychologist Michael S. Gazzaniga, in *Scientific American Mind*, June/July 2008, 32–39.

Chapter 19

1. Daniel C. Dennett, *Freedom Evolves* (New York: Penguin Putnam, 2003), p. 289.

2. Keith Ward, *Religion and Human Nature* (New York: Oxford University Press, 1998), pp. 145–147; Richard Swinburne, *The Evolution of the Soul* (Oxford: Clarendon Press, 1986); William Hasker, *The Emergent Self* (Ithaca: Cornell University Press, 1999). See also Kelly Nicholson, *Body and Soul: The Transcendence of Materialism* (Boulder: Westview Press, 1997), or A. G. Cairns-Smith, *Evolving the Mind: The Nature of Matter and the Origin of Consciousness* (New York: Cambridge University Press, 1996).

3. Paul M. Churchland, *The Engine of Reason, the Seat of the Soul: A Philosophical Journey into the Brain* (Cambridge, MA: MIT Press, 1995), pp. 208–213.

4. Freeman Dyson, "The World on a String," a review of Brian Green, *The Fabric of the Cosmos*, in the *New York Review of Books*, May 13, 2004, 19.

5. The clearest account of basic sociobiology is from Richard Dawkins—yes, the atheist—in *The Selfish Gene* (New York: Oxford University Press, 1976 & 1989). He was reporting and reflecting on the work of earlier biologists.

6. Thomas Aquinas, *Summa Theologica* (New York: Benziger, 1947), I-II. Q. 9, a. 1 "Whether the Will is Moved by the Intellect" and I-II, Q. 13, a. 6 "Whether Man Chooses of Necessity or Freely."

7. Benjamin Libet, *Mind Time: The Temporal Factor in Consciousness* (Cambridge, MA: Harvard University Press, 2004) is one of the pioneers of this field of study. The book summarizes the work of research by many different people.

8. C. S. Lewis, *Miracles: A Preliminary Study* (San Francisco: HarperSanFrancisco, 1996 [originally 1947]), pp. 35–42. For another example of this analogy, see John C. Polkinghorne, *Science and Providence: God's Interaction with the World* (West Conshohocken, PA: Templeton Foundation Press, 2005 [originally SPCK, 1989]), pp. 13–14.

Chapter 20

1. See, for example, John Polkinghorne, *The Faith of a Physicist: Reflections of a Bottom-Up Thinker* (Princeton, NJ: Princeton University Press, 1994); or his article, "God's Actions in the World," in *Cross Currents*, Fall, 1991, 293–307, a revision of a lecture printed in the *CTNS Bulletin* (10:2; Spring 1990).

2. "The Ethics of Belief " by William K. Clifford was first published in 1877 as an essay in *Contemporary Review* but can be found today in *The Ethics of Belief and Other Essays* by W. K. Clifford (Amherst, NY: Prometheus, 1999). Or see http://ajburger.homestead.com/files/book.htm

3. An impressive account of such differences in both Greek and Indian context can be found in Thomas McEvilly, *The Shape of Ancient Thought: Comparative Studies in Greek and Indian Philosophies* (New York: Allworth Press, 2002).

4. Edward E. Evans-Pritchard, *Theories of Primitive Religion* (New York: Oxford University Press, 1965), pp. 119–121.

5. Richard A. Shweder has cheered for the interpretive side, as in *Thinking through Cultures: Expeditions in Cultural Psychology* (Cambridge, MA: Harvard University Press, 1991).

6. Donald Brown, *Human Universals* (Philadelphia: Temple University Press, 1991) argues this case at length, and provides lists of universals from other anthropologists in an appendix.

7. Bryan Farha and Gary Steward, Jr., "Paranormal Beliefs: An Analysis of College Students" *Skeptical Inquirer*, Jan/Feb 2006, 30/1, 3740 or same journal, Jan–Feb 25/1, 2001, on Americans in general. "Science Indicators 200: Belief in the Paranormal or Pseudoscience" a report of the National Science Board.

8. Page 309 in James Lett "Interpretive Anthropology, Metaphysics, and the Paranormal," *Journal of Anthropological Research* 47/3 (Autumn, 1991), 305–329.

9. The 2009 February issue of the *National Center for Science Education Report*, a pro-evolution journal, has gathered many critical analyses of "Expelled" into one format.

10. Robin Dunbar, *The Trouble with Science* (Cambridge, MA: Harvard University Press, 1995), 176. For a similar analysis see Robert Kegan, *In Over Our Heads: The Mental Demands of Modern Life* (Cambridge, MA: Harvard University Press, 1998).

11. Brian Wenegrat, *The Divine Archetype: The Sociobiology and Psychology of Religion* (Lexington: MA: Lexington Books, 1990), pp. 84–85.

12. Phil Molé "9/11 Conspiracy Theories," 40–43 in *The Skeptic*, 12/4, 2006.

13. On Haidt's homepage find the link to "Moral Psychology and the Misunderstanding of Religion," at http://people.virginia.edu/~jdh6n/

14. Michael Ruse, *The Evolution-Creation Struggle* (Cambridge, MA: Harvard University Press, 2005).

15. As an example of cooperation, Edward O. Wilson, *The Creation: An Appeal to Save Life on Earth* (New York: W. W. Norton, 2006) writes as an agnostic, appealing to the Baptists he grew up among as well as to all religious people, to join together to save the earth.

Bibliography

Alexander, Richard D. "Evolution of the Human Psyche," in Paul Mellars and Chris Stringer, eds., *The Human Revolution: Behavioral and Biological Perspectives on the Origin of Modern Humans*. Princeton, NJ: Princeton University Press, 1989, 455–513.

Anderson, Carol Susan. *Divine Governance, Miracles, and Laws of Nature in the Early Middle Ages*. Ann Arbor: University of Michigan Dissertation Services, 1982.

Anselm of Canterbury. *Proslogion*. S. N. Deane, tran. Chicago: Open Court, 1903.

—. *The Augustine Catechism: The Enchiridion on Faith, Hope, and Love*. Bruce Harbert, tran. Hyde Park, NY: New City Press, 1999.

—. *The Literal Meaning of Genesis*. John Hammond Taylor, tran. Ramsey. NJ: Newman Press, 1982.

Applebaum, Wilbur. *The Scientific Revolution and the Foundations of Modern Science*. Westport, CT: Greenwood Press, 2005.

Appleyard, Bryan. *Understanding the Present: Science & the Soul of Modern Man*. New York: Doubleday, 1992.

Aquinas, Thomas. *Summa Theologica*. New York: Benzinger, 1947.

Armstrong, Karen. *A History of God*. New York: A. A. Knopf, 1993.

Asimov, Isaac. *The Universe: From Flat Earth to Quasar*. New York: Avon Books, 1966.

Asser, Seth M. and Rita Swan. "Child Fatalities from Religion-Motivated Medical Neglect." *Pediatrics*, 101, 1998, 625–629.

Augustine, St. Aurelius. *City of God*. Marcus Dodd, tran. New York: The Modern Library, 1950.

Axelrod, Robert. *The Evolution of Cooperation*. New York: Basic Books, 1984.

Barbour, Ian. *Religion in an Age of Science*. San Francisco: Harper & Row, 1990.

Barnes, Michael Horace. *Stages of Thought: The Co-Evolution of Religious Thought and Science*. New York: Oxford University Press, 2000.

Barrett, Justin L. *Why Would Anyone Believe in God?* New York: Altamira Press, 2004.

Barrow, J. D. and F. J. Tipler. *The Anthropic Cosmological Principle*. New York: Oxford University Press, 1986.

Barrow, John D. *Theories of Everything: The Quest for Ultimate Explanation*. Oxford: Clarendon Press, 1991.

Barth, Karl. *Dogmatics in Outline*. New York: Harper & Row, 1959.

Bausell, Barker R. *Snake Oil Science: The Truth about Complementary and Alternative Medicine*. New York: Oxford University Press, 2007.

Behe, Michael. *Darwin's Black Box*. New York: Free Press, 2006 (1996).

—. *The Edge of Evolution: The Search for the Limits of Darwinism*. New York: Simon & Schuster, 2007.

Ben-Ari, Moti. *Just a Theory: Exploring the Nature of Science*. Amherst, NY: Prometheus Books, 2005.

Bickerton, Derek. *Language and Human Behavior*. Seattle: University of Washington Press, 1995.

Bishop, John. *Believing by Faith: An Essay in the Epistemology and Ethics of Religious Belief*. New York: Oxford University Press, 2007.

Bliss, Richard B., Gary E. Parker, and Duane T. Gish. *Fossils: Key to the Present*. San Diego: Creation-Life, 1980.

Bowden, Malcolm. *The Rise of the Evolution Fraud*. London: Sovereign Publications, 1982.

Boyle, Robert. "A Free Inquiry." *The Works*. Hildesheim: George Olms. Vol. 5, 1965.

Bracken, Joseph. *The Divine Matrix: Creativity as Link between East and West*. New York: Orbis Books, 1995.

—. *The One in the Many: A Contemporary Reconstruction of the God-World Relationship*. Grand Rapids: Eerdmans, 2001.

Brady, Jules M. "St. Augustine's Theory of Seminal Reasons." *The New Scholasticism,* 38, 1964, 141–158.

Brooke, John Hedley. *Science and Religion: Some Historical Perspectives*. New York: Cambridge University Press, 1991.

Brooke, John and Geoffrey Cantor. *Reconstructing Nature: The Engagement of Science and Religion*. Edinburgh: T. & T. Clark, 1998.

Brown, Donald. *Human Universals*. Philadelphia: Temple University Press, 1991.

Brown, Neville. *Engaging the Cosmos: Astronomy, Philosophy, and Faith*. Portland, OR; Brighton: Sussex Academic Press, 2006.

Burns, R. M. *The Great Debate on Miracles: From Joseph Glanvill to David Hume*. Lewisburg, PA: Bucknell University Press, 1981.

Bynum, Caroline Walker. *The Resurrection of the Body in Western Christianity, 200–1336*. New York: Columbia University Press, 1995.

Byrne, Richard. *The Thinking Ape: Evolutionary Origins of Intelligence*. New York: Oxford University Press, 1995.

Cairns-Smith, A. G. *Evolving the Mind: The Nature of Matter and the Origin of Consciousness*. New York: Cambridge University Press, 1996.

Carter, Brandon. "Large Number Coincidences and the Anthropic Principle in Cosmology." *International Astronomical Union Symposium 63: Confrontation of Cosmological Theories with Observational Data*. Doredecht: Reidel, 1974, pp. 291–298.

Carter, Rita. *Mapping the Mind*. Berkeley: University of California Press, 1999.

Churchland, Paul M. *The Engine of Reason, the Seat of the Soul: A Philosophical Journey into the Brain*. Cambridge, MA: MIT Press, 1995.

Clagget, Marshall. *Greek Science in Antiquity*. Freeport, NY: Books for Libraries Press, 1955.

Clark, Ronald W. *The Survival of Charles Darwin*. New York: Random House, 1984.

Clark, Stuart. "The Scientific Status of Demonology." in Brian Vickers, ed. *Occult and Scientific Mentalities in the Renaissance*. New York: Cambridge University Press, 1984, pp. 351–369.

Clayton, Phillip and Jeffrey Schloss, eds. *Evolution and Ethics: Human Morality in Biological and Religious Perspective*. Grand Rapids: Eerdmans, 2004.

Clifford, William K. *The Ethics of Belief and Other Essays*. Amherst, NY: Prometheus Books, 1999.

Cobb, John B. and David R. Griffin. *Process Theology: An Introductory Exposition*. Philadelphia: Westminster, 1976.

Cohn, Norman. *Europe's Inner Demons: An Inquiry Inspired by the Great Witch-Hunt*. New York: New American Library Meridian Book, 1975.

Colanter, Eddie N. "Philosophical Implications of Neo-Darwinism and Intelligent Design," in H. Wayne House. *Intelligent Design 101: Leading Experts Explain the Key Issues*, 2008, pp. 153–176.

Collins, Francis S. *The Language of God: A Scientist Presents Evidence for Belief*. New York: Free Press, 2006.

Collins, John C. *The God of Miracles: An Exegetical Examination of God's Action in the World.* Wheaton, IL: Crossway Books, 2000.

Cooper, John W. *Body, Soul, and Life Everlasting: Biblical Anthropology and the Monism-Dualism Debate.* Grand Rapids: Eerdmans, 1989.

Corballis, Michael C. *The Lopsided Ape: Evolution of the Generative Mind.* New York: Oxford University Press, 1991.

Crabbe, James C. M., ed. *From Soul to Self.* New York: Routledge, 1999.

Crombie, A. C. *Medieval and Early Modern Science.* Vol. 2. Garden City, NJ: Doubleday Anchor Book, 1959.

Danielson, Dennis R. "The Great Copernican Cliché." *American Journal of Physics,* 69/10 Oct. 2001, 1029–1035.

Davies, Paul. *God and the New Physics.* New York: Simon & Schuster, 1983.

Dawkins, Richard. *A Devil's Chaplain: Reflections on Hope, Lies, Science, and Love.* New York: Mariner Books, 2004.

— *Climbing Mount Improbable.* New York: W. W. Norton, 1997.

—. *The Ancestor's Tale.* New York: Mariner Books, 2005.

—. *The Blind Watchmaker.* New York: Norton, 1986.

—. *The God Delusion.* New York: Houghton Mifflin, 2006a.

—. "The Improbability of God." *Free Inquiry,* 18, 1998, p. 6.

—. *The Selfish Gene.* New York: Oxford University Press, 2006b (3rd ed.).

—. *Unweaving the Rainbow.* New York: Mariner Books, 2000.

De Chardin, Teilhard. *The Divine Milieu.* New York: Harper, 1960.

—. *The Future of Man.* New York: Harper & Row, 1964.

—. The Human Phenomenon. Brighton: Sussex Academic Press, 2003 (originally *The Phenomenon of Man.* New York: Harper, 1959).

—. *Hymn of the Universe.* New York: Harper, 1960.

Demasio, Antonio. *Descartes' Error: Emotion, Reason, and the Human Brain.* New York: Vintage, 1995.

Dembski, William. *Intelligent Design: The Bridge between Science and Theology.* Downers Grove: InterVarsity Press, 1999.

—. *Mere Creation: Science, Faith & Intelligent Design.* Downers Grove: InterVarsity Press, 1998.

—. *No Free Lunch: Why Specified Complexity Cannot Be Purchased without Intelligence.* New York: Rowman & Littlefield, 2002.

—. *The Design Inference: Eliminating Chance through Small Probabilities.* New York: Cambridge University Press, 1998.

Dennett, Daniel. *Breaking the Spell: Religion as a Natural Phenomenon.* New York: Penguin, 2007.

—. *Darwin's Dangerous Idea: Evolution and the Meanings of Life.* New York: Simon & Schuster, 1995.

—. *Freedom Evolves.* New York: Penguin, 2004.

Descartes, René. "The World or Treatise on Light" in *The Philosophical Writings of Descartes.* John Cottingham, Robert Stoothoff, and Dugald Murdoch, eds. New York: Cambridge University Press, 1985, 81–98.

Desmond, Adrian and James Moore. *Darwin: The Life of a Tormented Evoutionist.* New York: Warner Books, 1991.

Dewart, Leslie. *Evolution and Consciousness.* Toronto: University of Toronto Press, 1989.

Diamond, Jared. *Guns, Germs, and Steel: The Fates of Human Societies.* New York: W. W. Norton, 2005 (1999).

Dick, Steven J. *Plurality of Worlds: The Origins of the Extra-Terrestrial Life Debate from Democritus to Kant.* New York: Cambridge University Press, 1982.

Donald, Merlin. *The Origins of the Modern Mind*. Cambridge, MA: Harvard University Press, 1992.

Downing, Crystal. *How Postmodernism Serves (My) Faith: Questioning Truth in Language, Philosophy and Art*. Downers Grove, IL: InterVarsity Press Academic, 2006.

Driesch, Hans. *History and Theory of Vitalism*. C. K. Ogden, tran. London: Macmillan, 1914.

Drubach, Daniel. *The Brain Explained*. New Jersey: Prentice-Hall, 2000.

Drummond, Henry. *The Ascent of Man*. New York: James Pott & Co., 1894.

Dunbar, Robin. *The Trouble with Science*. Cambridge, MA: Harvard University Press, 1995.

Durant, John. "Darwinism and Divinity: A Century of Debate" in John Durant, ed. *Darwinism and Divinity: Essays on Evolution and Religious Belief*. New York: Basil Blackwell, 1986, pp. 15–17.

Dyson, Freeman. "The World on a String." Review of *The Fabric of the Cosmos* by Brian Green. *The New York Review of Books* May 13, 2004, 19.

Edelman, Gerald M. *Neural Darwinism: The Theory of Neuronal Group Selection*. New York: Basic Books, 1987.

Edis, Taner. *Science and Nonbelief*. Westport, CT: Greenwood Press, 2006.

Eliade, Mircea. *The Sacred and the Profane: The Nature of Religion*. New York: Harcourt Brace, 1959.

Evans-Pritchard, Edward E. *Theories of Primitive Religion*. New York: Oxford, 1965.

Farha, Bryan and Gary Steward Jr. "Paranormal Beliefs: An Analysis of College Students." *Skeptical Inquirer,* 2006, 37–40, Vol. 30, No. 1.

—. "Science Indicators 200: Belief in the Paranormal or Pseudoscience." *Skeptical Inquirer,* 2001, pp. 12–15.

Feinberg, Todd M. *Altered Egos: How the Brain Creates the Self*. New York: Oxford University Press, 2001.

Feuerbach, Ludwig. *The Essence of Christianity*. New York: Harper & Row, 1957.

Foley, Robert. "Hominid Species and Stone Tool Assemblages." *Antiquity* 6, 1987, 380–392.

Fortey, Richard. *Life: A Natural History of the First Four Billion Years of Life on Earth*. New York: Alfred A. Knopf, 1998.

Freeman, Charles. *The Closing of the Western Mind: the Rise of Faith and the Fall of Reason*. New York: Vintage Books, 2002.

Freud, Sigmund. *The Future of an Illusion*. New York: Doubleday Anchor, 1955 (1927).

Fridrichsen, Anton Johnson. *The Problem of Miracle in Primitive Christianity*. Minneapolis: Augsburg, 1972.

Fuller, Steve. *Philosophy of Science and Its Discontents*. Boulder, CO: Westview Press, 1989.

Gale, George. *Theory of Science: An Introduction to the History, Logic, and Philosophy of Science*. New York: McGraw-Hill, 1976.

Gardner, Howard. *Frames of Mind: The Theory of Multiple Intelligences*. New York: Basic Books, 1983.

Gazzaniga, Michael S. *The Mind's Past*. Berkeley: University of California Press, 1998.

—. "Spheres of Influence." *Scientific American Mind,* 19, 2008, 32–39.

Geisler, Norman L. *Miracles and the Modern Mind: A Defense of Biblical Miracles*. Grand Rapids: Baker Book House, 1992.

Geivett, Douglas R. and Gary R. Habermas, eds. *In Defense of Miracles: A Comprehensive Case for God's Action in History*. Downers Grove, IL: InterVarsity Press, 1997.

Gellner, Ernest. *Plough, Sword, and Book: The Structure of Human History*. Chicago: University of Chicago, 1988.

Gillman, Neil. *The Death of Death: Resurrection and Immortality in Jewish Thought*. Woodstock, VT: Jewish Lights, 1997.

Gnuse, Robert. *No Other Gods: Emergent Monotheism in Israel*. Sheffield, England: Sheffield Academic Press, 1997.

Godfrey, Laurie R., ed. *Scientists Confront Creationism*. New York: W. W. Norton, 1983.

Gould, Stephen J. *Rocks of Ages*. New York: Ballantine, 1999.

Grant, Edward. "Science and Theology in the Middle Ages," in Ronald Numbers and David Lindberg, eds. *God and Nature*. Berkeley: University of California, 1986, 49–75.

—. *Planets, Stars, and Orbs: The Medieval Cosmos, 1200–1687*. New York: Cambridge University Press, 1995.

Greenstein, George. *The Symbiotic Universe: Life and Mind in the Cosmos*. New York: William Morrow and Company, 1988.

Griffin, David R. *Religion and Scientific Naturalism: Overcoming the Conflicts*. Albany: SUNY, 2000.

Griffin, Donald R. *Animal Minds*. Chicago: University of Chicago Press, 1994.

Griffiths, Paul J. and Reinhard Hutter, eds. *Reason and the Reasons of Faith*. New York: T. & T. Clark International, 2005.

Gross, Paul R. and Norman Levitt. *Higher Superstition: The Academic Left and Its Quarrels with Science*. Baltimore: Johns Hopkins, 1994.

Guthrie, Stewart. *Faces in the Clouds*. New York: Oxford University Press, 1993.

Haack, Susan. *Defending Science within Reason: Between Scientism and Cynicism*. Amherst, NY: Prometheus Books, 2003.

Hackman, Sandra, ed. *The Nova Reader: Science at the Turn of the Millennium*. New York: TV Books, 1999.

Hahn, Roger. "LaPlace & the Mechanistic Universe," in Ronald Numbers and David Lindberg, eds. *God and Nature*. Berkeley: University of California, 1986, pp. 265–266.

Hancock, Curtis L. and Brendan Sweetman, eds. *Faith and the Life of the Intellect*. Washington, DC: Catholic University of America Press, 2003.

Handy, Rollo. "Haeckel, Ernst Heinrich," in Paul Edwards, ed. *The Encyclopedia of Philosophy* 3, 399–402. New York: Macmillan, 1967.

Harris, Ruth. *Lourdes: Body and Spirit in the Secular Age*. New York: Penguin, 1999.

Hasker, William. *The Emergent Self*. Ithaca: Cornell University Press, 1999.

Haught, John F. *Deeper Than Darwin: The Prospect for Religion in an Age of Evolution*. Boulder, CO: Westview Press, 2003.

—. *God after Darwin: A Theology of Evolution*. Boulder, CO: Westview Press, 2000.

—. *God and the New Atheism: A Critical Response to Dawkins, Harris, and Hitchens*. Louisville: Westminster John Knox P, 2008.

—. *Is Nature Enough: Meaning and Truth in the Age of Science*. New York: Cambridge University Press, 2006.

—. *Science and Religion: From Conflict to Conversation*. New York: Paulist Press, 1995.

—. *What is God? How to Think about the Divine*. New York: Paulist Press, 1986.

Heinze, Thomas F. *The Creation vs. Evolution Handbook*. Grand Rapids: Baker Book House, 1972.

Hetherington, Norris S. *Cosmology: Historical, Literary, Philosophical, Religious and Scientific Perspectives*. New York: Garland, 1993.

Hitchens, Christopher. *God Is Not Great: How Religions Poison Everything*. New York: Twelve, 2007.

Horgan, John. *The End of Science: Facing the Limits of Knowledge in the Twilight of the Scientific Age*. Reading, MA: Addison-Wesley, 1996.

Hrobjartsson, Gotzsche PC A. "Is the Placebo Powerless? An Analysis of Clinical Trials Comparing Placebo with no Treatment." *New England Journal of Medicine* 344, 2001, 1594–1602.

Hume, David. *Writings on Religion*. Anthony Flew, ed. La Salle, IL: Open Court, 1992.

Huxley, Julian. "Evolutionary Vision," in Sol Tax and Charles Callender, eds. *Issues in Evolution: The University of Chicago Centennial discussions*. Vol. 3. Chicago: University of Chicago, 1960, 249.

Irenaeus. *The Writing of Irenaeus.* Alexander Roberts and W. H. Rambaut, tran. Edinburgh: T. & T. Clark, 1868.

Isaak, Mark. *The Counter-Creationism Handbook.* Westport, CT: Greenwood Press, 2005.

Jaki, Stanley. *Cosmos and Creator.* Edinburgh: Scottish Academic Press, 1980.

Johnson, Phillip E. *Defeating Darwinism by Opening Minds.* Downers Grove: InterVarsity Press, 1997.

—. *Reason in the Balance: The Case against Naturalism in Science, Law, and Education.* Downers Grove: InterVarsity Press, 1995.

—. *The Wedge of Truth: Splitting the Foundations of Naturalism.* Downers Grove: InterVarsity Press, 2000.

Johnson-Laird, Phillip N. *The Computer and the Mind: An Introduction to Cognitive Science.* Cambridge, MA: Harvard University Press, 1988.

Kaufmann, Stuart. *Reinventing the Sacred.* New York: Basic Books, 2008.

Kee, Howard Clark. *Medicine, Miracle, and Magic in New Testament Times.* Cambridge, MA: Cambridge University Press, 1986.

Kegan, Robert. *In Over Our Heads: The Mental Demands of Modern Life.* Cambridge, MA: Harvard University Press, 1998.

Kitcher, Phillip. *The Advancement of Science: Science without Legend, Objectivity without Illusions.* New York: Oxford University Press, 1993.

Kofahl, Robert E. *Handy Dandy Evolution Refuter.* Raleigh, NC: Beta Books, 1980.

Kraemer, David. *The Meanings of Death in Rabbinic Judaism.* New York: Routledge, 2000.

Kuhn, Thomas S. *The Copernican Revolution: Astronomy in the Development of Western Thought.* Cambridge, MA: Harvard University Press, 1957.

—. *The Essential Tension.* Chicago: University of Chicago Press, 1977.

—. *The Structure of Scientific Revolutions.* Chicago: University of Chicago Press, 1970.

Kwilecki, Susan. "A Scientific Approach to Religious Development: Proposals and a Case Illustration." *The Journal for the Scientific Study of Religion.* 27, 307–325, 1988.

Larmer, Robert A., ed. *Questions of Miracle.* Montreal: McGill-Queen's University Press, 1996.

Larson, Edward J. *Evolution: The Remarkable History of a Scientific Theory.* New York: Modern Library, 2006.

—. and Larry Witham, "Leading Scientists Still Reject God," *Nature* July 23, 1998, 313.

Leakey, Richard E. and Roger Lewin. *People of the Lake: Mankind and its Beginnings.* Garden City, NY: Doubleday, 1978.

LeHaye, Tim. *The Battle for the Mind.* Old Tappen, NJ: Fleming H. Revell Co, 1980.

—. and David Noebel. *Mind Seige: The Battle for Truth in the New Millennium.* London: Thomas Nelson, 2001/2003.

Lennox, John C. *God's Undertaker: Has Science Buried God?* Oxford: LionHutton, 2007.

Lett, James. "Interpretive Anthropology, Metaphysics, and the Paranormal." *Journal of Anthropological Research,* 47, 1991, 305–329.

Lewenstein, Bruce V. "Cold Fusion and Hot History," in Arnold Thackery, ed. *Osiris: Science after '40* [i.e., 1940]. 7, 1992, 135–163.

Lewis, C. S. *Miracles.* London: Collins/Fantana, 1947.

Libet, Benjamin. *Mind Time: The Temporal Factor in Consciousness.* Cambridge, MA: Harvard University Press, 2004.

Lieberman, Phillip. "The Origins of Some Aspects of Human Language and Cognition," in Paul Mellar and Christ Stringer, eds. *The Human Revolution: Behavioral and Biological Perspectives on the Origin of Modern Humans.* Princeton: Princeton University Press, 1989, pp. 391–414.

Lindbeck, George A. *The Nature of Doctrine*. New Haven: Yale University Press, 1984.

Lovejoy, Arthur O. *The Great Chain of Being: A Study of the History of an Idea*. New York: Harper, 1960.

Malik, Kenan. *Man, Beast, and Zombie: What Science Can and Cannot Tell us about Human Nature*. New Brunswick: Rutgers University Press, 2000.

Martin, Raymond and John Barresi. *The Rise and Fall of Soul and Self: An Intellectual History of Personal Identity*. New York: Columbia University Press, 2006.

May, Edwin C. "The American Institutes for Research Review of the Department of Defense's Star Gate Program: A Commentary." *The Journal of Parapsychology*, 60, 1996, 3–23.

McCabe, Herbert. *Faith within Reason*. New York: Continuum, 2007.

McCalla, Arthur. *The Creationist Debate: The Encounter between the Bible and the Historical Mind*. New York: T. & T. Clark, 2006.

McDonald, Paul S. *History of the Concept of Mind*. Burlington, VT: Ashgate, 2003.

McEvilly, Thomas. *The Shape of Ancient Thought: Comparative Studies in Greek and Indian Philosophies*. New York: Allworth Press, 2002.

McGee, Glenn and Arthur Kaplan. "Playing with God: Prayer is Not a Prescription." *The American Journal of Bioethics*, 7/12, 2007, 1.

McGrath, Alister E. *The Intellectual Origins of the European Reformation*. Oxford: Basil Blackwell, 1987.

—. *The Order of Things: Explorations in Scientific Theology*. Malden, MA: Blackwell, 2006.

McGraw, John J. *Brain and Belief: An Exploration of the Human Soul*. Del Mar, CA: Aegis Press, 2004.

Medin, Douglas L. and Scott Atran, eds. *Folkbiology*. Cambridge, MA: MIT Press, 1999.

Meek, Ronald L. *Social Science and the Ignoble Savage*. Cambridge, MA: Cambridge University Press, 1976.

Mellars, Paul and Chris Stringer. *The Human Revolution: Behavioral and Biological Perspectives on the Origin of Modern Humans*. Princeton: Princeton University Press, 1989.

Miller, Kenneth R. *Finding Darwin's God: A Scientist's Search for Common Ground between God and Evolution*. New York: HarperCollins, 1999.

Mithen, Steven. *Prehistory of the Mind: The Cognitive Origins of Art, Religion, and Science*. London: Thames & Hudson, 1996.

Molé, Phil. "9/11 Conspiracy Theories." *The Skeptic*, 12, 2006, 30–43.

Montaigne, Michel de. "Apology for Raimond Sebond." *The Essays of Michel de Montaigne*. George B. Ives, tran. Vol. 1. New York: Heritage, 1946, pp. 579–816.

Moore, John N. *Questions and Answers on Creation and Evolution*. Grand Rapids: Baker Book House, 1980.

Morris, Henry M. *Evolution and the Modern Christian*. Grand Rapids: Baker Book House, 1967.

—. *The Scientific Case for Creation*. San Diego: Institute for Creation Research, 1977 (also Green Forest, AZ: Master Books).

—. *The Twilight of Evolution*. Grand Rapids: Baker Book House, 1982.

Morris, Thomas V. *Our Idea of God: An Introduction to Philosophical Theology*. Downers Grove: InterVarsity Press, 1991.

Murphy, Nancey. *Bodies and Souls, or Spirited Bodies?* New York: Cambridge University Press, 2006.

Nebelsick, Harold. *Theology and Science in Mutual Modification*. New York: Oxford University Press, 1981.

Newberg, Andrew, Eugene D'Aquili, and Vince Rause. *Why God Won't Go Away: Brain Science and the Biology of Belief*. New York: Ballantine, 2001.

Newman, William R. *Promethean Ambitions: Alchemy and the Quest to Perfect Nature*. Chicago: University of Chicago Press, 2004.

Nicholson, Kelley. *Body and Soul: The Transcendence of Materialism*. Boulder, CO: Westview Press, 1997.

Nickell, Joe. *Looking for a Miracle: Weeping Icons, Relics, Stigmata, Visions & Healing Cures*. Amherst, NY: Prometheus Books, 1993.

Numbers, Ronald L. *The Creationists: The Evolution of Scientific Creationism*. Berkeley: University of California Press, 1992.

Oakley, Francis. *Omnipotence, Covenant, and Order*. Ithaca: Cornell University Press, 1984.

Olson, Richard G. *Science and Religion: From Copernicus to Darwin*. Baltimore: Johns Hopkins Press, 2004.

Otto, Rudolph. *The Idea of the Holy*. New York: Oxford University Press, 1958.

Page, George. *Inside the Animal Mind: A Groundbreaking Exploration of Animal Intelligence*. New York: Broadway, 2001.

Pascal, Blaise. *Pensées or Thoughts*. W. F Trotter, tran. New York: P. F. Collier, 1910.

Peacock, James A. and Thomas Kirsch. *The Human Direction: An Evolutionary Approach to Social and Cultural Anthropology*. New York: Appleton-Century-Crofts, 1970.

Penelhum, Terence. *Reason and Religious Faith*. Boulder, CO: Westview Press, 1995.

Pennock, Robert, ed. *Intelligent Design Creationism and Its Critics: Philosophical, Theological, and Scientific Perspectives*. Cambridge, MA: MIT Press, 2001.

—. *Tower of Babel: The Evidence against the New Creationism*. Cambridge, MA: MIT Press, 2000.

Pinker, Steven. *How the Mind Works*. New York: W. W. Norton, 1997.

Polkinghorne, John. *The Faith of a Physicist: Reflections of a Bottom-Up Thinker*. Princeton: Princeton University Press, 1994.

—. "God's Actions in the World." *Cross Currents*, 41, 1991, 293–307.

—. *Science and Providence: God's Interaction with the World*. West Conshohocken, PA: Templeton Foundation, 2005.

Pritchard, James B. *Ancient near Eastern Texts Relating to the Old Testament*. Princeton: Princeton University Press, 1955.

Prothero, Donald R. *Evolution: What the Fossils Say and Why It Matters*. New York: Columbia University Press, 2007.

Rees, Martin. *Before the Beginning: Our Universe and Others*. New York: Basic Books, 1998.

Reif, Worlf-Ernst. "Evolutionary Theory in German Paleontology," in Marjorie Grene, ed. *Dimensions of Darwinism*. Cambridge, MA: Cambridge University Press, 1983, pp. 173–203.

Richards, Jay W. "Why Are We Here: Accident or Purpose?" in H. Wayne House, ed. *Intelligent Design 101*. Grand Rapids, MI: Kregel, 2008, pp. 138–146.

Richards, Robert J. *Darwin and the Emergence of Evolutionary Theories of Mind and Behavior*. Chicago, IL: University of Chicago Press, 1987.

Rohr, Janelle. *Science and Religion: Opposing Viewpoints*. St. Paul, MN: Greenhaven Press, 1988.

Rombs, Ronnie J. *St. Augustine and the Fall of the Soul: Beyond O'Connell and His Critics*. Washington DC: Catholic University of America Press, 2006.

Ruse, Michael. *The Creation-Evolution Struggle*. Cambridge, MA: Harvard University Press, 2006.

—. *Mystery of Mysteries: Is Evolution a Social Construction?* Cambridge, MA: Harvard University Press, 1999.

Sagan, Carl. *Cosmos*. New York: Random House, 1980, 2002.

Schleiermacher, Friedrich. *The Christian Faith*. 2nd ed. Edinburgh: T. & T. Clark, 1928.

Schroeder, Gerald L. *Genesis and the Big Bang: The Discovery of Harmony between Modern Science and the Bible*. New York: Bantam, 1990.

Shepherd, Gordon M. *Creating Modern Neuroscience: The Revolutionary 1950s*. New York: Oxford University Press, 2009.

Shermer, Michael. *How We Believe: Science, Skepticism, and the Search for God*. New York: Holt, 2003.

Shweder, Richard A. *Thinking through Cultures: Expeditions in Cultural Psychology*. Cambridge, MA: Harvard University Press, 1991.

Silver, Brian L. *The Ascent of Science*. New York: Oxford University Press, 1998.

Smith, Mark S. *The Early History of God: Yahweh and the Other Deities in Ancient Israel*. Grand Rapids: Eerdmans, 2002.

Smolin, Lee. *The Life of the Cosmos*. New York: Oxford University Press, 1997.

Spencer, Herbert. *First Principles*. 1855. 4th ed. London: A. L. Burt Home Library, 1880 (Sutton Press, 2008).

Stark, Rodney. *For the Glory of God: How Monotheism Led to Reformation, Science, Witch-Hunts, and the End of Slavery*. Princeton: Princeton University Press, 2003.

Steele, David Ramsey. *Atheism Explained: From Folly to Philosophy*. Chicago: Open Court, 2008.

Stenger, Victor J. *God, the Failed Hypothesis: How Science Shows that God Does not Exist*. Amherst, NY: Prometheus Books, 2008.

Swinburne, Richard. *The Evolution of the Soul*. Oxford: Clarendon Press, 1986.

Teilhard de Chardin, Pierre. *The Phenomenon of Man*. New York: Harper & Bros., 1959. [New edition: *The Human Phenomenon*. Brighton: Sussex Academic Press, 2003.]

Thomas, Keith. *Religion and the Decline of Magic: Studies in Popular Belief in Sixteenth and Seventeenth Century England*. London: Weidenfeld & Nicolson, 1971.

Toulmin, Stephen and Jane Goodfield. *The Discovery of Time*. Chicago, IL: University of Chicago Press, 1965.

Tracy, Thomas S., ed. *The God Who Acts: Philosophical and Theological Explorations*. University Park, PA: Penn State University Press, 1994.

Vail, Tom. *Grand Canyon: A Different View*. Green Forest, AZ: Master Books, 2003.

Von Gebler, Karl. *Galileo Galilei and the Roman Curia*. Merrick, NY: Richwood Co, 1879.

Wallace, B. Alan. *The Taboo of Subjectivity: Toward a New Science of Consciousness*. New York: Oxford University Press, 2000.

Ward, Benedicta. *Miracles and the Medieval Mind: Theory, Record, and Event*. Philadelphia: University of Pennsylvania Press, 1982.

Ward, Keith. *Defending the Soul*. Chatham, NY: Oneworld, 1992.

—. *Pascal's Fire: Scientific Faith and Religious Understanding*. Oxford: Oneworld, 2006.

—. *Religion and Human Nature*. New York: Oxford University Press, 1998.

Waring, E. Graham, ed. *Deism & Natural Religion: A Source Book*. New York: F. Ungar, 1967.

Weinberg, Stan, ed. *Reviews of Thirty-One Creationist Books*. San Francisco: National Center for Science Education, 1984.

Weinberg, Stephen. *Dreams of a Final Theory: The Scientist's Search for the Ultimate Laws of Nature*. New York: Vintage Books, 1994.

Wells, Jonathan. *Icons of Evolution: Science or Myth? Why Much of What We Teach about Evolution is Wrong*. Washington DC: Regnery, 2000.

Wenegrat, Brian. *The Divine Archetype: The Sociobiology and Psychology of Religion*. Lexington, MA: Lexington Books, 1990.

Westfall, Richard. "The Rise of Science and the Decline of Orthodox Christianity," in David Lindberg and Ronald Numbers, eds. *God and Nature*, Berkeley: University of California Press, pp. 218–237.

Wightman, William P. *The Growth of Scientific Ideas.* New Haven: Yale, 1951.

Williams, Terence C. *The Idea of the Miraculous: The Challenge to Science and Religion.* New York: St. Martin's Press, 1991.

Wilson, Edward O. *The Creation: An Appeal to Save Life on Earth.* New York: W. W. Norton, 2006.

Wuthnow, Robert. *Meaning and Moral Order: Explorations in Cultural Analysis.* Berkeley: University of California Press, 1987.

Young, Davis A. *The Biblical Flood: A Case Study of the Church's Response to Extrabiblical Evidence.* Grand Rapids: Eerdmans, 1995.

Index